Praise for *Blueprints for Text Analysis Using Python*

This is the book I wish I had at the beginning of my research. Solidly written, well-researched, and substantiated with hands-on examples that can be replicated for a variety of business use cases that need ML.

—*K.V.S. Dileep, Head, Program Development, GreyAtom*

An excellent book for anyone looking to enter the world of text analytics in an efficient manner. Packed with well-thought-out examples that can jump start the process of developing real-world applications using text analytics and natural language processing.

—*Marcus Bender, Distinguished Solution Engineer and Oracle Fellow*

The authors provide a comprehensive view of all useful methods and techniques related to text analytics and NLP that are used today in any production system. All datasets and use cases are inspired by real-life problems which would help readers understand how complex business problems are solved in large organizations.

—*Dr. Soudip Roy Chowdhury, Cofounder and CEO, Eugenie.ai*

Text analytics as a field is advancing considerably, which mandates a solid foundation while building text-related applications. This book helps achieve exactly that, with detailed concepts and blueprints for the implementation of multiple applications on realistic datasets.

—*Kishore Ayyadevara, author of books on ML and AI*

A seamless melding of the methodical demands of the engineering discipline with the reactive nature of data science. This text is for the serious data engineer and balances an enterprise project's prescription nature with innovative techniques and exploratory scenarios.

—*Craig Trim, Senior Engineer at Causality Link*

This book bridges the gap between fanatically Googling and hoping that it works, and just knowing that it will. The extremely code-driven layout combined with clear names of methods and approaches is a perfect combination to save you tons of time and heartache.

—*Nirant Kasliwal, Verloop.io*

This book is high quality, very practical, and teaches necessary basics.

—*Oliver Zeigermann, book and video course author and machine learning practitioner*

Blueprints for Text Analysis Using Python
Machine Learning-Based Solutions for Common Real World (NLP) Applications

Jens Albrecht, Sidharth Ramachandran, and Christian Winkler

Beijing · Boston · Farnham · Sebastopol · Tokyo

Blueprints for Text Analytics Using Python

by Jens Albrecht, Sidharth Ramachandran, and Christian Winkler

Published by O'Reilly Media, Inc., 1005 Gravenstein Highway North, Sebastopol, CA 95472.

O'Reilly books may be purchased for educational, business, or sales promotional use. Online editions are also available for most titles (*http://oreilly.com*). For more information, contact our corporate/institutional sales department: 800-998-9938 or *corporate@oreilly.com*.

Acquisitions Editor: Michelle Smith
Development Editor: Amelia Blevins
Production Editor: Daniel Elfanbaum
Copyeditor: Kim Wimpsett
Proofreader: Piper Editorial LLC

Indexer: Sam Arnold-Boyd
Interior Designer: David Futato
Cover Designer: Jose Marzan
Illustrator: Kate Dullea

December 2020:   First Edition

Revision History for the First Edition
2020-12-03:   First Release

See *http://oreilly.com/catalog/errata.csp?isbn=9781492074083* for release details.

978-1-492-07408-3

[LSI]

Table of Contents

Preface

The written word is a powerful thing. The ancient Sumerians invented the first written language, and the introduction of the Gutenberg press allowed the written word to spread knowledge and enlightenment across the world. Language is in fact so important to human thinking that anthropologists claim that our ability for complex reasoning evolved at the same time that we developed language. Language represented in the form of text captures most of human thought, deeds, and actions, and our life is increasingly dominated by it. We communicate with colleagues through emails, with friends and family via messengers, and with others who share our passions using social media tools. Leaders inspire huge populations through speeches (and tweets) that are recorded as text, leading researchers communicate their findings via published research papers, and companies communicate their health through quarterly reports. Even this book uses text to spread knowledge. Analyzing and understanding text gives us the ability to gain knowledge and make decisions. Text analytics is about writing computer programs that can analyze vast amounts of information available in the form of text. Before making a product purchase or visiting a restaurant, we read customer reviews. A company could then use the same reviews to improve their product or service. A publisher could analyze discussions on the internet to estimate the demand for a certain programming language before commissioning a book on it.

It is much harder for a computer to understand text compared to other types of data. While there are rules of grammar and guidelines to forming sentences, these are often not strictly followed and depend heavily on context. Even with the correct grammar, it is hard for a machine to interpret the text correctly. The words that a person chooses while tweeting would be quite different from writing an email to express the same thought. There have been recent advances in statistical techniques and machine learning algorithms that allow us to get past many of these obstacles to derive value from text data. New models are able to capture the semantic meaning of text better than previous approaches based on word frequencies alone. But there are also many business tasks where these simple models perform surprisingly well.

In one of our client projects, for example, a home appliance manufacturer was able to understand the key topics affecting customer purchases by analyzing product reviews and adjust their marketing message to focus on these aspects. In another case, an e-commerce retailer used a deep neural network to classify customer queries and route them to the correct department for faster resolution. Analyzing abstracts from scientific journals has allowed an R&D company to detect trends in new materials and adjust their research accordingly. A fashion company identified mega-topics in their customer group by taking a look at posts in social networks. With this book we have tried to transfer our experiences from these and many other projects into blueprints that you can easily reuse in your own projects.

Approach of the Book

This book is intended to support data scientists and developers so they can quickly enter the area of text analytics and natural language processing. Thus, we put the focus on developing practical solutions that can serve as blueprints in your daily business. A blueprint, in our definition, is a best-practice solution for a common problem. It is a template that you can easily copy and adapt for reuse. For these blueprints we use production-ready Python frameworks for data analysis, natural language processing, and machine learning. Nevertheless, we also introduce the underlying models and algorithms.

We do not expect any previous knowledge in the field of natural language processing but provide you with the necessary background knowledge to get started quickly. In each chapter, we explain and discuss different solution approaches for the respective tasks with their potential strengths and weaknesses. Thus, you will not only acquire the knowledge about how to solve a certain kind of problem but also get a set of ready-to-use blueprints that you can take and customize to your data and requirements.

Each of the 13 chapters includes a self-contained use case for a specific aspect of text analytics (see Table P-1). Based on an example dataset, we develop and explain the blueprints step by step.

Table P-1. Overview of the chapters

Chapter	Dataset	Libraries
Chapter 1, *Gaining Early Insights from Textual Data* Getting started with the statistical exploration of textual data	UN General Debates	Pandas, Regex
Chapter 2, *Extracting Textual Insights with APIs* Using different Python modules to extract data from popular APIs	GitHub, Twitter, and Wikipedia API	Requests, Tweepy
Chapter 3, *Scraping Websites and Extracting Data* Using Python libraries to download web pages and extract content	Reuters website	Requests, Beautiful Soup, Readability-lxml, Scrapy

Chapter	Dataset	Libraries
Chapter 4, *Preparing Textual Data for Statistics and Machine Learning* Introduction to data cleaning and linguistic processing	Reddit Selfposts	Regex, spaCy
Chapter 5, *Feature Engineering and Syntactic Similarity* Introduction to features and vectorization	1 million headlines from ABC News	scikit-learn, NumPy
Chapter 6, *Text Classification Algorithms*. Text Classification Algorithms Using machine learning algorithms to classify software bugs	Java Development Tools bug reports	scikit-learn
Chapter 7, *How to Explain a Text Classifier* Explaining models and classification results	Java Development Tools bug reports	scikit-learn, Lime, Anchor, ELI5
Chapter 8, *Unsupervised Methods: Topic Modeling and Clustering* Using unsupervised methods to gain unbiased insights into text	UN General Debates	scikit-learn, Gensim
Chapter 9, *Text Summarization* Creating short summaries of news articles and forum threads using rule-based and machine learning approaches	Reuters News articles, Travel Forum threads	Sumy, scikit-learn
Chapter 10, *Exploring Semantic Relationships with Word Embeddings* Using word embeddings to explore and visualize semantic similarities in a specific data set	Reddit Selfposts	Gensim
Chapter 11, *Performing Sentiment Analysis on Text Data* Identifying customer sentiment in Amazon product reviews	Amazon product reviews	Transformers, scikit-learn, NLTK
Chapter 12, *Building a Knowledge Graph* How to extract named entities and their relationships using pretrained models and custom rules	Reuters news on mergers and acquisitions	spaCy
Chapter 13, *Using Text Analytics in Production* Deploy and scale the sentiment analysis blueprint as an API on Google Cloud Platform		FastAPI, Docker, conda, Kubernetes, gcloud

The choice of topics reflects the most common types of problems in our daily text analytics work. Typical tasks include data acquisition, statistical data exploration, and the use of supervised and unsupervised machine learning. The business questions range from content analysis ("What are people talking about?") to automatic text categorization.

Prerequisites

In this book you will learn how to solve text analytics problems efficiently with the Python ecosystem. We will explain all concepts specific to text analytics and machine learning in detail but assume that you already have basic knowledge of Python, including fundamental libraries like Pandas. You should also be familiar with Jupyter notebooks so that you can experiment with the code while reading the book. If not, check out the tutorials on *learnpython.org*, *docs.python.org*, or DataCamp (*https:// oreil.ly/oB-eH*).

Even though we explain the general ideas of the algorithms used, we won't go too much into the details. You should be able to follow the examples and reuse the code without completely understanding the mathematics behind it. College-level knowledge of linear algebra and statistics is helpful, though.

Some Important Libraries to Know

Every data analytics project starts with data exploration and data processing. The most popular Python library for those tasks is definitely *Pandas* (*https://pandas.pydata.org*). It offers rich functionality to access, transform, analyze, and visualize data. If you have never worked with this framework, we recommend checking out the official introduction, *10 minutes to Pandas* (*https://oreil.ly/eWlId*), or one of the other free tutorials available on the internet before reading the book.

For years, *scikit-learn* (*https://scikit-learn.org*) has been the machine learning toolkit for Python. It implements a large variety of supervised and unsupervised machine learning algorithms as well as many functions for data preprocessing. We use scikit-learn in several of the chapters to transform text into numerical vectors and for text classification.

When it comes to deep neural models, however, frameworks like PyTorch or TensorFlow are clearly superior to scikit-learn. Instead of using those libraries directly, we use the *Transformers library* (*https://oreil.ly/f5Ped*) from Hugging Face in Chapter 11 for sentiment analysis. Since the publication of BERT,[1] transformer-based models outperform previous approaches on tasks that require an understanding of the meaning of text, and the Transformers library provides easy access to many pretrained models.

Our favorite library for natural language processing is *spaCy*. Since its first release in 2016, spaCy enjoys a constantly growing user base. Though open source, it is primarily developed by the company Explosion (*https://explosion.ai*). Pretrained neural language models for part-of-speech tagging, dependency parsing, and named-entity recognition are available for many languages. We used spaCy version 2.3.2 for the development of this book, especially for data preparation (Chapter 4) and knowledge extraction (Chapter 12). At the time of publication, spaCy 3.0 will be out with completely new, transformer-based models, support for custom models in PyTorch and TensorFlow, and templates for defining end-to-end workflows.

Another NLP library we use is Gensim (*https://oreil.ly/YJ4Pz*), which is maintained by Radim Řehůřek. Gensim puts the focus on semantic analysis and provides all that is necessary to learn topic models (Chapter 8) and word embeddings (Chapter 10).

---

1 Devlin, Jacob, et al., "BERT: Pre-training of Deep Bidirectional Transformers for Language Understanding." 2018. *https://arxiv.org/abs/1810.04805*.

There are many other libraries for natural language processing that can be helpful but are not or only briefly mentioned in the book. These include NLTK (feature-rich grandfather of Python NLP libraries), TextBlob (easy to get started), Stanford's Stanza and CoreNLP, as well as Flair (state-of-the-art models for advanced tasks). Our goal was not to give an overview on everything that's out there but to choose and explain those libraries that worked best in our projects.

Books to Read

As we focus on practical solutions for our use cases, you might want to check out some additional books for further details or topics we did not cover. Below you will find some recommendations for books to read alongside this one:

Practical Natural Language Processing by Sowmya Vajjala, Bodhisattwa Majumder, Anuj Gupta, and Harshit Surana (O'Reilly, 2020), ISBN 978-1-492-05405-4.

Natural Language Processing in Action by Hobson Lane, Cole Howard, and Hannes Hapke (Manning Publications, 2019), ISBN 978-1-617-29463-1.

Mining the Social Web, 3rd Edition by Matthew A. Russell and Mikhail Klassen (O'Reilly, 2019), ISBN 978-1-491-98504-5.

Applied Text Analysis with Python by Benjamin Bengfort, Rebecca Bilbro, and Tony Ojeda (O'Reilly 2018), ISBN 978-1-491-96304-3.

Python for Data Analysis, 2nd Edition by Wes McKinney (O'Reilly, 2017), ISBN 978-1-491-95766-0.

Conventions Used in This Book

The following typographical conventions are used in this book:

Italic
Indicates new terms, URLs, email addresses, filenames, and file extensions.

`Constant width`
Used for program listings, as well as within paragraphs to refer to program elements such as variable or function names, databases, data types, environment variables, statements, and keywords.

`Constant width bold`
Shows commands or other text that should be typed literally by the user.

`Constant width italic`
Shows text that should be replaced with user-supplied values or by values determined by context.

This element signifies a tip or suggestion.

This element signifies a general note.

This element indicates a warning or caution.

This element indicates a blueprint.

Using Code Examples

The whole purpose of a blueprint is to be copied. Thus, we provide all the code developed in this book in our GitHub repository (*https://oreil.ly/btap-code*).

For each chapter, you will find an executable Jupyter notebook with the code from the book and possibly some additional functions or blueprints that have been omitted. The repository also contains the necessary datasets and some additional information.

The easiest way to run the notebooks is on Google Colab (*https://oreil.ly/colab*), Google's public cloud platform for machine learning. You don't even have to install Python on your local computer; just click on the Colab link for the respective chapter on GitHub (Google account required). However, we also added instructions for setting up your own (virtual) Python environment in the GitHub repository. We designed the Jupyter notebooks in a way that allows you to run them both locally and on Google Colab.

Libraries, data, and websites are subject to continuous change. Therefore, it can easily happen that the verbatim code in the book will not run properly in the future. To overcome this, we will keep the repository up to date. If you discover any technical problems or have recommendations on how to improve the code, do not hesitate to create an issue in the repository or send us a pull request.

If you have a technical question or a problem using the code examples, please email *bookquestions@oreilly.com*. In the case of technical problems, we recommend creating an issue in the GitHub repo (*https://oreil.ly/ApUgF*) and refer to O'Reilly's errata page for errors in the book.

This book is here to help you get your job done. In general, if example code is offered with this book, you may use it in your programs and documentation. You do not need to contact us for permission unless you're reproducing a significant portion of the code. For example, writing a program that uses several chunks of code from this book does not require permission. Selling or distributing examples from O'Reilly books does require permission. Answering a question by citing this book and quoting example code does not require permission. Incorporating a significant amount of example code from this book into your product's documentation does require permission.

You may use our code freely in your own projects without asking for permission. Especially if you publicly republish our code, we appreciate attribution. An attribution usually includes the title, author, publisher, and ISBN. For example: "*Blueprints for Text Analytics Using Python* by Jens Albrecht, Sidharth Ramachandran, and Christian Winkler (O'Reilly, 2021), 978-1-492-07408-3."

If you feel your use of code examples falls outside fair use or the permission given above, feel free to contact us at *permissions@oreilly.com*.

O'Reilly Online Learning

 For more than 40 years, *O'Reilly Media* has provided technology and business training, knowledge, and insight to help companies succeed.

Our unique network of experts and innovators share their knowledge and expertise through books, articles, and our online learning platform. O'Reilly's online learning platform gives you on-demand access to live training courses, in-depth learning paths, interactive coding environments, and a vast collection of text and video from O'Reilly and 200+ other publishers. For more information, visit *http://oreilly.com*.

How to Contact Us

Please address comments and questions concerning this book to the publisher:

O'Reilly Media, Inc.
1005 Gravenstein Highway North
Sebastopol, CA 95472

800-998-9938 (in the United States or Canada)
707-829-0515 (international or local)
707-829-0104 (fax)

We have a web page for this book, where we list errata, examples, and any additional information. You can access this page at *https://oreil.ly/text-analytics-with-python*.

Email *bookquestions@oreilly.com* to comment or ask technical questions about this book.

For news and information about our books and courses, visit *http://oreilly.com*.

Find us on Facebook: *http://facebook.com/oreilly*

Follow us on Twitter: *http://twitter.com/oreillymedia*

Watch us on YouTube: *http://youtube.com/oreillymedia*

Acknowledgments

Writing a book is a challenge, not only for the authors but also for their families and friends. All of us expected that it would take a lot of time, but still we were surprised by how much time we needed to develop the stories for each of the chapters. As we are all working full-time jobs, the time for discussing, coding, writing, and rewriting had to be taken from our families.

Working with O'Reilly has been a great pleasure for all of us. From the original proposal, during the time of writing, and in the production phase, we enjoyed working with professionals and immensely benefited from their hints and suggestions. The most intense time for us was writing the individual chapters. During that, we were perfectly supported by our development editor, Amelia Blevins. Without her help and improvements, the book would have been stuck in a less-readable state.

We would also like to express our gratitude to our reviewers, Oliver Zeigermann, Benjamin Bock, Alexander Schneider, and Darren Cook. They used their expertise and a lot of their time to make excellent suggestions and improvements and also to find errors in the text and the notebooks.

As we used state-of-the-art features of libraries, we sometimes encountered problems or incompatibilities. With spaCy as a central component in our analytics pipeline, working with the super responsive team from Explosion (Ines Montani, Sofie Van Landeghem, and Adriane Boyd) was a great pleasure. Their comments on the sections covering spaCy have been extremely helpful. Thanks also to Burton DeWilde, the developer behind textacy, for checking parts of the code.

## CHAPTER 1

Gaining Early Insights from Textual Data

One of the first tasks in every data analytics and machine learning project is to become familiar with the data. In fact, it is always essential to have a basic understanding of the data to achieve robust results. Descriptive statistics provide reliable and robust insights and help to assess data quality and distribution.

When considering texts, frequency analysis of words and phrases is one of the main methods for data exploration. Though absolute word frequencies usually are not very interesting, relative or weighted frequencies are. When analyzing text about politics, for example, the most common words will probably contain many obvious and unsurprising terms such as *people, country, government*, etc. But if you compare relative word frequencies in text from different political parties or even from politicians in the same party, you can learn a lot from the differences.

What You'll Learn and What We'll Build

This chapter presents blueprints for the statistical analysis of text. It gets you started quickly and introduces basic concepts that you will need to know in subsequent chapters. We will start by analyzing categorical metadata and then focus on word frequency analysis and visualization.

After studying this chapter, you will have basic knowledge about text processing and analysis. You will know how to tokenize text, filter stop words, and analyze textual content with frequency diagrams and word clouds. We will also introduce TF-IDF weighting as an important concept that will be picked up later in the book for text vectorization.

The blueprints in this chapter focus on quick results and follow the *KISS* principle: "Keep it simple, stupid!" Thus, we primarily use Pandas as our library of choice for data analysis in combination with regular expressions and Python core functionality. Chapter 4 will discuss advanced linguistic methods for data preparation.

Exploratory Data Analysis

Exploratory data analysis is the process of systematically examining data on an aggregated level. Typical methods include summary statistics for numerical features as well as frequency counts for categorical features. Histograms and box plots will illustrate the distribution of values, and time-series plots will show their evolution.

A dataset consisting of text documents such as news, tweets, emails, or service calls is called a *corpus* in natural language processing. The statistical exploration of such a corpus has different facets. Some analyses focus on metadata attributes, while others deal with the textual content. Figure 1-1 shows typical attributes of a text corpus, some of which are included in the data source, while others could be calculated or derived. The document metadata comprise multiple descriptive attributes, which are useful for aggregation and filtering. Time-like attributes are essential to understanding the evolution of the corpus. If available, author-related attributes allow you to analyze groups of authors and to benchmark these groups against one another.

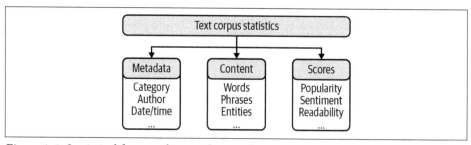

Figure 1-1. Statistical features for text data exploration.

Statistical analysis of the content is based on the frequencies of words and phrases. With the linguistic data preprocessing methods described in Chapter 4, we will extend the space of analysis to certain word types and named entities. Besides that, descriptive scores for the documents could be included in the dataset or derived by some kind of feature modeling. For example, the number of replies to a user's post could be taken as a measure of popularity. Finally, interesting soft facts such as sentiment or emotionality scores can be determined by one of the methods described later in this book.

Note that absolute figures are generally not very interesting when working with text. The mere fact that the word *problem* appears a hundred times does not contain any relevant information. But the fact that the relative frequency of *problem* has doubled within a week can be remarkable.

Introducing the Dataset

Analyzing political text, be it news or programs of political parties or parliamentary debates, can give interesting insights on national and international topics. Often, text from many years is publicly available so that an insight into the zeitgeist can be gained. Let's jump into the role of a political analyst who wants to get a feeling for the analytical potential of such a dataset.

For that, we will work with the UN General Debate dataset (*https://oreil.ly/lHHUm*). The corpus consists of 7,507 speeches held at the annual sessions of the United Nations General Assembly from 1970 to 2016. It was created in 2017 by Mikhaylov, Baturo, and Dasandi at Harvard "for understanding and measuring state preferences in world politics." Each of the almost 200 countries in the United Nations has the opportunity to present its views on global topics such international conflicts, terrorism, or climate change at the annual General Debate.

The original dataset on Kaggle is provided in the form of two CSV files, a big one containing the speeches and a smaller one with information about the speakers. To simplify matters, we prepared a single zipped CSV file containing all the information. You can find the code for the preparation as well as the resulting file in our GitHub repository (*https://oreil.ly/btap-code*).

In Pandas, a CSV file can be loaded with `pd.read_csv()`. Let's load the file and display two random records of the `DataFrame`:

```
file = "un-general-debates-blueprint.csv"
df = pd.read_csv(file)
df.sample(2)
```

Out:

	session	year	country	country_name	speaker	position	text
3871	51	1996	PER	Peru	Francisco Tudela Van Breughel Douglas	Minister for Foreign Affairs	At the outset, allow me,\nSir, to convey to you and to this Assembly the greetings\nand congratulations of the Peruvian people, as well as\ntheir...
4697	56	2001	GBR	United Kingdom	Jack Straw	Minister for Foreign Affairs	Please allow me\nwarmly to congratulate you, Sir, on your assumption of\nthe presidency of the fifty-sixth session of the General \nAssembly.\nThi...

The first column contains the index of the records. The combination of session number and year can be considered as the logical primary key of the table. The `country` column contains a standardized three-letter country ISO code and is followed by the textual description. Then we have two columns about the speaker and their position. The last column contains the actual text of the speech.

Our dataset is small; it contains only a few thousand records. It is a great dataset to use because we will not run into performance problems. If your dataset is larger, check out "Working with Large Datasets" for options.

Working with Large Datasets

Don't start data exploration with millions and billions of records. Instead, use a small sample of the data to get started. This way you can quickly develop the statements and visualizations you need. Once the analyses are prepared, you can rerun everything on the large dataset to get the full view.

There are multiple ways to select a sample of the data. The simplest and most useful one is Pandas's `sample` function, which is used in the following command to replace a `DataFrame` by a random sample of 10% of its records:

```
df = df.sample(frac=0.1)
```

The drawback of this method is that the full dataset must be loaded into main memory before it can be sampled. Alternatively, you can load only a subset of the data. For example, `pd.read_csv` has two optional parameters, `nrows` and `skiprows`, which can be used to read a slice of the whole file. However, this will select a range of subsequent rows, not a random sample. If your data is stored in a relational database, you should check whether it supports random sampling. You could also use some poor man's SQL for random sampling like this:

```
ORDER BY Rand() LIMIT 10000
```

Or:

```
WHERE id%10 = 0
```

Blueprint: Getting an Overview of the Data with Pandas

In our first blueprint, we use only metadata and record counts to explore data distribution and quality; we will not yet look at the textual content. We will work through the following steps:

1. Calculate summary statistics.
2. Check for missing values.

3. Plot distributions of interesting attributes.

4. Compare distributions across categories.

5. Visualize developments over time.

Before we can start analyzing the data, we need at least some information about the structure of the `DataFrame`. Table 1-1 shows some important descriptive properties or functions.

Table 1-1. Pandas commands to get information about dataframes

`df.columns`	List of column names	
`df.dtypes`	Tuples (column name, data type)	Strings are represented as object in versions before Pandas 1.0.
`df.info()`	Dtypes plus memory consumption	Use with `memory_usage='deep'` for good estimates on text.
`df.describe()`	Summary statistics	Use with `include='O'` for categorical data.

Calculating Summary Statistics for Columns

Pandas's `describe` function computes statistical summaries for the columns of the `DataFrame`. It works on a single series as well as on the complete `DataFrame`. The default output in the latter case is restricted to numerical columns. Currently, our `DataFrame` contains only the session number and the year as numerical data. Let's add a new numerical column to the `DataFrame` containing the text length to get some additional information about the distribution of the lengths of the speeches. We recommend transposing the result with `describe().T` to switch rows and columns in the representation:

```
df['length'] = df['text'].str.len()

df.describe().T
```

Out:

	count	mean	std	min	25%	50%	75%	max
session	7507.00	49.61	12.89	25.00	39.00	51.00	61.00	70.00
year	7507.00	1994.61	12.89	1970.00	1984.00	1996.00	2006.00	2015.00
length	7507.00	17967.28	7860.04	2362.00	12077.00	16424.00	22479.50	72041.00

`describe()`, without additional parameters, computes the total count of values, their mean and standard deviation, and a five-number summary (*https://oreil.ly/h2nrN*) of only the numerical columns. The `DataFrame` contains 7,507 entries for `session`, `year`, and `length`. Mean and standard deviation do not make much sense for `year` and `session`, but minimum and maximum are still interesting. Obviously, our dataset contains speeches from the 25th to the 70th UN General Debate sessions, spanning the years 1970 to 2015.

A summary for nonnumerical columns can be produced by specifying `include='O'` (the alias for `np.object`). In this case, we also get the count, the number of unique values, the top-most element (or one of them if there are many with the same number of occurrences), and its frequency. As the number of unique values is not useful for textual data, let's just analyze the `country` and `speaker` columns:

```
df[['country', 'speaker']].describe(include='O').T
```

Out:

	count	unique	top	freq
country	7507	199	ITA	46
speaker	7480	5428	Seyoum Mesfin	12

The dataset contains data from 199 unique countries and apparently 5,428 speakers. The number of countries is valid, as this column contains standardized ISO codes. But counting the unique values of text columns like `speaker` usually does not give valid results, as we will show in the next section.

Checking for Missing Data

By looking at the counts in the previous table, we can see that the `speaker` column has missing values. So, let's check all columns for null values by using `df.isna()` (the alias to `df.isnull()`) and compute a summary of the result:

```
df.isna().sum()
```

Out:

```
session          0
year             0
country          0
country_name     0
speaker         27
position      3005
text             0
length           0
dtype: int64
```

We need to be careful using the `speaker` and `position` columns, as the output tells us that this information is not always available! To prevent any problems, we could substitute the missing values with some generic value such as `unknown speaker` or `unknown position` or just the empty string.

Pandas supplies the function `df.fillna()` for that purpose:

```
df['speaker'].fillna('unknown', inplace=True)
```

But even the existing values can be problematic because the same speaker's name is sometimes spelled differently or even ambiguously. The following statement computes the number of records per speaker for all documents containing Bush in the speaker column:

```
df[df['speaker'].str.contains('Bush')]['speaker'].value_counts()
```

Out:

```
George W. Bush        4
Mr. George W. Bush    2
George Bush           1
Mr. George W Bush     1
Bush                  1
Name: speaker, dtype: int64
```

Any analysis on speaker names would produce the wrong results unless we resolve these ambiguities. So, we had better check the distinct values of categorical attributes. Knowing this, we will ignore the speaker information here.

Plotting Value Distributions

One way to visualize the five-number summary of a numerical distribution is a box plot (*https://oreil.ly/7xZJ_*). It can be easily produced by Pandas's built-in plot functionality. Let's take a look at the box plot for the `length` column:

```
df['length'].plot(kind='box', vert=False)
```

Out:

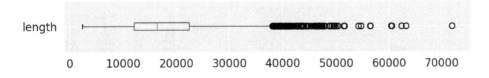

As illustrated by this plot, 50% percent of the speeches (the box in the middle) have a length between roughly 12,000 and 22,000 characters, with the median at about 16,000 and a long tail with many outliers to the right. The distribution is obviously left-skewed. We can get some more details by plotting a histogram:

```
df['length'].plot(kind='hist', bins=30)
```

Out:

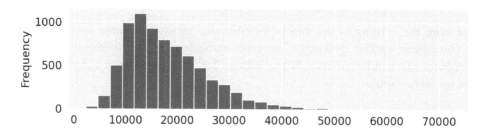

For the histogram, the value range of the length column is divided into 30 intervals of equal width, the *bins*. The y-axis shows the number of documents falling into each of these bins.

Comparing Value Distributions Across Categories

Peculiarities in the data often become visible when different subsets of the data are examined. A nice visualization to compare distributions across different categories is Seaborn's catplot (*https://oreil.ly/jhlEE*).

We show box and violin plots to compare the distributions of the speech length of the five permanent members of the UN security council (Figure 1-2). Thus, the category for the x-axis of sns.catplot is country:

```
where = df['country'].isin(['USA', 'FRA', 'GBR', 'CHN', 'RUS'])
sns.catplot(data=df[where], x="country", y="length", kind='box')
sns.catplot(data=df[where], x="country", y="length", kind='violin')
```

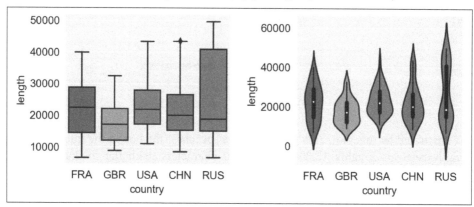

Figure 1-2. Box plots (left) and violin plots (right) visualizing the distribution of speech lengths for selected countries.

The violin plot is the "smoothed" version of a box plot. Frequencies are visualized by the width of the violin body, while the box is still visible inside the violin. Both plots reveal that the dispersion of values, in this case the lengths of the speeches, for Russia is much larger than for Great Britain. But the existence of multiple peaks, as in Russia, only becomes apparent in the violin plot.

Visualizing Developments Over Time

If your data contains date or time attributes, it is always interesting to visualize some developments within the data over time. A first time series can be created by analyzing the number of speeches per year. We can use the Pandas grouping function `size()` to return the number of rows per group. By simply appending `plot()`, we can visualize the resulting `DataFrame` (Figure 1-3, left):

```
df.groupby('year').size().plot(title="Number of Countries")
```

The timeline reflects the development of the number of countries in the UN, as each country is eligible for only one speech per year. Actually, the UN has 193 members today. Interestingly, the speech length needed to decrease with more countries entering the debates, as the following analysis reveals (Figure 1-3, right):

```
df.groupby('year').agg({'length': 'mean'}) \
    .plot(title="Avg. Speech Length", ylim=(0,30000))
```

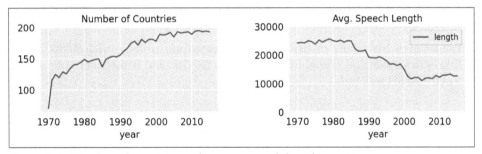

Figure 1-3. Number of countries and average speech length over time.

Pandas dataframes not only can be easily visualized in Jupyter notebooks but also can be exported to Excel (*.xlsx*), HTML, CSV, LaTeX, and many other formats by built-in functions. There is even a `to_clipboard()` function. Check the documentation (*https:// oreil.ly/HZDVN*) for details.

Resampling Time

In the UN dataset, we already have yearly data; the integer column `year` contains discrete values that we can use for grouping. But usually the dataset includes more fine-grained date or time values that need to be aggregated to an appropriate granularity for visualization. Depending on the scenario, this can range from hourly to yearly or even decades. Fortunately, Pandas has built-in functionality to access datetime values on different levels. For example, you can use the dt accessor of the underlying Pandas Series object to access certain properties such as dt.year directly. The following table shows some examples:[1]

Datetime property	Description	Datetime property	Description
dt.date	Date part of datetime	dt.hour	Hour part of datetime
dt.year	Year	dt.month	Month within year as number
dt.quarter	Quarter within year as number	dt.week	Week within year as number

Let's assume the datetime column in our dateframe actually has the name time as recommended for our blueprints. Then you could just create an additional year column in any DataFrame with this command:

```
df['year'] = df['time'].dt.year
```

Often you need combined values like 2020/Week 24 to plot a time series with appropriate labels. A flexible way to achieve this is to use dt.strftime(), which provides access to the common strftime (*https://oreil.ly/KvMjG*) (string from time) functionality in Pandas:

```
df['week'] = df['time'].dt.strftime("%Y/Week %W")
```

Pandas even has a built-in function called resample() (*https://oreil.ly/E0oOX*) for time-series resampling. However, it aggregates the data and is therefore not useful when working with text.

Blueprint: Building a Simple Text Preprocessing Pipeline

The analysis of metadata such as categories, time, authors, and other attributes gives some first insights on the corpus. But it's much more interesting to dig deeper into the actual content and explore frequent words in different subsets or time periods. In this section, we will develop a basic blueprint to prepare text for a quick first analysis consisting of a simple sequence of steps (Figure 1-4). As the output of one operation forms the input of the next one, such a sequence is also called a *processing pipeline* that transforms the original text into a number of tokens.

---

1 See the Pandas documentation (*https://oreil.ly/XjAKa*) for a complete list.

Figure 1-4. Simple preprocessing pipeline.

The pipeline presented here consists of three steps: case-folding into lowercase, tokenization, and stop word removal. These steps will be discussed in depth and extended in Chapter 4, where we make use of spaCy. To keep it fast and simple here, we build our own tokenizer based on regular expressions and show how to use an arbitrary stop word list.

Performing Tokenization with Regular Expressions

Tokenization is the process of extracting words from a sequence of characters. In Western languages, words are often separated by whitespaces and punctuation characters. Thus, the simplest and fastest tokenizer is Python's native `str.split()` method, which splits on whitespace. A more flexible way is to use regular expressions.

Regular expressions and the Python libraries `re` and `regex` will be introduced in more detail in Chapter 4. Here, we want to apply a simple pattern that matches words. Words in our definition consist of at least one letter as well as digits and hyphens. Pure numbers are skipped because they almost exclusively represent dates or speech or session identifiers in this corpus.

The frequently used expression `[A-Za-z]` is not a good option for matching letters because it misses accented letters like *ä* or *â*. Much better is the POSIX character class `\p{L}`, which selects all Unicode letters. Note that we need the `regex` library (*https://oreil.ly/hJ6M2*) instead of `re` to work with POSIX character classes. The following expression matches tokens consisting of at least one letter (`\p{L}`), preceded and followed by an arbitrary sequence of alphanumeric characters (`\w` includes digits, letters, and underscore) and hyphens (`-`):

```
import regex as re

def tokenize(text):
    return re.findall(r'[\w-]*\p{L}[\w-]*', text)
```

Let's try it with a sample sentence from the corpus:

```
text = "Let's defeat SARS-CoV-2 together in 2020!"
tokens = tokenize(text)
print("|".join(tokens))
```

Out:

```
Let|s|defeat|SARS-CoV-2|together|in
```

Treating Stop Words

The most frequent words in text are common words such as determiners, auxiliary verbs, pronouns, adverbs, and so on. These words are called *stop words*. Stop words usually don't carry much information but hide interesting content because of their high frequencies. Therefore, stop words are often removed before data analysis or model training.

In this section, we show how to discard stop words contained in a predefined list. Common stop word lists are available for many languages and are integrated in almost any NLP library. We will work with NLTK's list of stop words here, but you could use any list of words as a filter.[2] For fast lookup, you should always convert a list to a set. Sets are hash-based structures like dictionaries with nearly constant lookup time:

```
import nltk

stopwords = set(nltk.corpus.stopwords.words('english'))
```

Our approach to remove stop words from a given list, wrapped into the small function shown here, consists of a simple list comprehension. For the check, tokens are converted to lowercase as NLTK's list contains only lowercase words:

```
def remove_stop(tokens):
    return [t for t in tokens if t.lower() not in stopwords]
```

Often you'll need to add domain-specific stop words to the predefined list. For example, if you are analyzing emails, the terms *dear* and *regards* will probably appear in almost any document. On the other hand, you might want to treat some of the words in the predefined list not as stop words. We can add additional stop words and exclude others from the list using two of Python's set operators, | (union/or) and - (difference):

```
include_stopwords = {'dear', 'regards', 'must', 'would', 'also'}
exclude_stopwords = {'against'}

stopwords |= include_stopwords
stopwords -= exclude_stopwords
```

The stop word list from NLTK is conservative and contains only 179 words. Surprisingly, *would* is not considered a stop word, while *wouldn't* is. This illustrates a common problem with predefined stop word lists: inconsistency. Be aware that removing stop words can significantly affect the performance of semantically targeted analyses, as explained in "Why Removing Stop Words Can Be Dangerous" on page 13.

---

2 You can address spaCy's list similarly with `spacy.lang.en.STOP_WORDS`.

Why Removing Stop Words Can Be Dangerous

Stop word removal is a coarse-grained rule-based method. Be careful with the stop word lists you are using, and make sure that you don't delete valuable information. Look at this simple example: "I don't like ice cream."

Both NLTK and spaCy have *I* and *don't* (same as *do not*) in their stop word lists. If you remove those stop words, all that's left is *like ice cream*. This kind of preprocessing would heavily distort any kind of sentiment analysis. TF-IDF weighting, as introduced later in this section, automatically underweighs frequently occurring words but keeps those terms in the vocabulary.

In addition to or instead of a fixed list of stop words, it can be helpful to treat every word that appears in more than, say, 80% of the documents as a stop word. Such common words make it difficult to distinguish content. The parameter `max_df` of the scikit-learn vectorizers, as covered in Chapter 5, does exactly this. Another method is to filter words based on the word type (part of speech). This concept will be explained in Chapter 4.

Processing a Pipeline with One Line of Code

Let's get back to the `DataFrame` containing the documents of our corpus. We want to create a new column called `tokens` containing the lowercased, tokenized text without stop words for each document. For that, we use an extensible pattern for a processing pipeline. In our case, we will change all text to lowercase, tokenize it, and remove stop words. Other operations can be added by simply extending the pipeline:

```
pipeline = [str.lower, tokenize, remove_stop]

def prepare(text, pipeline):
    tokens = text
    for transform in pipeline:
        tokens = transform(tokens)
    return tokens
```

If we put all this into a function, it becomes a perfect use case for Pandas's `map` or `apply` operation. Functions such as `map` and `apply`, which take other functions as parameters, are called *higher-order functions* in mathematics and computer science.

Table 1-2. Pandas higher-order functions

Function	Description
Series.map	Works element by element on a Pandas Series
Series.apply	Same as map but allows additional parameters

Function	Description
DataFrame.applymap	Element by element on a Pandas DataFrame (same as map on Series)
DataFrame.apply	Works on rows or columns of a DataFrame and supports aggregation

Pandas supports the different higher-order functions on series and dataframes (Table 1-2). These functions not only allow you to specify a series of functional data transformations in a comprehensible way, but they can also be easily parallelized. The Python package pandarallel (*https://oreil.ly/qwPB4*), for example, provides parallel versions of map and apply.

Scalable frameworks like Apache Spark (*https://spark.apache.org*) support similar operations on dataframes even more elegantly. In fact, the map and reduce operations in distributed programming are based on the same principle of functional programming. In addition, many programming languages, including Python and JavaScript, have a native map operation for lists or arrays.

Using one of Pandas's higher-order operations, applying a functional transformation becomes a one-liner:

```
df['tokens'] = df['text'].apply(prepare, pipeline=pipeline)
```

The tokens column now consists of Python lists containing the extracted tokens for each document. Of course, this additional column basically doubles memory consumption of the DataFrame, but it allows you to quickly access the tokens directly for further analysis. Nevertheless, the following blueprints are designed in such a way that the tokenization can also be performed on the fly during analysis. In this way, performance can be traded for memory consumption: either tokenize once before analysis and consume memory or tokenize on the fly and wait.

We also add another column containing the length of the token list for summarizations later:

```
df['num_tokens'] = df['tokens'].map(len)
```

 tqdm (pronounced *taqadum* for "progress" in Arabic) is a great library for progress bars in Python. It supports conventional loops, e.g., by using tqdm_range instead of range, and it supports Pandas by providing progress_map and progress_apply operations on dataframes.[3] Our accompanying notebooks on GitHub use these operations, but we stick to plain Pandas here in the book.

---

3 Check out the documentation (*https://oreil.ly/gO_VN*) for further details.

Blueprints for Word Frequency Analysis

Frequently used words and phrases can give us some basic understanding of the discussed topics. However, word frequency analysis ignores the order and the context of the words. This is the idea of the famous bag-of-words model (see also Chapter 5): all the words are thrown into a bag where they tumble into a jumble. The original arrangement in the text is lost; only the frequency of the terms is taken into account. This model does not work well for complex tasks such as sentiment analysis or question answering, but it works surprisingly well for classification and topic modeling. In addition, it's a good starting point for understanding what the texts are all about.

In this section, we will develop a number of blueprints to calculate and visualize word frequencies. As raw frequencies overweigh unimportant but frequent words, we will also introduce TF-IDF at the end of the process. We will implement the frequency calculation by using a Counter because it is simple and extremely fast.

Blueprint: Counting Words with a Counter

Python's standard library has a built-in class Counter, which does exactly what you might think: it counts things.[4] The easiest way to work with a counter is to create it from a list of items, in our case strings representing the words or tokens. The resulting counter is basically a dictionary object containing those items as keys and their frequencies as values.

Let's illustrate its functionality with a simple example:

```
from collections import Counter

tokens = tokenize("She likes my cats and my cats like my sofa.")

counter = Counter(tokens)
print(counter)
```

Out:

```
Counter({'my': 3, 'cats': 2, 'She': 1, 'likes': 1, 'and': 1, 'like': 1,
        'sofa': 1})
```

The counter requires a list as input, so any text needs to be tokenized in advance. What's nice about the counter is that it can be incrementally updated with a list of tokens of a second document:

---

4 The NLTK class FreqDist (*https://oreil.ly/xQXUu*) is derived from Counter and adds some convenience functions.

```
more_tokens = tokenize("She likes dogs and cats.")
counter.update(more_tokens)
print(counter)
```

Out:

```
Counter({'my': 3, 'cats': 3, 'She': 2, 'likes': 2, 'and': 2, 'like': 1,
        'sofa': 1, 'dogs': 1})
```

To find the most frequent words within a corpus, we need to create a counter from the list of all words in all documents. A naive approach would be to concatenate all documents into a single, giant list of tokens, but that does not scale for larger datasets. It is much more efficient to call the update function of the counter object for each single document.

```
counter = Counter()

df['tokens'].map(counter.update)
```

We do a little trick here and put counter.update in the map function. The magic happens inside the update function under the hood. The whole map call runs extremely fast; it takes only about three seconds for the 7,500 UN speeches and scales linearly with the total number of tokens. The reason is that dictionaries in general and counters in particular are implemented as hash tables. A single counter is pretty compact compared to the whole corpus: it contains each word only once, along with its frequency.

Now we can retrieve the most common words in the text with the respective counter function:

```
print(counter.most_common(5))
```

Out:

```
[('nations', 124508),
 ('united', 120763),
 ('international', 117223),
 ('world', 89421),
 ('countries', 85734)]
```

For further processing and analysis, it is much more convenient to transform the counter into a Pandas DataFrame, and this is what the following blueprint function finally does. The tokens make up the index of the DataFrame, while the frequency values are stored in a column named freq. The rows are sorted so that the most frequent words appear at the head:

```
def count_words(df, column='tokens', preprocess=None, min_freq=2):

    # process tokens and update counter
    def update(doc):
        tokens = doc if preprocess is None else preprocess(doc)
```

```
        counter.update(tokens)

    # create counter and run through all data
    counter = Counter()
    df[column].map(update)

    # transform counter into a DataFrame
    freq_df = pd.DataFrame.from_dict(counter, orient='index', columns=['freq'])
    freq_df = freq_df.query('freq >= @min_freq')
    freq_df.index.name = 'token'

    return freq_df.sort_values('freq', ascending=False)
```

The function takes, as a first parameter, a Pandas `DataFrame` and takes the column name containing the tokens or the text as a second parameter. As we already stored the prepared tokens in the column `tokens` of the `DataFrame` containing the speeches, we can use the following two lines of code to compute the `DataFrame` with word frequencies and display the top five tokens:

```
    freq_df = count_words(df)
    freq_df.head(5)
```

Out:

token	freq
nations	124508
united	120763
international	117223
world	89421
countries	85734

If we don't want to use precomputed tokens for some special analysis, we could tokenize the text on the fly with a custom preprocessing function as the third parameter. For example, we could generate and count all words with 10 or more characters with this on-the-fly tokenization of the text:

```
    count_words(df, column='text',
                preprocess=lambda text: re.findall(r"\w{10,}", text))
```

The last parameter of `count_words` defines a minimum frequency of tokens to be included in the result. Its default is set to 2 to cut down the long tail of hapaxes, i.e., tokens occurring only once.

Blueprint: Creating a Frequency Diagram

There are dozens of ways to produce tables and diagrams in Python. We prefer Pandas with its built-in plot functionality because it is easier to use than plain Matplotlib. We assume a `DataFrame freq_df` generated by the previous blueprint for visualization. Creating a frequency diagram based on such a `DataFrame` now becomes basically a one-liner. We add two more lines for formatting:

```
ax = freq_df.head(15).plot(kind='barh', width=0.95)
ax.invert_yaxis()
ax.set(xlabel='Frequency', ylabel='Token', title='Top Words')
```

Out:

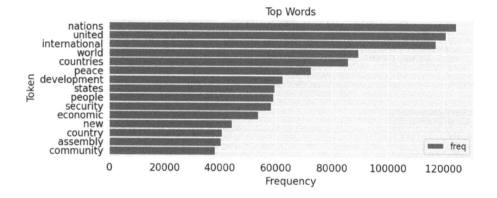

Using horizontal bars (barh) for word frequencies greatly improves readability because the words appear horizontally on the y-axis in a readable form. The y-axis is inverted to place the top words at the top of the chart. The axis labels and title can optionally be modified.

Blueprint: Creating Word Clouds

Plots of frequency distributions like the ones shown previously give detailed information about the token frequencies. But it is quite difficult to compare frequency diagrams for different time periods, categories, authors, and so on. Word clouds, in contrast, visualize the frequencies by different font sizes. They are much easier to comprehend and to compare, but they lack the precision of tables and bar charts. You should keep in mind that long words or words with capital letters get unproportionally high attraction.

The Python module wordcloud (*https://oreil.ly/RV0r5*) generates nice word clouds from texts or counters. The simplest way to use it is to instantiate a word cloud object with some options, such as the maximum number of words and a stop word list, and then let the wordcloud module handle the tokenization and stop word removal. The following code shows how to generate a word cloud for the text of the 2015 US speech and display the resulting image with Matplotlib:

```
from wordcloud import WordCloud
from matplotlib import pyplot as plt

text = df.query("year==2015 and country=='USA'")['text'].values[0]

wc = WordCloud(max_words=100, stopwords=stopwords)
wc.generate(text)
plt.imshow(wc, interpolation='bilinear')
plt.axis("off")
```

However, this works only for a single text and not a (potentially large) set of documents. For the latter use case, it is much faster to create a frequency counter first and then use the function generate_from_frequencies().

Our blueprint is a little wrapper around this function to also support a Pandas Series containing frequency values as created by count_words. The WordCloud class already has a magnitude of options to fine-tune the result. We use some of them in the following function to demonstrate possible adjustments, but you should check the documentation for details:

```
def wordcloud(word_freq, title=None, max_words=200, stopwords=None):

    wc = WordCloud(width=800, height=400,
                   background_color= "black", colormap="Paired",
                   max_font_size=150, max_words=max_words)

    # convert DataFrame into dict
    if type(word_freq) == pd.Series:
        counter = Counter(word_freq.fillna(0).to_dict())
    else:
        counter = word_freq

    # filter stop words in frequency counter
    if stopwords is not None:
        counter = {token:freq for (token, freq) in counter.items()
                              if token not in stopwords}
    wc.generate_from_frequencies(counter)

    plt.title(title)

    plt.imshow(wc, interpolation='bilinear')
    plt.axis("off")
```

The function has two convenience parameters to filter words. `skip_n` skips the top *n* words of the list. Obviously, in a UN corpus words like *united*, *nations*, or *international* are heading the list. It may be more interesting to visualize what comes next. The second filter is an (additional) list of stop words. Sometimes it is helpful to filter out specific frequent but uninteresting words for the visualization only.[5]

So, let's take a look at the 2015 speeches (Figure 1-5). The left word cloud visualizes the most frequent words unfiltered. The right word cloud instead treats the 50 most frequent words of the complete corpus as stop words:

```
freq_2015_df = count_words(df[df['year']==2015])
plt.figure()
wordcloud(freq_2015_df['freq'], max_words=100)
wordcloud(freq_2015_df['freq'], max_words=100, stopwords=freq_df.head(50).index)
```

Figure 1-5. Word clouds for the 2015 speeches including all words (left) and without the 50 most frequent words (right).

Clearly, the right word cloud without the most frequent words of the corpus gives a much better idea of the 2015 topics, but there are still frequent and unspecific words like *today* or *challenges*. We need a way to give less weight to those words, as shown in the next section.

Blueprint: Ranking with TF-IDF

As illustrated in Figure 1-5, visualizing the most frequent words usually does not reveal much insight. Even if stop words are removed, the most common words are usually obvious domain-specific terms that are quite similar in any subset (slice) of the data. But we would like to give more importance to those words that appear more frequently in a given slice of the data than "usual." Such

---

5 Note that the `wordcloud` module ignores the stop word list if `generate_from_frequencies` is called. Therefore, we apply an extra filter.

a slice can be any subset of the corpus, e.g., a single speech, the speeches of a certain decade, or the speeches from one country.

We want to highlight words whose actual word frequency in a slice is higher than their total probability would suggest. There is a number of algorithms to measure the "surprise" factor of a word. One of the simplest but best working approaches is to complement the term frequency with the inverse document frequency (see sidebar).

Inverse Document Frequency

The *inverse document frequency* (IDF) is a weighting factor that measures the "unusualness" of a term in a corpus. It is often used to reduce the influence of common terms for data analysis or machine learning. To explain it, let's first define the *document frequency* of a term t. Given a corpus (set of documents) C, the document frequency $df(t)$ is simply the number of documents d in C that contain the term t. Mathematically, it looks as follows:

$$df(t) = |\{d \in C \,|\, t \in d\}|$$

Terms appearing in many documents have a high document frequency. Based on this, we can define the *inverse document frequency* $idf(t)$ as follows:

$$idf(t) = log\left(\frac{|C|}{df(t)}\right)$$

The logarithm is used for sublinear scaling. Otherwise, rare words would get extremely high IDF scores. Note that $idf(t) = 0$ for terms that appear in all documents, i.e., $df(t) = |C|$. To not completely ignore those terms, some libraries add a constant to the whole term.[6] We add the term 0.1, which is roughly the value of tokens appearing in 90% of the documents ($log(1/0.9)$).[7]

For the weighting of a term t in a set of documents $D \subseteq C$, we compute the TF-IDF-score as the product of the term frequency $tf(t, D)$ and the IDF of term t:

$$tfidf(t, D) = tf(t, D) \cdot idf(t)$$

This score yields high values for terms appearing frequently in the selected document(s) D but rarely in the other documents of the corpus.

---

6 For example, scikit-learn's TfIdfVectorizer adds +1.

7 Another option is to add +1 in the denominator to prevent a division by zero for unseen terms with $df(t) = 0$. This technique is called *smoothing*.

Let's define a function to compute the IDF for all terms in the corpus. It is almost identical to count_words, except that each token is counted only once per document (counter.update(set(tokens))), and the IDF values are computed after counting. The parameter min_df serves as a filter for the long tail of infrequent words. The result of this function is again a DataFrame:

```
def compute_idf(df, column='tokens', preprocess=None, min_df=2):

    def update(doc):
        tokens = doc if preprocess is None else preprocess(doc)
        counter.update(set(tokens))

    # count tokens
    counter = Counter()
    df[column].map(update)

    # create DataFrame and compute idf
    idf_df = pd.DataFrame.from_dict(counter, orient='index', columns=['df'])
    idf_df = idf_df.query('df >= @min_df')
    idf_df['idf'] = np.log(len(df)/idf_df['df'])+0.1
    idf_df.index.name = 'token'
    return idf_df
```

The IDF values need to be computed once for the entire corpus (do not use a subset here!) and can then be used in all kinds of analyses. We create a DataFrame containing the IDF values for each token (idf_df) with this function:

```
idf_df = compute_idf(df)
```

As both the IDF and the frequency DataFrame have an index consisting of the tokens, we can simply multiply the columns of both DataFrames to calculate the TF-IDF score for the terms:

```
freq_df['tfidf'] = freq_df['freq'] * idf_df['idf']
```

Let's compare the word clouds based on word counts (term frequencies) alone and TF-IDF scores for the speeches of the first and last years in the corpus. We remove some more stop words that stand for the numbers of the respective debate sessions.

```
freq_1970 = count_words(df[df['year'] == 1970])
freq_2015 = count_words(df[df['year'] == 2015])

freq_1970['tfidf'] = freq_1970['freq'] * idf_df['idf']
freq_2015['tfidf'] = freq_2015['freq'] * idf_df['idf']

#wordcloud(freq_df['freq'], title='All years', subplot=(1,3,1))
wordcloud(freq_1970['freq'], title='1970 - TF',
          stopwords=['twenty-fifth', 'twenty-five'])
wordcloud(freq_2015['freq'], title='2015 - TF',
          stopwords=['seventieth'])
wordcloud(freq_1970['tfidf'], title='1970 - TF-IDF',
```

```
              stopwords=['twenty-fifth', 'twenty-five', 'twenty', 'fifth'])
   wordcloud(freq_2015['tfidf'], title='2015 - TF-IDF',
              stopwords=['seventieth'])
```

The word clouds in Figure 1-6 impressively demonstrate the power of TF-IDF
weighting. While the most common words are almost identical in 1970 and 2015, the
TF-IDF weighted visualizations emphasize the differences of political topics.

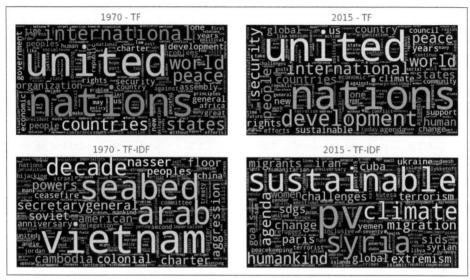

*Figure 1-6. Words weighted by plain counts (upper) and TF-IDF (lower) for speeches in
two selected years.*

The experienced reader might wonder why we implemented functions to count
words and compute IDF values ourselves instead of using the classes CountVector
izer and TfidfVectorizer of scikit-learn. Actually, there two reasons. First, the vectorizers produce a vector with weighted term frequencies for each single document
instead of arbitrary subsets of the dataset. Second, the results are matrices (good for
machine learning) and not dataframes (good for slicing, aggregation, and visualization). We would have to write about the same number of code lines in the end to
produce the results in Figure 1-6 but miss the opportunity to introduce this important concept from scratch. The scikit-learn vectorizers will be discussed in detail in
Chapter 5.

Blueprint: Finding a Keyword-in-Context

Word clouds and frequency diagrams are great tools to visually summarize textual data. However, they also often raise questions about why a certain term appears so prominently. For example, the *2015 TF-IDF* word cloud discussed earlier shows the terms *pv*, *sdgs*, or *sids*, and you probably do not know their meaning. To find that out, we need a way to inspect the actual occurrences of those words in the original, unprepared text. A simple yet clever way to do such an inspection is the keyword-in-context (KWIC) analysis. It produces a list of text fragments of equal length showing the left and right context of a keyword. Here is a sample of the KWIC list for *sdgs*, which gives us an explanation of that term:

```
5 random samples out of 73 contexts for 'sdgs':
  of our planet and its people. The   SDGs   are a tangible manifestation of th
nd, we are expected to achieve the    SDGs   and to demonstrate dramatic develo
ead by example in implementing the    SDGs   in Bangladesh. Attaching due impor
  the Sustainable Development Goals (  SDGs   ). We applaud all the Chairs of the
new Sustainable Development Goals (    SDGs   ) aspire to that same vision. The A
```

Obviously, *sdgs* is the lowercased version of SDGs, which stands for "sustainable development goals." With the same analysis we can learn that *sids* stands for "small island developing states." That is important information to interpret the topics of 2015! *pv*, however, is a tokenization artifact. It is actually the remainder of citation references like *(A/70/PV.28)*, which stands for "Assembly 70, Process Verbal 28," i.e., speech 28 of the 70th assembly.

Always look into the details when you encounter tokens that you do not know or that do not make sense to you! Often they carry important information (like *sdgs*) that you as an analyst should be able to interpret. But you'll also often find artifacts like *pv*. Those should be discarded if irrelevant or treated correctly.

KWIC analysis is implemented in NLTK and textacy. We will use textacy's KWIC function (*https://oreil.ly/-dSrA*) because it is fast and works on the untokenized text. Thus, we can search for strings spanning multiple tokens like "climate change," while NLTK cannot. Both NLTK and textacy's KWIC functions work on a single document only. To extend the analysis to a number of documents in a DataFrame, we provide the following function:

```
from textacy.text_utils import KWIC

def kwic(doc_series, keyword, window=35, print_samples=5):

    def add_kwic(text):
```

```
        kwic_list.extend(KWIC(text, keyword, ignore_case=True,
                              window_width=window, print_only=False))

    kwic_list = []
    doc_series.map(add_kwic)

    if print_samples is None or print_samples==0:
        return kwic_list
    else:
        k = min(print_samples, len(kwic_list))
        print(f"{k} random samples out of {len(kwic_list)} " + \
            f"contexts for '{keyword}':")
        for sample in random.sample(list(kwic_list), k):
            print(re.sub(r'[\n\t]', ' ', sample[0])+'  '+ \
                sample[1]+'  '+\
                re.sub(r'[\n\t]', ' ', sample[2]))
```

The function iteratively collects the keyword contexts by applying the add_kwic function to each document with map. This trick, which we already used in the word count blueprints, is very efficient and enables KWIC analysis also for larger corpora. By default, the function returns a list of tuples of the form (left context, keyword, right context). If print_samples is greater than 0, a random sample of the results is printed.[8] Sampling is especially useful when you work with lots of documents because the first entries of the list would otherwise stem from a single or a very small number of documents.

The KWIC list for *sdgs* from earlier was generated by this call:

```
    kwic(df[df['year'] == 2015]['text'], 'sdgs', print_samples=5)
```

Blueprint: Analyzing N-Grams

Just knowing that climate is a frequent word does not tell us too much about the topic of discussion because, for example, *climate change* and *political climate* have completely different meanings. Even *change climate* is not the same as *climate change*. It can therefore be helpful to extend frequency analyses from single words to short sequences of two or three words.

Basically, we are looking for two types of word sequences: compounds and collocations. A *compound* is a combination of two or more words with a specific meaning. In English, we find compounds in closed form, like *earthquake*; hyphenated form like *self-confident*; and open form like *climate change*. Thus, we may have to consider two

---

8 The parameter print_only in textacy's KWIC function works similarly but does not sample.

tokens as a single semantic unit. *Collocations*, in contrast, are words that are frequently used together. Often, they consist of an adjective or verb and a noun, like *red carpet* or *united nations*.

In text processing, we usually work with bigrams (sequences of length 2), sometimes even trigrams (length 3). *n*-grams of size 1 are single words, also called *unigrams*. The reason to stick to $n \le 3$ is that the number of different n-grams increases exponentially with respect to *n*, while their frequencies decrease in the same way. By far the most trigrams appear only once in a corpus.

The following function produces elegantly the set of n-grams for a sequence of tokens:[9]

```
def ngrams(tokens, n=2, sep=' '):
    return [sep.join(ngram) for ngram in zip(*[tokens[i:] for i in range(n)])]

text = "the visible manifestation of the global climate change"
tokens = tokenize(text)
print("|".join(ngrams(tokens, 2)))
```
Out:

```
the visible|visible manifestation|manifestation of|of the|the global|
global climate|climate change
```

As you can see, most of the bigrams contain stop words like prepositions and determiners. Thus, it is advisable to build bigrams without stop words. But we need to be careful: if we remove the stop words first and then build the bigrams, we generate bigrams that don't exist in the original text as a "manifestation global" in the example. Thus, we create the bigrams on all tokens but keep only those that do not contain any stop words with this modified `ngrams` function:

```
def ngrams(tokens, n=2, sep=' ', stopwords=set()):
    return [sep.join(ngram) for ngram in zip(*[tokens[i:] for i in range(n)])
            if len([t for t in ngram if t in stopwords])==0]

print("Bigrams:", "|".join(ngrams(tokens, 2, stopwords=stopwords)))
print("Trigrams:", "|".join(ngrams(tokens, 3, stopwords=stopwords)))
```
Out:

```
Bigrams: visible manifestation|global climate|climate change
Trigrams: global climate change
```

Using this `ngrams` function, we can add a column containing all bigrams to our `Data Frame` and apply the word count blueprint to determine the top five bigrams:

---

9 See Scott Triglia's blog post (*https://oreil.ly/7WwTe*) for an explanation.

```
df['bigrams'] = df['text'].apply(prepare, pipeline=[str.lower, tokenize]) \
                          .apply(ngrams, n=2, stopwords=stopwords)

count_words(df, 'bigrams').head(5)
```

Out:

token	freq
united nations	103236
international community	27786
general assembly	27096
security council	20961
human rights	19856

You may have noticed that we ignored sentence boundaries during tokenization. Thus, we will generate nonsense bigrams with the last word of one sentence and the first word of the next. Those bigrams will not be very frequent, so they don't really matter for data exploration. If we wanted to prevent this, we would need to identify sentence boundaries, which is much more complicated than word tokenization and not worth the effort here.

Now let's extend our TF-IDF-based unigram analysis from the previous section and include bigrams. We add the bigram IDF values, compute the TF-IDF-weighted bigram frequencies for all speeches from 2015, and generate a word cloud from the resulting DataFrame:

```
# concatenate existing IDF DataFrame with bigram IDFs
idf_df = pd.concat([idf_df, compute_idf(df, 'bigrams', min_df=10)])

freq_df = count_words(df[df['year'] == 2015], 'bigrams')
freq_df['tfidf'] = freq_df['freq'] * idf_df['idf']
wordcloud(freq_df['tfidf'], title='all bigrams', max_words=50)
```

As we can see in the word cloud on the left of Figure 1-7, *climate change* was a frequent bigram in 2015. But to understand the different contexts of *climate*, it may be interesting to take a look at the bigrams containing *climate* only. We can use a text filter on *climate* to achieve this and plot the result again as a word cloud (Figure 1-7, right):

```
where = freq_df.index.str.contains('climate')
wordcloud(freq_df[where]['freq'], title='"climate" bigrams', max_words=50)
```

Figure 1-7. Word clouds for all bigrams and bigrams containing the word climate.

The approach presented here creates and weights all n-grams that do not contain stop words. For a first analysis, the results look quite good. We just don't care about the long tail of infrequent bigrams. More sophisticated but also computationally expensive algorithms to identify collocations are available, for example, in NLTK's collocation finder (*https://oreil.ly/uW-2A*). We will show alternatives to identify meaningful phrases in Chapters 4 and 10.

Blueprint: Comparing Frequencies Across Time Intervals and Categories

You surely know Google Trends (*http://trends.google.com*), where you can track the development of a number of search terms over time. This kind of trend analysis computes frequencies by day and visualizes them with a line chart. We want to track the development of certain keywords over the course of the years in our UN Debates dataset to get an idea about the growing or shrinking importance of topics such as climate change, terrorism, or migration.

Creating Frequency Timelines

Our approach is to calculate the frequencies of given keywords per document and then aggregate those frequencies using Pandas's `groupby` function. The following function is for the first task. It extracts the counts of given keywords from a list of tokens:

```
def count_keywords(tokens, keywords):
    tokens = [t for t in tokens if t in keywords]
    counter = Counter(tokens)
    return [counter.get(k, 0) for k in keywords]
```

Let's demonstrate the functionality with a small example:

```
keywords = ['nuclear', 'terrorism', 'climate', 'freedom']
tokens = ['nuclear', 'climate', 'climate', 'freedom', 'climate', 'freedom']

print(count_keywords(tokens, keywords))
```

Out:

```
[1, 0, 3, 2]
```

As you can see, the function returns a list or vector of word counts. In fact, it's a very simple count-vectorizer for keywords. If we apply this function to each document in our `DataFrame`, we get a matrix of counts. The blueprint function `count_key words_by`, shown next, does exactly this as a first step. The matrix is then again converted into a `DataFrame` that is finally aggregated and sorted by the supplied grouping column.

```
def count_keywords_by(df, by, keywords, column='tokens'):

    freq_matrix = df[column].apply(count_keywords, keywords=keywords)
    freq_df = pd.DataFrame.from_records(freq_matrix, columns=keywords)
    freq_df[by] = df[by] # copy the grouping column(s)

    return freq_df.groupby(by=by).sum().sort_values(by)
```

This function is very fast because it has to take care of the keywords only. Counting the four keywords from earlier in the UN corpus takes just two seconds on a laptop. Let's take a look at the result:

```
freq_df = count_keywords_by(df, by='year', keywords=keywords)
```

Out:

	nuclear	terrorism	climate	freedom	year
1970	192	7	18	128
1971	275	9	35	205
...	...	...	...	...
2014	144	404	654	129
2015	246	378	662	148

 Even though we use only the attribute year as a grouping criterion in our examples, the blueprint function allows you to compare word frequencies across any discrete attribute, e.g., country, category, author—you name it. In fact, you could even specify a list of grouping attributes to compute, for example, counts per country and year.

The resulting `DataFrame` is already perfectly prepared for plotting as we have one data series per keyword. Using Pandas's `plot` function, we get a nice line chart similar to Google Trends (Figure 1-8):

```
freq_df.plot(kind='line')
```

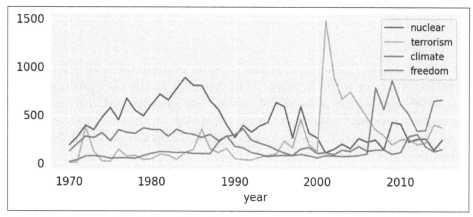

Figure 1-8. Frequencies of selected words per year.

Note the peak of *nuclear* in the 1980s indicating the arms race and the high peak of terrorism in 2001. It is somehow remarkable that the topic *climate* already got some attention in the 1970s and 1980s. Has it really? Well, if you check with a KWIC analysis ("Blueprint: Finding a Keyword-in-Context" on page 24), you'd find out that the word *climate* in those decades was almost exclusively used in a figurative sense.

Creating Frequency Heatmaps

Say we want to analyze the historic developments of global crises like the cold war, terrorism, and climate change. We could pick a selection of significant words and visualize their timelines by line charts as in the previous example. But line charts become confusing if you have more than four or five lines. An alternative visualization without that limitation is a heatmap, as provided by the Seaborn library. So, let's add a few more keywords to our filter and display the result as a heatmap (Figure 1-9).

```
keywords = ['terrorism', 'terrorist', 'nuclear', 'war', 'oil',
            'syria', 'syrian', 'refugees', 'migration', 'peacekeeping',
            'humanitarian', 'climate', 'change', 'sustainable', 'sdgs']

freq_df = count_keywords_by(df, by='year', keywords=keywords)

# compute relative frequencies based on total number of tokens per year
freq_df = freq_df.div(df.groupby('year')['num_tokens'].sum(), axis=0)
# apply square root as sublinear filter for better contrast
freq_df = freq_df.apply(np.sqrt)
```

```
sns.heatmap(data=freq_df.T,
            xticklabels=True, yticklabels=True, cbar=False, cmap="Reds")
```

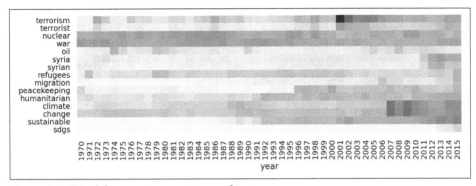

Figure 1-9. Word frequencies over time as heatmap.

There are a few things to consider for this kind of analysis:

Prefer relative frequencies for any kind of comparison.
Absolute term frequencies are problematic if the total number of tokens per year or category is not stable. For example, absolute frequencies naturally go up if more countries are speaking year after year in our example.

Be careful with the interpretation of frequency diagrams based on keyword lists.
Although the chart looks like a distribution of topics, it is not! There may be other words representing the same topic but not included in the list. Keywords may also have different meanings (e.g., "climate of the discussion"). Advanced techniques such as topic modeling (Chapter 8) and word embeddings (Chapter 10) can help here.

Use sublinear scaling.
As the frequency values differ greatly, it may be hard to see any change for less-frequent tokens. Therefore, you should scale the frequencies sublinearly (we applied the square root `np.sqrt`). The visual effect is similar to lowering contrast.

Closing Remarks

We demonstrated how to get started analyzing textual data. The process for text preparation and tokenization was kept simple to get quick results. In Chapter 4, we will introduce more sophisticated methods and discuss the advantages and disadvantages of different approaches.

Data exploration should not only provide initial insights but actually help to develop confidence in your data. One thing you should keep in mind is that you should always identify the root cause for any strange tokens popping up. The KWIC analysis is a good tool to search for such tokens.

For a first analysis of the content, we introduced several blueprints for word frequency analysis. The weighting of terms is based either on term frequency alone or on the combination of term frequency and inverse document frequency (TF-IDF). These concepts will be picked up later in Chapter 5 because TF-IDF weighting is a standard method to vectorize documents for machine learning.

There are many aspects of textual analysis that we did not cover in this chapter:

- Author-related information can help to identify influential writers, if that is one of your project goals. Authors can be distinguished by activity, social scores, writing style, etc.

- Sometimes it is interesting to compare authors or different corpora on the same topic by their readability. The `textacy` library (*https://oreil.ly/FRZJb*) has a function called `textstats` that computes different readability scores and other statistics in a single pass over the text.

- An interesting tool to identify and visualize distinguishing terms between categories (e.g., political parties) is Jason Kessler's `Scattertext` (*https://oreil.ly/R6Aw8*) library.

- Besides plain Python, you can also use interactive visual tools for data analysis. Microsoft's PowerBI has a nice word cloud add-on and lots of other options to produce interactive charts. We mention it because it is free to use in the desktop version and supports Python and R for data preparation and visualization.

- For larger projects, we recommend setting up a search engine like Apache SOLR (*https://oreil.ly/LqPvG*), Elasticsearch (*https://elastic.co*), or Tantivy (*https://oreil.ly/NCz1g*). Those platforms create specialized indexes (also using TF-IDF weighting) for fast full-text search. Python APIs are available for all of them.

## CHAPTER 2

Extracting Textual Insights with APIs

When you want to determine the approach to a research question or start working on a text analytics project, the availability of data is often the first stumbling block. A simple Google search or the more specific Dataset search (*https://oreil.ly/SJoyG*) will throw up curated datasets, and we will use some of these in subsequent chapters of this book. Depending on your project, such datasets may turn out to be generic and not suitable for your use case. You might have to create your own dataset, and application programming interfaces (APIs) are one way to extract data programmatically in an automated fashion.

What You'll Learn and What We'll Build

In this chapter, we will provide an overview of APIs and introduce blueprints to extract data for your project from popular websites like GitHub (*https://github.com*) and Twitter (*https://twitter.com*). You will learn about using authentication tokens, handling pagination, understanding rate limits, and automating data extraction. At the end of this chapter, you will be able to create your own datasets by making API calls to any identified service. While the blueprints are illustrated with specific examples such as GitHub and Twitter, they can be used to work with any API.

Application Programming Interfaces

APIs are interfaces that allow software applications or components to communicate with one another without having to know how they are implemented. The API provides a set of definitions and protocols including the kinds of requests that can be made, the data formats to be used, and the expected response. An API is a set of software interfaces that is commonly used by developers while building websites, apps, and services. For example, when you sign up for a new account with almost any service, you will be asked to verify your email address or telephone number with a one-time code or link. Typically, the developer would use the API provided by an authentication service to enable this functionality rather than build the entire flow. This allows decoupling of the core functionality that the service provides and uses APIs to build other necessary, but not unique, features. You can read an intuitive nontechnical introduction to APIs provided by Zapier (*https://oreil.ly/e9iUI*) for a better understanding.

How are programming APIs connected with data for text analytics projects? In addition to enabling basic functionality such as authentication, common functionality on websites is also offered as APIs, providing us with an alternative way of accessing data. For example, third-party tools make use of APIs to create a post or add comments on social media. We can use these same APIs to read and store this information locally to create our dataset. For instance, say you are an analyst working at a Consumer Packaged Goods firm looking to evaluate the performance of a marketing campaign. You could extract data using the Twitter Search API (*https://oreil.ly/PCJsx*), filter tweets that contain the campaign tagline or hashtag, and analyze the text to understand people's reactions. Or consider that you are asked by a training provider to help identify upcoming technology areas for new courses. One approach could be to extract data on questions being asked using the StackOverflow API (*https://oreil.ly/kMsGs*) and identify emerging topics using text analytics.

Using APIs is the preferred approach over scraping a website. They are designed to be callable functions, are easy to use, and can be automated. They are specifically recommended when working with data that changes frequently or when it's critical that the project reflects the latest information. When working with any API, it's important to take the time and read the documentation carefully. It provides granular information on the specific API call, data formats, and parameters as well as other details like user permissions, rate limits, and so on.

 Not all APIs are provided free of charge, and some providers have different plans to support different kinds of customers. For example, the Twitter API has Standard, Premium, and Enterprise versions. The Standard API is a public API (available to anyone with a developer account), while the Premium and Enterprise APIs are only for paying customers. We will use only public APIs in this chapter.

Blueprint: Extracting Data from an API Using the Requests Module

With the popularity of the web driven by the HTTP standard, a URL is most often the primary specification for an API. We will use the requests library that is included in the standard Python distribution as the primary way to access and extract data from an API. To illustrate this blueprint, we will use the GitHub API (*https://oreil.ly/oUIG1*). GitHub is a popular code hosting platform where several open source projects such as Python, scikit-learn, and TensorFlow, as well as the code for this book, are hosted. Let's say that you would like to determine the popularity of different programming languages such as Python, Java, and JavaScript. We could extract data from GitHub on the languages used by popular repositories and determine the prevalence of each language. Or consider that your organization is hosting a project on GitHub and wants to ensure that users and contributors adhere to the Code of Conduct. We can extract the issues and comments written by contributors and ensure that offensive language is not used. In this blueprint, we will read and understand the documentation of an API, make requests, and parse the output and create a dataset that can be used to solve our use case.

SOAP Versus REST Versus GraphQL

APIs have existed as a standard for software interfaces and communications for a long time, and the technology used to implement them has changed over the years. Simple Object Access Protocol (SOAP) was one of the earliest methods for different software modules to speak with one another using standard interfaces. SOAP uses a standard messaging format encapsulated using the Extensible Markup Language (XML) and can use any communication protocol (like HTTP, TCP) to transmit the message. The SOAP envelope contained in the XML follows a standard definition including the definition of data types, error codes, and so on. Representational State Transfer (REST), on the other hand, relies on HTTP as the communication protocol including the use of status codes to determine successful or failed calls. It defines data types much more loosely and uses JSON heavily, though other formats are also supported. SOAP is generally considered an older protocol and is typically used within legacy applications in large enterprises, while REST is a preferred format adopted by several web-based services. Graph Query Language (GraphQL) is a relatively new specification that defines a way to interact with APIs similar to writing SQL queries. One of the drawbacks of the REST architecture is that retrieving a single piece of information might require multiple calls to different resources. This will depend on how the resources are organized; for instance, to determine whether a user's phone number is active, one would have to make an API call to the /user endpoint to retrieve all details followed by a subsequent call to a different endpoint like /contacts with the phone number to check whether that phone number is active. In GraphQL this would be a single API call with a specific SQL-like query where all active phone numbers of a given user would be retrieved. While GraphQL has gained popularity since it was open sourced by Facebook in 2015, REST APIs are much more common. GitHub, for example, maintains version three of its APIs as a REST API (*https://oreil.ly/oUIG1*) that we will use in the blueprint, whereas the latest version four is a GraphQL API (*https://oreil.ly/ukpla*).

The first API we want to call is to list all the repositories on GitHub. The entry point to the REST API documentation can be found on GitHub (*https://oreil.ly/oUIG1*). You can either search for the specific method (also referred to as the *endpoint*) or navigate to the GitHub page (*https://oreil.ly/8HM5v*) to see its details, as shown in Figure 2-1.

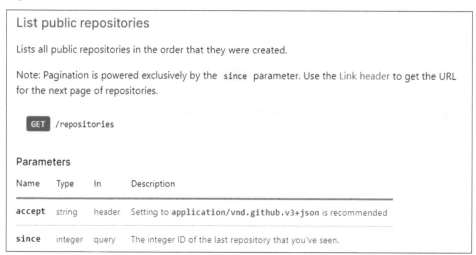

Figure 2-1. API documentation for listing public repositories.

As stated in the documentation, this is a GET method that will provide you with a list of repositories in the order they were created. Let's make a call using the `requests.get` method and view the response status:

```
import requests

response = requests.get('https://api.github.com/repositories',
                        headers={'Accept': 'application/vnd.github.v3+json'})
print(response.status_code)
```

Out:

```
200
```

A response code of 200 (*https://httpstatuses.com/200*) indicates that the call to the API was successful. We can also evaluate the encoding of the response object to ensure that we process it correctly. One of the important elements contained in the response object is the headers object. It is a dictionary that contains more detailed information, such as the name of the server, response timestamp, status, and so on. In the following code, we only extract the type of content and server details that have been returned by the API, but you are encouraged to look at all of the elements of this object. Most of this information is present in the detailed API documentation, but inspecting the response is another way to ensure that you parse the response accurately:

```
print (response.encoding)
print (response.headers['Content-Type'])
print (response.headers['server'])
```

Out:

```
utf-8
application/json; charset=utf-8
GitHub.com
```

Looking at the response parameters, we understand that the response follows a UTF-8 encoding, and the content is returned using the JSON format. The content can be directly accessed using the content element, which provides the payload in the form of bytes. Since we already know that the response is a JSON object, we can also use the json() command to read the response. This creates a list object where each element is a repository. We show the first element in the response that identifies the first GitHub repository that was created (*https://oreil.ly/L9b6L*). We have limited the output to the first 200 characters for the sake of brevity:

```
import json
print (json.dumps(response.json()[0], indent=2)[:200])
```

Out:

```
{
  "id": 1,
  "node_id": "MDEwOlJlcG9zaXRvcnkx",
  "name": "grit",
  "full_name": "mojombo/grit",
  "private": false,
  "owner": {
    "login": "mojombo",
    "id": 1,
    "node_id": "MDQ6VXNlcjE=",
```

While the previous response contains a list of repositories, it is not helpful when looking for specific programming languages. It might be better to use the Search API, which we will use next:

```
response = requests.get('https://api.github.com/search/repositories')
print (response.status_code)
```

Out:

```
422
```

The previous request was not successful as it returned with a status code of 422 (*https://httpstatuses.com/422*). This code indicates that the request was correct, but the server was not able to process the request. This is because we have not provided any search query parameter as specified in the documentation (*https://oreil.ly/5EtSw*). It is important to always check and understand the status before proceeding to view the response. You can view a detailed definition of each status code in the HTTP specification (*https://oreil.ly/SG6tf*).

Let's say that we want to identify GitHub repositories related to data science that are written in Python. We will modify the request by adding a second argument called params with the search terms. The search query needs to be constructed following the rules described in GitHub's documentation (*https://oreil.ly/jNCff*). Based on these rules, our search query is encoded to look for data_science, filter the language by Python (language:python), and combine the two (+). This constructed query is passed as the query argument q to params. We also pass the argument headers containing the Accept parameter where we specify text-match+json so that the response contains the matching metadata and provides the response in JSON format:

```
response = requests.get('https://api.github.com/search/repositories',
    params={'q': 'data_science+language:python'},
    headers={'Accept': 'application/vnd.github.v3.text-match+json'})
print(response.status_code)
```

Out:

```
200
```

As described in the example provided in the API documentation for the /search/repositories endpoint, the response contains a dictionary with total_count, incomplete_results, and items. It is important to note that this response format is different from the /repositories endpoint we saw earlier, and we must parse this structure accordingly. Here we list the names of the top five repositories returned by the search:

```
for item in response.json()['items'][:5]:
    printmd('**' + item['name'] + '**' + ': repository ' +
            item['text_matches'][0]['property'] + ' - \"*' +
```

```
      item['text_matches'][0]['fragment'] + '*\" matched with ' + '**' +
      item['text_matches'][0]['matches'][0]['text'] + '**')
```

Out:

DataCamp: repository description - *"DataCamp data-science courses"* matched with **data**

data-science-from-scratch: repository description - *"code for Data Science From Scratch book"* matched with **Data Science**

data-science-blogs: repository description - *"A curated list of data science blogs"* matched with **data science**

galaxy: repository description - *"Data intensive science for everyone."* matched with **Data**

data-scientist-roadmap: repository description - *"Tutorial coming with "data science roadmap" graphe."* matched with **data science**

We've seen how to make requests and parse the response. Let's consider the use case of monitoring the comments in a repository and ensuring that they adhere to community guidelines. We will use the List Repository Issues (*https://oreil.ly/9l-fy*) endpoint for this. Here we must specify the owner and the repository name to get all of the issue comments, and the response will contain a list of all comments in that repository. Let's make this request for the PyTorch repository, which is a popular deep learning framework:

```
response = requests.get(
    'https://api.github.com/repos/pytorch/pytorch/issues/comments')
print('Response Code', response.status_code)
print('Number of comments', len(response.json()))
```

Out:

```
Response Code 200
Number of comments 30
```

While we see that the response has succeeded, the number of comments returned is only 30. PyTorch is a popular framework with a lot of collaborators and users. Checking the issues page of the repository in a browser would show us that the number of comments is much higher. So, what are we missing?

Pagination

This is a technique used by many APIs to limit the number of elements in the response. The total number of comments in a repository can be large, and attempting to respond with all of them would be time-intensive and costly. As a result, the GitHub API implements the pagination concept where it returns only one page at a time, and in this case each page contains 30 results. The `links` field in the response object provides details on the number of pages in the response.

```
response.links
```

Out:

```
{'next': {'url': 'https://api.github.com/repositories/65600975/issues/
comments?page=2',
  'rel': 'next'},
 'last': {'url': 'https://api.github.com/repositories/65600975/issues/
comments?page=1334',
  'rel': 'last'}}
```

The `next` field provides us with a URL to the next page, which would contain the next 30 results, while the `last` field provides a link to the last page, which provides an indication of how many search results there are in total. The number of 30 results per page is also specified in the documentation and usually can be configured up to a certain maximum value. What does this mean for us? To get all the results, we must implement a function that will parse all the results on one page and then call the next URL until the last page has been reached. This is implemented as a recursive function where we check to see if a `next` link exists and recursively call the same function. The comments from each page are appended to the `output_json` object, which is finally returned. To restrict the number of comments that we retrieve, we use a filter parameter to fetch only the comments since July 2020. As per the documentation, the date must be specified using the ISO 8601 format and provided as a parameter using the `since` keyword:

```python
def get_all_pages(url, params=None, headers=None):
    output_json = []
    response = requests.get(url, params=params, headers=headers)
    if response.status_code == 200:
        output_json = response.json()
        if 'next' in response.links:
            next_url = response.links['next']['url']
            if next_url is not None:
                output_json += get_all_pages(next_url, params, headers)
    return output_json


out = get_all_pages(
    "https://api.github.com/repos/pytorch/pytorch/issues/comments",
    params={
        'since': '2020-07-01T10:00:01Z',
        'sorted': 'created',
        'direction': 'desc'
    },
    headers={'Accept': 'application/vnd.github.v3+json'})
df = pd.DataFrame(out)
```

```
print (df['body'].count())
df[['id','created_at','body']].sample(1)
```

Out:

```
3870
```

id	created_at	body
2176 286601372	2017-03-15T00:09:46Z	@soumith are you able to explain what dependency is broken? I can't find the PR you mentioned.

We have captured about 3,800 comments for the PyTorch repository by using the recursive pagination function, and we saw an example of one of these comments in the previous table. The dataset we have created here can be used to apply text analytics blueprints, for example, to identify comments that do not adhere to community guidelines and flag for moderation. It can also be augmented by running it at programmed time intervals to ensure that latest comments are always captured.

Rate Limiting

One issue that you might have noticed while extracting the comments is that we were able to retrieve only 3,800 comments. However, the actual number of comments is much more than that. This was a result of the API applying a rate limit. To ensure that an API can continue serving all users and avoid load on their infrastructure, providers will often enforce rate limits. The rate limit specifies how many requests can be made to an endpoint in a certain time frame. GitHub's Rate Limiting policy (*https:// oreil.ly/PH7hm*) states the following:

> For unauthenticated requests, the rate limit allows for up to 60 requests per hour. Unauthenticated requests are associated with the originating IP address, and not the user making requests.

The information about usage is contained in the headers section of the response object. We can make a call to the API to only retrieve the headers by using the head method and then peering into the X-Ratelimit-Limit, X-Ratelimit-Remaining, and X-RateLimit-Reset header elements:

```
response = requests.head(
    'https://api.github.com/repos/pytorch/pytorch/issues/comments')
print('X-Ratelimit-Limit', response.headers['X-Ratelimit-Limit'])
print('X-Ratelimit-Remaining', response.headers['X-Ratelimit-Remaining'])

# Converting UTC time to human-readable format
import datetime
print(
    'Rate Limits reset at',
    datetime.datetime.fromtimestamp(int(
        response.headers['X-RateLimit-Reset'])).strftime('%c'))
```

Out:

```
X-Ratelimit-Limit 60
X-Ratelimit-Remaining 0
Rate Limits reset at Sun Sep 20 12:46:18 2020
```

X-Ratelimit-Limit indicates how many requests can be made per unit of time (one hour in this case), X-Ratelimit-Remaining is the number of requests that can still be made without violating the rate limits, and X-RateLimit-Reset indicates the time at which the rate would be reset. It's possible for different API endpoints to have different rate limits. For example, the GitHub Search API has a per-minute rate limit (*https://oreil.ly/95Fw7*). If you exceed the rate limit by making requests that exceed the rate limit, then the API will respond with a status of 403.

While making API calls, we must honor the rate limits and also adjust the way we make our calls to ensure that we do not overload the server. While extracting comments from the repository as in the previous example, we are allowed to make 60 API calls every hour. We can make the requests one after the other, thereby quickly exhausting the limit, which is how our earlier blueprint works. The function handle_rate_limits shown next slows down the requests to ensure they are spaced out over the entire duration. It does so by distributing the remaining requests equally over the remaining time by applying a sleep function. This will ensure that our data extraction blueprint respects the rate limits and spaces the requests so that all the requested data is downloaded:

```
from datetime import datetime
import time

def handle_rate_limits(response):
    now = datetime.now()
    reset_time = datetime.fromtimestamp(
        int(response.headers['X-RateLimit-Reset']))
    remaining_requests = response.headers['X-Ratelimit-Remaining']
    remaining_time = (reset_time - now).total_seconds()
    intervals = remaining_time / (1.0 + int(remaining_requests))
    print('Sleeping for', intervals)
    time.sleep(intervals)
    return True
```

Network communication including API calls can fail for several reasons, such as interrupted connections, failed DNS lookups, connection timeouts, and so on. By default, the requests library does not implement any retries, and therefore a nice addition to our blueprint is an implementation of a retry strategy. This will allow API calls to be retried in case of specified failure conditions. It can be implemented with the HTTPAdapter library that allows more fine-grained control of the underlying HTTP connections being made. Here we initialize an adapter with the retry strategy that specifies five retries for a failed attempt. We also specify that these retries should be made only when the error status codes 500 (*https://httpstatuses.com/500*),

503 (*https://httpstatuses.com/503*), and 504 (*https://httpstatuses.com/504*) are received. In addition, we specify the `backoff_factor`[1] value that determines the exponentially increasing time delay between attempts after the second try to ensure that we don't hammer the server.

Every request object creates a default `Sessions` object that manages and persists connection settings across different requests, such as cookies, authentication, and proxies that should be stateless. Up to now we relied on the default `Sessions` object, but to override the connection behavior with our retry strategy, we have to specify a custom adapter that will enable us to use the retry strategy. This means that we will use the new `http Session` object to make our requests, as shown in the following code:

```
from requests.adapters import HTTPAdapter
from requests.packages.urllib3.util.retry import Retry

retry_strategy = Retry(
    total=5,
    status_forcelist=[500, 503, 504],
    backoff_factor=1
)

retry_adapter = HTTPAdapter(max_retries=retry_strategy)

http = requests.Session()
http.mount("https://", retry_adapter)
http.mount("http://", retry_adapter)

response = http.get('https://api.github.com/search/repositories',
                    params={'q': 'data_science+language:python'})

for item in response.json()['items'][:5]:
    print (item['name'])
```

Out:

```
DataCamp
data-science-from-scratch
data-science-blogs
galaxy
data-scientist-roadmap
```

Putting all this together, we can modify the blueprint to handle pagination, rate limits, and retries as follows:

```
from requests.adapters import HTTPAdapter
from requests.packages.urllib3.util.retry import Retry
```

---

1 Delay introduced between subsequent calls defined as `time_delay={backoff factor} * (2 ** ({number of total retries} - 1))`.

```
retry_strategy = Retry(
    total=5,
    status_forcelist=[500, 503, 504],
    backoff_factor=1
)

retry_adapter = HTTPAdapter(max_retries=retry_strategy)

http = requests.Session()
http.mount("https://", retry_adapter)
http.mount("http://", retry_adapter)

def get_all_pages(url, param=None, header=None):
    output_json = []
    response = http.get(url, params=param, headers=header)
    if response.status_code == 200:
        output_json = response.json()
        if 'next' in response.links:
            next_url = response.links['next']['url']
            if (next_url is not None) and (handle_rate_limits(response)):
                output_json += get_all_pages(next_url, param, header)
    return output_json
```

If you look closely at the rate limit documentation, you will observe that there are different rate limits based on the type of authentication used. All our requests up to now were unauthenticated requests, and the rate limits are much lower. We can identify our data extraction application to GitHub by registering for an account. We can then make authenticated requests to the API that increases the rate limits. This practice ensures that there is no abuse of the API by unidentified users or fraudulent applications, and most API providers do not allow access to an API without a form of authentication.

This blueprint shows you how to extract data from any API using the simple Python requests module and creating your own dataset. This is the fundamental way in which most API requests work and is useful for a one-off analysis and initial exploration of a new data source. Going back to our use case, if you were looking to identify the popular deep-learning frameworks for you to start learning, then this blueprint would be a good choice. Or let's say that your organization already has a sales forecasting model and you would like to evaluate the benefit of adding financial market news on the accuracy of this model. Assuming there is an API that provides financial news, you can easily create a dataset, apply text analytics blueprints, and test the relevance to the model.

Blueprint: Extracting Twitter Data with Tweepy

To make it easier for developers to work with their APIs, many of the popular services provide packages in multiple programming languages or at least have one or more community-supported modules. While the API is officially supported, these packages are well-maintained Python modules that incorporate additional functionality that makes them easy to use. This means you can focus on the kind of data that you would like to extract rather than the technical details of making API calls, authentication, and so on. In this blueprint, we will use one of the community-developed and supported Python modules for Twitter called Tweepy (*https://oreil.ly/yZOU7*). Twitter maintains a list of libraries for different languages (*https://oreil.ly/lwrFM*) that includes several libraries for Python. We chose Tweepy because it's actively maintained and used by many researchers. While this blueprint uses Tweepy to extract data from the Twitter API, the steps described would be similar for any other API.

We described earlier how you might use Twitter to analyze the effectiveness of a new marketing campaign. Another use case could be to perform text analytics to understand the popularity and sentiment for cryptocurrencies as a way to predict their adoption and value in the economy. Twitter is a social media network where users spontaneously share short messages, often reacting in real time to world events such as major calamities or popular sporting events. The user can also add the geolocation if they want to, and this gives us the ability to understand the most trending current events in a certain city or geographical area. During the government-imposed lockdowns due to COVID-19, several researchers used Twitter data to understand the spread of the virus and the impact of lockdowns (*https://oreil.ly/J7pDT*) and also used these as predictive variables of economic health.

Please note that when using a public API like Twitter, you will retrieve data from the public timelines of many users, and it could contain strong, maybe even offensive, language, including profanities. Please be aware of this and ensure that the data is handled appropriately depending on your use-case.

Obtaining Credentials

The first step when working with any API is authenticating yourself or your application. Twitter requires all users of their API to register as a developer and provide details for why they would like to use the API. This helps them identify you and prevent any unauthorized access. You must register yourself as a developer (*https://oreil.ly/vEnJp*). If you do not already have a Twitter account, then you will also be required to create one. You will be asked about your purpose for creating a developer account and additional questions on how you intend to use the Twitter API. Figure 2-2 shows some examples of these screens. Please provide detailed responses to ensure that Twitter fully understands your purpose for creating a developer account. For example, in this blueprint we are looking to extract tweets using the API to illustrate how this is done. Since we are only going to use the extraction capability, the question "Will your app use Tweet, Retweet, like, follow, or Direct Message functionality?" is not applicable and can be deselected. You must read and understand each question before proceeding. Note that this requirement will be different for each API and is also subject to change.

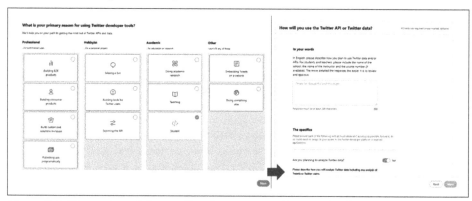

Figure 2-2. Illustration of sign-up flow for creating a Twitter developer account.

Now that you have a developer account, the next step is to create an app. The credentials of the app are used when making API calls, and it's important to specify the reason for creating the app. You have to provide details like the app name, the purpose for creating the app, and the website URL that is associated with the app. If you will use this app for research and learning purposes, then you could state this in the app description and provide the URL for your university page or GitHub repository associated with your project. Once the app is approved by Twitter, you can navigate to the tab *Keys and tokens*, as shown in Figure 2-3, where you will find the fields *API key* and *API secret key*. Please note that these are the credentials that will be used for authentication when making API calls, and it's important to not reveal them.

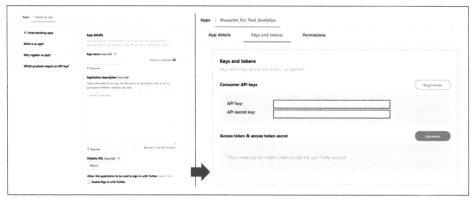

Figure 2-3. Creating a Twitter app and obtaining credentials.

Installing and Configuring Tweepy

The project repository for Tweepy (*https://oreil.ly/OHfnn*) and documentation (*https://oreil.ly/lDDo1*) are the best source for all information about using Tweepy. We can install Tweepy by entering **pip install tweepy** into the terminal. Next, we have to authenticate the app with the Twitter API, and we do this with the help of the **tweepy.AppAuthHandler** module to which we pass the API key and API secret key we obtained in the previous step. Finally, we instantiate the **tweepy.API** class, which will be used to make all subsequent calls to the Twitter API. Once the connection is made, we can confirm the host and version of the API object. Please note that since we are interested in read-only access to public information, we use application-only authentication (*https://oreil.ly/4oWbP*):

```
import tweepy

app_api_key = 'YOUR_APP_KEY_HERE'
app_api_secret_key = 'YOUR_APP_SECRET_HERE'


auth = tweepy.AppAuthHandler(app_api_key, app_api_secret_key)
api = tweepy.API(auth)

print ('API Host', api.host)
print ('API Version', api.api_root)
```

Out:

```
API Host api.twitter.com
API Version /1.1
```

Extracting Data from the Search API

Let's say we want to analyze the perception of cryptocurrency and determine its popularity. We will use the Search API to retrieve all tweets that mention this to create our dataset. The Twitter API also uses pagination to return multiple pages of results, but instead of implementing our own way of managing this, we will use the Cursor object provided by the Tweepy library to iterate through the results. We pass the search query to the API object and additionally specify the language of the tweets to be extracted (English in this case). We choose to retrieve only 100 items and create a DataFrame by loading the results as a JSON object:

```
search_term = 'cryptocurrency'

tweets = tweepy.Cursor(api.search,
                       q=search_term,
                       lang="en").items(100)

retrieved_tweets = [tweet._json for tweet in tweets]
df = pd.json_normalize(retrieved_tweets)

df[['text']].sample(3)
```

	text
59	Hi! I've been using OKEx which makes it really easy and safe to buy, sell, and store cryptocurrency (like Bitcoin).... https://t.co/4mOmpyQTSN
17	Get connected today 📺 #getconnected #bitcointrading #Bitcoin #BitcoinCash #bitcoinmining #cryptocurrency https://t.co/J60bCyFPUI
22	RT @stoinkies: We reached over 100 followers!\nGiveaway time!\nFOLLOW +RETWEET + LIKE THIS TWEET = Win 200 Dogecoin!\nEvery participant also g...

We have successfully completed the API call and can see the text of the retrieved tweets in the previous table, which already show interesting aspects. For example, we see the use of the word *RT*, which indicates a retweet (where the user has shared another tweet). We see the usage of emojis, which is a strong characteristic of the medium, and also notice that some tweets are truncated. Twitter actually imposes a limit on the number of characters that each tweet can contain, which was originally 140 characters and later extended to 280. This led to the creation of an extended tweet object (*https://oreil.ly/fvl-3*), which we must specify explicitly while retrieving results in Tweepy. Additionally, you must be aware that the standard version of the Twitter Search API provides results only from the last week, and one must sign up for the Premium or Enterprise versions for historical tweets.

For each endpoint, Twitter specifies a maximum value of count. This is the maximum number of results that is returned in a single page of the response. For example, the search endpoint specifies a maximum value of count=100, whereas user_timeline has a maximum value of count=200.

Let's expand our search to include an additional keyword relevant to the cryptocurrency topic like crypto and filter out retweets for now. This is done by using the filter keyword appended with a minus sign in the search term. We also specify that we would like to fetch tweets with the tweet_mode=extended parameter, which ensures that we retrieve the full text of all tweets. The Standard search API (*https://oreil.ly/4IGcB*) searches only a sample of recent Tweets published in the past seven days, but even this could potentially be a large number, and to avoid a large wait time to run the blueprint, we restrict ourselves to 12,000 tweets. We specify the parameter count=30, which is the maximum number of tweets that can be retrieved in one call. Therefore, we must make 400 such calls to obtain our dataset while taking into consideration the rate limits. This is within the rate limit of 450 requests every 15 minutes specified by the API. It's possible that you might exceed this rate limit while experimenting with this blueprint, and therefore we enable the automatic wait functionality provided by Tweepy by setting the wait_on_rate_limit parameter. We also set wait_on_rate_limit_notify so that we are notified of such wait times. If you are within the rate limits, the following function should execute in about five minutes:

```
api = tweepy.API(auth,
                 wait_on_rate_limit=True,
                 wait_on_rate_limit_notify=True,
                 retry_count=5,
                 retry_delay=10)

search_term = 'cryptocurrency OR crypto -filter:retweets'

tweets = tweepy.Cursor(api.search,
                       q=search_term,
                       lang="en",
                       tweet_mode='extended',
                       count=30).items(12000)

retrieved_tweets = [tweet._json for tweet in tweets]

df = pd.json_normalize(retrieved_tweets)
print('Number of retrieved tweets ', len(df))
df[['created_at','full_text','entities.hashtags']].sample(2)
```

Out:

```
Number of retrieved tweets  12000
```

	created_at	full_text	entities.hashtags
10505	Sat Sep 19 22:30:12 +0000 2020	Milk was created to let liquidity providers (people who have LP tokens) benefit because they can stake LP tokens at SpaceSwap, they get MILK token as a reward as well as 0.3% UniSwap commission.\n\n😍😍😍 \nhttps://t.co/M7sGblDq4W\n#DeFi #cryptocurrency #UniSwap #altcoin	[{'text': 'DeFi', 'indices': [224, 229]}, {'text': 'cryptocurrency', 'indices': [230, 245]}, {'text': 'UniSwap', 'indices': [246, 254]}, {'text': 'altcoin', 'indices': [256, 264]}]
11882	Sat Sep 19 20:57:45 +0000 2020	You can EARN dividends from our curation activity. The minimum to participate is 2000 #steem delegation... with delegation there is no risk of losing your principal. We can process the payout in #bitcoin and all major #cryptocurrencies .. #cryptocurrency \nhttps://t.co/4b3iH2AI4S	[{'text': 'steem', 'indices': [86, 92]}, {'text': 'bitcoin', 'indices': [195, 203]}, {'text': 'cryptocurrencies', 'indices': [218, 235]}, {'text': 'cryptocurrency', 'indices': [239, 254]}]

There is a lot of information that the API provides, as shown in the sample of two previous tweets that contain important elements such as the date when the tweet was sent out, the content of the tweet, and so on. Twitter also returns several entities such as hashtags contained within the tweet, and it would be interesting to see which hashtags are used heavily when discussing cryptocurrency:

```
def extract_entities(entity_list):
    entities = set()
    if len(entity_list) != 0:
        for item in entity_list:
            for key,value in item.items():
                if key == 'text':
                    entities.add(value.lower())
    return list(entities)

df['Entities'] = df['entities.hashtags'].apply(extract_entities)
pd.Series(np.concatenate(df['Entities'])).value_counts()[:25].plot(kind='barh')
```

The preceding code creates the graph shown in Figure 2-4, which shows us the important hashtags being used in conjunction with cryptocurrencies. It includes examples of cryptocurrencies such as *bitcoin* and *ethereum* as well as their trading short-codes *btc* and *eth*. It also throws up related activities such as *trading* and *airdrops*. There are also mentions of entities like *fintech* and *applecash*. At a first glance, it already gives you insight into the various terms and entities being discussed, and the presence of trading short-codes indicates that there might be some market information contained in these tweets. While this is a simple count of entities, we can use this dataset to apply more advanced text analytics techniques to determine popular sentiment about cryptocurrencies that derive relationships between entities. Please note that the results may differ depending on when the Twitter search was run and the random selection by the API.

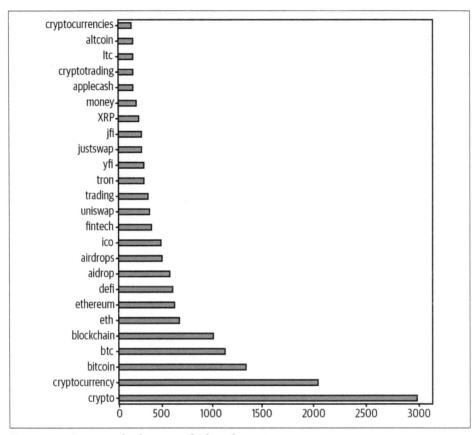

Figure 2-4. Common hashtags used when discussing cryptocurrency.

Extracting Data from a User's Timeline

Search is not the only way to interact with Twitter as we can use the API to also extract tweets by a specific user or account. This might be a person like a famous celebrity or world leader, or it might be an organization like a sports team. For instance, what if we would like to compare tweets from two popular Formula One teams, Mercedes and Ferrari? We can extract all the tweets that they have sent out and contrast their individual styles and the main themes that they focus on. We provide the screen name for the account (`MercedesAMGF1`) to retrieve all the tweets sent by this account:

```
api = tweepy.API(auth, wait_on_rate_limit=True, wait_on_rate_limit_notify=True)

tweets = tweepy.Cursor(api.user_timeline,
                       screen_name='MercedesAMGF1',
                       lang="en",
                       tweet_mode='extended',
```

```
                           count=100).items(5000)
    retrieved_tweets = [tweet._json for tweet in tweets]
    df = pd.io.json.json_normalize(retrieved_tweets)
    print ('Number of retrieved tweets ', len(df))
```

Out:

```
    Number of retrieved tweets  3232
```

As you can see, though we requested 5,000 tweets, we were able to retrieve only about 3,200 of them. This is a restriction placed on the API (*https://oreil.ly/RaNaQ*). Let's retrieve the tweets for the Ferrari team as well using their screen name (ScuderiaFerrari):

```
    def get_user_timeline(screen_name):
        api = tweepy.API(auth,
                            wait_on_rate_limit=True,
                            wait_on_rate_limit_notify=True)
        tweets = tweepy.Cursor(api.user_timeline,
                                screen_name=screen_name,
                                lang="en",
                                tweet_mode='extended',
                                count=200).items()
        retrieved_tweets = [tweet._json for tweet in tweets]
        df = pd.io.json.json_normalize(retrieved_tweets)
        df = df[~df['retweeted_status.id'].isna()]
        return df

    df_mercedes = get_user_timeline('MercedesAMGF1')
    print ('Number of Tweets from Mercedes', len(df_mercedes))
    df_ferrari = get_user_timeline('ScuderiaFerrari')
    print ('Number of Tweets from Ferrari', len(df_ferrari))
```

Out:

```
    Number of Tweets from Mercedes 180
    Number of Tweets from Ferrari 203
```

 One of the quirks of the Tweepy implementation is that in the case of retweets, the full_text column is truncated, and the retwee ted_status.full_text column must be used to retrieve all the characters of the tweet. For our use case, retweets are not important, and we filter them by checking if retweeted_status.id is empty. However, depending on the use case, you can add a condition to replace the column full_text with retweeted_sta tus.full_text in the case of retweets.

When we remove retweets, the number of tweets authored by each team handle significantly drops. We will reuse the word cloud blueprint from Chapter 1 with the function wordcloud to quickly visualize the tweets from each of the two teams and identify the keywords they focus on. Mercedes tweets seem to focus a lot on the races that the team participates in, such as *tuscangp, britishgp* and *race, day*. The Ferrari tweets, on the other hand, promote their merchandise, such as *ferraristore*, and drivers, such as *enzofitti* and *schumachermick*:

```
from blueprints.exploration import wordcloud

plt.figure()
wordcloud(df_mercedes['full_text'],
          max_words=100,
          stopwords=df_mercedes.head(5).index)

wordcloud(df_ferrari['full_text'],
          max_words=100,
          stopwords=df_ferrari.head(5).index)
```

Out:

Extracting Data from the Streaming API

Some APIs provide near real-time data, which might also be referred to as *streaming data*. In such a scenario, the API would like to *push* the data to us rather than waiting for a *get* request as we have been doing so far. An example of this is the Twitter Streaming API. This API provides us with a sample of the tweets being sent out in real time and can be filtered on several criteria. Since this is a continuous stream of data, we have to handle the data extraction process in a different manner. Tweepy already provides basic functionality in the StreamListener class that contains the on_data function. This function is called each time a new tweet is pushed by the streaming API, and we can customize it to implement logic that is specific to certain use cases.

Staying with the cryptocurrency use case, let's suppose that we want to have a continuously updated sentiment measure of different cryptocurrencies to make trading decisions. In this case, we would track real-time tweets mentioning cryptocurrencies and continuously update the popularity score. On the other hand, as researchers, we might be interested in analyzing the reactions of users during key live events such as the Super Bowl or announcement of election results. In such scenarios, we would listen for the entire duration of the event and store the results for subsequent analysis.

To keep this blueprint generic, we have created the FileStreamListener class as shown next, which will manage all the actions to be taken on the stream of incoming tweets. For every tweet pushed by the Twitter API, the on_data method is called. In our implementation, we gather incoming tweets into batches of 100 and then write to a file with the timestamp. The choice of 100 can be varied based on the memory available on the system:

```
from datetime import datetime
import math

class FileStreamListener(tweepy.StreamListener):

    def __init__(self, max_tweets=math.inf):
        self.num_tweets = 0
        self.TWEETS_FILE_SIZE = 100
        self.num_files = 0
        self.tweets = []
        self.max_tweets = max_tweets

    def on_data(self, data):
        while (self.num_files * self.TWEETS_FILE_SIZE < self.max_tweets):
            self.tweets.append(json.loads(data))
            self.num_tweets += 1
            if (self.num_tweets < self.TWEETS_FILE_SIZE):
                return True
            else:
                filename = 'Tweets_' + str(datetime.now().time()) + '.txt'
                print (self.TWEETS_FILE_SIZE, 'Tweets saved to', filename)
                file = open(filename, "w")
                json.dump(self.tweets, file)
                file.close()
                self.num_files += 1
                self.tweets = []
                self.num_tweets = 0
                return True
        return False

    def on_error(self, status_code):
        if status_code == 420:
            print ('Too many requests were made, please stagger requests')
            return False
        else:
            print ('Error {}'.format(status_code))
            return False
```

To get access to the streaming API, the basic app authentication is not enough. We must also provide the user authentication, which can be found on the same page as shown before. This means that the Streaming API requests are made by the app we created on behalf of the user (in this case our own account). This also means that we have to use the `OAuthHandler` class instead of the `AppAuthHandler` that we used up to now:

```
user_access_token = 'YOUR_USER_ACCESS_TOKEN_HERE'
user_access_secret = 'YOUR_USER_ACCESS_SECRET_HERE'

auth = tweepy.OAuthHandler(app_api_key, app_api_secret_key)
auth.set_access_token(user_access_token, user_access_secret)
api = tweepy.API(auth, wait_on_rate_limit=True, wait_on_rate_limit_notify=True)
```

When initializing an object of `FileStreamListener`, we also specify the maximum number of tweets that we would like to extract. This acts like a stopping condition, and if not specified, the process will run as long as it is not terminated by the user or stopped due to a server error. We initialize the Twitter stream by passing in the authentication object (`api.auth`) and the object that will manage the stream (`file StreamListener`). We also ask for the extended tweets to be provided. Once this is done, we can start tracking live tweets from the stream using the filter function and providing keywords that we would like to track:

```
fileStreamListener = FileStreamListener(5000)
fileStream = tweepy.Stream(auth=api.auth,
                           listener=fileStreamListener,
                           tweet_mode='extended')
fileStream.filter(track=['cryptocurrency'])
```

If you would like to run the extractor in a separate thread, you can pass the keyword `async=True` to the filter function, and this will run continuously in a separate thread. Once it has run for some time and stored tweets, we can read this into a Pandas `DataFrame` as before. When an error occurs, the `FileStreamListener` does not attempt retries but only prints the error `status_code`. You are encouraged to implement failure handling and customize the `on_data` method to suit the use case.

These blueprints only provide guidance on accessing popular APIs for data extraction. Since each API is different, the functionality provided by the corresponding Python module will also be different. For instance, Wikipedia (*https://oreil.ly/zruJt*) is another popular source for extracting text data, and `wikipediaapi` (*https://oreil.ly/ Eyon3*) is one of the supported Python modules for extracting this data. It can be installed by using the command **pip install wikipediaapi**, and since this is a publicly available data source, the authentication and generation of access tokens is not necessary. You only need to specify the version of Wikipedia (language) and the topic name for which you want to extract data. The following code snippet shows the steps to download the Wikipedia entry for "Cryptocurrency" and shows the initial few lines of this article:

```
import wikipediaapi

wiki_wiki = wikipediaapi.Wikipedia(
        language='en',
```

```
        extract_format=wikipediaapi.ExtractFormat.WIKI
)

p_wiki = wiki_wiki.page('Cryptocurrency')
print (p_wiki.text[:200], '....')
```

Out:

```
A cryptocurrency (or crypto currency) is a digital asset designed to work
as a medium of exchange wherein individual coin ownership records are stored
in a ledger existing in a form of computerized da ....
```

Closing Remarks

In this chapter, we first introduced blueprints that make use of the Python requests library to make API calls and extract data. We also introduced ways to work with paginated results, rate limits, and retries. These blueprints work for any kind of API and are great if you would like to control and customize several aspects for your data extraction. In the next set of blueprints, we used Tweepy to extract data from the Twitter API. This is an example of a community-developed Python library that supports a popular API and provides tested functionality out of the box. You often don't have to worry about implementing your own pagination or backoff strategy and is therefore one less thing to worry about. If your use case needs to get data from a popular API, then it is convenient to use such a preexisting package.

## CHAPTER 3

Scraping Websites and Extracting Data

Often, it will happen that you visit a website and find the content interesting. If there are only a few pages, it's possible to read everything on your own. But as soon as there is a considerable amount of content, reading everything on your own will not be possible.

To use the powerful text analytics blueprints described in this book, you have to acquire the content first. Most websites won't have a "download all content" button, so we have to find a clever way to download ("scrape") the pages.

Usually we are mainly interested in the content part of each individual web page, less so in navigation, etc. As soon as we have the data locally available, we can use powerful extraction techniques to dissect the pages into elements such as title, content, and also some meta-information (publication date, author, and so on).

What You'll Learn and What We'll Build

In this chapter, we will show you how to acquire HTML data from websites and use powerful tools to extract the content from these HTML files. We will show this with content from one specific data source, the Reuters news archive.

In the first step, we will download single HTML files and extract data from each one with different methods.

Normally, you will not be interested in single pages. Therefore, we will build a blueprint solution. We will download and analyze a news archive page (which contains links to all articles). After completing this, we know the URLs of the referred documents. Then you can download the documents at the URLs and extract their content to a Pandas `DataFrame`.

After studying this chapter, you will have a good overview of methods that download HTML and extract data. You will be familiar with the different extraction methods for content provided by Python. We will have seen a complete example for downloading and extracting data. For your own work, you will be able to select an appropriate framework. In this chapter, we will provide standard blueprints for extracting often-used elements that you can reuse.

Scraping and Data Extraction

Scraping websites is a complex process consisting of typically three different phases, as illustrated in Figure 3-1.

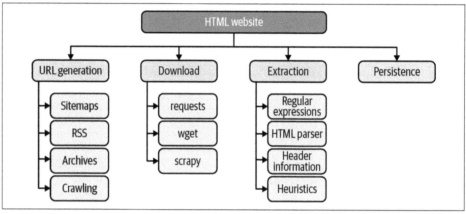

Figure 3-1. Outline of scraping process.

In the first step, we have to generate all interesting URLs of a website. Afterward, we can use different tools to download the pages from the corresponding URLs. Finally, we will extract the "net" data from the downloaded pages; we can also use different strategies in this phase. Of course, it is crucial to permanently save extracted data. In this chapter, we use a Pandas `DataFrame` that offers a variety of persistence mechanisms.

Scraping Is Not Always Necessary: Sources for Existing Datasets

Often, datasets are already available, and you can download them as a whole. This might be special datasets that have a focus on specific content or use cases. If you are interested in sentiment detection, both the comment dataset from the Internet Movie Database (*https://oreil.ly/mljhA*) and the Rotten Tomatoes dataset (*https://oreil.ly/CszzV*) for movies are used quite frequently. Using more structured data, the Yelp dataset (*https://oreil.ly/3la0V*) contains both text and metadata.

Apart from these domain-specific datasets, there more generic ones like Common Crawl (*http://commoncrawl.org*). To generate this, almost each month, parts of the whole Internet are crawled and stored. For compression purposes, data is stored in a special format called WARC. The dataset is really huge, containing roughly two billion web pages. You can freely download the archive or access it directly via an S3 bucket on Amazon Web Services (AWS).

For experimenting, one of the simplest and directly accessible datasets is the so-called newsgroups dataset, which is directly built into scikit-learn (*https://oreil.ly/h2mIl*). Although it is quite dated, it is useful to have a dataset for immediate experimentation without having to download and transform anything.

As we want to show how to download and extract HTML content from the Internet in this chapter, these existing datasets will not be used.

Introducing the Reuters News Archive

Let's assume we are interested in analyzing the current and past political situation and are looking for an appropriate dataset. We want to find some trends, uncover when a word or topic was introduced for the first time, and so on. For this, our aim is to convert the documents to a Pandas `DataFrame`.

Obviously, news headlines and articles are well suited as a database for these requirements. If possible, we should find an archive that goes back a few years, ideally even some decades.

Some newspapers have such archives, but most of them will also have a certain political bias that we want to avoid if possible. We are looking for content that is as neutral as possible.

This is why we decided to use the Reuters news archive. Reuters is an international news organization and works as a news agency; in other words, it provides news to many different publications. It was founded more than a hundred years ago and has a lot of news articles in its archives. It's a good source of content for many reasons:

- It is politically neutral.
- It has a big archive of news.
- News articles are categorized in sections.
- The focus is not on a specific region.
- Almost everybody will find some interesting headlines there.
- It has a liberal policy for downloading data.
- It is very well connected, and the website itself is fast.

Searching for Data

If we are interested in news, using the archive of a large newspaper or news agency is an obvious solution. Sometimes, however, finding appropriate content is not easy. Let's assume we are interested in diggers and want to download content for that. As we do not know which websites carry the corresponding content, we have to find them first.

Fortunately, today's internet search engines use extremely sophisticated algorithms and yield good results when you provide them with specific search queries. If data is (openly) available on the web, search engines will almost certainly be able to find it. One of the most difficult parts of searching for data is knowing which search terms to use.

Running various search terms across different search engines, we can use statistics (or more sophisticated methods) to find the most relevant websites. This requires the repetition of many search requests and counting the number of results. APIs are helpful for running these searches and are available for the big search engines (like Google and Bing).

After finding a useful data source, you must check its number of pages. Search engines can also help in this case, by using specialized idioms as your search term:

- Use `site:domain` to restrict searches to a single domain.

- In more specific cases, `inurl:/path/` can also be helpful, but the syntax differs among different search engines.

- The approaches can be combined; let's assume you want to search for Python articles with NumPy in the URL and compare stackoverflow.com with quora.com. The corresponding search terms would be `site:quora.com python inurl:numpy` versus `site:stackoverflow.com python inurl:numpy`.

- More information is available at the help pages of the search engines, such as Google's Programmable Search Engine page.

Note that search engines are built for interactive operations. If you perform too many (automated) searches, the engines will start sending captchas and eventually block you.

URL Generation

For downloading content from the Reuters' archive, we need to know the URLs of the content pages. After we know the URLs, the download itself is easy as there are powerful Python tools available to accomplish that.

At first sight it might seem easy to find URLs, but in practice it is often not so simple. The process is called *URL generation*, and in many crawling projects it is one of the most difficult tasks. We have to make sure that we do not systematically miss URLs; therefore, thinking carefully about the process in the beginning is crucial. Performed correctly, URL generation can also be a tremendous time-saver.

Before You Download

Be careful: sometimes downloading data is illegal. The rules and legal situation might depend on the country where the data is hosted and into which country it is downloaded. Often, websites have a page called "terms of use" or something similar that might be worth taking a look at.

If data is saved only temporarily, the same rules for search engines might apply. As search engines like Google cannot read and understand the terms of use of every single page they index, there is a really old protocol called the robots exclusion standard (*https://oreil.ly/IWysG*). Websites using this have a file called *robots.txt* at the top level. This file can be downloaded and interpreted automatically. For single websites, it is also possible to read it manually and interpret the data. The rule of thumb is that if there is no `Disal low: *`, you should be allowed to download and (temporarily) save the content.

There are many different possibilities:

Crawling
Start on the home page (or a section) of the website and download all links on the same website. Crawling might take some time.

URL generators
Writing a URL generator is a slightly more sophisticated solution. This is most suitable for use on hierarchically organized content like forums, blogs, etc.

Search engines
Ask search engines for specific URLs and download only these specific URLs.

Sitemaps

A standard called *sitemap.xml* (*https://oreil.ly/XANO0*), which was originally conceived for search engines, is an interesting alternative. A file called *sitemap.xml* contains a list of all pages on a website (or references to sub-sitemaps). Contrary to *robots.txt*, the filename is not fixed and can sometimes be found in *robots.txt* itself. The best guess is to look for *sitemap.xml* on the top level of a website.

RSS

The RSS format (*https://oreil.ly/_aOOM*) was originally conceived for newsfeeds and is still in wide use for subscribing to frequently changing content sources. It works via XML files and does not only contain URLs but also document titles and sometimes summaries of articles.

Specialized programs

Downloading data from social networks and similar content is often simplified by using specialized programs that are available on GitHub (such as Facebook Chat Downloader (*https://oreil.ly/ThyNf*) for Facebook Chats, Instaloader (*https://oreil.ly/utGsC*) for Instagram, and so on).

In the following sections, we focus on *robots.txt*, *sitemaps.xml*, and RSS feeds. Later in the chapter, we show a multistage download that uses URL generators.

Note: Use an API for Downloading Data If It's Available

Instead of generating the URLs, downloading the content, and extracting it, using an API is much easier and more stable. You will find more information about that in Chapter 2.

Blueprint: Downloading and Interpreting robots.txt

Finding the content on a website is often not so easy. To see the techniques mentioned earlier in action, we'll take a look at the Reuters news archive. Of course, (almost) any other website will work in a similar fashion.

As discussed, *robots.txt* (*https://www.reuters.com/robots.txt*) is a good starting point:

```
# robots_allow.txt for www.reuters.com
# Disallow: /*/key-developments/article/*

User-agent: *
Disallow: /finance/stocks/option
[...]
Disallow: /news/archive/commentary
```

```
SITEMAP: https://www.reuters.com/sitemap_index.xml
SITEMAP: https://www.reuters.com/sitemap_news_index.xml
SITEMAP: https://www.reuters.com/sitemap_video_index.xml
SITEMAP: https://www.reuters.com/sitemap_market_index.xml
SITEMAP: https://www.reuters.com/brandfeature/sitemap

User-agent: Pipl
Disallow: /
[...]
```

Some user agents are not allowed to download anything, but the rest may do that. We can check that programmatically in Python:

```
import urllib.robotparser
rp = urllib.robotparser.RobotFileParser()
rp.set_url("https://www.reuters.com/robots.txt")
rp.read()
rp.can_fetch("*", "https://www.reuters.com/sitemap.xml")
```

Out:

```
True
```

Blueprint: Finding URLs from sitemap.xml

Reuters is even nice enough to mention the URLs of the sitemap for the news (*https://reuters.com/sitemap_news_index.xml*), which actually contains only a reference to other sitemap files. Let's download that. An excerpt at the time of writing looks like this:[1]

```
[...]
<url>
  <loc>https://www.reuters.com/article/
us-health-vaping-marijuana-idUSKBN1WG4KT</loc>
  <news:news>
    <news:publication>
      <news:name>Reuters</news:name>
      <news:language>eng</news:language>
    </news:publication>
    <news:publication_date>2019-10-01T08:37:37+00:00</news:publication_date>
    <news:title>Banned in Boston: Without vaping, medical marijuana patients
            must adapt</news:title>
    <news:keywords>Headlines,Credit RSS</news:keywords>
```

---

1 Reuters is a news website and changes daily. Therefore, expect completely different results when running the code!

```
      </news:news>
    </url>
    [...]
```

The most interesting part is the line with <loc>, as it contains the URL of the article. Filtering out all these <loc> lines leads to a list of URLs for news articles that can be downloaded afterward.

As Python has an incredibly rich ecosystem of libraries, it's not hard to find a sitemap parser. There are several available, such as ultimate-sitemap-parser (*https://oreil.ly/XgY9z*). However, this parser downloads the whole sitemap hierarchy, which is a bit too sophisticated for us as we just want the URLs.

It's easy to convert *sitemap.xml* to an associative array (hash) that is called a dict in Python:[2]

```
import xmltodict
import requests

sitemap = xmltodict.parse(requests.get(
        'https://www.reuters.com/sitemap_news_index1.xml').text)
```

Let's check what is in the dict before actually downloading the files[3]:

```
urls = [url["loc"] for url in sitemap["urlset"]["url"]]
# just print the first few URLs to avoid using too much space
print("\n".join(urls[0:3]))
```

Out:

```
https://www.reuters.com/article/us-japan-fukushima/ex-tepco-bosses-cleared-
over-fukushima-nuclear-disaster-idUSKBN1W40CP
https://www.reuters.com/article/us-global-oil/oil-prices-rise-as-saudi-supply-
risks-come-into-focus-idUSKBN1W405X
https://www.reuters.com/article/us-saudi-aramco/iran-warns-against-war-as-us-
and-saudi-weigh-response-to-oil-attack-idUSKBN1W40VN
```

We will use this list of URLs in the following section and download their content.

---

2 You might have to install the package first with **pip install xmltodict**.

3 Reuters is a news site, and the content is continually updated. Note that your results will definitely be different!

Blueprint: Finding URLs from RSS

As Reuters is a news website, it also offers access to its articles via an RSS feed. Several years ago, browsers would show an RSS icon next to the URL if you could subscribe to this source. While those days are gone, it is still not too difficult to find the URLs for RSS feeds. At the bottom of the website, we can see a line with navigation icons, as shown in Figure 3-2.

Figure 3-2. Part of the Reuters website that links to the RSS feed.

The icon that looks like a WIFI indicator is the link to the RSS feeds page. Often (and sometimes more easily) this can be found by taking a look at the source code of the corresponding webpage and searching for *RSS*.

The world news RSS feed has the URL *http://feeds.reuters.com/Reuters/worldNews*[4] and can easily be parsed in Python, as follows:

```
import feedparser
feed = feedparser.parse('http://feeds.reuters.com/Reuters/worldNews')
```

The individual format of the RSS file might differ from site to site. However, most of the time we will find title and link as fields[5]:

```
[(e.title, e.link) for e in feed.entries]
```

Out:

```
[('Cambodian police search for British woman, 21, missing from beach',
  'http://feeds.reuters.com/~r/Reuters/worldNews/~3/xq6Hy6R9lxo/cambodian-
police-search-for-british-woman-21-missing-from-beach-idUSKBN1X70HX'),
 ('Killing the leader may not be enough to stamp out Islamic State',
  'http://feeds.reuters.com/~r/Reuters/worldNews/~3/jbDXkbcQFPA/killing-the-
leader-may-not-be-enough-to-stamp-out-islamic-state-idUSKBN1X7203'), [...]
]
```

In our case, we are more interested in the "real" URLs, which are contained in the id field:

```
[e.id for e in feed.entries]
```

---

4 Just after the time of writing, Reuters stopped providing RSS feeds, which led to a public outcry. We hope that RSS feeds will be restored. The Jupyter notebook for this chapter on GitHub (*https://oreil.ly/Wamlu*) uses an archived version of the RSS feed from the Internet archive.

5 As stated previously, Reuters is a dynamically generated website, and your results will be different!

Out:

```
['https://www.reuters.com/article/us-cambodia-britain-tourist/cambodian-
police-search-for-british-woman-21-missing-from-beach-
idUSKBN1X70HX?feedType=RSS&feedName=worldNews',
 'https://www.reuters.com/article/us-mideast-crisis-baghdadi-future-analys/
killing-the-leader-may-not-be-enough-to-stamp-out-islamic-state-
idUSKBN1X7203?feedType=RSS&feedName=worldNews',
 'https://www.reuters.com/article/us-britain-eu/eu-approves-brexit-delay-
until-january-31-as-pm-johnson-pursues-election-
idUSKBN1X70NT?feedType=RSS&feedName=worldNews', [...]
]
```

Great, we have found an alternative way to get a list of URLs that can be used when no *sitemap.xml* is available.

Sometimes you will still encounter so-called *Atom feeds* (*https://oreil.ly/Jcdgi*), which basically offer the same information as RSS in a different format.

If you wanted to implement a website monitoring tool, taking a periodic look at Reuters news (or other news sources) or RSS (or Atom) would be a good way to go ahead.

If you are interested in whole websites, looking for *sitemap.xml* is an excellent idea. Sometimes it might be difficult to find (hints might be in *robots.txt*), but it is almost always worth the extra effort to find it.

If you cannot find *sitemap.xml* and you plan to regularly download content, going for RSS is a good second choice.

Whenever possible, try to avoid crawling websites for URLs. The process is largely uncontrollable, can take a long time, and might yield incomplete results.

Downloading Data

At first sight, downloading data might seem like the most difficult and time-consuming part of the scraping process. Often, that's not true as you can accomplish it in a highly standardized way.

In this section, we show different methods for downloading data, both with Python libraries and external tools. Especially for big projects, using external programs has some advantages.

Compared to several years ago, the Internet is much faster today. Big websites have reacted to this development by using content-delivery networks, which can speed them up by orders of magnitude. This helps us a lot as the actual downloading process is not as slow as it used to be but is more or less limited by our own bandwidth.

Tips for Efficient Downloads

The following strategies will help you download websites efficiently:

Compression
> HTML normally is very verbose and can easily be compressed by several factors. To save bandwidth, a download program supporting gzip compression (deflate or brotli is also possible) will save considerable bandwidth and time.

Content distribution networks (CDNs)
> Cloud servers like AWS have an immensely powerful connection to the internet. To avoid overloading servers, parallel downloads should be used carefully. Definitely work with a "grace period" and wait some time between requests. To make the traffic look more human (and avoid automatic exclusions from the servers), randomizing this period is often a good idea.

Keep alive
> For the past few years, most servers have begun using the HTTPS/TLS protocol for secure data transmission. The handshake of the protocol is quite complicated. It includes checking public/private keys and creating a symmetric session key before the actual encrypted transmission can start (Diffie-Hellman key exchange (*https://oreil.ly/rOzKH*)).
>
> Browsers are quite clever and have a special cache for this session key. When looking for a dedicated download program, choose one that also has such a cache. To achieve even smaller latencies, HTTP keep-alive can be used to recycle TCP connections. The Python requests library supports this functionality using the `Session` abstraction.

Save files
> In many projects, it has proven useful to save the downloaded HTML pages (temporarily) in the filesystem. Of course, the structured content can be extracted on the fly, but if something goes wrong or pages have a different structure than expected, it will be hard to find and debug. This is extremely useful, especially during development.

Start simple
> In most blueprints, `requests` is well-suited for downloading pages. It offers a decent interface and works in Python environments.

Avoid getting banned
> Most websites are not keen on getting scraped, and quite a few have implemented countermeasures. Be polite and add a grace period between requests if you plan to download many pages.

If you get banned anyway, you should actively notice this by checking the content and the response code. Changing IP addresses or using using IPv6, proxy servers, VPNs, or even the Tor network are possible options then.

Legal aspects

Depending on where you live and the terms of use of a website, scraping might not be allowed at all.

Blueprint: Downloading HTML Pages with Python

To download HTML pages, it's necessary to know the URLs. As we have seen, the URLs are contained in the sitemap. Let's use this list to download the content:

```
%%time
s = requests.Session()
for url in urls[0:10]:
    # get the part after the last / in URL and use as filename
    file = url.split("/")[-1]

    r = s.get(url)
    if r.ok:
        with open(file, "w+b") as f:
            f.write(r.text.encode('utf-8'))
    else:
        print("error with URL %s" % url)
```

Out:

```
CPU times: user 117 ms, sys: 7.71 ms, total: 124 ms
Wall time: 314 ms
```

Depending on your Internet connection, it might take longer, but that was quite fast. Using the session abstraction, we make sure to have maximum speed by leveraging keep-alive, SSL session caching, and so on.

Use Proper Error Handling When Downloading URLs

When downloading URLs, you are using a network protocol to communicate with remote servers. There are many kinds of errors that can happen, such as changed URLs, servers not responding, etc. The example just shows an error message; in real life, your solution should probably be more sophisticated.

Blueprint: Downloading HTML Pages with wget

A good tool for mass downloading pages is wget (*https://oreil.ly/wget*), which is a command line tool available for almost all platforms. On Linux and macOS, wget should already be installed or can easily be installed using a package manager. On Windows, there is a port available at *https://oreil.ly/2Nl0b*.

wget supports lists of URLs for downloads and HTTP keep-alive. Normally, each HTTP request needs a separate TCP connection (or a Diffie-Hellman key exchange; see "Tips for Efficient Downloads" on page 67). The -nc option of wget will check whether files have already been downloaded. This way, we can avoid downloading content twice. We can now stop the process at any time and restart without losing data, which is important if a web server blocks us, our Internet connection goes down, etc. Let's save the list of URLs from the last blueprint to a file and use that as a template for downloading:

```
with open("urls.txt", "w+b") as f:
    f.write("\n".join(urls).encode('utf-8'))
```

Now go to your command line (or a terminal tab in Jupyter) and call wget:

```
wget -nc -i urls.txt
```

The -i option tells wget the list of URLs to download. It's fun to see how wget skips the existing files (due to the -nc option) and how fast the downloading works.

wget can also be used for recursively downloading websites with the option -r.

Danger of Lockout!

Be careful, this might lead to long-running processes, and eventually you might get locked out of the website. It's often a good idea to combine -r with -l (recursion level) when experimenting with recursive downloads.

There are several different ways to download data. For a moderate number of pages (like a few hundred to a thousand), a download directly in a Python program is the standard way to go. We recommend the requests library, as it is easy to use.

Downloading more than a few thousand pages normally works better in a multistage process by first generating a list of URLs and then downloading them externally via a dedicated program like wget.

Extracting Semistructured Data

In the following section, we will explore different methods to extract data from Reuters articles. We will start with using regular expressions and then turn to a full-fledged HTML parser.

Eventually we will be interested in the data of more than one article, but as a first step we will concentrate on a single one. Let's take "Banned in Boston: Without vaping, medical marijuana patients must adapt" (*https://oreil.ly/jg0Jr*) as our example.

Blueprint: Extracting Data with Regular Expressions

The browser will be one of the most important tools for dissecting the article. Start by opening the URL and using the View Source functionality. In the first step, we can see that the title is interesting. Taking a look at the HTML, the title is surrounded by both <title> and <h1>.

```
[...]
<title>Banned in Boston: Without vaping, medical marijuana patients
must adapt - Reuters</title>
[...]
<h1 class="ArticleHeader_headline">Banned in Boston: Without vaping,
medical marijuana patients must adapt</h1>
[...]
```

HTML Code Changes Over Time

The programs described in this section work with the HTML code that was current when the book was written. However, publishers are free to change their website structure anytime and even remove content. An alternative is to use the data from the Wayback Machine (*https://archive.org*). The Reuters website is mirrored there, and snapshots are kept that preserve the layout and the HTML structure.

Also take a look at the GitHub archive of the book. If the layout has changed and the programs would not work anymore, alternative links (and sitemaps) will be provided there.

Programmatically, the extraction of the title can be achieved with regular expressions without using any other libraries. Let's first download the article and save it to a local file called *us-health-vaping-marijuana-idUSKBN1WG4KT.html*.

```
import requests

url = 'https://www.reuters.com/article/us-health-vaping-marijuana-idUSKBN1WG4KT'

# use the part after the last / as filename
file = url.split("/")[-1] + ".html"
r = requests.get(url)
with open(file, "w+b") as f:
    f.write(r.text.encode('utf-8'))
```

A Python blueprint for extracting the title might look like this:

```
import re

with open(file, "r") as f:
    html = f.read()
    g = re.search(r'<title>(.*)</title>', html, re.MULTILINE|re.DOTALL)
    if g:
        print(g.groups()[0])
```

Out:

```
Banned in Boston: Without vaping, medical marijuana patients must adapt - Reuters
```

The re library is not fully integrated into Python string handling. In other words, it cannot be invoked as methods of string. As our HTML documents consist of many lines, we have to use re.MULTILINE|re.DOTALL. Sometimes cascaded calls to re.search are necessary, but they do make the code harder to read.

It is crucial to use re.search and not re.match in Python, which is different than in many other programming languages. The latter tries to match the whole string, and as there is data before <title> and after </title>, it fails.

Blueprint: Using an HTML Parser for Extraction

The article has more interesting parts that are tedious to extract with regular expressions. There's text in the article, a publication date is associated with it, and the authors are named. This is much easier to accomplish with an HTML parser.[6] Fortunately, with the Python package called Beautiful Soup (*https://oreil.ly/I2VJh*), we have an extremely powerful library for handling this. If you don't have Beautiful Soup installed, install it now with pip install bs4 or conda install bs4. Beautiful Soup is tolerant and can also parse "bad" HTML that is often found on sloppily managed websites.

---

6 HTML cannot be parsed with regular expressions (*https://oreil.ly/EeCjy*).

The next sections make use of the fact that all articles have the same structure in the news archive. Fortunately, this is true for most big websites as the pages are not hand-crafted but rather generated by a content management system from a database.

Extracting the title/headline

Selecting content in Beautiful Soup uses so-called selectors that need to be given in the Python program. Finding them is a bit tricky, but there are structural approaches for that. Almost all modern browsers support a Web Inspector, which is useful for finding the CSS selectors. Open the Web Inspector in the browser (most commonly achieved by pressing F12) when the article is loaded, and click the Web Inspector icon, as shown in Figure 3-3.

Figure 3-3. Web Inspector icon in the Chrome browser.

Hover over the headline and you will see the corresponding element highlighted, as shown in Figure 3-4.

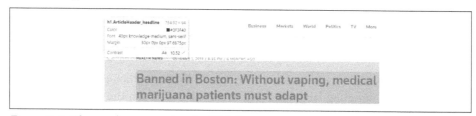

Figure 3-4. Chrome browser using the Web Inspector.

Clicking the headline to show it in the Web Inspector. It should look like this:

```
<h1 class="ArticleHeader_headline">Banned in Boston: Without vaping, medical
marijuana patients must adapt</h1>
```

Using CSS notation,[7] this element can be selected with h1.ArticleHeader_headline. Beautiful Soup understands that:

```
from bs4 import Beautiful Soup
soup = Beautiful Soup(html, 'html.parser')
soup.select("h1.ArticleHeader_headline")
```

Out:

```
[<h1 class="ArticleHeader_headline">Banned in Boston: Without vaping, medical
marijuana patients must adapt</h1>]
```

---

7 See *CSS: The Definitive Guide, 4th Edition* by Eric A. Meyer and Estelle Weyl (O'Reilly, 2017)

Beautiful Soup makes it even easier and lets us use the tag names directly:

```
soup.h1
```

Out:

```
<h1 class="ArticleHeader_headline">Banned in Boston: Without vaping, medical
marijuana patients must adapt</h1>
```

Normally, the most interesting part of the previous HTML fragment is the real text without the HTML clutter around it. Beautiful Soup can extract that:

```
soup.h1.text
```

Out:

```
'Banned in Boston: Without vaping, medical marijuana patients must adapt'
```

Note that in contrast to the regular expression solution, unnecessary whitespaces have been stripped by Beautiful Soup.

Unfortunately, that does not work as well for the title:

```
soup.title.text
```

Out:

```
'\n            Banned in Boston: Without vaping, medical marijuana patients
must adapt - Reuters'
```

Here, we would need to manually strip the data and eliminate the - Reuters suffix.

Extracting the article text

In a similar way to the previously described procedure for finding the headline selector, you can easily find the text content at the selector div.StandardArticle Body_body. When using select, Beautiful Soup returns a list. Often it is clear from the underlying HTML structure that the list consists of only one item or we are interested only in the first element. We can use the convenience method select_one here:

```
soup.select_one("div.StandardArticleBody_body").text
```

Out:

```
"WASHINGTON (Reuters) - In the first few days of the four-month ban [...]"
```

Extracting image captions

But wait, apart from the text, this part also contains images with captions that might be relevant separately. So again, use the Web Inspector to hover over the images and find the corresponding CSS selectors. All images are contained in <figure> elements, so let's select them:

```
soup.select("div.StandardArticleBody_body figure img")
```

Out:

```
[<img aria-label="FILE PHOTO: An employee puts down an eighth of an ounce
  marijuana after letting a customer smell it outside the Magnolia cannabis
  lounge in Oakland, California, U.S. April 20, 2018. REUTERS/Elijah Nouvelage"
  src="//s3.reutersmedia.net/resources/r/
  ?m=02&amp;d=20191001&amp;t=2&amp;i=1435991144&amp;r=LYNXMPEF90
  39L&amp;w=20"/>, <img src="//s3.reutersmedia.net/resources/r/
  ?m=02&amp;d=20191001&amp;t=2&amp;i=1435991145&amp;r=LYNXMPEF90
  39M"/>]
```

Inspecting the result closely, this code contains only one image, whereas the browser displays many images. This is a pattern that can often be found in web pages. Code for the images is not in the page itself but is added later by client-side JavaScript. Technically this is possible, although it is not the best style. From a content perspective, it would be better if the image source were contained in the original server-generated page and made visible by CSS later. This would also help our extraction process. Anyway, we are more interested in the caption of the image, so the correct selector would be to replace img with figcaption.

```
soup.select("div.StandardArticleBody_body figcaption")
```

Out:

```
[<figcaption><div class="Image_caption"><span>FILE PHOTO:
  An employee puts down an eighth of an ounce marijuana after letting a
  customer smell it outside the Magnolia cannabis lounge in Oakland,
  California, U.S. April 20, 2018. REUTERS/Elijah Nouvelage</span></
  div></figcaption>,

  <figcaption class="Slideshow_caption">Slideshow<span class="Slideshow_count">
  (2 Images)</span></figcaption>]
```

Extracting the URL

When downloading many HTML files, it is often difficult to find the original URLs of the files if they have not been saved separately. Moreover, URLs might change, and normally it is best to use the standard (called *canonical*) URL. Fortunately, there is an HTML tag called <link rel="canonical"> that can be used for this purpose. The tag is not mandatory, but it is extremely common, as it is also taken into account by search engines and contributes to a good ranking:

```
soup.find("link", {'rel': 'canonical'})['href']
```

Out:

```
'https://www.reuters.com/article/us-health-vaping-marijuana-idUSKBN1WG4KT'
```

Extracting list information (authors)

Taking a look at the source code, the author of the article is mentioned in a <meta name="Author"> tag.

```
soup.find("meta", {'name': 'Author'})['content']
```

Out:

```
'Jacqueline Tempera'
```

However, this returns only one author. Reading the text, there is another author, which is unfortunately not contained in the meta-information of the page. Of course, it can be extracted again by selecting the elements in the browser and using the CSS selector:

```
sel = "div.BylineBar_first-container.ArticleHeader_byline-bar \
    div.BylineBar_byline span"
soup.select(sel)
```

Out:

```
[<span><a href="/journalists/jacqueline-tempera" target="_blank">
  Jacqueline Tempera</a>, </span>,
 <span><a href="/journalists/jonathan-allen" target="_blank">
  Jonathan Allen</a></span>]
```

Extracting the author names is then straightforward:

```
[a.text for a in soup.select(sel)]
```

Out:

```
['Jacqueline Tempera, ', 'Jonathan Allen']
```

Semantic and nonsemantic content

In contrast to the previous examples, the sel selector is not *semantic*. Selection is performed based on layout-like classes. This works well for the moment but is likely to break if the layout is changed. Therefore, it's a good idea to avoid these kinds of selections if the code is likely to be executed not only once or in a batch but should also run in the future.

Extracting text of links (section)

The section is easy to extract. Using the Web Inspector again, we can find that the CSS selector is the following:

```
soup.select_one("div.ArticleHeader_channel a").text
```

Out:

```
'Politics'
```

Extracting reading time

Reading time can be found easily via the Web Inspector:

```
soup.select_one("p.BylineBar_reading-time").text
```

Out:

```
'6 Min Read'
```

Extracting attributes (ID)

Having a primary key that uniquely identifies an article is helpful. The ID is also present in the URL, but there might be some heuristics and advanced splitting necessary to find it. Using the browser's View Source functionality and searching for this ID, we see that it is the id attribute of the article container:

```
soup.select_one("div.StandardArticle_inner-container")['id']
```

Out:

```
'USKBN1WG4KT'
```

Extracting attribution

Apart from the authors, the article carries more attributions. They can be found at the end of the text and reside in a special container:

```
soup.select_one("p.Attribution_content").text
```

Out:

```
'Reporting Jacqueline Tempera in Brookline and Boston, Massachusetts, and
Jonathan Allen in New York; Editing by Frank McGurty and Bill Berkrot'
```

Extracting timestamp

For many statistical purposes, it is crucial to know the time that the article was posted. This is mentioned next to the section, but unfortunately it is constructed to be human-readable (like "3 days ago"). This can be parsed but is tedious. Knowing the real publishing time, the correct element can be found in the HTML head element:

```
ptime = soup.find("meta", { 'property': "og:article:published_time"})['content']
print(ptime)
```

Out:

```
2019-10-01T19:23:16+0000
```

A string is already helpful (especially in this notation, as we will see later), but Python offers facilities to convert that to a datetime object easily:

```
from dateutil import parser
parser.parse(ptime)
```

Out:

```
datetime.datetime(2019, 10, 1, 19, 23, 16, tzinfo=tzutc())
```

The same can be done for `modified_time` instead of `published_time`, if that is more relevant.

Use regular expressions only for crude extraction. An HTML parser is slower but much easier to use and more stable.

Often, it makes sense to take a look at the semantic structure of the documents and use HTML tags that have semantic class names to find the value of structural elements. These tags have the advantage that they are the same over a large class of web pages. Extraction of their content therefore has to be implemented only once and can be reused.

Apart from extremely simple cases, try to use an HTML parser whenever possible. Some standard structures that can be found in almost any HTML document are discussed in the following sidebar.

Standardized Extraction

Normally, it is a good idea to extract at least these standardized parts of each document:

- Title: Use the `<title>` or `<h1>` tag.
- Summary of web page: Look for `<meta name="description">`.
- Structured header information: Standardized in the OpenGraph (*https://ogp.me*). Search for `og:` in the source code of a page.
- URL of a web page: The URL itself might contain valuable information and can be found in `<link rel="canonical>`.
- URL structure: Modern URLs are often not cryptic but contain a lot of information, like categories (sections) organized in folders, IDs, or even timestamps in blogs.

Blueprint: Spidering

So far we have taken a look at how we can download web pages and extract the content using HTML parsing techniques. From a business perspective, looking at single pages is often not so interesting, butyou want to see the whole picture. For this, you need much more content.

Fortunately, our acquired knowledge can be combined to download content archives or whole websites. This is often a multistage process where you need to generate URLs first, download the content, find more URLs, and so on.

This section explains one of these "spidering" examples in detail and creates a scalable blueprint that can be used for downloading thousands (or millions) of pages.

Introducing the Use Case

Parsing a single Reuters article is a nice exercise, but the Reuters archive is much larger and contains many articles. It is also possible to use the techniques we have covered to parse a larger amount. Imagine that you want to download and extract, for example, a whole forum with user-generated content or a website with scientific articles. As mentioned previously, it is often most difficult to find the correct URLs of the articles.

Not in this case, though. It would be possible to use *sitemap.xml*, but Reuters is generous enough to offer a dedicated archive page at *https://www.reuters.com/news/archive*. A paging functionality is also available, so it's possible to go backward in time.

Figure 3-5 shows the steps for downloading part of the archive (called *spidering*). The process works as follows:

1. Define how many pages of the archive should be downloaded.
2. Download each page of the archive into a file called *page-000001.html*, *page-000002.html*, and so on for easier inspection. Skip this step if the file is already present.
3. For each *page-*.html* file, extract the URLs of the referenced articles.
4. For each article URL, download the article into a local HTML file. Skip this step if the article file is already present.
5. For each article file, extract the content into a dict and combine these dicts into a Pandas DataFrame.

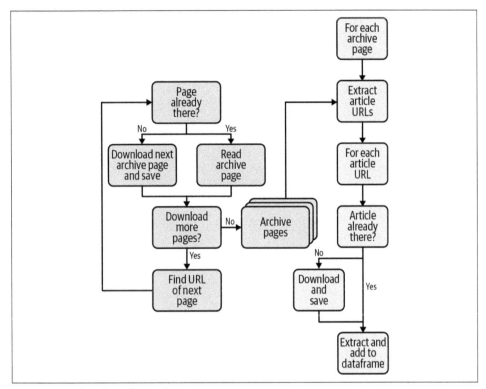

Figure 3-5. Flowchart for spidering process.

In a more generic approach, it might be necessary to create intermediate URLs in step 3 (if there is an overview page for years, months, etc.) before we finally arrive at the article URLs.

The procedure is constructed in a way that each step can be run individually and downloads have to be performed only once. This has proven to be useful, especially when we have to extract a large number of articles/URLs, as a single missing download or malformed HTML page does not mean that the whole procedure including downloading has to be started again. Moreover, the process can be restarted anytime and downloads only data that has not yet been downloaded. This is called *idempotence* and is often a useful concept when interacting with "expensive" APIs.

The finished program looks like this:

```
import requests
from bs4 import Beautiful Soup
import os.path
from dateutil import parser

def download_archive_page(page):
    filename = "page-%06d.html" % page
```

```
        if not os.path.isfile(filename):
            url = "https://www.reuters.com/news/archive/" + \
                "?view=page&page=%d&pageSize=10" % page
            r = requests.get(url)
            with open(filename, "w+") as f:
                f.write(r.text)

    def parse_archive_page(page_file):
        with open(page_file, "r") as f:
            html = f.read()

        soup = Beautiful Soup(html, 'html.parser')
        hrefs = ["https://www.reuters.com" + a['href']
                    for a in soup.select("article.story div.story-content a")]
        return hrefs

    def download_article(url):
        # check if article already there
        filename = url.split("/")[-1] + ".html"
        if not os.path.isfile(filename):
            r = requests.get(url)
            with open(filename, "w+") as f:
                f.write(r.text)

    def parse_article(article_file):
        with open(article_file, "r") as f:
            html = f.read()
        r = {}
        soup = Beautiful Soup(html, 'html.parser')
        r['id'] = soup.select_one("div.StandardArticle_inner-container")['id']
        r['url'] = soup.find("link", {'rel': 'canonical'})['href']
        r['headline'] = soup.h1.text
        r['section'] = soup.select_one("div.ArticleHeader_channel a").text
        r['text'] = soup.select_one("div.StandardArticleBody_body").text
        r['authors'] = [a.text
                            for a in soup.select("div.BylineBar_first-container.\
                                            ArticleHeader_byline-bar\
                                            div.BylineBar_byline span")]
        r['time'] = soup.find("meta", { 'property':
                                            "og:article:published_time"})['content']
        return r
```

Having defined these functions, they can be invoked with parameters (which can easily be changed):

```
# download 10 pages of archive
for p in range(1, 10):
    download_archive_page(p)

# parse archive and add to article_urls
import glob

article_urls = []
```

```
for page_file in glob.glob("page-*.html"):
    article_urls += parse_archive_page(page_file)

# download articles
for url in article_urls:
    download_article(url)

# arrange in pandas DataFrame
import pandas as pd

df = pd.DataFrame()
for article_file in glob.glob("*-id???????????.html"):
    df = df.append(parse_article(article_file), ignore_index=True)

df['time'] = pd.to_datetime(df.time)
```

Error Handling and Production-Quality Software

For simplicity, all example programs discussed in this chapter do not use error handling. For production software, however, you should use exception handling. As HTML can change frequently and pages might be incomplete, errors can happen at any time, so it is a good idea to use try/except generously and log the errors. If systematic errors occur, you should look for the root cause and eliminate it. If errors occur only sporadically or due to malformed HTML, you can probably ignore them, as they might also be due to server software.

Using the download and save file mechanism described earlier, the extraction procedure can be restarted anytime or also be applied to certain problematic files separately. This is often a big advantage and helps to achieve a cleanly extracted dataset fast.

Generating URLs is often as difficult as extracting content and is frequently related to it. In many cases, this has to be repeated several times to download, for example, hierarchical content.

When you download data, always find a filename for each URL and save it to the filesystem. You will have to restart the process more often than you think. Not having to download everything over and over is immensely useful, especially during the development process.

If you have downloaded and extracted the data, you will probably want to persist it for later use. An easy way is to save it in individual JSON files. If you have many files, using a directory structure might be a good option. With an increasing number of pages, even this might not scale well, and it's a better idea to use a database or another columnar data store.

Density-Based Text Extraction

Extracting structured data from HTML is not complicated, but it is tedious. If you want to extract data from a whole website, it is well worth the effort as you only have to implement the extraction for a limited number of page types.

However, you may need to extract text from many different websites. Implementing the extraction for each of them does not scale well. There is some metadata that can be found easily, such as title, description, etc. But the text itself is not so easy to find.

Taking a look at the information density, there are some heuristics that allow extraction of the text. The algorithm behind it measures the *density of information* and therefore automatically eliminates repeated information such as headers, navigation, footers, and so on. The implementation is not so simple but is fortunately available in a library called `python-readability` (*https://oreil.ly/AemZh*). The name originates from a now-orphaned browser plugin called Readability, which was conceived to remove clutter from web pages and make them easily readable—exactly what is needed here. To get started, we must first install `python-readability` (**pip install readability-lxml**).

Extracting Reuters Content with Readability

Let's see how this works in the Reuters example. We keep the HTML we have downloaded, but of course you can also use a file or URL:

```
from readability import Document

doc = Document(html)
doc.title()
```

Out:

```
'Banned in Boston: Without vaping, medical marijuana patients must adapt -
Reuters'
```

As you can see, that was easy. The title can be extracted via the corresponding element. However, the library can do some additional tricks, such as finding the title or the summary of the page:

```
doc.short_title()
```

Out:

```
'Banned in Boston: Without vaping, medical marijuana patients must adapt'
```

That is already quite good. Let's check how well it works for the actual content:

```
doc.summary()
```

Out:

```
'<html><body><div><div class="StandardArticleBody_body"><p>BOSTON (Reuters) -
In the first few days of [...] </p>

<div class="Attribution_container"><div class="Attribution_attribution">
<p class="Attribution_content">Reporting Jacqueline Tempera in Brookline
and Boston, Massachusetts, and Jonathan Allen in New York; Editing by Frank
McGurty and Bill Berkrot</p></div></div></div></div></body></html>'
```

The data still has some remaining HTML structure, which can be useful to keep because paragraphs are included. Of course, the body part can be extracted again with Beautiful Soup:

```
density_soup = Beautiful Soup(doc.summary(), 'html.parser')
density_soup.body.text
```

Out:

```
'BOSTON (Reuters) - In the first few days of the four-month ban on all vaping
products in Massachusetts, Laura Lee Medeiros, a medical marijuana patient,
began to worry.\xa0 FILE PHOTO: An employee puts down an eighth of an ounce
marijuana after letting a customer smell it outside the Magnolia cannabis
lounge in Oakland, California, U.S. [...]

Reporting Jacqueline Tempera in Brookline and Boston, Massachusetts, and
Jonathan Allen in New York; Editing by Frank McGurty and Bill Berkrot'
```

In this case, the results are excellent. In most of the cases, python-readability works reasonably well and removes the need to implement too many special cases. However, the cost of using this library is uncertainty. Will it always work in the expected way with the impossibility of extracting structured data such as timestamps, authors, and so on (although there might be other heuristics for that)?

Summary Density-Based Text Extraction

Density-based text extraction is powerful when using both heuristics and statistical information about information distribution on an HTML page. You should keep in mind that the results are almost always worse when compared to implementing a specific extractor. However, if you need to extract content from many different page types or from an archive where you don't have a fixed layout at all, it might well be worth it to go that way.

Performing a detailed quality assurance afterward is even more essential compared to the structured approach as both the heuristics and the statistics might sometimes go in the wrong direction.

All-in-One Approach

Scrapy (*https://scrapy.org*) is another Python package that offers an all-in-one approach to spidering and content extraction. The methods are similar to the ones described in the earlier sections, although Scrapy is more suited for downloading *whole* websites and not only parts of them.

The object-oriented, holistic approach of Scrapy is definitely nice, and the code is readable. However, it turns out to be quite difficult to restart spidering and extraction without having to download the whole website again.

Compared to the approach described earlier, downloading must also happen in Python. For websites with a huge number of pages, HTTP keep-alive cannot be used, and gzip encoding is also difficult. Both can be easily integrated in the modular method by externalizing the downloads via tools such as wget.

Blueprint: Scraping the Reuters Archive with Scrapy

Let's see how the download of the archive and the articles would look in Scrapy. Go ahead and install Scrapy (either via **conda install scrapy** or **pip install scrapy**).

```
import scrapy
import logging

class ReutersArchiveSpider(scrapy.Spider):
    name = 'reuters-archive'

    custom_settings = {
        'LOG_LEVEL': logging.WARNING,
        'FEED_FORMAT': 'json',
        'FEED_URI': 'reuters-archive.json'
    }

    start_urls = [
        'https://www.reuters.com/news/archive/',
    ]

    def parse(self, response):
        for article in response.css("article.story div.story-content a"):
            yield response.follow(article.css("a::attr(href)").extract_first(),
                                  self.parse_article)
        next_page_url = response.css('a.control-nav-next::attr(href)').\
                        extract_first()
```

```
    if (next_page_url is not None) & ('page=2' not in next_page_url):
        yield response.follow(next_page_url, self.parse)

def parse_article(self, response):
    yield {
      'title': response.css('h1::text').extract_first().strip(),
      'section': response.css('div.ArticleHeader_channel a::text').\
              extract_first().strip(),
      'text': "\n".join(response.\
              css('div.StandardArticleBody_body p::text').extract())
    }
```

Scrapy works in an object-oriented way. For each so-called spider, a class needs to be implemented that is derived from scrapy.Spider. Scrapy adds a lot of debug output, which is reduced in the previous example by logging.WARNING. The base class automatically calls the parse function with the start_urls. This function extracts the links to the article and invokes yield with the function parse_article as a parameter. This function in turn extracts some attributes from the articles and yields them in a dict. Finally, the next page link is crawled, but we stop here before getting the second page.

yield has a double functionality in Scrapy. If a dict is yielded, it is added to the results. If a Request object is yielded, the object is fetched and gets parsed.

Scrapy and Jupyter

Scrapy is optimized for command-line usage, but it can also be invoked in a Jupyter notebook. Because of Scrapy's usage of the (ancient) Twisted environment (*https://oreil.ly/j6HCm*), the scraping cannot be restarted, so you have only one shot if you try it in the notebook (otherwise you have to restart the notebook):

```
# this can be run only once from a Jupyter notebook
# due to Twisted
from scrapy.crawler import CrawlerProcess
process = CrawlerProcess()

process.crawl(ReutersArchiveSpider)
process.start()
```

Here are a few things worth mentioning:

- The all-in-one approach looks elegant and concise.
- As most of the coding is spent in extracting data in the articles, this code has to change frequently. For this, spidering has to be restarted (and if you are running the script in Jupyter, you also have to start the Jupyter notebook server), which tremendously increases turnaround times.

- It's nice that JSON can directly be produced. Be careful as the JSON file is appended, which can result in an invalid JSON if you don't delete the file before starting the spidering process. This can be solved by using the so-called jl format (JSON lines), but it is a workaround.

- Scrapy has some nice ideas. In our day-to-day work, we do not use it, mainly because debugging is hard. If persistence of the HTML files is needed (which we strongly suggest), it loses lots of advantages. The object-oriented approach is useful and can be implemented outside of Scrapy without too much effort.

As Scrapy also uses CSS selectors for extracting HTML content, the basic technologies are the same as with the other approaches. There are considerable differences in the downloading method, though. Having Twisted as a backend creates some overhead and imposes a special programming model.

Decide carefully whether an all-in-one approach suits your project needs. For some websites, ready-made Scrapy spiders might already be available and can be reused.

Possible Problems with Scraping

Before scraping content, it is always worthwhile to consider possible copyright and data protection issues.

More and more web applications are constructed using frameworks like React (*https://reactjs.org*). They have only a single page, and data is transferred via an API. This often leads to websites not working without JavaScript. Sometimes there are specialized URLs constructed for search engines that are also useful for spidering. Usually, those can be found in *sitemap.xml*. You can try it by switching off JavaScript in your browser and then see whether the website still works.

If JavaScript is needed, you can find requests on the Network tab by using the Web Inspector of the browser and clicking around the application. Sometimes, JSON is used to transfer the data, which makes extraction often much easier compared to HTML. However, the individual JSON URLs still have to be generated, and there might be additional parameters to avoid cross-site request forgery (CSRF) (*https://oreil.ly/_6O_Q*).

Requests can become quite complicated, such as in the Facebook timeline, on Instagram, or on Twitter. Obviously, these websites try to keep their content for themselves and avoid spidering.

For complicated cases, it can be useful to "remote control" the browser by using Selenium (*https://oreil.ly/YssLD*), a framework that was originally conceived for the automated testing of web applications, or a headless browser (*https://oreil.ly/CH2ZI*).

Websites like Google try to detect automatic download attempts and start sending captchas. This can also happen with other websites. Most of the time this is bound to certain IP addresses. The website must then be "unlocked" with a normal browser, and the automatic requests should be sent with larger pauses between them.

Another method to avoid content extraction is obfuscated HTML code where CSS classes have totally random names. If the names do not change, this is more work initially to find the correct selectors but should work automatically afterward. If the names change every day (for example), content extraction becomes extremely difficult.

Closing Remarks and Recommendation

Web scraping is a powerful and scalable technique to acquire content. The necessary Python infrastructure supports scraping projects in an excellent way. The combination of the requests library and Beautiful Soup is comfortable and works well for moderately large scraping jobs.

As we have seen throughout the chapter, we can systematically split up large scraping projects into URL generation and downloading phases. If the number of documents becomes really big, external tools like wget might be more appropriate compared to requests. As soon as everything is downloaded, Beautiful Soup can be used to extract the content.

If you want to minimize waiting time, all stages can be run in parallel.

In any case, you should be aware of the legal aspects and behave as an "ethical scraper" by respecting the rules in *robots.txt*.

## CHAPTER 4

Preparing Textual Data for Statistics and Machine Learning

Technically, any text document is just a sequence of characters. To build models on the content, we need to transform a text into a sequence of words or, more generally, meaningful sequences of characters called *tokens*. But that alone is not sufficient. Think of the word sequence *New York*, which should be treated as a single named-entity. Correctly identifying such word sequences as compound structures requires sophisticated linguistic processing.

Data preparation or data preprocessing in general involves not only the transformation of data into a form that can serve as the basis for analysis but also the removal of disturbing noise. What's noise and what isn't always depends on the analysis you are going to perform. When working with text, noise comes in different flavors. The raw data may include HTML tags or special characters that should be removed in most cases. But frequent words carrying little meaning, the so-called *stop words*, introduce noise into machine learning and data analysis because they make it harder to detect patterns.

What You'll Learn and What We'll Build

In this chapter, we will develop blueprints for a text preprocessing pipeline. The pipeline will take the raw text as input, clean it, transform it, and extract the basic features of textual content. We start with regular expressions for data cleaning and tokenization and then focus on linguistic processing with *spaCy*. spaCy is a powerful NLP library with a modern API and state-of-the-art models. For some operations we will make use of *textacy*, a library that provides some nice add-on functionality especially for data preprocessing. We will also point to NLTK and other libraries whenever it appears helpful.

After studying this chapter, you will know the required and optional steps of data preparation. You will know how to use regular expressions for data cleaning and how to use spaCy for feature extraction. With the provided blueprints you will be able to quickly set up a data preparation pipeline for your own project.

A Data Preprocessing Pipeline

Data preprocessing usually involves a sequence of steps. Often, this sequence is called a *pipeline* because you feed raw data into the pipeline and get the transformed and preprocessed data out of it. In Chapter 1 we already built a simple data processing pipeline including tokenization and stop word removal. We will use the term *pipeline* in this chapter as a general term for a sequence of processing steps. Figure 4-1 gives an overview of the blueprints we are going to build for the preprocessing pipeline in this chapter.

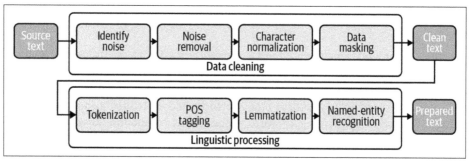

Figure 4-1. A pipeline with typical preprocessing steps for textual data.

The first major block of operations in our pipeline is *data cleaning*. We start by identifying and removing noise in text like HTML tags and nonprintable characters. During *character normalization*, special characters such as accents and hyphens are transformed into a standard representation. Finally, we can mask or remove identifiers like URLs or email addresses if they are not relevant for the analysis or if there are privacy issues. Now the text is clean enough to start linguistic processing.

Here, *tokenization* splits a document into a list of separate tokens like words and punctuation characters. *Part-of-speech (POS) tagging* is the process of determining the word class, whether it's a noun, a verb, an article, etc. *Lemmatization* maps inflected words to their uninflected root, the lemma (e.g., "are" → "be"). The target of *named-entity recognition* is the identification of references to people, organizations, locations, etc., in the text.

In the end, we want to create a database with preprared data ready for analysis and machine learning. Thus, the required preparation steps vary from project to project. It's up to you to decide which of the following blueprints you need to include in your problem-specific pipeline.

Introducing the Dataset: Reddit Self-Posts

The preparation of textual data is particularly challenging when you work with user-generated content (UGC). In contrast to well-redacted text from professional reports, news, and blogs, user contributions in social media usually are short and contain lots of abbreviations, hashtags, emojis, and typos. Thus, we will use the Reddit Self-Posts (*https://oreil.ly/0pnqO*) dataset, which is hosted on Kaggle. The complete dataset contains roughly 1 million user posts with title and content, arranged in 1,013 different subreddits, each of which has 1,000 records. We will use a subset of only 20,000 posts contained in the autos category. The dataset we prepare in this chapter is the basis for the analysis of word embeddings in Chapter 10.

Loading Data Into Pandas

The original dataset consists of two separate CSV files, one with the posts and the other one with some metadata for the subreddits, including category information. Both files are loaded into a Pandas `DataFrame` by `pd.read_csv()` and then joined into a single `DataFrame`.

```
import pandas as pd

posts_file = "rspct.tsv.gz"
posts_df = pd.read_csv(posts_file, sep='\t')

subred_file = "subreddit_info.csv.gz"
subred_df = pd.read_csv(subred_file).set_index(['subreddit'])

df = posts_df.join(subred_df, on='subreddit')
```

 ## Blueprint: Standardizing Attribute Names

Before we start working with the data, we will change the dataset-specific column names to more generic names. We recommend always naming the main `DataFrame` df, and naming the column with the text to analyze text. Such naming conventions for common variables and attribute names make it easier to reuse the code of the blueprints in different projects.

Let's take a look at the columns list of this dataset:

```
print(df.columns)
```

Out:

```
Index(['id', 'subreddit', 'title', 'selftext', 'category_1', 'category_2',
       'category_3', 'in_data', 'reason_for_exclusion'],
      dtype='object')
```

For column renaming and selection, we define a dictionary `column_mapping` where each entry defines a mapping from the current column name to a new name. Columns mapped to `None` and unmentioned columns are dropped. A dictionary is perfect documentation for such a transformation and easy to reuse. This dictionary is then used to select and rename the columns that we want to keep.

```
column_mapping = {
    'id': 'id',
    'subreddit': 'subreddit',
    'title': 'title',
    'selftext': 'text',
    'category_1': 'category',
    'category_2': 'subcategory',
    'category_3': None, # no data
    'in_data': None, # not needed
    'reason_for_exclusion': None # not needed
}

# define remaining columns
columns = [c for c in column_mapping.keys() if column_mapping[c] != None]

# select and rename those columns
df = df[columns].rename(columns=column_mapping)
```

As already mentioned, we limit the data to the autos category:

```
df = df[df['category'] == 'autos']
```

Let's take a brief look at a sample record to get a first impression of the data:

```
df.sample(1).T
```

	14356
id	7jc2k4
subreddit	volt
title	Dashcam for 2017 volt
text	Hello.<lb>I'm looking into getting a dashcam. <lb>Does anyone have any recommendations? <lb><lb>I'm generally looking for a rechargeable one so that I don't have to route wires down to the cigarette lighter. <lb>Unless there are instructions on how to wire it properly without wires showing. <lb><lb><lb>Thanks!
category	autos
subcategory	chevrolet

Saving and Loading a DataFrame

After each step of data preparation, it is helpful to write the respective DataFrame to disk as a checkpoint. Pandas directly supports a number of serialization options (*https://oreil.ly/VaXTx*). Text-based formats like CSV or JSON can be imported into most other tools easily. However, information about data types is lost (CSV) or only saved rudimentarily (JSON). The standard serialization format of Python, pickle, is supported by Pandas and therefore a viable option. It is fast and preserves all information but can only be processed by Python. "Pickling" a data frame is easy; you just need to specify the filename:

```
df.to_pickle("reddit_dataframe.pkl")
```

We prefer, however, storing dataframes in SQL databases because they give you all the advantages of SQL, including filters, joins, and easy access from many tools. But in contrast to pickle, only SQL data types are supported. Columns containing objects or lists, for example, cannot simply be saved this way and need to be serialized manually.

In our examples, we will use SQLite to persist data frames. SQLite is well integrated with Python. Moreover, it's just a library and does not require a server, so the files are self-contained and can be exchanged between different team members easily. For more power and safety, we recommend a server-based SQL database.

We use pd.to_sql() to save our DataFrame as table posts into an SQLite database. The DataFrame index is not stored, and any existing data is overwritten:

```
import sqlite3

db_name = "reddit-selfposts.db"
con = sqlite3.connect(db_name)
df.to_sql("posts", con, index=False, if_exists="replace")
con.close()
```

The DataFrame can be easily restored with pd.read_sql():

```
con = sqlite3.connect(db_name)
df = pd.read_sql("select * from posts", con)
con.close()
```

Cleaning Text Data

When working with user requests or comments as opposed to well-edited articles, you usually have to deal with a number of quality issues:

Special formatting and program code
> The text may still contain special characters, HTML entities, Markdown tags, and things like that. These artifacts should be cleaned in advance because they complicate tokenization and introduce noise.

Salutations, signatures, addresses, etc.
> Personal communication often contains meaningless polite phrases and salutations by name that are usually irrelevant for the analysis.

Replies
> If your text contains answers repeating the question text, you need to delete the duplicate questions. Keeping them will distort any model and statistics.

In this section, we will demonstrate how to use regular expressions to identify and remove unwanted patterns in the data. Check out the following sidebar for some more details on regular expressions in Python.

Regular Expressions

Regular expressions are an essential tool for text data preparation. They can be used not only for tokenization and data cleaning but also for the identification and treatment of email addresses, salutations, program code, and more.

Python has the standard library re for regular expressions and the newer, backward-compatible library regex (*https://oreil.ly/x2dYf*) that offers support for POSIX character classes and some more flexibility.

A good overview about the available meta-characters like ^ as well as character classes like \w is available at W3Schools (*https://oreil.ly/pZgG1*). There is also a number of interactive websites to develop and test regular expressions, e.g., *https://regex101.com* (make sure to set the flavor to Python).

In many packages, you will find the precompiled regular expressions like this:

```
RE_BRACKET = re.compile('\[[^\[\]]*\]')
text = RE_BRACKET.sub(' ', text)
```

Precompilation was originally a mechanism to improve performance, but modern Python automatically caches compiled versions of regular expressions. However, it still gives some benefit for frequently accessed expressions and improves readability.

Take a look at the following text example from the Reddit dataset:

```
text = """
After viewing the [PINKIEPOOL Trailer](https://www.youtu.be/watch?v=ieHRoHUg)
it got me thinking about the best match ups.
<lb>Here's my take:<lb><lb>[](/sp)[](/ppseesyou) Deadpool<lb>[](/sp)[](/ajsly)
Captain America<lb>"""
```

It will definitely improve the results if this text gets some cleaning and polishing. Some tags are just artifacts from web scraping, so we will get rid of them. And as we are not interested in the URLs and other links, we will discard them as well.

Blueprint: Identify Noise with Regular Expressions

The identification of quality problems in a big dataset can be tricky. Of course, you can and should take a look at a sample of the data. But the probability is high that you won't find all the issues. It is better to define rough patterns indicating likely problems and check the complete dataset programmatically.

The following function can help you to identify noise in textual data. By *noise* we mean everything that's not plain text and may therefore disturb further analysis. The function uses a regular expression to search for a number of suspicious characters and returns their share of all characters as a score for impurity. Very short texts (less than min_len characters) are ignored because here a single special character would lead to a significant impurity and distort the result.

```
import re

RE_SUSPICIOUS = re.compile(r'[&#<>{}\[\]\\]')

def impurity(text, min_len=10):
    """returns the share of suspicious characters in a text"""
    if text == None or len(text) < min_len:
        return 0
    else:
        return len(RE_SUSPICIOUS.findall(text))/len(text)

print(impurity(text))
```

Out:

```
0.09009009009009009
```

You almost never find these characters in well-redacted text, so the scores in general should be very small. For the previous example text, about 9% of the characters are "suspicious" according to our definition. The search pattern may of course need adaption for corpora containing hashtags or similar tokens containing special characters. However, it doesn't need to be perfect; it just needs to be good enough to indicate potential quality issues.

For the Reddit data, we can get the most "impure" records with the following two statements. Note that we use Pandas `apply()` instead of the similar `map()` because it allows us to forward additional parameters like `min_len` to the applied function.[1]

```
# add new column to data frame
df['impurity'] = df['text'].apply(impurity, min_len=10)

# get the top 3 records
df[['text', 'impurity']].sort_values(by='impurity', ascending=False).head(3)
```

	text	impurity
19682	Looking at buying a 335i with 39k miles and 11 months left on the CPO warranty. I asked the deal...	0.21
12357	I'm looking to lease an a4 premium plus automatic with the nav package.\<lb>\<lb>Vehicle Price:\<ta...	0.17
2730	Breakdown below:\<lb>\<lb>Elantra GT\<lb>\<lb>2.0L 4-cylinder\<lb>\<lb>6-speed Manual Transmission\<lb>...	0.14

Obviously, there are many tags like `<lb>` (linebreak) and `<tab>` included. Let's check if there are others by utilizing our word count blueprint from Chapter 1 in combination with a simple regex tokenizer for such tags:

```
from blueprints.exploration import count_words
count_words(df, column='text', preprocess=lambda t: re.findall(r'<[\w/]*>', t))
```

	freq	token
\<lb>	100729	
\<tab>	642	

Now we know that although these two tags are common, they are the only ones.

Blueprint: Removing Noise with Regular Expressions

Our approach to data cleaning consists of defining a set of regular expressions and identifying problematic patterns and corresponding substitution rules.[2] The blueprint function first substitutes all HTML escapes (e.g.,

---

1 The Pandas operations `map` and `apply` were explained in "Blueprint: Building a Simple Text Preprocessing Pipeline" on page 10.

2 Libraries specialized in HTML data cleaning such as Beautiful Soup were introduced in Chapter 3.

&) by their plain-text representation and then replaces certain patterns by spaces. Finally, sequences of whitespaces are pruned:

```
import html

def clean(text):
    # convert html escapes like &amp; to characters.
    text = html.unescape(text)
    # tags like <tab>
    text = re.sub(r'<[^<>]*>', ' ', text)
    # markdown URLs like [Some text](https://....)
    text = re.sub(r'\[([^\[\]]*)\]\(([^\(\)]*\)', r'\1', text)
    # text or code in brackets like [0]
    text = re.sub(r'\[[^\[\]]*\]', ' ', text)
    # standalone sequences of specials, matches &# but not #cool
    text = re.sub(r'(?:^|\s)[&#<>{}\[\]+|\\:-]{1,}(?:\s|$)', ' ', text)
    # standalone sequences of hyphens like --- or ==
    text = re.sub(r'(?:^|\s)[\-=\+]{2,}(?:\s|$)', ' ', text)
    # sequences of white spaces
    text = re.sub(r'\s+', ' ', text)
    return text.strip()
```

 Be careful: if your regular expressions are not defined precisely enough, you can accidentally delete valuable information during this process without noticing it! The repeaters + and * can be especially dangerous because they match unbounded sequences of characters and can remove large portions of the text.

Let's apply the `clean` function to the earlier sample text and check the result:

```
clean_text = clean(text)
print(clean_text)
print("Impurity:", impurity(clean_text))
```

Out:

```
After viewing the PINKIEPOOL Trailer it got me thinking about the best
match ups. Here's my take: Deadpool Captain America
Impurity: 0.0
```

That looks pretty good. Once you have treated the first patterns, you should check the impurity of the cleaned text again and add further cleaning steps if necessary:

```
df['clean_text'] = df['text'].map(clean)
df['impurity']   = df['clean_text'].apply(impurity, min_len=20)

df[['clean_text', 'impurity']].sort_values(by='impurity', ascending=False) \
                              .head(3)
```

	clean_text	impurity
14058	Mustang 2018, 2019, or 2020? Must Haves!! 1. Have a Credit score of 780\+ for the best low interest rates! 2. Join a Credit Union to finance the vehicle! 3. Or Find a Lender to finance the vehicle...	0.03
18934	At the dealership, they offered an option for foot-well illumination, but I cannot find any reference to this online. Has anyone gotten it? How does it look? Anyone have pictures. Not sure if this...	0.03
16505	I am looking at four Caymans, all in a similar price range. The major differences are the miles, the years, and one isn't a S. https://www.cargurus.com/Cars/inventorylisting/viewDetailsFilterV...	0.02

Even the dirtiest records, according to our regular expression, look pretty clean now. But besides those rough patterns we were searching for, there are also more subtle variations of characters that can cause problems.

Blueprint: Character Normalization with textacy

Take a look at the following sentence, which contains typical issues related to variants of letters and quote characters:

```
text = "The café "Saint-Raphaël" is loca-\nted on Côte d'Azur."
```

Accented characters can be a problem because people do not consistently use them. For example, the tokens `Saint-Raphaël` and `Saint-Raphael` will not be recognized as identical. In addition, texts often contain words separated by a hyphen due to the automatic line breaks. Fancy Unicode hyphens and apostrophes like the ones used in the text can be a problem for tokenization. For all of these issues it makes sense to normalize the text and replace accents and fancy characters with ASCII equivalents.

We will use *textacy* (*https://textacy.readthedocs.io*) for that purpose. textacy is an NLP library built to work with spaCy. It leaves the linguistic part to spaCy and focuses on pre- and postprocessing. Thus, its preprocessing module comprises a nice collection of functions to normalize characters and to treat common patterns such as URLs, email addresses, telephone numbers, and so on, which we will use next. Table 4-1 shows a selection of textacy's preprocessing functions. All of these functions work on plain text, completely independent from spaCy.

Table 4-1. Subset of textacy's preprocessing functions

Function	Description
`normalize_hyphenated_words`	Reassembles words that were separated by a line break
`normalize_quotation_marks`	Replaces all kind of fancy quotation marks with an ASCII equivalent
`normalize_unicode`	Unifies different codes of accented characters in Unicode
`remove_accents`	Replaces accented characters with ASCII, if possible, or drops them
`replace_urls`	Similar for URLs like https://xyz.com

Function	Description
replace_emails	Replaces emails with _EMAIL_
replace_hashtags	Similar for tags like #sunshine
replace_numbers	Similar for numbers like 1235
replace_phone_numbers	Similar for telephone numbers +1 800 456-6553
replace_user_handles	Similar for user handles like @pete
replace_emojis	Replaces smileys etc. with _EMOJI_

Our blueprint function shown here standardizes fancy hyphens and quotes and removes accents with the help of textacy:

```
import textacy.preprocessing as tprep

def normalize(text):
    text = tprep.normalize_hyphenated_words(text)
    text = tprep.normalize_quotation_marks(text)
    text = tprep.normalize_unicode(text)
    text = tprep.remove_accents(text)
    return text
```

When this is applied to the earlier example sentence, we get the following result:

```
print(normalize(text))
```

Out:

```
The cafe "Saint-Raphael" is located on Cote d'Azur.
```

As Unicode normalization has many facets, you can check out other libraries. *unidecode* (*https://oreil.ly/eqKI-*), for example, does an excellent job here.

Blueprint: Pattern-Based Data Masking with textacy

Text, in particular content written by users, often contains not only ordinary words but also several kinds of identifiers, such as URLs, email addresses, or phone numbers. Sometimes we are interested especially in those items, for example, to analyze the most frequently mentioned URLs. In many cases, though, it may be better to remove or mask this information, either because it is not relevant or for privacy reasons.

textacy has some convenient `replace` functions for data masking (see Table 4-1). Most of the functions are based on regular expressions, which are easily accessible via the open source code (*https://oreil.ly/Ly6Ce*). Thus, whenever you need to treat any of these items, textacy has a regular expression for it that you can directly use or adapt to your needs. Let's illustrate this with a simple call to find the most frequently used URLs in the corpus:

```
from textacy.preprocessing.resources import RE_URL

count_words(df, column='clean_text', preprocess=RE_URL.findall).head(3)
```

token	freq
www.getlowered.com	3
http://www.ecolamautomotive.com/#!2/kv7fq	2
https://www.reddit.com/r/Jeep/comments/4ux232/just_ordered_an_android_head_unit_joying_jeep/	2

For the analysis we want to perform with this dataset (in Chapter 10), we are not interested in those URLs. They rather represent a disturbing artifact. Thus, we will substitute all URLs in our text with `replace_urls`, which is in fact just a call to `RE_URL.sub`. The default substitution for all of textacy's replace functions is a generic tag enclosed by underscores like `_URL_`. You can choose your own substitution by specifying the `replace_with` parameter. Often it makes sense to not completely remove those items because it leaves the structure of the sentences intact. The following call illustrates the functionality:

```
from textacy.preprocessing.replace import replace_urls

text = "Check out https://spacy.io/usage/spacy-101"

# using default substitution _URL_
print(replace_urls(text))
```

Out:

```
Check out _URL_
```

To finalize data cleaning, we apply the normalization and data masking functions to our data:

```
df['clean_text'] = df['clean_text'].map(replace_urls)
df['clean_text'] = df['clean_text'].map(normalize)
```

Data cleaning is like cleaning your house. You'll always find some dirty corners, and you won't ever get your house totally clean. So you stop cleaning when it is *sufficiently* clean. That's what we assume for our data at the moment. Later in the process, if analysis results are suffering from remaining noise, we may need to get back to data cleaning.

We finally rename the text columns so that `clean_text` becomes `text`, drop the impurity column, and store the new version of the `DataFrame` in the database.

```
df.rename(columns={'text': 'raw_text', 'clean_text': 'text'}, inplace=True)
df.drop(columns=['impurity'], inplace=True)

con = sqlite3.connect(db_name)
df.to_sql("posts_cleaned", con, index=False, if_exists="replace")
con.close()
```

Tokenization

We already introduced a regex tokenizer in Chapter 1, which used a simple rule. In practice, however, tokenization can be quite complex if we want to treat everything correctly. Consider the following piece of text as an example:

```
text = """
2019-08-10 23:32: @pete/@louis - I don't have a well-designed
solution for today's problem. The code of module AC68 should be -1.
Have to think a bit... #goodnight ;-) 😀😀"""
```

Obviously, the rules to define word and sentence boundaries are not that simple. So what exactly is a token? Unfortunately, there is no clear definition. We could say that a token is a linguistic unit that is semantically useful for analysis. This definition implies that tokenization is application dependent to some degree. For example, in many cases we can simply discard punctuation characters, but not if we want to keep emoticons like :-) for sentiment analysis. The same is true for tokens containing numbers or hashtags. Even though most tokenizers, including those used in NLTK and spaCy, are based on regular expressions, they apply quite complex and sometimes language-specific rules.

We will first develop our own blueprint for tokenization-based regular expressions before we briefly introduce NLTK's tokenizers. Tokenization in spaCy will be covered in the next section of this chapter as part of spaCy's integrated process.

Blueprint: Tokenization with Regular Expressions

Useful functions for tokenization are `re.split()` and `re.findall()`. The first one splits a string at matching expressions, while the latter extracts all character sequences matching a certain pattern. For example, in Chapter 1 we used the regex library with the POSIX pattern `[\w-]*\p{L}[\w-]*` to find sequences of alphanumeric characters with at least one letter. The scikit-learn `CountVectorizer` uses the pattern `\w\w+` for its default tokenization. It matches all sequences of two or more alphanumeric characters. Applied to our sample sentence, this yields the following result:[3]

```
tokens = re.findall(r'\w\w+', text)
print(*tokens, sep='|')
```

Out:

```
2019|08|10|23|32|pete|louis|don|have|well|designed|solution|for|today
problem|The|code|of|module|AC68|should|be|Have|to|think|bit|goodnight
```

Unfortunately, all special characters and the emojis are lost. To improve the result, we add some additional expressions for the emojis and create a reusable regular expression RE_TOKEN. The VERBOSE option allows readable formatting of complex expressions. The following tokenize function and the example illustrate the use:

```
RE_TOKEN = re.compile(r"""
             ( [#]?[@\w'’\.\-\:]*\w    # words, hashtags and email addresses
             | [:;<]\-?[\)\(3]         # coarse pattern for basic text emojis
             | [\U0001F100-\U0001FFFF] # coarse code range for unicode emojis
             )
             """, re.VERBOSE)

def tokenize(text):
    return RE_TOKEN.findall(text)

tokens = tokenize(text)
print(*tokens, sep='|')
```

Out:

```
2019-08-10|23:32|@pete|@louis|I|don't|have|a|well-designed|solution
for|today's|problem|The|code|of|module|AC68|should|be|-1|Have|to|think
a|bit|#goodnight|;-)|☺|☺
```

This expression should yield reasonably good results on most user-generated content. It can be used to quickly tokenize text for data exploration, as explained in Chapter 1. It's also a good alternative for the default tokenization of the scikit-learn vectorizers, which will be introduced in the next chapter.

Tokenization with NLTK

Let's take a brief look at NLTK's tokenizers, as NLTK is frequently used for tokenization. The standard NLTK tokenizer can be called by the shortcut word_tokenize. It produces the following result on our sample text:

---

3 The asterisk operator (*) unpacks the list into separate arguments for print.

```
import nltk

tokens = nltk.tokenize.word_tokenize(text)
print(*tokens, sep='|')
```

Out:

```
2019-08-10|23:32|:|@|pete/|@|louis|-|I|do|n't|have|a|well-designed
solution|for|today|'s|problem|.|The|code|of|module|AC68|should|be|-1|.
Have|to|think|a|bit|...|#|goodnight|;|-|)|| ☺☺
```

The function internally uses the TreebankWordTokenizer in combination with the PunktSentenceTokenizer. It works well for standard text but has its flaws with hashtags or text emojis. NLTK also provides a RegexpTokenizer, which is basically a wrapper for re.findall() with some added convenience functionality. Besides that, there are other regular-expression-based tokenizers in NLTK, like the TweetToken izer or the multilingual ToktokTokenizer, which you can check out in the notebook on GitHub (*https://oreil.ly/zLTEl*) for this chapter.

Recommendations for Tokenization

You will probably need to use custom regular expressions if you aim for high precision on domain-specific token patterns. Fortunately, you can find regular expressions for many common patterns in open source libraries and adapt them to your needs.[4]

In general, you should be aware of the following problematic cases in your application and define how to treat them:[5]

- Tokens containing periods, such as Dr., Mrs., U., xyz.com
- Hyphens, like in rule-based
- Clitics (connected word abbreviations), like in couldn't, we've or je t'aime
- Numerical expressions, such as telephone numbers ((123) 456-7890) or dates (August 7th, 2019)
- Emojis, hashtags, email addresses, or URLs

The tokenizers in common libraries differ especially with regard to those tokens.

---

4 For example, check out NLTK's tweet tokenizer (*https://oreil.ly/R45_t*) for regular expressions for text emoticons and URLs, or see textacy's compile regexes (*https://oreil.ly/i0HhJ*).

5 A good overview is "The Art of Tokenization" by Craig Trim (*https://oreil.ly/LyGvt*).

Linguistic Processing with spaCy

spaCy is a powerful library for linguistic data processing. It provides an integrated pipeline of processing components, by default a tokenizer, a part-of-speech tagger, a dependency parser, and a named-entity recognizer (see Figure 4-2). Tokenization is based on complex language-dependent rules and regular expressions, while all subsequent steps use pretrained neural models.

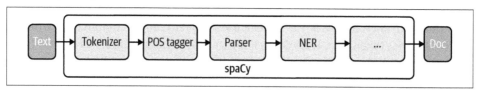

Figure 4-2. spaCy's NLP pipeline.

The philosophy of spaCy is that the original text is retained throughout the process. Instead of transforming it, spaCy adds layers of information. The main object to represent the processed text is a `Doc` object, which itself contains a list of `Token` objects. Any range selection of tokens creates a `Span`. Each of these object types has properties that are determined step-by-step.

In this section, we explain how to process a document with spaCy, how to work with tokens and their attributes, how to use part-of-speech tags, and how to extract named entities. We will dive even deeper into spaCy's more advanced concepts in Chapter 12, where we write our own pipeline components, create custom attributes, and work with the dependency tree generated by the parser for knowledge extraction.

 For the development of the examples in this book, we used spaCy version 2.3.2. If you already use spaCy 3.0, which is still under development at the time of writing, your results may look slightly different.

Instantiating a Pipeline

Let's get started with spaCy. As a first step we need to instantiate an object of spaCy's `Language` class by calling `spacy.load()` along with the name of the model file to use.[6] We will use the small English language model `en_core_web_sm` in this chapter. The variable for the `Language` object is usually called `nlp`:

```
import spacy
nlp = spacy.load('en_core_web_sm')
```

---

6 See spaCy's website (*https://oreil.ly/spaCy*) for a list of available models.

This `Language` object now contains the shared vocabulary, the model, and the processing pipeline. You can check the pipeline components via this property of the object:

```
nlp.pipeline
```

Out:

```
[('tagger', <spacy.pipeline.pipes.Tagger at 0x7fbd766f84c0>),
 ('parser', <spacy.pipeline.pipes.DependencyParser at 0x7fbd813184c0>),
 ('ner', <spacy.pipeline.pipes.EntityRecognizer at 0x7fbd81318400>)]
```

The default pipeline consists of a tagger, parser, and named-entity recognizer (`ner`), all of which are language-dependent. The tokenizer is not explicitly listed because this step is always necessary.

spaCy's tokenizer is pretty fast, but all other steps are based on neural models and consume a significant amount of time. Compared to other libraries, though, spaCy's models are among the fastest. Processing the whole pipeline takes about 10–20 times as long as just tokenization, where each step is taking a similar share of the total time. If tokenization of 1,000 documents takes, for example, one second, tagging, parsing, and NER may each take an additional five seconds. This may become a problem if you process big datasets. So, it's better to switch off the parts that you don't need.

Often you will only need the tokenizer and the part-of-speech tagger. In this case, you should disable the parser and named-entity recognition like this:

```
nlp = spacy.load("en_core_web_sm", disable=["parser", "ner"])
```

If you just want the tokenizer and nothing else, you can also simply call `nlp.make_doc` on a text.

Processing Text

The pipeline is executed by calling the `nlp` object. The call returns an object of type `spacy.tokens.doc.Doc`, a container to access the tokens, spans (ranges of tokens), and their linguistic annotations.

```
nlp = spacy.load("en_core_web_sm")
text = "My best friend Ryan Peters likes fancy adventure games."
doc = nlp(text)
```

spaCy is object-oriented as well as nondestructive. The original text is always retained. When you print the `doc` object, it uses `doc.text`, the property containing the original text. But `doc` is also a container object for the tokens, and you can use it as an iterator for them:

```
for token in doc:
    print(token, end="|")
```

Out:

```
My|best|friend|Ryan|Peters|likes|fancy|adventure|games|.|
```

Each token is actually an object of spaCy's class Token. Tokens, as well as docs, have a number of interesting properties for language processing. Table 4-2 shows which of these properties are created by each pipeline component.[7]

Table 4-2. Selection of attributes created by spaCy's built-in pipeline

Component	Creates
Tokenizer	`Token.is_punct, Token.is_alpha, Token.like_email, Token.like_url`
Part-of-speech tagger	`Token.pos_`
Dependency parser	`Token.dep_, Token.head, Doc.sents, Doc.noun_chunks`
Named-entity recognizer	`Doc.ents, Token.ent_iob_, Token.ent_type_`

We provide a small utility function, `display_nlp`, to generate a table containing the tokens and their attributes. Internally, we create a `DataFrame` for this and use the token position in the document as an index. Punctuation characters are skipped by default in this function. Table 4-3 shows the output of this function for our example sentence:

```
def display_nlp(doc, include_punct=False):
    """Generate data frame for visualization of spaCy tokens."""
    rows = []
    for i, t in enumerate(doc):
        if not t.is_punct or include_punct:
            row = {'token': i,  'text': t.text, 'lemma_': t.lemma_,
                   'is_stop': t.is_stop, 'is_alpha': t.is_alpha,
                   'pos_': t.pos_, 'dep_': t.dep_,
                   'ent_type_': t.ent_type_, 'ent_iob_': t.ent_iob_}
            rows.append(row)

    df = pd.DataFrame(rows).set_index('token')
    df.index.name = None
    return df
```

Table 4-3. Result of spaCy's document processing as generated by display_nlp

	text	lemma_	is_stop	is_alpha	pos_	dep_	ent_type_	ent_iob_
0	My	-PRON-	True	True	DET	poss		O
1	best	good	False	True	ADJ	amod		O
2	friend	friend	False	True	NOUN	nsubj		O
3	Ryan	Ryan	False	True	PROPN	compound	PERSON	B

---

7 See spaCy's API (*https://oreil.ly/cvNhV*) for a complete list.

---

	text	lemma_	is_stop	is_alpha	pos_	dep_	ent_type_	ent_iob_
4	Peters	Peters	False	True	PROPN	appos	PERSON	I
5	likes	like	False	True	VERB	ROOT		O
6	fancy	fancy	False	True	ADJ	amod		O
7	adventure	adventure	False	True	NOUN	compound		O
8	games	game	False	True	NOUN	dobj		O

For each token, you find the lemma, some descriptive flags, the part-of-speech tag, the dependency tag (not used here, but in Chapter 12), and possibly some information about the entity type. The is_<something> flags are created based on rules, but all part-of-speech, dependency, and named-entity attributes are based on neural network models. So, there is always some degree of uncertainty in this information. The corpora used for training contain a mixture of news articles and online articles. The predictions of the model are fairly accurate if your data has similar linguistic characteristics. But if your data is very different—if you are working with Twitter data or IT service desk tickets, for example—you should be aware that this information is unreliable.

spaCy uses the convention that token attributes with an underscore like pos_ yield the readable textual representation. pos without an underscore returns spaCy's numeric identifier of a part-of-speech tag.[8] The numeric identifiers can be imported as constants, e.g., spacy.symbols.VERB. Make sure not to mix them up!

Blueprint: Customizing Tokenization

Tokenization is the first step in the pipeline, and everything depends on the correct tokens. spaCy's tokenizer does a good job in most cases, but it splits on hash signs, hyphens, and underscores, which is sometimes not what you want. Therefore, it may be necessary to adjust its behavior. Let's look at the following text as an example:

```
text = "@Pete: choose low-carb #food #eat-smart. _url_ ;-) 😎🍔"
doc = nlp(text)

for token in doc:
    print(token, end="|")
```

---

8 See spaCy's API (https://oreil.ly/EpmEI) for a complete list of attributes.

Out:

```
@Pete|:|choose|low|-|carb|#|food|#|eat|-|smart|.|_|url|_|;-)|☺|👋|
```

spaCy's tokenizer is completely rule-based. First, it splits the text on whitespace characters. Then it uses prefix, suffix, and infix splitting rules defined by regular expressions to further split the remaining tokens. Exception rules are used to handle language-specific exceptions like *can't*, which should be split into *ca* and *n't* with lemmas *can* and *not*.[9]

As you can see in the example, spaCy's English tokenizer contains an infix rule for splits at hyphens. In addition, it has a prefix rule to split off characters like # or _. It works well for tokens prefixed with @ and emojis, though.

One option is to merge tokens in a postprocessing step using `doc.retokenize`. However, that will not fix any miscalculated part-of-speech tags and syntactical dependencies because these rely on tokenization. So it may be better to change the tokenization rules and create correct tokens in the first place.

The best approach for this is to create your own variant of the tokenizer with individual rules for infix, prefix, and suffix splitting.[10] The following function creates a tokenizer object with individual rules in a "minimally invasive" way: we just drop the respective patterns from spaCy's default rules but retain the major part of the logic:

```python
from spacy.tokenizer import Tokenizer
from spacy.util import compile_prefix_regex, \
                       compile_infix_regex, compile_suffix_regex

def custom_tokenizer(nlp):

    # use default patterns except the ones matched by re.search
    prefixes = [pattern for pattern in nlp.Defaults.prefixes
                if pattern not in ['-', '_', '#']]
    suffixes = [pattern for pattern in nlp.Defaults.suffixes
                if pattern not in ['_']]
    infixes  = [pattern for pattern in nlp.Defaults.infixes
                if not re.search(pattern, 'xx-xx')]

    return Tokenizer(vocab         = nlp.vocab,
                     rules         = nlp.Defaults.tokenizer_exceptions,
                     prefix_search = compile_prefix_regex(prefixes).search,
                     suffix_search = compile_suffix_regex(suffixes).search,
                     infix_finditer = compile_infix_regex(infixes).finditer,
                     token_match   = nlp.Defaults.token_match)

nlp = spacy.load('en_core_web_sm')
```

---

9 See spaCy's tokenization usage docs (*https://oreil.ly/HMWja*) for details and an illustrative example.

10 See spaCy's tokenizer usage docs (*https://oreil.ly/45yU4*) for details.

```
nlp.tokenizer = custom_tokenizer(nlp)

doc = nlp(text)
for token in doc:
    print(token, end="|")
```

Out:

```
@Pete|:|choose|low-carb|#food|#eat-smart|.|_url_|;-)|☺|🍮|
```

Be careful with tokenization modifications because their effects can be subtle, and fixing a set of cases can break another set of cases. For example, with our modification, tokens like Chicago-based won't be split anymore. In addition, there are several Unicode characters for hyphens and dashes that could cause problems if they have not been normalized.

Blueprint: Working with Stop Words

spaCy uses language-specific stop word lists to set the is_stop property for each token directly after tokenization. Thus, filtering stop words (and similarly punctuation tokens) is easy:

```
text = "Dear Ryan, we need to sit down and talk. Regards, Pete"
doc = nlp(text)

non_stop = [t for t in doc if not t.is_stop and not t.is_punct]
print(non_stop)
```

Out:

```
[Dear, Ryan, need, sit, talk, Regards, Pete]
```

The list of English stop words with more than 300 entries can be accessed by importing spacy.lang.en.STOP_WORDS. When an nlp object is created, this list is loaded and stored under nlp.Defaults.stop_words. We can modify spaCy's default behavior by setting the is_stop property of the respective words in spaCy's vocabulary:[11]

```
nlp = spacy.load('en_core_web_sm')
nlp.vocab['down'].is_stop = False
```

---

11 Modifying the stop word list this way will probably become deprecated with spaCy 3.0. Instead, it is recommended to create a modified subclass of the respective language class. See the GitHub notebook (*https://oreil.ly/CV2Cz*) for this chapter for details.

```
nlp.vocab['Dear'].is_stop = True
nlp.vocab['Regards'].is_stop = True
```

If we rerun the previous example, we get the following result:

```
[Ryan, need, sit, down, talk, Pete]
```

Blueprint: Extracting Lemmas Based on Part of Speech

Lemmatization is the mapping of a word to its uninflected root. Treating words like *housing*, *housed*, and *house* as the same has many advantages for statistics, machine learning, and information retrieval. It can not only improve the quality of the models but also decrease training time and model size because the vocabulary is much smaller if only uninflected forms are kept. In addition, it is often helpful to restrict the types of the words used to certain categories, such as nouns, verbs, and adjectives. Those word types are called *part-of-speech tags*.

Let's first take a closer look at lemmatization. The lemma of a token or span can be accessed by the lemma_ property, as illustrated in the following example:

```
text = "My best friend Ryan Peters likes fancy adventure games."
doc = nlp(text)

print(*[t.lemma_ for t in doc], sep='|')
```

Out:

```
-PRON-|good|friend|Ryan|Peters|like|fancy|adventure|game|.
```

The correct assignment of the lemma requires a lookup dictionary and knowledge about the part of speech of a word. For example, the lemma of the noun *meeting* is *meeting*, while the lemma of the verb is *meet*. In English, spaCy is able to make this distinction. In most other languages, however, lemmatization is purely dictionary-based, ignoring the part-of-speech dependency. Note that personal pronouns like *I*, *me*, *you*, and *her* always get the lemma -PRON- in spaCy.

The other token attribute we will use in this blueprint is the part-of-speech tag. Table 4-3 shows that each token in a spaCy doc has two part-of-speech attributes: pos_ and tag_. tag_ is the tag from the tagset used to train the model. For spaCy's English models, which have been trained on the OntoNotes 5 corpus, this is the Penn Treebank tagset. For a German model, this would be the Stuttgart-Tübingen tagset. The pos_ attribute contains the simplified tag of the universal part-of-speech tagset.[12]

---

12 See Universal Part-of-speech tags (*https://oreil.ly/lAKtm*) for more.

We recommend using this attribute as the values will remain stable across different models. Table 4-4 shows the complete tag set descriptions.

Table 4-4. Universal part-of-speech tags

Tag	Description	Examples
ADJ	Adjectives (describe nouns)	big, green, African
ADP	Adpositions (prepositions and postpositions)	in, on
ADV	Adverbs (modify verbs or adjectives)	very, exactly, always
AUX	Auxiliary (accompanies verb)	can (do), is (doing)
CCONJ	Connecting conjunction	and, or, but
DET	Determiner (with regard to nouns)	the, a, all (things), your (idea)
INTJ	Interjection (independent word, exclamation, expression of emotion)	hi, yeah
NOUN	Nouns (common and proper)	house, computer
NUM	Cardinal numbers	nine, 9, IX
PROPN	Proper noun, name, or part of a name	Peter, Berlin
PRON	Pronoun, substitute for noun	I, you, myself, who
PART	Particle (makes sense only with other word)	
PUNCT	Punctuation characters	, . ;
SCONJ	Subordinating conjunction	before, since, if
SYM	Symbols (word-like)	$, ©
VERB	Verbs (all tenses and modes)	go, went, thinking
X	Anything that cannot be assigned	grlmpf

Part-of-speech tags are an excellent alternative to stop words as word filters. In linguistics, pronouns, prepositions, conjunctions, and determiners are called *function words* because their main function is to create grammatical relationships within a sentence. Nouns, verbs, adjectives, and adverbs are content words, and the meaning of a sentence depends mainly on them.

Often, we are interested only in content words. Thus, instead of using a stop word list, we can use part-of-speech tags to select the word types we are interested in and discard the rest. For example, a list containing only the nouns and proper nouns in a doc can be generated like this:

```
text = "My best friend Ryan Peters likes fancy adventure games."
doc = nlp(text)

nouns = [t for t in doc if t.pos_ in ['NOUN', 'PROPN']]
print(nouns)
```

Out:

```
[friend, Ryan, Peters, adventure, games]
```

We could easily define a more general filter function for this purpose, but textacy's `extract.words` function conveniently provides this functionality. It also allows us to filter on part of speech and additional token properties such as `is_punct` or `is_stop`. Thus, the filter function allows both part-of-speech selection and stop word filtering. Internally it works just like we illustrated for the noun filter shown previously.

The following example shows how to extract tokens for adjectives and nouns from the sample sentence:

```
import textacy

tokens = textacy.extract.words(doc,
            filter_stops = True,          # default True, no stopwords
            filter_punct = True,          # default True, no punctuation
            filter_nums = True,           # default False, no numbers
            include_pos = ['ADJ', 'NOUN'], # default None = include all
            exclude_pos = None,           # default None = exclude none
            min_freq = 1)                 # minimum frequency of words

print(*[t for t in tokens], sep='|')
```

Out:

```
best|friend|fancy|adventure|games
```

Our blueprint function to extract a filtered list of word lemmas is finally just a tiny wrapper around that function. By forwarding the keyword arguments (`**kwargs`), this function accepts the same parameters as textacy's `extract.words`.

```
def extract_lemmas(doc, **kwargs):
    return [t.lemma_ for t in textacy.extract.words(doc, **kwargs)]

lemmas = extract_lemmas(doc, include_pos=['ADJ', 'NOUN'])
print(*lemmas, sep='|')
```

Out:

```
good|friend|fancy|adventure|game
```

 Using lemmas instead of inflected words is often a good idea, but not always. For example, it can have a negative effect on sentiment analysis where "good" and "best" make a difference.

Blueprint: Extracting Noun Phrases

In Chapter 1 we illustrated how to use n-grams for analysis. n-grams are simple enumerations of subsequences of *n* words in a sentence. For example, the sentence we used earlier contains the following bigrams:

```
My_best|best_friend|friend_Ryan|Ryan_Peters|Peters_likes|likes_fancy
fancy_adventure|adventure_games
```

Many of those bigrams are not very useful for analysis, for example, `likes_fancy` or `my_best`. It would be even worse for trigrams. But how can we detect word sequences that have real meaning? One way is to apply pattern-matching on the part-of-speech tags. spaCy has a quite powerful rule-based matcher (*https://oreil.ly/VjOJK*), and textacy has a convenient wrapper for pattern-based phrase extraction (*https://oreil.ly/Xz70U*). The following pattern extracts sequences of nouns with a preceding adjective:

```
text = "My best friend Ryan Peters likes fancy adventure games."
doc = nlp(text)

patterns = ["POS:ADJ POS:NOUN:+"]
spans = textacy.extract.matches(doc, patterns=patterns)
print(*[s.lemma_ for s in spans], sep='|')
```

Out:

```
good friend|fancy adventure|fancy adventure game
```

Alternatively, you could use spaCy's `doc.noun_chunks` for noun phrase extraction. However, as the returned chunks can also include pronouns and determiners, this function is less suited for feature extraction:

```
print(*doc.noun_chunks, sep='|')
```

Out:

```
My best friend|Ryan Peters|fancy adventure games
```

Thus, we define our blueprint for noun phrase extraction based on part-of-speech patterns. The function takes a doc, a list of part-of-speech tags, and a separator character to join the words of the noun phrase. The constructed pattern searches for sequences of nouns that are preceded by a token with one of the specified part-of-speech tags. Returned are the lemmas. Our example extracts all phrases consisting of an adjective or a noun followed by a sequence of nouns:

```
def extract_noun_phrases(doc, preceding_pos=['NOUN'], sep='_'):
    patterns = []
    for pos in preceding_pos:
        patterns.append(f"POS:{pos} POS:NOUN:+")
```

```
    spans = textacy.extract.matches(doc, patterns=patterns)
    return [sep.join([t.lemma_ for t in s]) for s in spans]

print(*extract_noun_phrases(doc, ['ADJ', 'NOUN']), sep='|')
```
Out:
```
good_friend|fancy_adventure|fancy_adventure_game|adventure_game
```

Blueprint: Extracting Named Entities

Named-entity recognition refers to the process of detecting entities such as people, locations, or organizations in text. Each entity can consist of one or more tokens, like *San Francisco*. Therefore, named entities are represented by Span objects. As with noun phrases, it can be helpful to retrieve a list of named entities for further analysis.

If you look again at Table 4-3, you see the token attributes for named-entity recognition, ent_type_ and ent_iob_. ent_iob_ contains the information if a token begins an entity (B), is inside an entity (I), or is outside (O). Instead of iterating through the tokens, we can also access the named entities directly with doc.ents. Here, the property for the entity type is called label_. Let's illustrate this with an example:

```
text = "James O'Neill, chairman of World Cargo Inc, lives in San Francisco."
doc = nlp(text)

for ent in doc.ents:
    print(f"({ent.text}, {ent.label_})", end=" ")
```
Out:
```
(James O'Neill, PERSON) (World Cargo Inc, ORG) (San Francisco, GPE)
```

spaCy's display module also provides visualization for the named-entity recognition, which makes the result much more readable and visually supports the identification of misclassified entities:

```
from spacy import display

display.render(doc, style='ent')
```

James O'Neill **PERSON** , chairman of   World Cargo Inc **ORG** , lives in   San Francisco **GPE** .

The named entities were identified correctly as a person, an organization, and a geopolitical entity (GPE). But be aware that the accuracy for named-entity recognition may not be very good if your corpus is missing a clear grammatical structure. Check out "Named-Entity Recognition" on page 329 for a detailed discussion.

For the extraction of named entities of certain types, we again make use of one of textacy's convenient functions:

```
def extract_entities(doc, include_types=None, sep='_'):

    ents = textacy.extract.entities(doc,
            include_types=include_types,
            exclude_types=None,
            drop_determiners=True,
            min_freq=1)

    return [sep.join([t.lemma_ for t in e])+'/'+e.label_ for e in ents]
```

With this function we can, for example, retrieve the named entities of types PERSON and GPE (geo-political entity) like this:

```
print(extract_entities(doc, ['PERSON', 'GPE']))
```

Out:

```
["James_O'Neill/PERSON", 'San_Francisco/GPE']
```

Feature Extraction on a Large Dataset

Now that we know the tools spaCy provides, we can finally build our linguistic feature extractor. Figure 4-3 illustrates what we are going to do. In the end, we want to create a dataset that can be used as input to statistical analysis and various machine learning algorithms. Once extracted, we will persist the preprocessed data "ready to use" in a database.

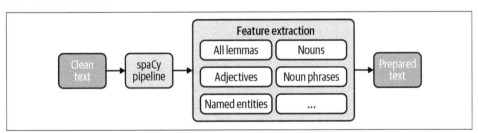

Figure 4-3. Feature extraction from text with spaCy.

Blueprint: Creating One Function to Get It All

This blueprint function combines all the extraction functions from the previous section. It neatly puts everything we want to extract in one place in the code so that the subsequent steps do not need to be adjusted if you add or change something here:

```
def extract_nlp(doc):
    return {
    'lemmas'           : extract_lemmas(doc,
                                     exclude_pos = ['PART', 'PUNCT',
                                        'DET', 'PRON', 'SYM', 'SPACE'],
                                     filter_stops = False),
    'adjs_verbs'       : extract_lemmas(doc, include_pos = ['ADJ', 'VERB']),
    'nouns'            : extract_lemmas(doc, include_pos = ['NOUN', 'PROPN']),
    'noun_phrases'     : extract_noun_phrases(doc, ['NOUN']),
    'adj_noun_phrases' : extract_noun_phrases(doc, ['ADJ']),
    'entities'         : extract_entities(doc, ['PERSON', 'ORG', 'GPE', 'LOC'])
    }
```

The function returns a dictionary with everything we want to extract, as shown in this example:

```
text = "My best friend Ryan Peters likes fancy adventure games."
doc = nlp(text)
for col, values in extract_nlp(doc).items():
    print(f"{col}: {values}")
```

Out:

```
lemmas: ['good', 'friend', 'Ryan', 'Peters', 'like', 'fancy', 'adventure', \
        'game']
adjs_verbs: ['good', 'like', 'fancy']
nouns: ['friend', 'Ryan', 'Peters', 'adventure', 'game']
noun_phrases: ['adventure_game']
adj_noun_phrases: ['good_friend', 'fancy_adventure', 'fancy_adventure_game']
entities: ['Ryan_Peters/PERSON']
```

The list of returned column names is needed for the next steps. Instead of hard-coding it, we just call extract_nlp with an empty document to retrieve the list:

```
nlp_columns = list(extract_nlp(nlp.make_doc('')).keys())
print(nlp_columns)
```

Out:

```
['lemmas', 'adjs_verbs', 'nouns', 'noun_phrases', 'adj_noun_phrases', 'entities']
```

Blueprint: Using spaCy on a Large Dataset

Now we can use this function to extract features from all the records of a dataset. We take the cleaned texts that we created and saved at the beginning of this chapter and add the titles:

```
db_name = "reddit-selfposts.db"
con = sqlite3.connect(db_name)
df = pd.read_sql("select * from posts_cleaned", con)
con.close()

df['text'] = df['title'] + ': ' + df['text']
```

Before we start NLP processing, we initialize the new DataFrame columns we want to fill with values:

```
for col in nlp_columns:
    df[col] = None
```

spaCy's neural models benefit from running on GPU. Thus, we try to load the model on the GPU before we start:

```
if spacy.prefer_gpu():
    print("Working on GPU.")
else:
    print("No GPU found, working on CPU.")
```

Now we have to decide which model and which of the pipeline components to use. Remember to disable unneccesary components to improve runtime! We stick to the small English model with the default pipeline and use our custom tokenizer that splits on hyphens:

```
nlp = spacy.load('en_core_web_sm', disable=[])
nlp.tokenizer = custom_tokenizer(nlp) # optional
```

When processing larger datasets, it is recommended to use spaCy's batch processing for a significant performance gain (roughly factor 2 on our dataset). The function nlp.pipe takes an iterable of texts, processes them internally as a batch, and yields a list of processed Doc objects in the same order as the input data.

To use it, we first have to define a batch size. Then we can loop over the batches and call nlp.pipe.

```
batch_size = 50

for i in range(0, len(df), batch_size):
    docs = nlp.pipe(df['text'][i:i+batch_size])

    for j, doc in enumerate(docs):
```

```
    for col, values in extract_nlp(doc).items():
        df[col].iloc[i+j] = values
```

In the inner loop we extract the features from the processed doc and write the values back into the DataFrame. The whole process takes about six to eight minutes on the dataset without using a GPU and about three to four minutes with the GPU on Colab.

The newly created columns are perfectly suited for frequency analysis with the functions from Chapter 1. Let's check for the most frequently mentioned noun phrases in the autos category:

```
count_words(df, 'noun_phrases').head(10).plot(kind='barh').invert_yaxis()
```

Out:

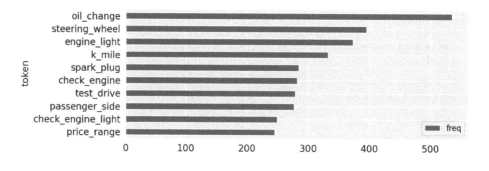

Persisting the Result

Finally, we save the complete DataFrame to SQLite. To do so, we need to serialize the extracted lists to space-separated strings, as lists are not supported by most databases:

```
df[nlp_columns] = df[nlp_columns].applymap(lambda items: ' '.join(items))

con = sqlite3.connect(db_name)
df.to_sql("posts_nlp", con, index=False, if_exists="replace")
con.close()
```

The resulting table provides a solid and ready-to-use basis for further analyses. In fact, we will use this data again in Chapter 10 to train word embeddings on the extracted lemmas. Of course, the preprocessing steps depend on what you are going to do with the data. Working with sets of words like those produced by our blueprint is perfect for any kind of statistical analysis on word frequencies and machine learning based on a bag-of-words vectorization. You will need to adapt the steps for algorithms that rely on knowledge about word sequences.

A Note on Execution Time

Complete linguistic processing is *really* time-consuming. In fact, processing just the 20,000 Reddit posts with spaCy takes several minutes. A simple regexp tokenizer, in contrast, takes only a few seconds to tokenize all records on the same machine. It's the tagging, parsing, and named-entity recognition that's expensive, even though spaCy is really fast compared to other libraries. So if you don't need named entities, you should definitely disable the parser and name-entity recognition to save more than 60% of the runtime.

Processing the data in batches with `nlp.pipe` and using GPUs is one way to speed up data processing for spaCy. But data preparation in general is also a perfect candidate for parallelization. One option to parallelize tasks in Python is using the library `multi processing` (*https://oreil.ly/hoqxv*). Especially for the parallelization of operations on dataframes, there are some scalable alternatives to Pandas worth checking, namely Dask (*https://dask.org*), Modin (*https://oreil.ly/BPMLh*), and Vaex (*https://oreil.ly/hb66b*). pandarallel (*https://oreil.ly/-PCJa*) is a library that adds parallel apply operators directly to Pandas.

In any case, it is helpful to watch the progress and get a runtime estimate. As already mentioned in Chapter 1, the *tqdm* library is a great tool for that purpose because it provides progress bars (*https://oreil.ly/Rbh_-*) for iterators and dataframe operations. Our notebooks on GitHub use tqdm whenever possible.

There Is More

We started out with data cleaning and went through a whole pipeline of linguistic processing. Still, there some aspects that we didn't cover in detail but that may be helpful or even necessary in your projects.

Language Detection

Many corpora contain text in different languages. Whenever you are working with a multilingual corpus, you have to decide on one of these options:

- Ignore other languages if they represent a negligible minority, and treat every text as if it were of the corpus's major language, e.g., English.
- Translate all texts to the main language, for example, by using Google Translate.
- Identify the language and do language-dependent preprocessing in the next steps.

There are good libraries for language detection. Our recommendation is Facebook's fastText library (*https://oreil.ly/6QhAj*). fastText provides a pretrained model that identifies 176 languages really fast and accurately. We provide an additional blueprint for language detection with fastText in the GitHub repository (*https://oreil.ly/c3dsK*) for this chapter.

textacy's `make_spacy_doc` function allows you to automatically load the respective language model for linguistic processing if available. By default, it uses a language detection model based on Google's Compact Language Detector v3 (*https://oreil.ly/mJLfx*), but you could also hook in any language detection function (for example, fastText).

Spell-Checking

User-generated content suffers from a lot of misspellings. It would be great if a spell-checker could automatically correct these errors. SymSpell (*https://oreil.ly/puo2S*) is a popular spell-checker with a Python port (*https://oreil.ly/yNs_k*). However, as you know from your smartphone, automatic spelling correction may itself introduce funny artifacts. So, you should definitely check whether the quality really improves.

Token Normalization

Often, there are different spellings for identical terms or variations of terms that you want to treat and especially count identically. In this case, it is useful to normalize these terms and map them to a common standard. Here are some examples:

- U.S.A. or U.S. → USA
- dot-com bubble → dotcom bubble
- München → Munich

You could use spaCy's phrase matcher to integrate this kind of normalization as a post-processing step into its pipeline. If you don't use spaCy, you can use a simple Python dictionary to map different spellings to their normalized forms.

Closing Remarks and Recommendations

"Garbage in, garbage out" is a frequently cited problem in data projects. This is especially true for textual data, which is inherently noisy. Therefore, data cleaning is one of the most important tasks in any text analysis project. Spend enough effort to ensure high data quality and check it systematically. We have shown many solutions to identify and resolve quality issues in this section.

The second prerequisite for reliable analyses and robust models is normalization. Many machine learning algorithms for text are based on the bag-of-words model, which generates a notion of similarity between documents based on word frequencies. In general, you are better off with lemmatized text when you do text classification, topic modeling, or clustering based on TF-IDF. You should avoid or use only sparingly those kinds of normalization or stop word removal for more complex machine learning tasks such as text summarization, machine translation, or question answering where the model needs to reflect the variety of the language.

## CHAPTER 5

Feature Engineering and Syntactic Similarity

As we saw in Chapter 1, text is significantly different from structured data. One of the most striking differences is that text is represented by words, while structured data (mostly) uses numbers. From a scientific point of view, centuries of mathematical research have led to an extremely good understanding of numbers and sophisticated methods. Information science has picked up that mathematical research, and many creative algorithms have been invented on top of that. Recent advances in machine learning have generalized a lot of formerly very specific algorithms and made them applicable to many different use cases. These methods "learn" directly from data and provide an unbiased view.

To use these instruments, we have to find a mapping of text to numbers. Considering the richness and complexity of text, it is clear that a single number will not be enough to represent the meaning of a document. Something more complex is needed. The natural extension of real numbers in mathematics is a tuple of real numbers, called a *vector*. Almost all text representations in text analytics and machine learning use vectors; see Chapter 6 for more.

Vectors live in a vector space, and most vector spaces have additional properties such as norms and distances, which will be helpful for us as they imply the concept of similarity. As we will see in subsequent chapters, measuring the similarity between documents is absolutely crucial for most text analytics applications, but it is also interesting on its own.

What You'll Learn and What We'll Build

In this chapter we talk about the vectorization of documents. This means we will convert unstructured text into vectors that contain numbers.

There are quite a few ways to vectorize documents. As document vectorization is the basis for all machine learning tasks, we will spend some time designing and implementing our own vectorizer. You can use that as a blueprint if you need a specialized vectorizer for your own projects.

Afterward, we will focus on two popular models that are already implemented in scikit-learn: the bag-of words model and the TF-IDF improvements to it. We will download a large dataset of documents and vectorize it with these methods. As you will see, there can be many problems that are related to data volume and scalability.

Although vectorization is a base technology for more sophisticated machine learning algorithms, it can also be used on its own to calculate similarities between documents. We will take a detailed look at how this works, how it can be optimized, and how we can make it scalable. For a richer representation of words, see Chapter 10, and for a more contextualized approach, see Chapter 11.

After studying this chapter, you will understand how to convert documents to numbers (*vectors*) using words or combinations as *features*.[1] We will try different methods of vectorizing documents, and you will be able to determine the correct method for your use case. You will learn why the similarity of documents is important and a standard way to calculate it. We will go into detail with an example that has many documents and show how to vectorize them and calculate similarities effectively.

The first section introduces the concept of a vectorizer by actually building your own simple one. This can be used as a blueprint for more sophisticated vectorizers that you might have to build in your own projects. Counting word occurrences and using them as vectors is called *bag-of-words* and already creates very versatile models.

Together with the dataset (which has more than 1,000,000 news headlines), we introduce a use case and present a scalable blueprint architecture in the TF-IDF section. We will build a blueprint for vectorizing documents and a similarity search for documents. Even more challenging, we will try to identify the most similar (but nonidentical) headlines in this corpus.

---

1 In later chapters, we will take a look at other possibilities of vectorizing words (Chapter 10) and documents (Chapter 11).

A Toy Dataset for Experimentation

Quite surprisingly, a lot of experiments have shown that for many text analytics problems it is enough to know which words appear in documents. It is not necessary to understand the meaning of the words or take word order into account. As the underlying mappings are particularly easy and fast to calculate, we will start with these mappings and use the words as features.

For the first blueprints, we will concentrate on the methods and therefore use a few sentences from the novel *A Tale of Two Cities* (*https://oreil.ly/rfmPH*) by Charles Dickens as a toy dataset. We will use the following sentences:

- It was the best of times.
- It was the worst of times.
- It was the age of wisdom.
- It was the age of foolishness.

Blueprint: Building Your Own Vectorizer

As vectorizing documents is the base for nearly all of the following chapters in this book, we take an in-depth look at how vectorizers work. This works best by implementing our own vectorizer. You can use the methods in this section if you need to implement a custom vectorizer in your own projects or need to adapt an existing vectorizer to your specific requirements.

To make it as simple as possible, we will implement a so-called *one-hot vectorizer*. This vectorizer creates binary vectors from documents by noting if a word appears in a document or not, yielding 1 or 0, respectively.

We will start by creating a vocabulary and assigning numbers to words, then perform the vectorization, and finally analyze similarity in this binary space.

Enumerating the Vocabulary

Starting with the words as features, we have to find a way to convert words to the dimensions of the vectors. Extracting the words from the text is done via tokenization, as explained in Chapter 2.[2]

---

2 There are much more sophisticated algorithms for determining the vocabulary, like SentencePiece (*https://oreil.ly/A6TEl*) and BPE (*https://oreil.ly/tVDgu*), which are worth taking a look at if you want to reduce the number of features.

As we are interested only in whether a word appears in a document or not, we can just enumerate the words:

```
sentences = ["It was the best of times",
             "it was the worst of times",
             "it was the age of wisdom",
             "it was the age of foolishness"]

tokenized_sentences = [[t for t in sentence.split()] for sentence in sentences]
vocabulary = set([w for s in tokenized_sentences for w in s])

import pandas as pd
pd.DataFrame([[w, i] for i,w in enumerate(vocabulary)])
```

Out:

It	0
age	1
best	2
foolishness	3
it	4
of	5
the	6
times	7
was	8
wisdom	9
worst	10

As you can see, the words have been numbered according to their first occurrence. This is what we call a *dictionary*, consisting of words (the vocabulary) and their respective numbers. Instead of having to refer to words, we can now use the numbers and arrange them in the following vectors.

Vectorizing Documents

To compare vectors, calculate similarities, and so forth, we have to make sure that vectors for each document have the same number of dimensions. To achieve that, we use the same dictionary for all documents. If the document doesn't contain a word, we just put a 0 at the corresponding position; otherwise, we will use a 1. By convention, row vectors are used for documents. The dimension of the vectors is as big as the length of the dictionary. In our example, this is not a problem as we have only a few words. However, in large projects, the vocabulary can easily exceed 100,000 words.

Let's calculate the one-hot encoding of all sentences before actually using a library for this:

```
def onehot_encode(tokenized_sentence):
    return [1 if w in tokenized_sentence else 0 for w in vocabulary]

onehot = [onehot_encode(tokenized_sentence)
          for tokenized_sentence in tokenized_sentences]

for (sentence, oh) in zip(sentences, onehot):
    print("%s: %s" % (oh, sentence))
```

Out:

```
[0, 1, 1, 0, 0, 1, 1, 0, 0, 1, 1]: It was the best of times
[1, 1, 1, 0, 0, 0, 1, 1, 0, 1, 0]: it was the worst of times
[0, 1, 1, 0, 1, 0, 0, 1, 1, 1, 0]: it was the age of wisdom
[0, 1, 1, 1, 1, 0, 0, 1, 0, 1, 0]: it was the age of foolishness
```

For each sentence, we have now calculated a vector representation. Converting documents to one-hot vectors, we have lost information about how often words occur in documents and in which order.

Out-of-vocabulary documents

What happens if we try to keep the vocabulary fixed and add new documents? That depends on whether the words of the documents are already contained in the dictionary. Of course, it can happen that all words are already known:

```
onehot_encode("the age of wisdom is the best of times".split())
```

Out:

```
[0, 1, 0, 0, 1, 0, 1, 0, 1, 1, 1]
```

However, the opposite is also quite possible. If we try to vectorize a sentence with only unknown words, we get a null vector:

```
onehot_encode("John likes to watch movies. Mary likes movies too.".split())
```

Out:

```
[0, 0, 0, 0, 0, 0, 0, 0, 0, 0, 0]
```

This sentence does not "interact" with the other sentences in the corpus. From a strict point of view, this sentence is not similar to any sentence in the corpus. This is no problem for a single sentence; if this happens more frequently, the vocabulary or the corpus needs to be adjusted.

The Document-Term Matrix

Arranging the row vectors for each document in a matrix with the rows enumerating the documents, we arrive at the document-term matrix. The document-term matrix is the vector representation of all documents and the most basic building block for nearly all machine learning tasks throughout this book. In this chapter, we will use it for calculating document similarities:

```
pd.DataFrame(onehot, columns=vocabulary)
```

Out:

It	Age	Best	Foolishness	It	Of	The	Times	Was	Wisdom	Worst
1	0	1	0	0	1	1	1	1	0	0
0	0	0	0	1	1	1	1	1	0	1
0	1	0	0	1	1	1	0	1	1	0
0	1	0	1	1	1	1	0	1	0	0

Be careful: using lists and arrays for the document-term matrix works best with a small vocabulary. With large vocabularies, we will have to find a cleverer representation. Scikit-learn takes care of this and uses so-called sparse vectors and matrices from SciPy (*https://oreil.ly/yk1wx*).

Calculating similarities

Calculating the similarities between documents works by calculating the number of common 1s at the corresponding positions. In one-hot encoding, this is an extremely fast operation, as it can be calculated on the bit level by ANDing the vectors and counting the number of 1s in the resulting vector. Let's calculate the similarity of the first two sentences:

```
sim = [onehot[0][i] & onehot[1][i] for i in range(0, len(vocabulary))]
sum(sim)
```

Out:

```
4
```

Another possible way to calculate the similarity that we will encounter frequently is using *scalar product* (often called *dot product*) of the two document vectors. The scalar product is calculated by multiplying corresponding components of the two vectors and adding up these products. By observing the fact that a product can only be 1 if both factors are 1, we effectively calculate the number of common 1s in the vectors. Let's try it:

```
np.dot(onehot[0], onehot[1])
```

Out:

```
4
```

The Similarity Matrix

If we are interested in finding the similarity of all documents to each other, there is a fantastic shortcut for calculating all the numbers with just one command! Generalizing the formula from the previous section, we find the similarity of document i and document j to be as follows:

$$S_{ij} = d_i \cdot d_j$$

If we want to use the document-term matrix from earlier, we can write the scalar product as a sum:

$$S_{ij} = \Sigma_k D_{ik} D_{jk} = \Sigma_k D_{ik}(D^T)_{kj} = (D \cdot D^T)_{ij}$$

So, this is just the matrix product of our document-term matrix with itself transposed. In Python, that's now easy to calculate (the sentences in the output have been added for easier checking the similarity):[3]

```
np.dot(onehot, np.transpose(onehot))
```

Out:

```
array([[6, 4, 3, 3],      # It was the best of times
       [4, 6, 4, 4],      # it was the worst of times
       [3, 4, 6, 5],      # it was the age of wisdom
       [3, 4, 5, 6]])     # it was the age of foolishness
```

Obviously, the highest numbers are on the diagonal, as each document is most similar to itself. The matrix has to be symmetric, as document A has the same similarity to B

---

3 Confusingly, numpy.dot is used both for the dot product (inner product) and for matrix multiplication. If Numpy detects two row or column vectors (i.e., one-dimensional arrays) with the same dimension, it calculates the dot product and yields a scalar. If not and the passed two-dimensional arrays are suitable for matrix multiplication, it performs this operation and yields a matrix. All other cases produce errors. That's convenient, but it's a lot of heuristics.

as *B* to *A*. Apart from that, we can see that the second sentence is on average most similar to all others, whereas the third and last document is the most similar pairwise (they differ only by one word). The same would be true of the first and second documents if we ignored case.

One-Hot Encoding with scikit-learn

As discussed earlier, the same vectorization can be achieved with scikit-learn. Don't be tempted to use OneHotEncoder, which is suitable only for categorical features. As each sentence has several words, the correct class to use in this case is MultiLabelBinarizer:

```
from sklearn.preprocessing import MultiLabelBinarizer
lb = MultiLabelBinarizer()
lb.fit([vocabulary])
lb.transform(words)
```

Out:

```
array([[1, 0, 1, 0, 0, 1, 1, 1, 1, 0, 0],
       [0, 0, 0, 0, 1, 1, 1, 1, 1, 0, 1],
       [0, 1, 0, 0, 1, 1, 1, 0, 1, 1, 0],
       [0, 1, 0, 1, 1, 1, 1, 0, 1, 0, 0]])
```

Here we can already see a pattern that is typical for scikit-learn. All vectorizers (and many other classes) have a fit method and a transform method. The fit method "learns" the vocabulary, whereas the transform method converts the documents to vectors. Fortunately, we got the same results as in our own vectorizer.

Understanding how a document vectorizer works is crucial for implementing your own, but it's also helpful for appreciating all the functionalities and parameters of existing vectorizers. This is why we have implemented our own. We have taken a detailed look at the different stages of vectorization, starting with building a vocabulary and then converting the documents to binary vectors.

Afterward, we analyzed the similarity of the documents. It turned out that the dot product of their corresponding vectors is a good measure for this similarity.

One-hot vectors are also used in practice, for example, in document classification and clustering. However, scikit-learn also offers more sophisticated vectorizers, which we will use in the next sections.

Bag-of-Words Models

One-hot encoding has already provided us with a basic representation of documents as vectors. However, it did not take care of words appearing many times in documents. If we want to calculate the frequency of words for each document, then we should use what is called a *bag-of-words* representation.

Although somewhat simplistic, these models are in wide use. For cases such as classification and sentiment detection, they work reasonably. Moreover, there are topic modeling methods like Latent Dirichlet Allocation (LDA), which explicitly requires a bag-of-words model.[4]

Blueprint: Using scikit-learn's CountVectorizer

Instead of implementing a bag-of-words model on our own, we use the algorithm that scikit-learn provides.

Notice that the corresponding class is called CountVectorizer, which is our first encounter with feature extraction in scikit-learn. We will take a detailed look at the design of the classes and in which order their methods should be called:

```
from sklearn.feature_extraction.text import CountVectorizer
cv = CountVectorizer()
```

Our example sentences from the one-hot encoder is really trivial, as no sentence in our dataset contains words more than once. Let's add some more sentences and use that as a basis for the CountVectorizer:

```
more_sentences = sentences + \
                ["John likes to watch movies. Mary likes movies too.",
                 "Mary also likes to watch football games."]
```

CountVectorizer works in two distinct phases: first it has to learn the vocabulary; afterward it can transform the documents to vectors.

Fitting the vocabulary

First, it needs to learn about the vocabulary. This is simpler now, as we can just pass the array with the sentences:

```
cv.fit(more_sentences)

CountVectorizer(analyzer='word', binary=False, decode_error='strict',
                dtype=<class 'numpy.int64'>, encoding='utf-8', input='content',
                lowercase=True, max_df=1.0, max_features=None, min_df=1,
```

---

4 See Chapter 8 for more on LDA.

```
        ngram_range=(1, 1), preprocessor=None, stop_words=None,
        strip_accents=None, token_pattern='(?u)\\b\\w\\w+\\b',
        tokenizer=None, vocabulary=None)
```

Don't worry about all these parameters; we will talk about the important ones later.
Let's first see what CountVectorizer used as vocabulary, which is called *feature names*
here:

```
print(cv.get_feature_names())
```

Out:

```
['age', 'also', 'best', 'foolishness', 'football', 'games',
 'it', 'john', 'likes', 'mary', 'movies', 'of', 'the', 'times',
 'to', 'too', 'was', 'watch', 'wisdom', 'worst']
```

We have created a vocabulary and so-called features using CountVectorizer. Conveniently, the vocabulary is sorted alphabetically, which makes it easier for us to
decide whether a specific word is included.

Transforming the documents to vectors

In the second step, we will use CountVectorizer to transform the documents to the
vector representation:

```
dt = cv.transform(more_sentences)
```

The result is the document-term matrix that we have already encountered in the previous section. However, it is a different object, as CountVectorizer has created a
sparse matrix. Let's check:

```
dt
```

Out:

```
<6x20 sparse matrix of type '<class 'numpy.int64'>'
with 38 stored elements in Compressed Sparse Row format>
```

Sparse matrices are extremely efficient. Instead of storing $6 \times 20 = 120$ elements, it
just has to save 38! Sparse matrices achieve that by skipping all zero elements.

Let's try to recover our former document-term matrix. For this, we must transform
the sparse matrix to a (dense) array. To make it easier to read, we convert it into a
Pandas DataFrame:

```
pd.DataFrame(dt.toarray(), columns=cv.get_feature_names())
```

Age	Also	Best	Foolishness	Football	Games	It	John	Likes	Many	Movies	Of	The	Times	To	Too	Was	Watch	Wisdom	Worst
0	0	0	0	0	0	1	0	0	0	0	1	1	1	0	0	1	0	0	0
0	0	0	0	0	0	1	0	0	0	0	1	1	1	0	0	1	0	0	1
1	0	0	0	0	0	1	0	0	0	0	1	1	0	0	0	1	0	1	0
1	0	0	1	0	0	1	0	0	0	0	1	1	0	0	0	1	0	0	0
0	0	0	0	0	0	0	1	2	1	2	0	0	0	1	1	0	1	1	1
0	1	0	0	1	1	1	0	1	1	0	0	0	0	1	0	0	1	1	0

The document-term matrix looks very similar to the one from our one-hot vectorizer. Note, however, that the columns are in alphabetical order, and observe several 2s in the fifth row. This originates from the document "John likes to watch movies. Mary likes movies too.", which has many duplicate words.

Blueprint: Calculating Similarities

Finding similarities between documents is now more difficult as it is not enough to count the common 1s in the documents. In general, the number of occurrences of each word can be bigger, and we have to take that into account. The dot product cannot be used for this, as it is also sensitive to the length of the vector (the number of words in the documents). Also, a Euclidean distance is not very useful in high-dimensional vector spaces. This is why most commonly the angle between document vectors is used as a measure of similarity. The cosine of the angle between two vectors is defined by the following:

$$\cos(\mathbf{a}, \mathbf{b}) = \frac{\mathbf{a} \cdot \mathbf{b}}{||\mathbf{a}|| \cdot ||\mathbf{b}||} = \frac{\Sigma a_i b_i}{\sqrt{\Sigma a_i a_i} \sqrt{\Sigma b_i b_i}}$$

Scikit-learn simplifies this calculation by offering a cosine_similarity utility function. Let's check the similarity of the first two sentences:

```
from sklearn.metrics.pairwise import cosine_similarity
cosine_similarity(dt[0], dt[1])
```

Out:

```
array([[0.83333333]])
```

Compared to our handmade similarity in the earlier sections, `cosine_similarity` offers some advantages, as it is properly normalized and can take only values between 0 and 1.

Calculating the similarity of all documents is of course also possible; scikit-learn has optimized the `cosine_similarity`, so it is possible to directly pass matrices:

```
pd.DataFrame(cosine_similarity(dt, dt)))
```

Out:

	0	1	2	3	4	5
0	1.000000	0.833333	0.666667	0.666667	0.000000	0.000000
1	0.833333	1.000000	0.666667	0.666667	0.000000	0.000000
2	0.666667	0.666667	1.000000	0.833333	0.000000	0.000000
3	0.666667	0.666667	0.833333	1.000000	0.000000	0.000000
4	0.000000	0.000000	0.000000	0.000000	1.000000	0.524142
5	0.000000	0.000000	0.000000	0.000000	0.524142	1.000000

Again, the matrix is symmetric with the highest values on the diagonal. It's also easy to see that document pairs 0/1 and 2/3 are most similar. Documents 4/5 have no similarity at all to the other documents but have some similarity to each other. Taking a look back at the sentences, this is exactly what one would expect.

Bag-of-words models are suitable for a variety of use cases. For classification, sentiment detection, and many topic models, they create a bias toward the most frequent words as they have the highest numbers in the document-term matrix. Often these words do not carry much meaning and could be defined as stop words.

As these would be highly domain-specific, a more generic approach "punishes" words that appear too often in the corpus of all documents. This is called a *TF-IDF model* and will be discussed in the next section.

TF-IDF Models

In our previous example, many sentences started with the words "it was the time of." This contributed a lot to their similarity, but in reality, the actual information you get by the words is minimal. TF-IDF will take care of that by counting the number of total word occurrences. It will reduce weights of frequent words and at the same time increase the weights of uncommon words. Apart from the information-theoretical measure,[5] this is also something that you can observe when reading documents: if you encounter uncommon words, it is likely that the author wants to convey an important message with them.

Optimized Document Vectors with TfidfTransformer

As we saw in Chapter 2, a better measure for information compared to counting is calculating the inverted document frequency and using a penalty for very common words. The TF-IDF weight can be calculated from the bag-of-words model. Let's try this again with the previous model and see how the weights of the document-term matrix change:

```
from sklearn.feature_extraction.text import TfidfTransformer
tfidf = TfidfTransformer()
tfidf_dt = tfidf.fit_transform(dt)
pd.DataFrame(tfidf_dt.toarray(), columns=cv.get_feature_names())
```

Out:

Age	Also	Best	Foolishness	Football	Games	It	John	Likes	Many	Movies	Of	The	Times	To	Too	Was	Watch	Wisdom	Worst
0.00	0.00	0.57	0.00	0.00	0.00	0.34	0.00	0.00	0.00	0.00	0.34	0.34	0.47	0.00	0.00	0.34	0.00	0.00	0.00
0.00	0.00	0.00	0.00	0.00	0.00	0.34	0.00	0.00	0.00	0.00	0.34	0.34	0.47	0.00	0.00	0.34	0.00	0.00	0.57
0.47	0.00	0.00	0.00	0.00	0.00	0.34	0.00	0.00	0.00	0.00	0.34	0.34	0.00	0.00	0.00	0.34	0.00	0.57	0.00
0.47	0.00	0.00	0.57	0.00	0.00	0.34	0.00	0.00	0.00	0.00	0.34	0.34	0.00	0.00	0.00	0.34	0.00	0.00	0.00
0.00	0.00	0.00	0.00	0.00	0.00	0.00	0.31	0.50	0.25	0.61	0.00	0.00	0.00	0.25	0.35	0.00	0.25	0.00	0.00
0.00	0.42	0.00	0.00	0.42	0.42	0.00	0.00	0.34	0.34	0.00	0.00	0.00	0.00	0.34	0.00	0.00	0.34	0.00	0.00

As you can see, some words have been scaled to smaller values (like "it"), while others have not been scaled down so much (like "wisdom"). Let's see the effect on the similarity matrix:

```
pd.DataFrame(cosine_similarity(tfidf_dt, tfidf_dt))
```

Out:

	0	1	2	3	4	5
0	1.000000	0.675351	0.457049	0.457049	0.00000	0.00000
1	0.675351	1.000000	0.457049	0.457049	0.00000	0.00000
2	0.457049	0.457049	1.000000	0.675351	0.00000	0.00000

---

5 See, for example, the definition of entropy (*https://oreil.ly/3qTpX*) as a measure of uncertainty and information. Basically, this says that a low-probability value carries more information than a more likely value.

	0	1	2	3	4	5
3	0.457049	0.457049	0.675351	1.000000	0.00000	0.00000
4	0.000000	0.000000	0.000000	0.000000	1.000000	0.43076
5	0.000000	0.000000	0.000000	0.000000	0.43076	1.000000

We get exactly the effect we have hoped for! Document pairs 0/1 and 2/3 are still very similar, but the number has also decreased to a more reasonable level as the document pairs differ in *significant words*. The more common words now have lower weights.

Introducing the ABC Dataset

As a real-word use case, we will take a dataset from Kaggle (*https://oreil.ly/hg5R3*) that contains news headlines. Headlines originate from Australian news source ABC and are from 2003 to 2017. The CSV file contains only a timestamp and the headline without punctuation in lowercase. We load the CSV file into a Pandas `DataFrame` and take a look at the first few documents:

```
headlines = pd.read_csv("abcnews-date-text.csv", parse_dates=["publish_date"])
print(len(headlines))
headlines.head()
```

Out:

```
1103663
```

	publish_date	headline_text
0	2003-02-19	aba decides against community broadcasting lic...
1	2003-02-19	act fire witnesses must be aware of defamation
2	2003-02-19	a g calls for infrastructure protection summit
3	2003-02-19	air nz staff in aust strike for pay rise
4	2003-02-19	air nz strike to affect australian travellers

There are 1,103,663 headlines in this dataset. Note that the headlines do not include punctuation and are all transformed to lowercase. Apart from the text, the dataset includes the publication date of each headline.

As we saw earlier, the TF-IDF vectors can be calculated using the bag-of-words model (the *count vectors* in scikit-learn terminology). As it is so common to use TF-IDF document vectors, scikit-learn has created a "shortcut" to skip the count vectors and directly calculate the TF-IDF vectors. The corresponding class is called `TfidfVector izer`, and we will use it next.

In the following, we have also combined the calls to fit and to transform in `fit_trans` `form`, which is convenient:

```
from sklearn.feature_extraction.text import TfidfVectorizer
tfidf = TfidfVectorizer()
dt = tfidf.fit_transform(headlines["headline_text"])
```

This might take a while, as so many documents have to be analyzed and vectorized. Take a look at the dimensions of the document-term matrix:

```
dt
```

Out:

```
<1103663x95878 sparse matrix of type '<class 'numpy.float64'>'
with 7001357 stored elements in Compressed Sparse Row format>
```

The number of rows was expected, but the number of columns (the vocabulary) is really large, with almost 100,000 words. Doing the math shows that a naive storage of data would have led to 1,103,663 * 95,878 elements with 8 bytes per float and have used roughly 788 GB RAM. This shows the incredible effectiveness of sparse matrices as the real memory used is "only" 56,010,856 bytes (roughly 0.056 GB; found out via `dt.data.nbytes`). It's still a lot, but it's manageable.

Calculating the similarity between two vectors is another story, though. Scikit-learn (and SciPy as a basis) is highly optimized for working with sparse vectors, but it still takes some time doing the sample calculation (similarities of the first 10,000 documents):

```
%%time
cosine_similarity(dt[0:10000], dt[0:10000])
```

Out:

```
CPU times: user 154 ms, sys: 261 ms, total: 415 ms

Wall time: 414 ms

array([[1.       , 0.       , 0.       , ..., 0.       , 0.       , 0.       ],
       [0.       , 1.       , 0.       , ..., 0.       , 0.       , 0.       ],
       [0.       , 0.       , 1.       , ..., 0.       , 0.       , 0.       ],
       ...,
       [0.       , 0.       , 0.       , ..., 1.       , 0.16913596, 0.16792138],
       [0.       , 0.       , 0.       , ..., 0.16913596, 1.       , 0.33258708],
       [0.       , 0.       , 0.       , ..., 0.16792138, 0.33258708, 1.       ]])
```

For machine learning in the next chapters, many of these linear algebra calculations are necessary and have to be repeated over and over. Often operations scale quadratically with the number of features ($O(N^2)$). Optimizing the vectorization by removing unnecessary features is therefore not only helpful for calculating the similarities but also crucial for scalable machine learning.

Blueprint: Reducing Feature Dimensions

We have now found features for our documents and used them to calculate document vectors. As we have seen in the example, the number of features can get quite large. Lots of machine learning algorithms are computationally intensive and scale with the number of features, often even polynomially. One part of feature engineering is therefore focused on reducing these features to the ones that are really necessary.

In this section, we show a blueprint for how this can be achieved and measure their impact on the number of features.

Removing stop words

In the first place, we can think about removing the words that carry the least meaning. Although this is domain-dependent, there are lists of the most common English words that common sense tells us can normally be neglected. These words are called *stop words*. Common stop words are determiners, auxiliary verbs, and pronouns. For a more detailed discussion, see Chapter 4. Be careful when removing stop words as they can contain certain words that might carry a domain-specific meaning in special texts!

This does not reduce the number of dimensions tremendously as there are only a few hundred common stop words in almost any language. However, it should drastically decrease the number of stored elements as stop words are so common. This leads to less memory consumption and faster calculations, as fewer numbers need to be multiplied.

Let's use the standard spaCy stop words and check the effects on the document-term matrix. Note that we pass stop words as a named parameter to the `TfidfVectorizer`:

```
from spacy.lang.en.stop_words import STOP_WORDS as stopwords
print(len(stopwords))
tfidf = TfidfVectorizer(stop_words=stopwords)
dt = tfidf.fit_transform(headlines["headline_text"])
dt
```

Out:

```
305
<1103663x95600 sparse matrix of type '<class 'numpy.float64'>'
with 5644186 stored elements in Compressed Sparse Row format>
```

With only 305 stop words, we managed to reduce the number of stored elements by 20%. The dimensions of the matrix are almost the same, with fewer columns due to the 95,878 – 95,600 = 278 stop words that actually appeared in the headlines.

Minimum frequency

Taking a look at the definition of the cosine similarity, we can easily see that components can contribute only if both vectors have a nonzero value at the corresponding index. This means that we can neglect all words occurring less than twice! TfidfVectorizer (and CountVectorizer) have a parameter for that called min_df.

```
tfidf = TfidfVectorizer(stop_words=stopwords, min_df=2)
dt = tfidf.fit_transform(headlines["headline_text"])
dt
```

Out:

```
<1103663x58527 sparse matrix of type '<class 'numpy.float64'>'
with 5607113 stored elements in Compressed Sparse Row format>
```

Obviously, there are a lot of words appearing just once (95,600 – 58,527 = 37,073). Those words should also be stored only once; checking with the number of stored elements, we should get the same result: 5,644,186 – 5,607,113 = 37,073. Performing this kind of transformation, it is always useful to integrate such plausibility checks.

Losing Information

Be careful: by using min_df=2, we have not lost any information in vectorizing the headlines of this document corpus. If we plan to vectorize more documents later with the same vocabulary, we might lose information, as words appearing again in the new documents that were only present once in the original documents will not be found in the vocabulary.

min_df can also take float values. This means that a word has to occur in a minimum fraction of documents. Normally, this reduces the vocabulary drastically even for low numbers of min_df:

```
tfidf = TfidfVectorizer(stop_words=stopwords, min_df=.0001)
dt = tfidf.fit_transform(headlines["headline_text"])
dt
```

Out:

```
<1103663x6772 sparse matrix of type '<class 'numpy.float64'>'
with 4816381 stored elements in Compressed Sparse Row format>
```

This transformation is probably too strict and reduces the vocabulary too far. Depending on the number of documents, you should set min_df to a low integer and check the effects on the vocabulary.

Maximum frequency

Sometimes a text corpus might have a special vocabulary with lots of repeating terms that are too specific to be contained in stop word lists. For this use case, scikit-learn offers the max_df parameter, which eliminates terms occurring too often in the corpus. Let's check how the dimensions are reduced when we eliminate all the words that appear in at least 10% of the headlines:

```
tfidf = TfidfVectorizer(stop_words=stopwords, max_df=0.1)
dt = tfidf.fit_transform(headlines["headline_text"])
dt
```

Out:

```
<1103663x95600 sparse matrix of type '<class 'numpy.float64'>'
    with 5644186 stored elements in Compressed Sparse Row format>
```

Setting max_df to a low value of 10% does not eliminate a single word![6] Our news headlines are very diverse. Depending on the type of corpus you have, experimenting with max_df can be quite useful. In any case, you should always check how the dimensions change.

Blueprint: Improving Features by Making Them More Specific

So far, we have only used the original words of the headlines and reduced the number of dimensions by stop words and counting frequencies. We have not yet changed the features themselves. Using linguistic analysis, there are more possibilities.

Performing linguistic analysis

Using spaCy, we can lemmatize all headlines and just keep the lemmas. This takes some time, but we expect to find a smaller vocabulary. First, we have to perform a linguistic analysis, which might take some time to finish (see Chapter 4 for more details):

```
import spacy

nlp = spacy.load("en")
nouns_adjectives_verbs = ["NOUN", "PROPN", "ADJ", "ADV", "VERB"]
```

---

6 This is, of course, related to the stop word list that has already been used. In news articles, the most common words are stop words. In domain-specific texts, it might be completely different. Using stop words is often the safer choice, as these lists have been curated.

```
for i, row in headlines.iterrows():
    doc = nlp(str(row["headline_text"]))
    headlines.at[i, "lemmas"] = " ".join([token.lemma_ for token in doc])
    headlines.at[i, "nav"] = " ".join([token.lemma_ for token in doc
                            if token.pos_ in nouns_adjectives_verbs])
```

Blueprint: Using Lemmas Instead of Words for Vectorizing Documents

Now, we can vectorize the data using the lemmas and see how the vocabulary decreased:

```
tfidf = TfidfVectorizer(stop_words=stopwords)
dt = tfidf.fit_transform(headlines["lemmas"].map(str))
dt
```

Out:

```
<1103663x71921 sparse matrix of type '<class 'numpy.float64'>'
with 5053610 stored elements in Compressed Sparse Row format>
```

Saving almost 25,000 dimensions is a lot. In news headlines, lemmatizing the data probably does not lose any information. In other use cases like those in Chapter 11, it's a completely different story.

Features, Dimensions, and Precision/Recall

Lemmatizing considerably reduces the vocabulary size. For news headlines, the tense, for example, is not important. When interpreting a novel, it might play a crucial role, however. Depending on your use case, you should think carefully about which text/NLP transformation is useful.

Reducing the feature dimensions with min_df and max_df is also a double-sided sword. Removing infrequent features might be good for a corpus, but if you add additional documents, there might be too few features.

In later chapters, we will introduce precision and recall as quality metrics for information retrieval. We can then quantify the effects of reducing dimensions (with NLP and vectorization tuning) and increasing dimensions (with bigrams, for example) by observing the impact on these metrics.

Blueprint: Limit Word Types

Using the data generated earlier, we can restrict ourselves to considering just nouns, adjectives, and verbs for the vectorization, as prepositions, conjugations, and so on are supposed to carry little meaning. This again reduces the vocabulary:

```
tfidf = TfidfVectorizer(stop_words=stopwords)
dt = tfidf.fit_transform(headlines["nav"].map(str))
dt
```

Out:

```
<1103663x68426 sparse matrix of type '<class 'numpy.float64'>'
with 4889344 stored elements in Compressed Sparse Row format>
```

There's not much to win here, which is probably due to the headlines mainly containing nouns, adjectives, and verbs. But this might look totally different in your own projects. Depending on the type of texts you are analyzing, restricting word types will not only reduce the size of the vocabulary but will also lead to much lower noise. It's a good idea to try this with a small part of the corpus first to avoid long waiting times due to the expensive linguistic analysis.

Blueprint: Remove Most Common Words

As we learned, removing frequent words can lead to document-term matrices with far fewer entries. This is especially helpful when you perform unsupervised learning, as you will normally not be interested in common words that are common anyway.

To remove even more noise, we will now try to eliminate the most common English words. Be careful, as there will normally also be words involved that might carry important meaning. There are various lists with those words; they can easily be found on the internet. The list from Google (*https://oreil.ly/bOho1*) is rather popular and directly available on GitHub. Pandas can directly read the list if we tell it to be a CSV file without column headers. We will then instruct the TfidfVectorizer to use that list as stop words:

```
top_10000 = pd.read_csv("https://raw.githubusercontent.com/first20hours/\
google-10000-english/master/google-10000-english.txt", header=None)
tfidf = TfidfVectorizer(stop_words=set(top_10000.iloc[:,0].values))
dt = tfidf.fit_transform(headlines["nav"].map(str))
dt
```

Out:

```
<1103663x61630 sparse matrix of type '<class 'numpy.float64'>'
with 1298200 stored elements in Compressed Sparse Row format>
```

As you can see, the matrix now has 3.5 million fewer stored elements. The vocabulary shrunk by 68,426 – 61,630 = 6,796 words, so more than 3,000 of the most frequent English words were not even used in the ABC headlines.

Removing frequent words is an excellent method to remove noise from the dataset and concentrate on the uncommon words. However, you should be careful using this from the beginning as even frequent words do have a meaning, and they might also have a special meaning in your document corpus. We recommend performing such analyses additionally but not exclusively.

Blueprint: Adding Context via N-Grams

So far, we have used only single words as features (dimensions of our document vectors) as the basis for our vectorization. With this strategy, we have lost a lot of context information. Using single words as features does not respect the context in which the words appear. In later chapters we will learn how to overcome that limitation with sophisticated models like word embeddings. In our current example, we will use a simpler method and take advantage of word combinations, so called *n-grams*. Two-word combinations are called *bigrams*; for three words, they are called *trigrams*.

Fortunately, CountVectorizer and TfidfVectorizer have the corresponding options. Contrary to the last few sections where we tried to reduce the vocabulary, we now enhance the vocabulary with word combinations. There are many such combinations; their number (and vocabulary size) is growing almost exponentially with n.[7] We will therefore be careful and start with bigrams:

```
tfidf = TfidfVectorizer(stop_words=stopwords, ngram_range=(1,2), min_df=2)
dt = tfidf.fit_transform(headlines["headline_text"])
print(dt.shape)
print(dt.data.nbytes)
tfidf = TfidfVectorizer(stop_words=stopwords, ngram_range=(1,3), min_df=2)
dt = tfidf.fit_transform(headlines["headline_text"])
print(dt.shape)
print(dt.data.nbytes)
```

---

7 It would be growing exponentially if all word combinations were possible and would be used. As this is unlikely, the dimensions are growing subexponentially.

Out:

```
(1103663, 559961)
67325400
(1103663, 747988)
72360104
```

Increasing the feature dimensions from 95,600 to 2,335,132 or even 5,339,558 is quite painful even though the RAM size has not grown too much. For some tasks that need context-specific information (like sentiment analysis), n-grams are extremely useful. It is always useful to keep an eye on the dimensions, though.

Combining n-grams with linguistic features and common words is also possible and reduces the vocabulary size considerably:

```
tfidf = TfidfVectorizer(ngram_range=(1,2),
        stop_words=set(top_10000.iloc[:,0].values))
dt = tfidf.fit_transform(headlines["nav"].map(str))
dt
```

Out:

```
<1103663x385857 sparse matrix of type '<class 'numpy.float64'>'
with 1753239 stored elements in Compressed Sparse Row format>
Compared to the original bigram vectorization with min_df=2 above,
there are just 82,370 dimensions left from 67,325,400
```

Scikit-learn offers many different vectorizers. Normally, starting with TfidfVector izer is a good idea, as it is one of the most versatile.

Options of TfidfVectorizer

TF-IDF can even be switched off so there is a seamless fallback to CountVectorizer. Because of the many parameters, it can take some time to find the perfect set of options.

Finding the correct set of features is often tedious and requires experimentation with the (many) parameters of TfidfVectorizer, like min_df, max_df, or simplified text via NLP. In our work, we have had good experiences with setting min_df to 5, for example, and max_df to 0.7. In the end, this time is excellently invested as the results will depend heavily on correct vectorization. There is no golden bullet, though, and this *feature engineering* depends heavily on the use case and the planned use of the vectors.

The TF-IDF method itself can be improved by using a subnormal term frequency or normalizing the resulting vectors. The latter is useful for quickly calculating similarities, and we demonstrate its use later in the chapter. The former is mainly interesting for long documents to avoid repeating words getting a too high-weight.

Think very carefully about feature dimensions. In our previous examples, we have used single words and bigrams as features. Depending on the use case, this might already be enough. This works well for texts with common vocabulary, like news. But often you will encounter special vocabularies (for example, scientific publications or letters to an insurance company), which will require more sophisticated feature engineering.

Keep number of dimensions in mind. As we have seen, using parameters like ngram_range can lead to large feature spaces. Apart from the RAM usage, this will also be a problem for many machine learning algorithms due to overfitting. Therefore, it's a good idea to always consider the (increase of) feature dimensions when changing parameters or vectorization methods.

Syntactic Similarity in the ABC Dataset

Similarity is one of the most basic concepts in machine learning and text analytics. In this section, we take a look at some challenging problems finding similar documents in the ABC dataset.

After taking a look at possible vectorizations in the previous section, we will now use one of them to calculate the similarities. We will present a blueprint to show how you can perform these calculations efficiently from both a CPU and a RAM perspective. As we are handling large amounts of data here, we have to make extensive use of the NumPy library (*https://numpy.org*).

In the first step, we vectorize the data using stop words and bigrams:

```
# there are "test" headlines in the corpus
stopwords.add("test")
tfidf = TfidfVectorizer(stop_words=stopwords, ngram_range=(1,2), min_df=2, \
                        norm='l2')
dt = tfidf.fit_transform(headlines["headline_text"])
```

We are now ready to use these vectors for our blueprints.

Blueprint: Finding Most Similar Headlines to a Made-up Headline

Let's say we want to find a headline in our data that most closely matches a headline that we remember, but only roughly. This is quite easy to solve, as we just have to vectorize our new document:

```
made_up = tfidf.transform(["australia and new zealand discuss optimal apple \
                          size"])
```

Now we have to calculate the cosine similarity to each headline in the corpus. We could implement this in a loop, but it's easier with the `cosine_similarity` function of scikit-learn:

```
sim = cosine_similarity(made_up, dt)
```

The result is a "number of headlines in the corpus" × 1 matrix, where each number represents the similarity to a document in the corpus. Using `np.argmax` gives us the index of the most similar document:

```
headlines.iloc[np.argmax(sim)]
```

Out:

```
publish_date          2011-08-17 00:00:00
headline_text     new zealand apple imports
Name: 633392, dtype: object
```

No *sizes* of apples and no *Australia* are present in the most similar headline, but it definitely bears some similarity with our invented headline.

Blueprint: Finding the Two Most Similar Documents in a Large Corpus (Much More Difficult)

When handling a corpus of many documents, you might often be asked questions such as "Are there duplicates?" or "Has this been mentioned before?" They all boil down to finding the most similar (maybe even identical) documents in the corpus. We will explain how to accomplish this and again use the ABC dataset as our example. The number of headlines will turn out to be a challenge.

You might think that finding the most similar documents in the corpus is as easy as calculating the `cosine_similarity` between all documents. However, this is not possible as 1,103,663 × 1,103,663 = 1,218,072,017,569. More than one trillion elements do not fit in the RAM of even the most advanced computers. It is perfectly possible to perform the necessary matrix multiplications without having to wait for ages.

Clearly, this problem needs optimization. As text analytics often has to cope with many documents, this is a very typical challenge. Often, the first optimization is to take an intensive look at all the needed numbers. We can easily observe that the document similarity relation is symmetrical and normalized.

In other words, we just need to calculate the subdiagonal elements of the similarity matrix (Figure 5-1)

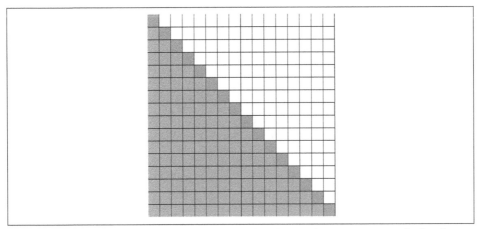

Figure 5-1. Elements that need to be calculated in the similarity matrix. Only the elements below the diagonal need to be calculated, as their numbers are identical to the ones mirrored on the diagonal. The diagonal elements are all 1.

This reduces the number of elements to 1,103,663 × 1,103,662 / 2 = 609,035,456,953, which could be calculated in loop iterations, keeping only the most similar documents. However, calculating all these elements separately is not a good option, as the necessary Python loops (where each iteration calculates just a single matrix element) will eat up a lot of CPU performance.

Instead of calculating individual elements of the similarity matrix, we divide the problem into different blocks and calculate 10,000 × 10,000 similarity submatrices[8] at once by taking blocks of 10,000 TF-IDF vectors from the document matrix. Each of these matrices contains 100,000,000 similarities, which will still fit in RAM. Of course, this leads to calculating too many elements, and we have to perform this for 111 × 110 / 2 = 6,105 submatrices (see Figure 5-2).

From the previous section, we know that iteration takes roughly 500 ms to calculate. Another advantage of this approach is that leveraging data locality gives us a bigger chance of having the necessary matrix elements already in the CPU cache. We estimate that everything should run in about 3,000 seconds, which is roughly one hour.

---

8 We have chosen 10,000 dimensions, as the resulting matrix can be kept in RAM (using roughly 1 GB should be possible even on moderate hardware).

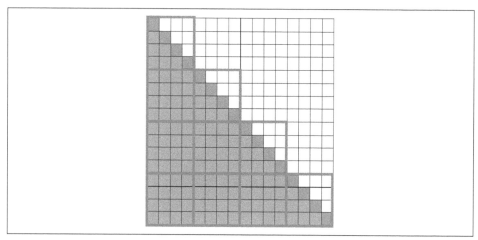

Figure 5-2. Dividing the matrix into submatrices, which we can calculate more easily; the problem is divided into blocks (here, 4 × 4), and the white and diagonal elements within the blocks are redundantly calculated.

Can we improve this? Yes, indeed another speedup of a factor of 10 is actually possible. This works by normalizing the TF-IDF vectors via the corresponding option of TfidfVectorizer. Afterward, the similarity can be calculated with np.dot:[9]

```
%%time
np.dot(dt[0:10000], np.transpose(dt[0:10000]))
```

Out:

```
CPU times: user 16.4 ms, sys: 0 ns, total: 16.4 ms
Wall time: 16 ms
<10000x10000 sparse matrix of type '<class 'numpy.float64'>'
with 1818931 stored elements in Compressed Sparse Row format>
```

In each iteration we save the most similar documents and their similarity and adjust them during the iterations. To skip identical documents (or more precisely, documents with identical document vectors), we only consider similarities < 0.9999. As it turns out, using < relations with a sparse matrix is extremely inefficient, as all nonexistent elements are supposed to be 0. Therefore, we must be creative and find another way:

```
%%time
batch = 10000
```

---

9 All calculations can be sped up considerably by using processor-specific libraries, e.g., by subscribing to the Intel channel in Anaconda. This will use AVX2, AVX-512, and similar instructions and use parallelization. MKL (*https://oreil.ly/pa1zj*) and OpenBlas (*https://oreil.ly/jZYSG*) are good candidates for linear algebra libraries.

```
max_sim = 0.0
max_a = None
max_b = None
for a in range(0, dt.shape[0], batch):
    for b in range(0, a+batch, batch):
        print(a, b)
        r = np.dot(dt[a:a+batch], np.transpose(dt[b:b+batch]))
        # eliminate identical vectors
        # by setting their similarity to np.nan which gets sorted out
        r[r > 0.9999] = np.nan
        sim = r.max()
        if sim > max_sim:
            # argmax returns a single value which we have to
            # map to the two dimensions
            (max_a, max_b) = np.unravel_index(np.argmax(r), r.shape)
            # adjust offsets in corpus (this is a submatrix)
            max_a += a
            max_b += b
            max_sim = sim
```

Out:

```
CPU times: user 6min 12s, sys: 2.11 s, total: 6min 14s
Wall time: 6min 12s
```

That did not take too long, fortunately! max_a and max_b contain the indices of the headlines with maximum similarity (avoiding identical headlines). Let's take a look at the results:

```
print(headlines.iloc[max_a])
print(headlines.iloc[max_b])
```

Out:

```
publish_date                        2014-09-18 00:00:00
headline_text     vline fails to meet punctuality targets report
Name: 904965, dtype: object
publish_date                        2008-02-15 00:00:00
headline_text     vline fails to meet punctuality targets
Name: 364042, dtype: object
```

Using the block calculation approach, we have calculated almost a trillion similarities in just a few minutes. The results are interpretable as we have found similar, but not identical, documents. The different date shows that these are definitely also separate headlines.

Blueprint: Finding Related Words

Until now, we have analyzed documents with respect to their similarity. But the corpus implicitly has much more information, specifically information about related words. In our sense, words are related if they are used in the same documents. Words should be "more" related if they frequently appear together in the documents. As an example, consider the word *zealand*, which almost always occurs together with *new*; therefore, these two words are *related*.

Instead of working with a document-term matrix, we would like to work with a term-document matrix, which is just its transposed form. Instead of taking row vectors, we now take column vectors. However, we need to re-vectorize the data. Assume two words are infrequently used and that both happen to be present only once in the same headline. Their vectors would then be identical, but this is not what we are looking for. As an example, let's think of a person named *Zaphod Beeblebrox*, who is mentioned in two articles. Our algorithm would assign a 100% related score to these words. Although this is correct, it is not very significant. We therefore only consider words that appear at least 1,000 times to get a decent statistical significance:

```
tfidf_word = TfidfVectorizer(stop_words=stopwords, min_df=1000)
dt_word = tfidf_word.fit_transform(headlines["headline_text"])
```

The vocabulary is quite small, and we can directly calculate the cosine similarity. Changing row for column vectors, we just transpose the matrix, using the convenient .T method of NumPy:

```
r = cosine_similarity(dt_word.T, dt_word.T)
np.fill_diagonal(r, 0)
```

Finding the largest entries is easiest if we convert it to a one-dimensional array, get the index of the sorted elements via `np.argsort`, and restore the original indices for the vocabulary lookup:

```
voc = tfidf_word.get_feature_names()
size = r.shape[0] # quadratic
for index in np.argsort(r.flatten())[::-1][0:40]:
    a = int(index/size)
    b = index%size
    if a > b:  # avoid repetitions
        print('"%s" related to "%s"' % (voc[a], voc[b]))
```

Out:

```
"sri" related to "lanka"
"hour" related to "country"
"seekers" related to "asylum"
"springs" related to "alice"
"pleads" related to "guilty"
```

```
"hill" related to "broken"
"trump" related to "donald"
"violence" related to "domestic"
"climate" related to "change"
"driving" related to "drink"
"care" related to "aged"
"gold" related to "coast"
"royal" related to "commission"
"mental" related to "health"
"wind" related to "farm"
"flu" related to "bird"
"murray" related to "darling"
"world" related to "cup"
"hour" related to "2014"
"north" related to "korea"
```

It's quite easy to interpret these results. For some word combinations like *climate change*, we have restored frequent bigrams. On the other hand, we can also see related words that don't appear next to each other in the headlines, such as *drink* and *driving*. By using the transposed document-term matrix, we have performed a kind of *co-occurrence analysis*.

Improving Similarity Measures

Does using n-grams, certain word types, or combinations to find most similar documents change the results?

Documents that have a high similarity and are also published at roughly the same time probably describe the same event. Find a way to remove these from the similarities or—the other way around—focus on these events to detect duplication of news.

Tips for Long-Running Programs like Syntactic Similarity

The following are some efficiency tips for long-running programs:

Perform benchmarking before waiting too long
> Before performing calculations on the whole dataset, it is often useful to run a single calculation and extrapolate how long the whole algorithm will run and how much memory it will need. You should definitely try to understand how runtime and memory grow with increased complexity (linear, polynomial, exponential). Otherwise, you might have to wait for a long time and find out that after a few hours (or even days) only 10% progress memory is exhausted.

Try to divide your problem into smaller parts

Dividing a problem into smaller blocks can help here tremendously. As we have seen in the most similar document of the news corpus, this took only 20 minutes or so to run and used no significant memory. Compared to a naive approach, we would have found out after considerable runtime that the RAM would not have been enough. Furthermore, by dividing the problem into parts, you can make use of multicore architectures or even distribute the problem on many computers.

Summary and Conclusion

In this section, we have prepared blueprints for vectorization and syntactic similarity. Almost all machine learning projects with text (such as classification, topic modeling, and sentiment detection) need document vectors at their very base.

It turns out that feature engineering is one of the most powerful levers for achieving outstanding performance with these sophisticated machine learning algorithms. Therefore, it's an excellent idea to try different vectorizers, play with their parameters, and watch the resulting feature space. There are really many possibilities, and for good reason: although optimizing this takes some time, it is usually well-invested as the results of the subsequent steps in the analysis pipeline will benefit tremendously.

The similarity measure used in this chapter is just an example for document similarities. For more complicated requirements, there are more sophisticated similarity algorithms that you will learn about in the following chapters.

Finding similar documents is a well-known problem in information retrieval. There are more sophisticated scores, such as BM25 (*https://oreil.ly/s47TC*). If you want a scalable solution, the very popular Apache Lucene (*http://lucene.apache.org*) library (which is the basis of search engines like Apache Solr (*https://oreil.ly/R5y0E*) and Elasticsearch (*https://oreil.ly/2qfAL*)) makes use of this and is used for really big document collections in production scenarios.

In the following chapters, we will revisit similarity quite often. We will take a look at integrating word semantics and document semantics, and we will use transfer learning to leverage predefined language models that have been trained with extremely large documents corpora to achieve state-of-the-art performance.

## CHAPTER 6

Text Classification Algorithms

The internet is often referred to as the great enabler: it allows us to accomplish a lot in our daily lives with the help of online tools and platforms. On the other hand, it can also be a source of information overload and endless search. Whether it is communicating with colleagues and customers, partners, or vendors, emails and other messaging tools are an inherent part of our daily work lives. Brands interact with customers and get valuable feedback on their products through social media channels like Facebook and Twitter. Software developers and product managers communicate using ticketing applications like Trello (*https://trello.com*) to track development tasks, while open source communities use GitHub (*https://github.com*) issues and Bugzilla (*https://bugzilla.org*) to track software bugs that need to be fixed or new functionality that needs to be added.

While these tools are useful for getting work done, they can also become overwhelming and quickly turn into a deluge of information. A lot of emails contain promotional content, spam, and marketing newsletters that are often a distraction. Similarly, software developers can easily get buried under a mountain of bug reports and feature requests that take away their productivity. In order to make the best use of these tools, we must also use techniques to categorize, filter, and prioritize the more important information from the less relevant pieces, and text classification is one such technique that can help us achieve this.

The most common example of this is spam detection that is provided by email providers. In this application of text classification, every incoming email is analyzed to determine whether it contains meaningful and useful content or irrelevant information that is not useful. This allows the email application to show only the relevant and important emails and take away the deluge of less useful information. Another application is the classification of incoming customer service requests or software bug reports. If we are able to classify and assign them to the right person or department, then they will be resolved faster. There are several applications of text classification, and in this chapter we will develop a blueprint that can be applied across several of them.

What You'll Learn and What We'll Build

In this chapter, we will build a blueprint for text classification using a supervised learning technique. We will use a dataset containing bug reports of a software application and use the blueprint to predict the priority of these bugs and the specific module that a particular bug belongs to. After studying this chapter, you will understand how to apply supervised learning techniques, splitting the data into train and test parts, validating model performance using accuracy measures, and applying cross-validation techniques. You will also learn about different types of text classification such as binary and multiclass classifications.

Introducing the Java Development Tools Bug Dataset

Software technology products are often complex and consist of several interacting components. For example, let's say you are part of a team developing an Android application that plays podcasts. Apart from the player itself, there can be separate components such as the library manager, search and discover, and so on. If a user reports that they are unable to play any podcasts, then it's important to recognize that this is a critical bug that needs immediate attention. Another user might report an issue with their favorite podcast not showing up. This may not be as critical, but it's important to determine whether this needs to be looked at by the library manager team or if it's actually a problem for the search and discover team. To ensure fast response times, it's important to classify issues accurately and assign them to the right team. Bugs are an inevitable part of any software product, but a quick response will ensure that customers will be happy and continue to use your product.

In this chapter, we will use blueprints to classify bugs and issues raised during the development of the Java Development Tools (JDT) open source project (*https://eclipse.org/jdt*). The JDT project is a part of the Eclipse foundation, which develops the Eclipse integrated development environment (IDE). JDT provides all the functionality needed by software developers to write code using Java in the Eclipse IDE. Users of JDT report bugs and track issues with the tool Bugzilla, a popular open source bug tracking software. Bugzilla is also used by other open source projects like Firefox and the Eclipse Platform. A dataset containing the bugs for all these projects can be found on GitHub (*https://oreil.ly/giRWx*), and we will use the bugs dataset of the JDT project.

The following section loads a *CSV* file that contains the JDT bugs dataset. This dataset contains 45,296 bugs and some of the available characteristics for each bug. We print a list of all the features reported for a bug and look at some of them in more detail to see what the bug reports look like:

```
df = pd.read_csv('eclipse_jdt.csv')
print (df.columns)
df[['Issue_id','Priority','Component','Title','Description']].sample(2)
```

Out:

```
Index(['Issue_id', 'Priority', 'Component', 'Duplicated_issue', 'Title',
       'Description', 'Status', 'Resolution', 'Version', 'Created_time',
       'Resolved_time'],
      dtype='object')
```

	Issue_id	Priority	Component	Title	Description
38438	239715	P3	UI	No property tester for TestCaseElement for property projectNature	I20080613-2000; ; Not sure if this belongs to JDT/Debug or Platform/Debug.; ; I saw this error message several times today in my error log but Im not yet sure how to reproduce it.; ; -- Error Deta...
44129	395007	P3	UI	[package explorer] Refresh action not available on Java package folders	M3.; ; F5 (Refresh) is available as a context menu entry for ordinary source folders but not for Java package folders in the e4 Java Package explorer.; ; Please restore the 3.x functionality.

Based on the details shown in the previous table, we can see that each bug report contains the following important features:

Issue_id
> The primary key for the issue used to track the bug.

Priority
> This varies from P1 (most critical) to P5 (least critical) and defines the severity of the bug (a categorical field).

Component
> This refers to the specific architectural part of the project where the bug occurs. This could be the UI, the APT, etc. (a categorical field).

Title
> This is a short summary entered by the user that briefly describes the bug (a full text field).

Description
> This is a more detailed description of the software behavior that produces the bug and its impact on usage (a full text field).

While creating the bug reports, users follow the guidelines mentioned on the JDT Bugzilla website. This describes what information the user needs to provide while raising a bug so that the developer can find a quick resolution. The website also includes guidelines that help the user identify what priority should be given for a particular bug. Our blueprint will use these bug reports to develop a supervised learning algorithm that can be used to automatically assign a priority to any bug that is raised in the future.

In the previous section, we got a high-level understanding of the dataset and the various features for each bug report. Let's now explore a single bug report in more detail. We randomly sample a single bug (you can choose a different value for `random_state` to see a different bug) and transpose the results so that the results can be displayed with more detail. If we do not transpose, the Description feature would be shown in a truncated manner, whereas now we can see all the contents:

```
df.sample(1).T
```

Out:

	11811
Issue_id	33113
Priority	P3
Component	Debug
Title	Evaluating for loop suspends in URLClassLoader
Description	Debug to a breakpoint in some HelloWorld program. In the DisplayView; highlight and ; Display the following code snippet:; ; for (int i = 0; i < 10; i++) {; System.out.println(i);; }; ; Instead of just reporting No explicit return value; the debugger suspends in the ; URLClassLoader; apparently trying to load the class int. You have hit Resume several ; more times before the evaluation completes. The DebugView does not indicate why it ; has stopped (the thread is just labeled Evaluating). This behavior does not happen if ; you turn off the Suspend on uncaught exceptions preference.
Status	VERIFIED
Resolution	FIXED
Version	2.1
Created_time	2003-02-25 15:40:00 -0500
Resolved_time	2003-03-05 17:11:17 -0500

We can see from the previous table that this bug was raised in the Debug component where the program would crash while evaluating a for loop. We can also see that the user has assigned a medium priority (P3) and that this bug was fixed in a week's time. We can see that the reporter of this bug has followed the guidelines and provided a lot of information that also helps the software developer understand and identify the problem and provide a fix. Most software users are aware that the more information they provide, the easier it would be for a developer to understand the issue and provide a fix. Therefore, we can assume that most bug reports contain enough information for us to create a supervised learning model.

The output graph describes the distribution of bug reports across different priorities. We can see that most bugs have been assigned a level of P3. While this might be because Bugzilla assigns P3 as the default option, it is more likely that this reflects the natural tendency of users to pick a medium level for their bug reports. They believe that the bug does not have a high priority (P1) and at the same time do not want their bug to not be looked at all by choosing a P5. This is reflected in a lot of real-world phenomena and is generally referred to as the normal distribution, where a lot of observations are found at the center or mean with fewer observations at the ends. This could be also visualized as a bell curve.

```
df['Priority'].value_counts().sort_index().plot(kind='bar')
```

Out:

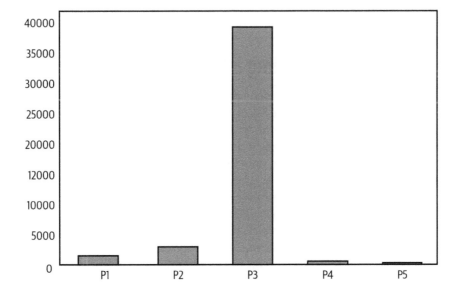

The vast difference between the number of bugs with priority P3 versus other priorities is a problem for building a supervised learning model and is referred to as *class imbalance*. Because the class P3 has an order of magnitude greater number of observations than the other classes, the text classification algorithm will have much more information on P3 bugs than the other priorities: P1, P2, P4, and P5. We will see how the class imbalance of the Priority feature impacts our solution and also attempt to overcome it later in the blueprint. This is similar to learning something as a human. If you have seen more examples of one outcome, you will "predict" more of the same.

In the following snippet, we can see how many bugs are reported against each component of the JDT. The UI and Core components have a much greater number of bugs than the Doc or APT components. This is expected since some components of a software system are larger and more important than others. The Doc component, for example, consists of the documentation section of the software and is used by software developers to understand the functionality but is probably not a working component. The Core component, on the other hand, is an important functional component of JDT and therefore has many more bugs assigned to it:

```
df['Component'].value_counts()
```

Out:

```
    UI       17479
    Core     13669
    Debug    7542
    Text     5901
    APT      406
    Doc      299
    Name: Component, dtype: int64
```

Blueprint: Building a Text Classification System

We will take a step-by-step approach to building a text classification system and then combine all of these steps to present a unified blueprint. This *text classification* system falls under the broader category of *supervised learning* models. *Supervised learning* refers to a domain of machine learning algorithms that uses labeled data points as training data to learn the relationship between independent variables and the target variable. The process of learning the relationship is also referred to as *training a machine learning model*. If the target variable is a continuous numeric variable like distance, sales units, or transaction amounts, we would train a *regression* model. However, in our case, the target variable (Priority) is a categorical variable like the priority or component, and we will choose a *classification* method to train a supervised learning model. This model will use independent variables such as title or description to predict the priority or component of the bug. A supervised machine learning method aims to learn the mapping function from input to output variable(s), defined mathematically as follows:

$$y = f(X)$$

In the preceding equation, y is the output or target variable, f is the mapping function, and X is the input variable or set of variables.

Since we are using data that contains the labeled target variable, this is referred to as *supervised learning*. Figure 6-1 illustrates the workflow of a supervised learning model. There are two phases of the workflow: the training phase and the predicting phase. The training phase starts with the training data that includes the training observations (which could be text data like bug reports) and the associated labels (which is what we would want to predict like priority or software component). While many features of the training observations could be used as is, this alone may not be enough to learn the mapping function, and we would like to add domain knowledge to help the model understand the relationship better. For example, we could add a feature that shows on which day of the week the bug was reported since bugs are likely to be fixed sooner if they are reported earlier in the week. This step is referred to as *feature engineering*, and the result is a set of *feature vectors* for each document. The training step of a supervised learning model accepts as input the feature vectors and their associated labels and tries to learn the mapping function. At the end of the training step, we have the mapping function, which is also called the trained model and can be used to generate predictions.

During the prediction phase, the model receives a new input observation (for example, a bug report) and transforms the documents in the same way as applied during the training phase to produce the feature vectors. The new feature vectors are fed into the trained model to generate the prediction (for example, a bug priority). In this manner we have achieved an automated way of predicting a label.

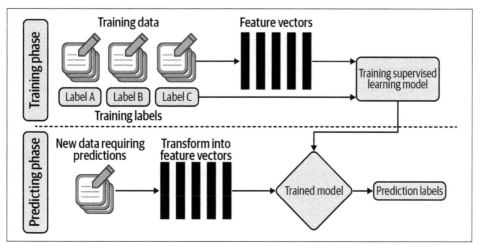

Figure 6-1. Workflow of a supervised learning algorithm used for classification.

Text classification is an example of a supervised learning algorithm where we use text data and NLP techniques such as text vectorization to assign a categorical target variable to a given document. Classification algorithms can be characterized into the following categories:

Binary classification
> This is actually a special case of multiclass classification where an observation can have any one of two values (binary). For example, a given email can be marked as spam or not spam. But each observation will have only one label.

Multiclass classification

In this type of classification algorithm, each observation is associated with one label. For example, a bug report can have a single value of priority from any of the five categories P1, P2, P3, P4, or P5. Similarly, when attempting to identify the software component that a bug is reported in, each bug can be in one of six categories (UI, Core, Debug, Text, APT, or Doc).

Multilabel classification

In this type of classification algorithm each observation can be assigned to multiple labels. For example, a single news article could be tagged with multiple labels, such as Security, Tech, and Blockchain. Several strategies can be used to solve a multilabel classification problem, including the use of multiple binary classification models to generate the final result, but we will not cover this in our blueprint.

Step 1: Data Preparation

Before proceeding to build the text classification model, we must perform some necessary preprocessing steps to clean the data and format it in a manner that is suitable for the application of machine learning algorithms. Since our objective is to identify the priority of a bug report given its title and description, we select only those columns that are relevant for the text classification model. We also remove any rows that contain empty values using the `dropna` function. Finally, we combine the title and description columns to create a single text value and apply the text cleaning blueprint from Chapter 4 to remove special characters. After removing the special characters, we filter out those observations that have fewer than 50 characters in the text field. These bug reports have not been filled out correctly and contain very little description of the problem and are not helpful in training the model:

```
df = df[['Title','Description','Priority']]
df = df.dropna()
df['text'] = df['Title'] + ' ' + df['Description']
df = df.drop(columns=['Title','Description'])
df.columns
```

Out:

```
Index(['Priority', 'text'], dtype='object')
```

Then:

```
df['text'] = df['text'].apply(clean)
df = df[df['text'].str.len() > 50]
df.sample(2)
```

```
Out:
```

	Priority	text
28311	P3	Need to re-run APT on anti-dependencies when files are generated If a generated file satisfies a missing type in another file we should rerun APT on the file which would be fixed by the new type. Currently java compilation does the correct thing but APT does not. Need to keep track of files with missing types and recompile at the end of the round if new types are generated. For good perf need to track the names and only compile those missing types that were generated
25026	P2	Externalize String wizard: usability improvements M6 Test pass Since most of the Java developers will not be faces with the Eclipses mode I would move the check box down to the area of the Accessor class. Furthermore the wizard shouldnt provide the option if org.eclipse.osgi.util.NLS isnt present in the workspace. This will avoid that normal Java developers are faces with the option at all

We can see from the preceding summary of the text feature for two bug reports that our cleaning steps have removed a lot of special characters; we still have retained a lot of the code structure and statements that form part of the description. This is useful information that the model can use to understand the bug and will have an impact on whether it belongs to a higher priority.

Step 2: Train-Test Split

During the process of training a supervised learning model, we are attempting to learn a function that most closely resembles the real-world behavior. We use the information available in the training data to learn this function. Afterward, it is important to evaluate how close our learned function is to the real world, and we split our entire data into train and test splits to achieve this. We split the data, typically using a percentage, with the larger share assigned to the train split. For example, if we have a dataset with 100 observations and apply a train-test split in the ratio of 80-20, then 80 observations will become part of the train split and 20 observations will become part of the test split. The model is now trained on the train split, which uses only the 80 observations to learn the function. We will use the test split of 20 observations to evaluate the learned function. An illustration of this is shown in Figure 6-2.

During training phase:

$$y_{train} = F(X_{train})$$

During evaluation:

$$y_{prediction} = F(X_{test})$$

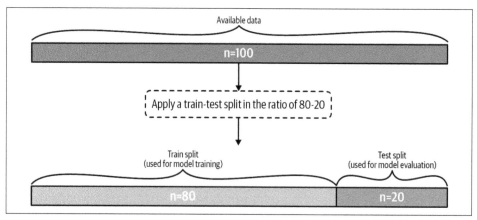

Figure 6-2. A train-test split in the ratio 80-20.

The model has seen only the 80 observations in the train split, and the learned function is now applied on a completely independent and unseen test split to generate the predictions. We know the real values of the target variable in the test split, and comparing these with the predictions will give us a true measure of how well the learned function performs and how close it is to real-world behavior:

$$accuracy = error\_metric\left(y_{prediction}, y_{true}\right)$$

Evaluating the learned model on the test split provides an unbiased estimate of the error of the text classification model since the observations in the test split have been randomly sampled from the training observations and are not part of the learning process. The test split will be used during model evaluation, and there are several metrics that can be used to measure this error, which will be discussed in "Step 4: Model Evaluation" on page 165.

We use the `sklearn.model_selection.train_test_split` function to implement the train-test split, and we provide 0.2 as the argument for the `test_size` (denoting 20% of our data as our test split). In addition, we must also specify our independent and target variables, and the method returns to us a list of four elements; the first two elements are the independent variables split into train and test splits, and the next two elements are the target variable splits. One important argument of the function to note is the `random_state`. This number influences how the rows are sampled and therefore which set of observations goes to the train split and which set of observations goes to the test split. If you provide a different number, the 80-20 split will remain the same, but a different selection of observations will go to the train and test splits. It's important to remember that to reproduce the same results you must choose the same value of the `random_state`. For example, if you want to check what happens to the model on adding a new independent variable, you must be able to compare the accuracy before and after adding the new variable. Therefore, you must use the same `random_state` so that you can determine whether a change occurred. The last parameter to take note of is `stratify`, which ensures that the distribution of the target variable is maintained in the train and test splits. If this is not maintained, then the training split can have a much higher number of observations of a certain class, which does not reflect the distribution in the training data and leads to the model learning an unrealistic function:

```
X_train, X_test, Y_train, Y_test = train_test_split(df['text'],
                                                    df['Priority'],
                                                    test_size=0.2,
                                                    random_state=42,
                                                    stratify=df['Priority'])

print('Size of Training Data ', X_train.shape[0])
print('Size of Test Data ', X_test.shape[0])
```

Out:

```
Size of Training Data  36024
Size of Test Data  9006
```

Step 3: Training the Machine Learning Model

Our next step in creating the text classification blueprint is to train a supervised machine learning model using a suitable algorithm. SVM is one of the popular algorithms used when working with text classification, and we will first provide an introduction to the method and then illustrate why it's well-suited to our task.

Consider a set of points in the X-Y plane with each point belonging to one of two classes: cross or circle, as represented in Figure 6-3. The SVM works by choosing a line that clearly separates the two classes. Of course, there could be several such lines (shown by the dotted options), and the algorithm chooses the line that provides the maximum separation between the closest cross and circle points (identified with a box around them). These closest cross and circle points are referred to as *support vectors*. In the illustration, we are able to identify a hyperplane that clearly separates the cross and circle points, but in reality, it might be difficult to achieve this. For example, there may be a few circle points that lie on the extreme left, and it would be impossible to then generate a hyperplane. The algorithm manages this with the tolerance parameter `tol` that allows for some flexibility and accepts an error in the form of misclassified points when deciding a hyperplane.

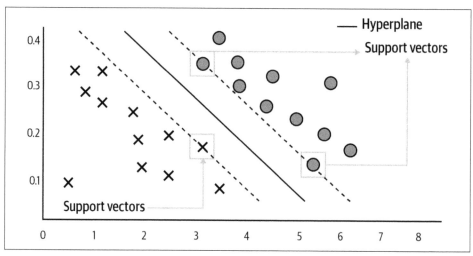

Figure 6-3. Hyperplane and support vectors in a simple two-dimensional classification example.

Before proceeding to run the SVM model, we must prepare our text data in a suitable format that can be used by the algorithm. This means that we must find a way to represent text data in a numeric format. The simplest way is to count the number of times each word occurs in a bug report and combine the counts of all words to create a numeric representation for each observation. This technique has the disadvantage that commonly occurring words will have large values and could be understood as important features when this is not true. Therefore, we use the preferred option of representing the text using a Term-Frequency Inverse Document Frequency (TF-IDF) vectorization, which is explained in more detail in Chapter 5:

```
tfidf = TfidfVectorizer(min_df = 10, ngram_range=(1,2), stop_words="english")
X_train_tf = tfidf.fit_transform(X_train)
```

The TF-IDF vectorization performed in the previous step results in a sparse matrix. The SVM algorithm is preferred when working with text data because it is more suited to work with sparse data compared to other algorithms like Random Forest (*https://oreil.ly/uFkYZ*). They are also better suited to work with input features that are purely numeric (as in our case), while other algorithms are capable of handling a mixture of numeric and categorical input features. For our text classification model we will use the sklearn.svm.LinearSVC module that is provided by the scikit-learn library. SVMs can actually be initialized with different kernel functions, and the linear kernel is recommended for use with text data as there are a large number of features that can be considered linearly separable. It is also faster to fit since it has fewer parameters to optimize. The scikit-learn package provides different implementations of a linear SVM, and if you are interested, you can learn the differences between them as described in "SVC Versus LinearSVC Versus SGDClassifier" on page 165.

In the following code, we initialize the model with a certain `random_state` and specify a tolerance value of 0.00001. The arguments are specific to the type of model we use, and we will show later in this chapter how we can arrive at the optimal parameter values for these arguments. For now we start by specifying some default values and then call the `fit` method, making sure to use the vectorized independent variables that we created in the previous step:

```
model1 = LinearSVC(random_state=0, tol=1e-5)
model1.fit(X_train_tf, Y_train)
```

Out:

```
LinearSVC(C=1.0, class_weight=None, dual=True, fit_intercept=True,
          intercept_scaling=1, loss='squared_hinge', max_iter=1000,
          multi_class='ovr', penalty='l2', random_state=0, tol=1e-05,
          verbose=0)
```

On executing the preceding code, we fit a model using the training data, and the result shows us the various parameters of the model that was generated. Most of these are the default values since we specified only the `random_state` and tolerance.

SVC Versus LinearSVC Versus SGDClassifier

`sklearn.svm.SVC` is the generic implementation of the support vector machine algorithm provided by scikit-learn. This can be used to build models with different kernel functions, including linear, polynomial, and radial basis functions. The `sklearn.svm.LinearSVC` is a specific implementation of a linear SVM. Ideally, it should produce the same results as an SVC with linear kernel. However, the key difference is that LinearSVC uses the liblinear implementation (*https://oreil.ly/5UzQ8*), while SVC is based on the libsvm (*https://oreil.ly/IR1Ji*) implementation. Both of them are popular open source libraries in C++ that implement the SVM algorithm but use different approaches. LinearSVC is much faster, whereas SVC is more generic and supports multiple kernels. `sklearn.linear_model.SGDClassifier` is actually an optimization algorithm called *stochastic gradient descent* (SGD), and is used to optimize a given objective function. When we specify the loss of an SGDClassifier to "hinge," this equates to a linear SVM and should arrive at the same result. Again, the approach is different, and therefore the results may not be the same. To summarize, all three methods can be used to implement an SVM with a linear kernel, but LinearSVC is normally the fastest, whereas the other two methods are more generic.

Step 4: Model Evaluation

We now have a model that can be used to predict the target variable for all the observations in the test split. For these observations, we also know the real target variable, and therefore we can calculate the performance of our model. There are many metrics that can be used to quantify the accuracy of our model, and we will introduce three of them in this section.

The simplest way to validate our text classification model is accuracy: the ratio of the number of predictions that the model got right to the total number of observations. This can be expressed mathematically as follows:

$$Accuracy = \frac{Number\ of\ correct\ predictions}{Total\ number\ of\ predictions\ made}$$

To measure the accuracy of the model, we use the trained model to generate predictions and compare with the real values. To generate the predictions, we must apply the same vectorization to the test split of the independent variable and then call the predict method of the trained model. Once we have the predictions, we can use the accuracy_score method shown next that automatically generates this metric by comparing the true values and the model predictions of the test split:

```
X_test_tf = tfidf.transform(X_test)

Y_pred = model1.predict(X_test_tf)
print ('Accuracy Score - ', accuracy_score(Y_test, Y_pred))
```

Out:

```
Accuracy Score -  0.8748612036420165
```

As you can see, we have achieved a high accuracy score of 87.5%, which indicates that we have a good model that is able to predict the priority of bugs accurately. Please note that if you initialized the model with a different random_state, you might not get the same score, but it would be similar. It is always a good idea to compare the performance of a trained model with a simple baseline approach that could be based on simple rules of thumb or business knowledge. The objective is to check whether the trained model performs better than the baseline and therefore adds value. We can use the sklearn.svm.DummyClassifier module, which provides simple strategies like most_frequent, where the baseline model always predicts the class with highest frequency, or which is stratified, which generates predictions that respect the training data distribution:

```
clf = DummyClassifier(strategy='most_frequent')
clf.fit(X_train, Y_train)
Y_pred_baseline = clf.predict(X_test)
print ('Accuracy Score - ', accuracy_score(Y_test, Y_pred_baseline))
```

Out:

```
Accuracy Score -  0.8769709082833667
```

We can clearly see that our trained model is not adding any value since it performs just as well as a baseline that always chooses the class P3. Another aspect that we must dig deeper to investigate is how well the model is performing for the different priority levels. Is it better at predicting priority P1 or P5? To analyze this, we can use another evaluation tool known as the *confusion matrix*. The confusion matrix is a grid that compares the predicted values with the actual values for all the classified observations. The most common representation of a confusion matrix is for a binary classification problem with only two labels.

We can modify our multiclass classification problem to suit this representation by considering one class as P3 and the other class as all of the rest. Let's look at Figure 6-4, a sample representation of the confusion matrix that predicts only whether a particular bug has a priority P3 or not.

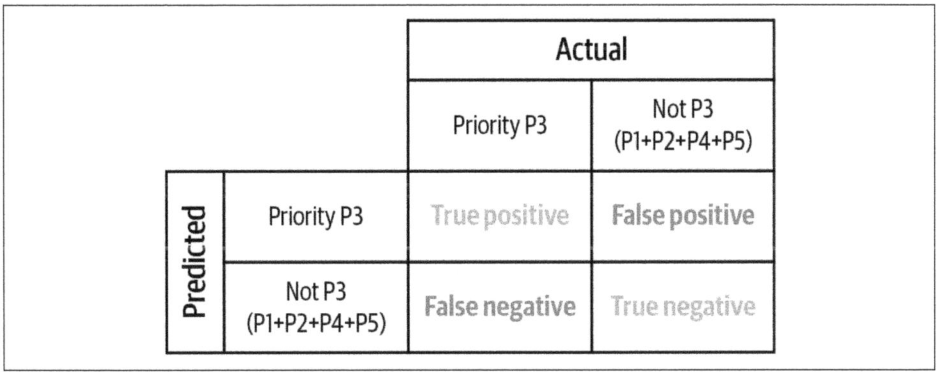

		Actual	
		Priority P3	Not P3 (P1+P2+P4+P5)
Predicted	Priority P3	True positive	False positive
	Not P3 (P1+P2+P4+P5)	False negative	True negative

Figure 6-4. Confusion matrix for priority P3 and not P3.

The rows depict the predictions, and the columns depict the actual values. Each slot in the matrix is the count of observations falling in that slot:

True Positive
The count of those observations that were predicted to be positive and are indeed positive.

True Negative
The count of those observations that were predicted to be negative and are indeed negative.

False Positive
The count of those observations that were predicted to be positive but are actually negative.

False Negative
The count of those observations that were predicted to be negative but are actually positive.

Based on this list, we can automatically derive the accuracy measure using the following equation:

$$Accuracy = \frac{(True\ Positive\ +\ True\ Negative)}{(True\ Positive\ +\ True\ Negative\ +\ False\ Positive\ +\ False\ Negative)}$$

This is nothing but a ratio of all the predictions that were correct and the total number of predictions.

Precision and recall

The real value of using the confusion matrix is in other measures like Precision and Recall, which give us more insight into how the model performs for different classes.

Let's take the positive (P3) class and consider the Precision:

$$Precision = \frac{True\ Positive}{(True\ Positive\ +\ False\ Positive)}$$

This metric tells us what proportion of predicted positives is actually positive, or how accurate our model is at predicting the positive class. If we want to be sure of our positive predictions, then this is a metric we must maximize. For example, if we are classifying emails as spam (positive), then we must be accurate at this; otherwise, a good email might accidentally be sent to the spam folder.

Another metric that is derived from the confusion matrix is Recall:

$$Recall = \frac{True\ Positive}{(True\ Positive\ +\ False\ Negative)}$$

This metric tells us what proportion of real positive values is actually identified by our model. A high recall means that our model is able to capture most of the positive classifications in reality. This is especially important when the cost of not identifying a positive case is very high, for example, if a patient has cancer but our model does not identify it.

From the previous discussion, we can conclude that both precision and recall are important metrics depending on the application of the model. The *F1 score* is a metric that creates a harmonic mean of both of these measures and can also be used as a proxy to evaluate the overall accuracy of the model:

$$F1\ Score = \frac{2\ *\ (Precision\ *\ Recall)}{(Precision\ +\ Recall)}$$

Now that we have developed an understanding of the confusion matrix, let's come back to our blueprint and add the step to evaluate the confusion matrix of the trained model. Note that the earlier representation was simplified as a binary classification, whereas our model is actually a multiclass classification problem, and therefore the confusion matrix will change accordingly. For example, the confusion matrix for our model can be generated with the function confusion_matrix, as shown here:

```
Y_pred = model1.predict(X_test_tf)
confusion_matrix(Y_test, Y_pred)
```

Out:

```
array([[  17,    6,  195,    5,    0],
       [   7,   14,  579,    7,    0],
       [  21,   43, 7821,   13,    0],
       [   0,    7,  194,   27,    0],
       [   0,    0,   50,    0,    0]])
```

This can also be visualized in the form of a heatmap by using the plot_confu sion_matrix function as shown here:

```
plot_confusion_matrix(model1,X_test_tf,
                      Y_test, values_format='d',
                      cmap=plt.cm.Blues)
plt.show()
```

We can define the precision and recall for each category using the same methodology as described earlier but will now include the count of observations that were incorrectly classified into other categories as well.

For example, the precision of the category P3 can be calculated as the ratio of correctly predicted P3 values (7,821) and all predicted P3 values (195 + 579 + 7,821 + 194 + 50), resulting in the following:

Precision (P3) = 7,821 / 8,839 = 0.88

Similarly, the recall for P3 can be calculated as the ratio of correctly predicted P3 values and all actual P3 values (21 + 43 + 7,821 + 13 + 0), resulting in the following:

Recall (P2) = 7,821 / 7,898 = 0.99

An easier way to determine these measures directly is to use the `classifica` `tion_report` function from scikit-learn that automatically calculates these values for us:

```
print(classification_report(Y_test, Y_pred))
```
Out:

	precision	recall	f1-score	support
P1	0.38	0.08	0.13	223
P2	0.20	0.02	0.04	607
P3	0.88	0.99	0.93	7898
P4	0.52	0.12	0.19	228
P5	0.00	0.00	0.00	50
accuracy			0.87	9006
macro avg	0.40	0.24	0.26	9006
weighted avg	0.81	0.87	0.83	9006

Based on our calculations and the previous classification report, one issue becomes glaringly obvious: while the recall and precision values for the class P3 are quite high, these values for the other classes are low and even 0 in some cases (P5). The overall accuracy of the model is 88%, but if we hard-coded our prediction to always be P3, this would also be correct 88% of the time. This makes it clear that our model has not learned much of significance and is merely predicting the majority class. This highlights the fact that during model evaluation we must analyze several metrics and not rely on the accuracy alone.

Class imbalance

The reason for the model to behave in this manner is due to the *class imbalance* in the priority classes that we observed earlier. While there were close to 36,000 bugs with a priority of P3, the number of bugs with other priority classes was only about 4,000 and even fewer in other cases. This means that when we trained our model, it was able to learn the characteristics of the P3 class alone.

There are several techniques we can use to overcome the issue of class imbalance. They belong to two categories of upsampling and downsampling techniques. Upsampling techniques refer to methods used to artificially increase the number of observations of the minority class (non-P3 classes in our example). These techniques can vary from simply adding multiple copies to generating new observations using a method like SMOTE.[1] Downsampling techniques refer to methods that are used to reduce the number of observations of the majority class (P3 in our example). We will choose to randomly downsample the P3 class to have a similar number of observations as the other classes:

```
# Filter bug reports with priority P3 and sample 4000 rows from it
df_sampleP3 = df[df['Priority'] == 'P3'].sample(n=4000)

# Create a separate DataFrame containing all other bug reports
df_sampleRest = df[df['Priority'] != 'P3']

# Concatenate the two DataFrame to create the new balanced bug reports dataset
df_balanced = pd.concat([df_sampleRest, df_sampleP3])

# Check the status of the class imbalance
df_balanced['Priority'].value_counts()
```

Out:

```
P3    4000
P2    3036
P4    1138
P1    1117
P5    252
Name: Priority, dtype: int64
```

Please note that in performing the downsampling, we are losing information, and this is not generally a good idea. However, whenever we come across a class imbalance problem, this prevents our model from learning the right information. We try to overcome this by using upsampling and downsampling techniques, but this will always involve a compromise with regard to data quality. While we have chosen a simplistic approach, please see the following sidebar to understand various ways to deal with the situation.

---

1 Nitesh Chawla et al. "Synthetic Minority Over-Sampling Technique." *Journal of Artificial Intelligence Research* 16 (June 2002). *https://arxiv.org/pdf/1106.1813.pdf.*

Dealing with Class Imbalance

One of the straightforward ways of dealing with class imbalance is by randomly upsampling or downsampling. However, there are several more creative ways to deal with this situation, the first of which is the *synthetic-minority oversampling technique* (SMOTE). Using this method we don't just create copies of the same observation but instead synthetically generate new observations that are similar to the minority class. From the paper (*https://oreil.ly/Se_qS*), we have the following simple description:

> Take the difference between the feature vector (sample) under consideration and its nearest neighbor. Multiply this difference by a random number between 0 and 1, and add it to the feature vector under consideration. This causes the selection of a random point along the line segment between two specific features.

This creates new samples that lie close to existing minority samples but are not exactly the same. The most useful Python package for dealing with class imbalance is *imbalanced-learn* (*https://oreil.ly/tuzV3*), which is also compatible with scikit-learn. In addition to the methods discussed, it also provides additional sampling techniques such as *NearMiss* (for undersampling using nearest neighbors).

Final Blueprint for Text Classification

We will now combine all the steps we have listed so far to create our blueprint for text classification:

```
# Loading the balanced DataFrame

df = df_balanced[['text', 'Priority']]
df = df.dropna()

# Step 1 - Data Preparation

df['text'] = df['text'].apply(clean)

# Step 2 - Train-Test Split
X_train, X_test, Y_train, Y_test = train_test_split(df['text'],
                                                    df['Priority'],
                                                    test_size=0.2,
                                                    random_state=42,
                                                    stratify=df['Priority'])
print('Size of Training Data ', X_train.shape[0])
print('Size of Test Data ', X_test.shape[0])

# Step 3 - Training the Machine Learning model
```

```
tfidf = TfidfVectorizer(min_df=10, ngram_range=(1, 2), stop_words="english")
X_train_tf = tfidf.fit_transform(X_train)

model1 = LinearSVC(random_state=0, tol=1e-5)
model1.fit(X_train_tf, Y_train)

# Step 4 - Model Evaluation

X_test_tf = tfidf.transform(X_test)
Y_pred = model1.predict(X_test_tf)
print('Accuracy Score - ', accuracy_score(Y_test, Y_pred))
print(classification_report(Y_test, Y_pred))
```

Out:

```
Size of Training Data  7634
Size of Test Data  1909
Accuracy Score -  0.4903090623363017
              precision    recall  f1-score   support

         P1       0.45      0.29      0.35       224
         P2       0.42      0.47      0.44       607
         P3       0.56      0.65      0.61       800
         P4       0.39      0.29      0.33       228
         P5       0.00      0.00      0.00        50

   accuracy                           0.49      1909
  macro avg       0.37      0.34      0.35      1909
weighted avg       0.47      0.49      0.48      1909
```

Based on the results, we can see that our accuracy is now at 49%, which is not good. Analyzing further, we can see that precision and recall values have improved for priority P1 and P2, indicating that we are able to better predict bugs with this priority. However, it's also obvious that for bugs with priority P5, this model does not offer anything. We see that this model does perform better than a simple baseline using a *stratified* strategy, as shown next. Even though the earlier model had a higher accuracy, it wasn't actually a good model because it was ineffective. This model is also not good but at least presents a true picture and informs us that we must not use it for generating predictions:

```
clf = DummyClassifier(strategy='stratified')
clf.fit(X_train, Y_train)
Y_pred_baseline = clf.predict(X_test)
print ('Accuracy Score - ', accuracy_score(Y_test, Y_pred_baseline))
```

Out:

```
Accuracy Score -  0.30434782608695654
```

The following are some examples of where our model predictions for these priorities are accurate:

```
# Create a DataFrame combining the Title and Description,
# Actual and Predicted values that we can explore
frame = { 'text': X_test, 'actual': Y_test, 'predicted': Y_pred }
result = pd.DataFrame(frame)

result[((result['actual'] == 'P1') | (result['actual'] == 'P2')) &
       (result['actual'] == result['predicted'])].sample(2)
```

Out:

	text	actual	predicted
64	Java launcher: Dont prompt for element to launch if theres only one I went to debug a CU by selecting it and clicking the debug tool item. I was prompted to select a launcher and I also had to select the only available class on the second page. The second step shouldnt be necessary. The next button on the first page should be disabled. NOTES: DW The first time you launch something in your workspace you must go through this pain...This is due to the debugger being pluggable for different lauguages. In this case the launcher selection is generic debug support and the choosing of a class to launch is java specific debug support. To promote lazy plugin loading and to avoid launchers doing exhaustive searching for launchable targets the launcher selection page does not poll the pluggable launch page to see if it can finish with the current selection. Once you have selected a defualt launcher for a project the launcher selection page will not bother you again. Moved to inactive for post-June consideratio	P2	P2
5298	Rapid stepping toString When you do rapid stepping and have an object selected displaying details we get exceptions in the log. This is because the toString attempts an evaluation while a step is in progress. We have to allow stepping during evaluations so this is a tricky timing issue. </log-entr	P1	P1

Here are some cases where the model prediction is inaccurate:

```
result[((result['actual'] == 'P1') | (result['actual'] == 'P2')) &
       (result['actual'] != result['predicted'])].sample(2)
```

Out:

	text	actual	predicted
4707	Javadoc wizard: Problems with default package 20020328 1. empty project. create A.java in default package 2. Start export wizard select the default package press Finish 3. Creation fails javadoc: No source files for package A Loading source files for package A... 1 error Dont know if this is a general javadoc probl	P1	P2
16976	Breakpoint condition compiler should not matter about NON-NLS strings Ive a project in which Ive set compiler option usage of non-externalized strings to Warning. When I want to set a condition on a breakpoint which contains a string object.equals for example I break all the time at this point due to a compilation error... Then Im obliged to write my condition as: boolean cond = object.equals //$NON-NLS-1$ return cond to avoid this problem. Wont it be possible that debugger uses a specific compiler which would ignore current project/workspace compiler options but only uses default one	P2	P3

Our model is not accurate, and from observing the predictions, it is not clear whether a relationship between description and priority exists. To improve the accuracy of our model, we have to perform additional data cleaning steps and perform steps such as lemmatization, removing noisy tokens, modifying `min_df` and `max_df`, including trigrams, and so on. We recommend that you modify the current `clean` function provided in "Feature Extraction on a Large Dataset" on page 115 and check the performance. Another option is also to determine the right hyperparameters for the selected model, and in the next section, we will introduce the cross-validation and grid search techniques, which can help us better understand model performance and arrive at an optimized model.

Blueprint: Using Cross-Validation to Estimate Realistic Accuracy Metrics

Before training the model, we created a train-test split so that we can accurately evaluate our model. Based on the test split, we got an accuracy of 48.7%. However, it is desirable to improve this accuracy. Some of the techniques that we could use include adding additional features such as trigrams, adding additional text cleaning steps, choosing different model parameters, and then checking performance on the test split. Our result is always based on a single hold-out dataset that we created using the train-test split. If we go back and change the `random_state` or `shuffle` our data, then we might get a different test split, which might have different accuracy for the same model. Therefore, we rely heavily on a given test split to determine the accuracy of our model.

Cross-validation is a technique that allows us to train on different splits of data and validate also on different splits of data in a repetitive manner so that the final model that is trained achieves the right balance between *underfitting* and *overfitting*. Underfitting is the phenomenon where our trained model does not learn the underlying relationship well and makes similar predictions for every observation that are far away from the real value. This is because the chosen model is not complex enough to model the phenomenon (wrong choice of model) or there are insufficient observations from which to learn the relationship. Overfitting is the phenomenon where the chosen model is complex and has fit the underlying pattern very well during training but produces significant deviations on the test data. This indicates that the trained model does not generalize well to unseen data. By using a cross-validation technique, we become aware of these drawbacks by training and testing on multiple splits of the data and can arrive at a more realistic performance of our model.

There are many variants of cross-validation, and the most widely used is K-fold cross-validation. Figure 6-5 demonstrates a K-fold strategy, where we first divide the entire training dataset into K folds. In each iteration, a model is trained on a different set of K-1 folds of the data, and validation is performed on the held-out Kth fold. The overall performance is taken to be the average of the performance on all hold-out K folds. In this way we are not basing our model accuracy on just one test split but multiple such splits, and similarly we are also training the model on multiple splits of the training data. This allows us to use all the observations for training our model as we do not need to have a separate hold-out test split.

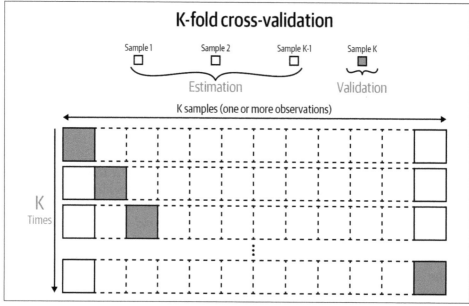

Figure 6-5. A K-fold cross-validation strategy where a different hold-out set (shaded) is chosen each time the model is trained. The rest of the sets form part of the training data.

To perform cross-validation, we will use the `cross_val_score` method from scikit-learn. This takes as arguments the model that needs to be fit, the training dataset, and the number of folds that we want to use. In this case, we use a five-fold cross-validation strategy, and, depending on the number of training observations and availability of computing infrastructure, this can vary between 5 and 10. The method returns the validation score for each iteration of the cross-validation, and we can calculate the mean value obtained across all validation folds. From the results, we can see that the validation score varies from 36% up to 47%. This indicates that the model accuracy we reported earlier on the test dataset was optimistic and an artifact of the specific way in which the train-test split occurred. A more realistic accuracy that we can expect from this model is actually the average score of 44% derived from cross-validation. It's important to perform this exercise to understand the true potential of any model. We perform the vectorization step again because we are going to use the entire dataset and not just the train split:

```
# Vectorization

tfidf = TfidfVectorizer(min_df = 10, ngram_range=(1,2), stop_words="english")
df_tf = tfidf.fit_transform(df['text']).toarray()

# Cross Validation with 5 folds

scores = cross_val_score(estimator=model1,
                         X=df_tf,
                         y=df['Priority'],
                         cv=5)

print ("Validation scores from each iteration of the cross validation ", scores)
print ("Mean value across of validation scores ", scores.mean())
print ("Standard deviation of validation scores ", scores.std())
```

Out:

```
Validation scores from each iteration of the cross validation
[0.47773704 0.47302252 0.45468832 0.44054479 0.3677318 ]
Mean value across of validation scores  0.44274489261393396
Standard deviation of validation scores  0.03978852971586144
```

Using a cross-validation technique allows us to use all observations, and we do not need to create a separate hold-out test split. This gives the model more data to learn from.

Blueprint: Performing Hyperparameter Tuning with Grid Search

Grid search is a useful technique to improve the accuracy of the model by evaluating different parameters that are used as arguments for the model. It does so by trying different combinations of hyperparameters that can maximize a given metric (e.g., accuracy) for the machine learning model. For example, if we use the sklearn.svm.SVC model, it has a parameter named kernel (*https://oreil.ly/30Xsq*) that can take several values: linear, rbf (radial basis function), poly (polynomial), and so on. Furthermore, by setting up a preprocessing pipeline, we could also test with different values of ngram_range for the TF-IDF vectorization. When we do a grid search, we provide the set of parameter values that we would like to evaluate, and combined with the cross-validation method of training a model, this identifies the set of hyperparameters that maximizes model accuracy. The biggest drawback of this technique is that it is CPU- and time-intensive; in a way we, are testing many possible combinations of hyperparameters to arrive at the set of values that perform best.

To test the right choice of hyperparameters for our model, we first create a `train ing_pipeline` where we define the steps that we would like to run. In this case, we specify the TF-IDF vectorization and the LinearSVC model training. We then define a set of parameters that we would like to test using the variable `grid_param`. Since a parameter value is specific to a certain step in the pipeline, we use the name of the step as the prefix when specifying the `grid_param`. For example, `min_df` is a parameter used by the vectorization step and is therefore referred to as `tfidf__min_df`. Finally, we use the `GridSearchCV` method, which provides the functionality to test multiple versions of the entire pipeline with different sets of hyperparameters and produces the cross-validation scores from which we pick the best-performing version:

```
training_pipeline = Pipeline(
    steps=[('tfidf', TfidfVectorizer(stop_words="english")),
           ('model', LinearSVC(random_state=42, tol=1e-5))])

grid_param = [{
    'tfidf__min_df': [5, 10],
    'tfidf__ngram_range': [(1, 3), (1, 6)],
    'model__penalty': ['l2'],
    'model__loss': ['hinge'],
    'model__max_iter': [10000]
}, {
    'tfidf__min_df': [5, 10],
    'tfidf__ngram_range': [(1, 3), (1, 6)],
    'model__C': [1, 10],
    'model__tol': [1e-2, 1e-3]
}]

gridSearchProcessor = GridSearchCV(estimator=training_pipeline,
                                   param_grid=grid_param,
                                   cv=5)
gridSearchProcessor.fit(df['text'], df['Priority'])

best_params = gridSearchProcessor.best_params_
print("Best alpha parameter identified by grid search ", best_params)

best_result = gridSearchProcessor.best_score_
print("Best result identified by grid search ", best_result)
```

Out:

```
Best alpha parameter identified by grid search  {'model__loss': 'hinge',
'model__max_iter': 10000, 'model__penalty': 'l2', 'tfidf__min_df': 10,
```

```
'tfidf__ngram_range': (1, 6)}
Best result identified by grid search  0.46390780513357777
```

We have evaluated two values of `min_df` and `ngram_range` with two different sets of model parameters. In the first set, we tried with the l2 `model_penalty` and hinge `model_loss` with a maximum of 1,000 iterations. In the second set, we tried to vary the value of the regularization parameter C and `tolerance` values of the model. While we saw the parameters of the best model earlier, we can also check the performance of all other models that were generated to see how the parameter values interact. You can see the top five models and their parameter values as in the following:

```
gridsearch_results = pd.DataFrame(gridSearchProcessor.cv_results_)
gridsearch_results[['rank_test_score', 'mean_test_score',
                    'params']].sort_values(by=['rank_test_score'])[:5]
```

	rank_test_score	mean_test_score	params
3	1	0.46	{'model__loss': 'hinge', 'model__max_iter': 10000, 'model__penalty': 'l2', 'tfidf__min_df': 10, 'tfidf__ngram_range': (1, 6)}
2	2	0.46	{'model__loss': 'hinge', 'model__max_iter': 10000, 'model__penalty': 'l2', 'tfidf__min_df': 10, 'tfidf__ngram_range': (1, 3)}
0	3	0.46	{'model__loss': 'hinge', 'model__max_iter': 10000, 'model__penalty': 'l2', 'tfidf__min_df': 5, 'tfidf__ngram_range': (1, 3)}
1	4	0.46	{'model__loss': 'hinge', 'model__max_iter': 10000, 'model__penalty': 'l2', 'tfidf__min_df': 5, 'tfidf__ngram_range': (1, 6)}
5	5	0.45	{'model__C': 1, 'model__tol': 0.01, 'tfidf__min_df': 5, 'tfidf__ngram_range': (1, 6)}

Blueprint Recap and Conclusion

Let's recap the steps of the blueprint for text classification by applying this to a different classification task. If you recall, we mentioned at the beginning of the chapter that to enable quick bug fixes, we must identify the priority of the bug and also assign it to the right team. The assignment can be done automatically by identifying which part of the software the bug belongs to. We have seen that the bug reports have a feature named `Component` with values including `Core`, `UI`, and `Doc`. This can be helpful in assigning the bug to the right team or individual, leading to a faster resolution. This task is similar to identifying the bug priority and will help us understand how the blueprint can be applied to any other application.

We update the blueprint with the following changes:

- Additional step to include grid search to identify the best hyperparameters and limit the number of options tested to increase runtime
- Additional option to use the `sklearn.svm.SVC` function to compare performance and try nonlinear kernels

```python
# Flag that determines the choice of SVC and LinearSVC
runSVC = True

# Loading the DataFrame

df = pd.read_csv('eclipse_jdt.csv')
df = df[['Title', 'Description', 'Component']]
df = df.dropna()
df['text'] = df['Title'] + df['Description']
df = df.drop(columns=['Title', 'Description'])

# Step 1 - Data Preparation
df['text'] = df['text'].apply(clean)
df = df[df['text'].str.len() > 50]

if (runSVC):
    # Sample the data when running SVC to ensure reasonable run-times
    df = df.groupby('Component', as_index=False).apply(pd.DataFrame.sample,
                                                       random_state=21,
                                                       frac=.2)

# Step 2 - Train-Test Split
X_train, X_test, Y_train, Y_test = train_test_split(df['text'],
                                                    df['Component'],
                                                    test_size=0.2,
                                                    random_state=42,
                                                    stratify=df['Component'])
print('Size of Training Data ', X_train.shape[0])
print('Size of Test Data ', X_test.shape[0])

# Step 3 - Training the Machine Learning model
tfidf = TfidfVectorizer(stop_words="english")

if (runSVC):
    model = SVC(random_state=42, probability=True)
    grid_param = [{
        'tfidf__min_df': [5, 10],
        'tfidf__ngram_range': [(1, 3), (1, 6)],
        'model__C': [1, 100],
        'model__kernel': ['linear']
    }]
else:
    model = LinearSVC(random_state=42, tol=1e-5)
    grid_param = {
```

```
        'tfidf__min_df': [5, 10],
        'tfidf__ngram_range': [(1, 3), (1, 6)],
        'model__C': [1, 100],
        'model__loss': ['hinge']
    }

training_pipeline = Pipeline(
    steps=[('tfidf', TfidfVectorizer(stop_words="english")), ('model', model)])

gridSearchProcessor = GridSearchCV(estimator=training_pipeline,
                                   param_grid=grid_param,
                                   cv=5)

gridSearchProcessor.fit(X_train, Y_train)

best_params = gridSearchProcessor.best_params_
print("Best alpha parameter identified by grid search ", best_params)

best_result = gridSearchProcessor.best_score_
print("Best result identified by grid search ", best_result)

best_model = gridSearchProcessor.best_estimator_

# Step 4 - Model Evaluation

Y_pred = best_model.predict(X_test)
print('Accuracy Score - ', accuracy_score(Y_test, Y_pred))
print(classification_report(Y_test, Y_pred))
```

Out:

```
Size of Training Data  7204
Size of Test Data  1801
Best alpha parameter identified by grid search  {'model__C': 1,
'model__kernel': 'linear', 'tfidf__min_df': 5, 'tfidf__ngram_range': (1, 6)}
Best result identified by grid search  0.739867279666898
Accuracy Score -   0.7368128817323709
              precision    recall  f1-score   support

         APT       1.00      0.25      0.40        16
        Core       0.74      0.77      0.75       544
       Debug       0.89      0.77      0.82       300
         Doc       0.50      0.17      0.25        12
        Text       0.61      0.45      0.52       235
          UI       0.71      0.81      0.76       694

    accuracy                           0.74      1801
   macro avg       0.74      0.54      0.58      1801
weighted avg       0.74      0.74      0.73      1801
```

Based on the accuracy and classification report, we have achieved an accuracy of 73%, and we can conclude that this model is able to predict the software component that a bug is referring to more accurately than the priority. While some of the improvement is due to the additional steps of grid search and cross-validation, most of it is simply because there is a relationship that the model could identify between the bug description and the Component it refers to. The Component feature does not show the same level of the class imbalance problem that we noticed earlier. However, even within Component, we can see the poor results for the software component Doc, which has few observations compared to the other components. Also, comparing with the baseline, we can see that this model improves in performance. We can try to balance our data, or we can make an informed business decision that it's more important for the model to predict those software components that have a larger number of bugs:

```
clf = DummyClassifier(strategy='most_frequent')
clf.fit(X_train, Y_train)
Y_pred_baseline = clf.predict(X_test)
print ('Accuracy Score - ', accuracy_score(Y_test, Y_pred_baseline))
```

Out:

```
Accuracy Score -  0.38534147695724597
```

Let's also attempt to understand how this model tries to make its predictions by looking at where it works well and where it fails. We will first sample two observations where the predictions were accurate:

```
# Create a DataFrame combining the Title and Description,
# Actual and Predicted values that we can explore
frame = { 'text': X_test, 'actual': Y_test, 'predicted': Y_pred }
result = pd.DataFrame(frame)

result[result['actual'] == result['predicted']].sample(2)
```

Out:

	text	actual	predicted
28225	Move static initializer lacks atomic undo.When a method is moved the move can be atomically undone with a single Undo command. But when a static initializer is moved it can only be undone with an Undo command issued in both the source and destination files	UI	UI
30592	Debug view steals focus when breakpoint hitM5 - I20060217-1115 When you debug a program that has breakpoints when the debugger hits a breakpoint pressing Ctrl+Sht+B does not remove the breakpoint even though the line looks like it has the focus. To actually remove the breakpoint one has to click in the editor on the proper line and repress the keys	Debug	Debug

We can see that when a bug is classified as belonging to the Debug component the description makes use of terms like *debugger* and *breakpoint*, whereas when a bug is classified in UI, we see an indication of *Undo* and *movement*. This seems to indicate that the trained model is able to learn associations between words in the description and the corresponding software component. Let's also look at some observations where the predictions were incorrect:

```
result[result['actual'] != result['predicted']].sample(2)
```

Out:

	text	actual	predicted
16138	Line wrapping on @see tags creates a new warning Invalid parameters declarationIn Eclipce 3.0M5 with the javadoc checking enabled linewrapping will cause a warning Javadoc: Invalid parameters declaration This will cause the warning: /** * @see com.xyz.util.monitoring.MonitoringObserver#monitorSetValue */ where this will not : /** * @see com.xyz.util.monitoring.MonitoringObserver#monitorSetValue *	Text	Core
32903	After a String array is created eclipse fails to recognize methods for an object.Type these lines in any program. String abc = new String {a b c} System. After System. eclipse wont list all the available methods	Core	UI

Here, it becomes more difficult to identify reasons for an incorrect classification, but we must analyze further if we want to improve the accuracy of our model. After we build a model, we must investigate our predictions and understand why the model made these predictions. There are several techniques that we can use to explain model predictions, and this will be covered in more detail in Chapter 7.

Closing Remarks

In this chapter, we presented a blueprint for performing the different steps in building a supervised text classification model. It starts with the data preparation steps, including the balancing of classes, if required. We then showed the steps for creating train and test splits, including the use of cross-validation as the preferred technique to arrive at an accurate measure of model accuracy. We then presented grid search as one of the techniques to validate different settings of hyperparameters to find the most optimal combination. Supervised machine learning is a broad area with multiple applications like loan default prediction, ad-click prediction, etc. This blueprint presents an end-to-end technique for building a supervised machine learning model and can be extended to problems outside of text classification as well.

Further Reading

Bergstra, James, and Yoshua Bengio. "Random Search for Hyper-Parameter Optimization." 2012. *http://www.jmlr.org/papers/volume13/bergstra12a/bergstra12a.pdf*.

Berwick, R. "An Idiot's guide to Support Vector Machines." *http://web.mit.edu/6.034/wwwbob/svm-notes-long-08.pdf*.

Kohavi, Ron. "A Study of CrossValidation and Bootstrap for Accuracy Estimation and Model Selection." *http://ai.stanford.edu/~ronnyk/accEst.pdf*.

Raschka, Sebastian. "Model Evaluation, Model Selection, and Algorithm Selection in Machine Learning." 2018. *https://arxiv.org/pdf/1811.12808.pdf*.

## CHAPTER 7

How to Explain a Text Classifier

In the previous chapters, we have learned a lot about advanced analytical methods for unstructured text data. Starting with statistics and using NLP, we have found interesting insights from text.

Using supervised methods for classification, we have assigned text documents to already-given categories by training algorithms. Although we have checked the quality of the classification process, we have skipped an important aspect: we have no idea *why* the model has decided to assign a category to a text.

This might sound unimportant if the category was correct. However, in daily life you often have to *explain* your own decisions and make them *transparent* to others. The same is true for machine learning algorithms.

In real-life projects, you will more often than not hear the question "Why has the algorithm assigned this category/sentiment?" Even before that, understanding how the algorithm has learned something will help you to improve the classification by using different algorithms, adding features, changing weights, and so on. Compared to structured data, the question is much more important with text as humans can interpret the text itself. Moreover, text has many artifacts such as signatures in emails that you better avoid and make sure that they are not the dominant features in your classification.

In addition to the technological perspective, there are also some legal aspects to keep in mind. You might be responsible for proving that your algorithm is not biased or does not discriminate. The GDPR in the European Union even demands that for algorithms that make decisions (like allowing only certain kinds of payment) on public websites.

Last but not least, trust needs information. If you make your results as transparent as possible, you will enormously increase the confidence and trust that somebody has in your method.

What You'll Learn and What We'll Build

In this chapter, we will take a look at several methods for explaining the results of a supervised machine learning model. Wherever possible, we will build on classification examples that have been part of the previous chapters.

We will start by revisiting the classification of the bug reports from Chapter 6. Some reports were classified correctly, some not. We will take a step back and analyze whether classification is always a binary decision. For some models, it is not, and we will calculate the probabilities of bug reports belonging to a certain class and check with the correct values (the so-called *ground truth*).

In the next section, we will analyze which features were responsible for the decision of the model. We can calculate this using support vector machines. We will try to interpret the results and see if we can use that knowledge to improve the method.

Afterward, we will take a more general approach and introduce *local interpretable model-agnostic explanations* (LIME). LIME is (almost) agnostic to the specific machine learning model and can explain the results of many algorithms.

People have been researching explainable AI a lot in recent years and came up with a more sophisticated model called *Anchor*, which we will present in the last part of this chapter.

After studying this chapter, you will know different methods for explaining the results of supervised machine learning models. You will be able to use this for your own projects and decide which of the methods is best suited for your specific requirements. You will be able to interpret the results and create intuitive visualizations to make them easily understandable for nonexperts.

Blueprint: Determining Classification Confidence Using Prediction Probability

You might remember the example from Chapter 6 where we tried to classify the bug reports according to their component. We will now train a support vector machine with the optimal parameters found in that chapter. The rest of the notation stays the same:

```
svc = SVC(kernel="linear", C=1, probability=True, random_state=42)
svc.fit(X_train_tf, Y_train)
```

If you recall the classification report, we had a good average precision and recall of 75%, so the classification worked rather well. But there were some cases where the prediction differed from the actual value. We will try to look at the results of these predictions in more detail now to understand if there is a pattern that we can use to distinguish between "good" and "bad" prediction without taking a look at the actual results as those will be unknown in real classification scenarios.

For this, we will use the function `predict_proba` of the support vector machine model, which tells us about the internals of the SVM, namely, the probabilities it calculated for the respective classes (obviously the prediction itself has the highest probability).[1] As a parameter, it expects a matrix consisting of document vectors. The result is the probability for the different classes. As a first step, we are going to construct a `DataFrame` from the prediction results:

```
X_test_tf = tfidf.transform(X_test)
Y_pred = svc.predict(X_test_tf)
result = pd.DataFrame({ 'text': X_test.values, 'actual': Y_test.values,
                       'predicted': Y_pred })
```

Let's try it with one document of the test dataset and assume that we want to optimize our classification and are mainly interested in cases where the predictions are wrong:

```
result[result["actual"] != result["predicted"]].head()
```

Out:

	text	actual	predicted
2	NPE in Delta processor while executing JDT/UI ...	Core	UI
15	Inserting a block of text in editor badly alig...	UI	Text
16	Differences when debugging identical objects W...	Debug	Core
20	Foreach template doesnt work for class members...	Core	UI
21	exchange left and right operands for compariso...	UI	Core

Document 21 looks like a good candidate. The predicted class "Core" is wrong, but "left" and "right" also sound like UI (which would be correct). Let's take a deeper look at that:

```
text = result.iloc[21]["text"]
print(text)
```

---

1 Graphically, you can think of the probabilities as the distance of the samples to the hyperplane defined by the SVM.

Out:

```
exchange left and right operands for comparison operators changes semantics
Fix for Bug 149803 was not good.; ; The right fix should do the following;
if --> if --> if ; if ; if
```

This looks like a good candidate for a more detailed analysis as it contains words that would naively speak for both Core and for UI. Maybe we can understand that in more detail if we look at the probabilities. Calculating this is quite easy:

```
svc.predict_proba(X_test_tf[21])
```

Out:

```
array([[0.002669, 0.46736578, 0.07725225, 0.00319434, 0.06874877,
        0.38076986]])
```

Remembering that the classes had the order APT, Core, Debug, Doc, Text, and UI, the algorithm was a bit more convinced of Core compared to UI, which would have been its second choice.

Is this always the case? We will try to find out and calculate the decision probability for all documents in the test dataset and add it to a DataFrame:

```
class_names = ["APT", "Core", "Debug", "Doc", "Text", "UI"]
prob = svc.predict_proba(X_test_tf)
# new dataframe for explainable results
er = result.copy().reset_index()
for c in enumerate(class_names):
    er[c] = prob[:, i]
```

Let's take a look at some samples of the data frame and find out whether the predictions are better if the algorithm was quite convinced about its decision (i.e., the probability for the chosen category was much higher than the others):

```
er[["actual", "predicted"] + class_names].sample(5, random_state=99)
```

Out:

	actual	predicted	APT	Core	Debug	Doc	Text	UI
266	UI	UI	0.000598	0.000929	0.000476	0.001377	0.224473	0.772148
835	Text	Text	0.002083	0.032109	0.001481	0.002085	0.696666	0.265577
998	Text	Text	0.000356	0.026525	0.003425	0.000673	0.942136	0.026884
754	Core	Text	0.003862	0.334308	0.011312	0.015478	0.492112	0.142927
686	UI	UI	0.019319	0.099088	0.143744	0.082969	0.053174	0.601705

Looking at the table, there is only one wrong prediction (754). In this case, the algorithm was quite "unsure" and decided for the category with a probability of less than 50%. Can we find a pattern for this?

Let's try to build two `DataFrames`, one with correct and another with wrong predictions. Afterward, we will analyze the distribution of the highest probability and see whether we can find any differences:

```
er['max_probability'] = er[class_names].max(axis=1)
correct = (er[er['actual'] == er['predicted']])
wrong   = (er[er['actual'] != er['predicted']])
```

We will now plot this as a histogram:

```
correct["max_probability"].plot.hist(title="Correct")
wrong["max_probability"].plot.hist(title="Wrong")
```

Out:

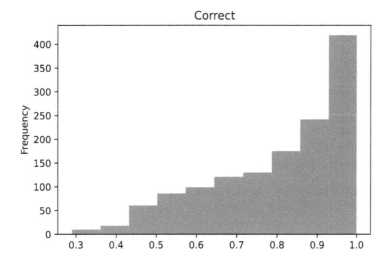

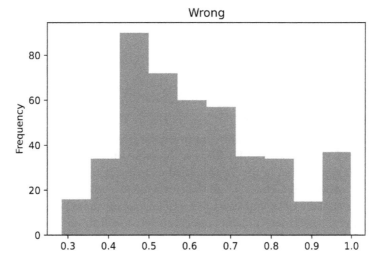

We can see that in the case of correct predictions, the model often decided with high probabilities, whereas the probabilities were considerably lower when the decision was wrong. As we will see later, the small peak in the wrong category with high probability is due to short texts or missing words.

Finally, we will take a look at whether we can improve the results if we only consider decisions that have been made with a probability of more than 80%:

```
high = er[er["max_probability"] > 0.8]
print(classification_report(high["actual"], high["predicted"]))
```

Out:

	precision	recall	f1-score	support
APT	0.90	0.75	0.82	12
Core	0.94	0.89	0.92	264
Debug	0.94	0.99	0.96	202
Doc	1.00	0.67	0.80	3
Text	0.78	0.75	0.77	72
UI	0.90	0.92	0.91	342
accuracy			0.91	895
macro avg	0.91	0.83	0.86	895
weighted avg	0.91	0.91	0.91	895

Compare this to the original result, shown here:

```
print(classification_report(er["actual"], er["predicted"]))
```

Out:

	precision	recall	f1-score	support
APT	0.90	0.56	0.69	16
Core	0.76	0.77	0.76	546
Debug	0.90	0.78	0.84	302
Doc	1.00	0.25	0.40	12
Text	0.64	0.51	0.57	236
UI	0.72	0.82	0.77	699
accuracy			0.75	1811
macro avg	0.82	0.62	0.67	1811
weighted avg	0.75	0.75	0.75	1811

We can see that we have considerably improved the precision for predicting the components Core, Debug, Text, and UI while at the same time increasing the recall. This is great, as the explanation of the SVM has led us to a smaller subset of data in which the classifier works better. However, in the components with few samples (Apt, Doc), the result has actually only improved the recall. It seems that there are just too few samples in these categories, and the algorithm has too little information to decide based on the text. In the case of Doc, we just removed most of the documents belonging to this class and so increased the recall.

The improvement came with a price, though. We have excluded more than 900 documents, roughly half of the dataset. So, overall, we have actually found fewer documents in the smaller dataset! In some projects, it might be useful to let the model only decide in cases where it is quite "sure" and discard ambiguous cases (or classify them by hand). This often depends on the business requirements.

In this section, we have found a correlation between the predicting probability and the quality of results. However, we have not yet understood how the model predicts (i.e., which words are used). We will analyze this in the next section.

Blueprint: Measuring Feature Importance of Predictive Models

In this section, we want to find out which features were relevant for the model to find the correct class. Fortunately, our SVM class can tell us the necessary parameters (called *coefficients*):

```
svc.coef_
```

Out:

```
<15x6403 sparse matrix of type '<class 'numpy.float64'>'
    with 64451 stored elements in Compressed Sparse Row format>
```

6403 is the size of the vocabulary (check with `len(tfidf.get_feature_names())`, but where does the 15 originate from? That is a bit more complicated. Technically, the coefficients are organized in a matrix as each class competes against each other in a one-to-one way. As we have six classes and classes do not have to compete against themselves, there are 15 combinations (the binomial coefficient 6 over 2). The 15 coefficients are organized as described in Table 7-1.

Table 7-1. Coefficient layout for a multiclass SVC classifier

	APT	Core	Debug	Doc	Text	UI
APT	0	1	2	3	4	
Core		5	6	7	8	
Debug			9	10	11	
Doc				12	13	
Text					14	
UI						

Coefficient Structure Depends on Machine Learning Model

The coefficients might have a completely different organization if you use other classifiers. Even for SVM, using a nonlinear model (created by SGDClassifier) creates only one coefficient set per class. We will see some examples of this when we talk about ELI5.

The rows should be read first, so if we want to find out how the model distinguishes APT from Core, we should take index 0 of the coefficients. However, we are more interested in the difference of Core and UI, so we take index 8. In the first step, we sort the coefficients by their values and keep the indices, which are the vocabulary positions:

```
# coef_[8] yields a matrix, A[0] converts to array and takes first row
coef = svc.coef_[8].A[0]
vocabulary_positions = coef.argsort()
vocabulary = tfidf.get_feature_names()
```

Afterward, we now take the top positive and negative contributions:

```
top_words = 10
top_positive_coef = vocabulary_positions[-top_words:].tolist()
top_negative_coef = vocabulary_positions[:top_words].tolist()
```

Then we will aggregate this to a `DataFrame` to make it easier to display the results:

```
core_ui = pd.DataFrame([[vocabulary[c],
                       coef[c]] for c in top_positive_coef + top_negative_coef],
                       columns=["feature", "coefficient"]).sort_values("coefficient")
```

We would like to visualize the contributions of the coefficients to make it easy to understand. Positive values favor the Core component, and negative values prefer UI, as shown in Figure 7-1. To obtain this, we use the following:

```
core_ui.set_index("feature").plot.barh()
```

These results are quite easy to interpret. The SVM model has nicely learned that the words *compiler* and *ast* are specific to the Core component, whereas *wizard*, *ui*, and *dialog* are used to identify bugs in the UI component. It seems a quick fix is more popular in the UI, which emphasizes the long-term stability of the core.

We have just found the features that are important for the whole SVM model to choose between Core and UI. But this does not indicate which features are important to identify a bug that can be categorized as Core given any bug report. If we want to get these features for the Core component and consider the previous matrix, we need indices 5, 6, 7, and 8. With this strategy, we have ignored the difference between APT and Core. To take this into account, we need to subtract index 0:

```
c = svc.coef_
coef = (c[5] + c[6] + c[7] + c[8] - c[0]).A[0]
vocabulary_positions = coef.argsort()
```

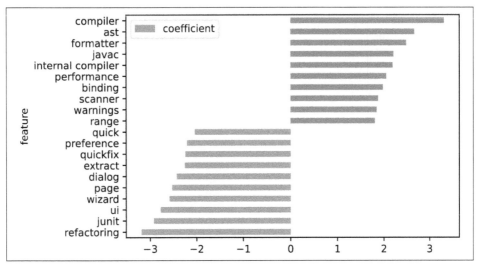

Figure 7-1. Word contributions to UI (negative) and Core (positive).

The rest of the code is almost identical to the previous code. We now extend the diagram to 20 words (Figure 7-2):

```
top_words = 20
top_positive_coef = vocabulary_positions[-top_words:].tolist()
top_negative_coef = vocabulary_positions[:top_words].tolist()
core = pd.DataFrame([[vocabulary[c], coef[c]]
                        for c in top_positive_coef + top_negative_coef],
                    columns=["feature", "coefficient"]).\
            sort_values("coefficient")
core.set_index("feature").plot.barh(figsize=(6, 10),
                color=[['red']*top_words + ['green']*top_words])
```

In the diagram, you can see a lot of words that the model uses to identify the Core component and in the lower part those that are used to primarily identify other components.

You can use the methods described in this blueprint to make the results of the SVM model transparent and explainable. In many projects, this has proved to be valuable as it takes away the "magic" and the subjectivity of machine learning.

This works quite well, but we do not yet know how sensitive the model is to changes in certain words. This is a more complicated question that we will try to answer in the next section.

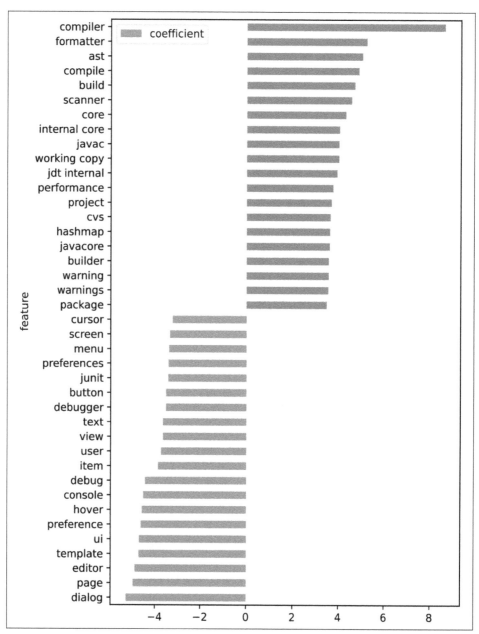

Figure 7-2. Coefficients favoring or opposing the Core component.

Blueprint: Using LIME to Explain the Classification Results

LIME is an acronym for "Local Interpretable Model-Agnostic Explanations" (*https://oreil.ly/D8cIN*) and is a popular framework for explainable machine learning. It was conceived at the University of Washington (*https://oreil.ly/Q8zly*) and is publicly available on GitHub (*https://oreil.ly/bErrv*).

Let's take a look at the defining features of LIME. It works *locally* by taking a look at each prediction separately. This is achieved by modifying the input vector to find the local components that the predictions are sensitive to.

Explainability Needs Computation Time

Running the explainer code can take considerable time. We tried to tailor the examples in a way that you don't have to wait for more than 10 minutes on normal computers. However, by increasing the sample size, this can easily take hours.

From the behavior in the vicinity of the vector, it will draw conclusions about which components are more or less important. LIME will visualize the contributions and explain the decision mechanism of the algorithm *for individual documents*.

LIME does not depend on a specific machine learning model and can be applied to a multitude of problems. Not every model qualifies; the model needs to predict the probabilities of the categories. Not all support vector machine models can do that. In addition, using complicated models where predictions take considerable time is not very practical in high-dimensional feature spaces like those common in text analytics. As LIME attempts to locally modify the feature vectors, it needs to perform a lot of predictions and in this case takes a long time to finish.

Finally, LIME will generate an explanation for the model on a per-sample basis and allow you to understand the model. You can use this to improve your model but also to explain how a classification works. Although the model will still be a black box, you will gain some knowledge of what might be going on in the box.

Let's get back to the classification problem of the previous section and try to find a LIME explanation for a few samples. As LIME wants text as input and classification probabilities as output, we arrange the vectorizer and classifier in a *pipeline*:

```
from sklearn.pipeline import make_pipeline
pipeline = make_pipeline(tfidf, best_model)
```

The pipeline should be able to make predictions if we give it some text, as done here:

```
pipeline.predict_proba(["compiler not working"])
```

Out:

```
array([[0.00240522, 0.95605684, 0.00440957, 0.00100242, 0.00971824,
        0.02640771]])
```

The classifier suggests with very high probability to put this in class 2, which is Core. So, our pipeline works exactly in the way we want it: we can give it text documents as parameters, and it returns the probabilities for the documents belonging to each category. Now it's time to turn on LIME by first importing the package (you might have to install the package first with `pip` or `conda`). Afterward, we will create an explainer, which is one of the central elements of LIME and is responsible for explaining individual predictions:

```
from lime.lime_text import LimeTextExplainer
explainer = LimeTextExplainer(class_names=class_names)
```

We check the `DataFrame` for classes that have been wrongly predicted in the following:

```
er[er["predicted"] != er["actual"]].head(5)
```

Out:

	index	text	actual	predicted	APT	Core	Debug	Doc	Text	UI
2	2	NPE in Delta processor while executing JDT/UI ...	Core	UI	0.003357	0.309548	0.046491	0.002031	0.012309	0.626265
15	15	Inserting a block of text in editor badly alig...	UI	Text	0.001576	0.063076	0.034610	0.003907	0.614473	0.282356
16	16	Differences when debugging identical objects W...	Debug	Core	0.002677	0.430862	0.313465	0.004193	0.055838	0.192965
20	20	Foreach template doesnt work for class members...	Core	UI	0.000880	0.044018	0.001019	0.000783	0.130766	0.822535
21	21	exchange left and right operands for compariso...	UI	Core	0.002669	0.467366	0.077252	0.003194	0.068749	0.380770

Take a look at the corresponding record (row 21 in our case):

```
id = 21
print('Document id: %d' % id)
```

```
print('Predicted class =', er.iloc[id]["predicted"])
print('True class: %s' % er.iloc[id]["actual"])
```

Out:

```
Document id: 21
Predicted class = Core
True class: UI
```

Now it's time for LIME to explain this to us!

```
exp = explainer.explain_instance(result.iloc[id]["text"],
        pipeline.predict_proba, num_features=10, labels=[1, 5])
print('Explanation for class %s' % class_names[1])
print('\n'.join(map(str, exp.as_list(label=1))))
print()
print('Explanation for class %s' % class_names[5])
print('\n'.join(map(str, exp.as_list(label=5))))
```

Out:

```
Explanation for class Core
('fix', -0.14306948642919184)
('Bug', 0.14077384623641856)
('following', 0.11150012169630388)
('comparison', 0.10122423126000728)
('Fix', -0.0884162779420967)
('right', 0.08315255286108318)
('semantics', 0.081438570054730141)
('changes', -0.079427782008582)
('left', 0.03188240169394561)
('good', -0.0027133756042246504)

Explanation for class UI
('fix', 0.15069083664026453)
('Bug', -0.14853911521141774)
('right', 0.11283930406785869)
('comparison', -0.10654654371478504)
('left', -0.10391669738035045)
('following', -0.1003931859632352)
('semantics', -0.056644426928774076)
('Fix', 0.05365037666619837)
('changes', 0.040806391076561165)
('good', 0.0401761761717476)
```

LIME shows us which words it thinks are in favor (positive) or against (negative) a certain class. This is quite easy and similar to what we have achieved in the SVM example. Even better, now it's independent of the model itself; it just needs to support predict_proba (which is also true for Random Forest and so on).

With LIME, you can extend the analysis to more classes and create a graphics representation of their specific words:

```
exp = explainer.explain_instance(result.iloc[id]["text"],
            pipeline.predict_proba, num_features=6, top_labels=3)
exp.show_in_notebook(text=False)
```

Out:

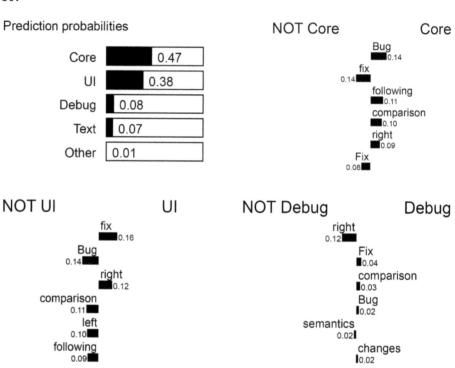

This looks intuitive and much more suitable for interpretation and even inclusion in a presentation. We can clearly see that *fix* and *right* are crucial for assigning the UI class and at the same time against Core. Bug, however, speaks for Core, as do *comparison* and *semantics*. Unfortunately, this is not what a human would accept as rules for classification; they seem too specific, and there is no abstraction. In other words, our model looks *overfitted*.

Improving Models

With this knowledge and the expertise of people familiar with the tickets, you could improve the model. We could, for example, ask if *Bug* is really specific to Core or if we'd better make it a stop word. It might also prove useful to convert everything to lowercase.

LIME can even support you in finding representative samples that help you interpret the model performance as a whole. The feature is called *submodular picks* and works like this:

```
from lime import submodular_pick
import numpy as np
np.random.seed(42)
lsm = submodular_pick.SubmodularPick(explainer, er["text"].values,
                                     pipeline.predict_proba,
                                     sample_size=100,
                                     num_features=20,
                                     num_exps_desired=5)
```

The individual "picks" can be visualized as shown previously in the notebook and are even more complete now with highlighting. We show only the first of the picks here:

```
lsm.explanations[0].show_in_notebook()
```

Out:

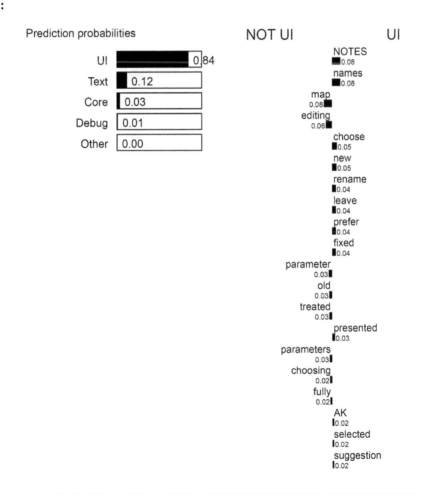

In the following case, we can interpret the results, but it does not look like the model learned the abstraction, which is again a sign of *overfitting*.

Text with highlighted words

Rename parameter - should leave existing parameter names for editing When performing a rename on parameters; a map of parameter names is; presented; which is nice.; However when choosing one to rename; its new name is emptied which is somewhat disruptive. I; would prefer having it fully selected; so as to easily choose to rename or discard; i.e. the; old name could be treated as a suggestion .; ; NOTES:; ; AK ; fixed

The LIME software module works for linear support vector machines in scikit-learn but not for those with more complex kernels. The graphical presentation is nice but is not directly suitable for presentations. Therefore, we will take a look at ELI5, which is an alternative implementation and tries to overcome these problems.

Blueprint: Using ELI5 to Explain the Classification Results

ELI5 ("Explain it to me like I'm 5") is another popular software library for machine learning explanation also using the LIME algorithm. As it can be used for nonlinear SVMs and has a different API, we will take a short look at it and show how to use it in our case.

ELI5 needs a model that has been trained with libsvm, which our SVC model from before unfortunately is not. Luckily, training an SVM is really fast, so we can create a new classifier with the same data, but with a libsvm-based model, and check its performance. You might remember the classification report from Chapter 6, which gives a good summary about the quality of the model:

```
from sklearn.linear_model import SGDClassifier
svm = SGDClassifier(loss='hinge', max_iter=1000, tol=1e-3, random_state=42)
svm.fit(X_train_tf, Y_train)
Y_pred_svm = svm.predict(X_test_tf)
print(classification_report(Y_test, Y_pred_svm))
```

Out:

	precision	recall	f1-score	support
APT	0.89	0.50	0.64	16
Core	0.77	0.78	0.77	546
Debug	0.85	0.84	0.85	302
Doc	0.75	0.25	0.38	12

```
       Text        0.62      0.59      0.60       236
         UI        0.76      0.79      0.78       699

   accuracy                            0.76      1811
  macro avg        0.77      0.62      0.67      1811
weighted avg       0.76      0.76      0.76      1811
```

Taking a look at the last line, this is roughly as good as what we have achieved with SVC. Thus, it makes sense to explain it! Using ELI5, finding explanations for this model is easy:

```
import eli5
eli5.show_weights(svm, top=10, vec=tfidf, target_names=class_names)
```

y=APT top features		y=Core top features		y=Debug top features		y=Doc top features		y=Text top features		y=UI top features	
Weight[?]	Feature	Weight[?]	Feature	Weight[?]	Feature	Weight[?]	Feature	Weight[?]	Feature	Weight[?]	Feature
+3.972	apt	+4.208	compiler	+6.390	debug	+1.732	htm	+3.196	javadoc	+4.683	junit
+2.497	factory path	+3.115	ast	+4.827	breakpoint	+1.700	guide		view	+4.326	refactoring
+1.844	processor	+2.829	javac	+3.950	debugger	+1.092	help	+2.621	folded	+3.222	quickfix
+1.435	factory	+2.460	formatter	+3.921	console	+1.052	whats	+2.543	dictionary	+3.148	wizard
+1.229	jdt apt	+2.428	compile	+3.206	variables	+0.927	jdt doc	+2.501	jface text	+2.947	working set
+1.071	reconcile	+2.427	build		view	+0.911	tutorial	+2.490	breadcrumb	+2.934	refactor
+0.969	testing	+2.418	internal	+3.140	internal	+0.881	jdt	+2.474	hover	+2.909	extract
+0.884	annotation		compiler		debug	+0.880	developer	+2.330	workaround	+2.857	organize
	processing	+2.365	working	+3.099	breakpoints	...822 more positive...		+2.290	template	...3028 more positive...	
...998 more positive...			copy	+2.841	step	...2251 more negative...		...2674 more positive...		-3.118	breakpoint
...2861 more negative...		...3162 more positive...		+2.804	debug ui	-1.255	apt	...3567 more negative...		-4.042	debug
-0.881	jdt core	...3210 more negative...		+2.783	launching	-1.385	<BIAS>	-2.296	notes		
-1.329	<BIAS>	-2.578	wizard	...2500 more positive...				-2.355	debug		
		-2.893	refactoring	...3750 more negative...							

The positive features (i.e., words) are shown in green. More intense shades of green mean a larger contribution of the word to the corresponding class. The red colors work exactly opposite: words appearing in red "repel" the classes (for example, "refactoring" in the lower part of the second row strongly rejects class Core). <BIAS> is a special case and contains the so-called *intercept*, i.e., systematic failures of the model.

As you can see, we now get weights for the individual classes. This is due to the non-linear SVM model working differently in multiclass scenarios compared to SVC. Each class is "scored" on its own, and there is no competition. At first sight, the words look very plausible.

ELI5 can also explain individual observations:

```
eli5.show_prediction(svm, X_test.iloc[21], vec=tfidf, target_names=class_names)
```

y=APT (score **-1.603**) top features

Contribution[?]	Feature
-0.273	Highlighted in text (sum)
-1.329	<BIAS>

exchange left and right operands for comparison operators changes semantics fix for bug 149803 was not good.; ; the right fix should do the following; if --> if --> if ; if ; if

y=Core (score **-0.342**) top features

Contribution[?]	Feature
+0.530	Highlighted in text (sum)
-0.872	<BIAS>

exchange left and right operands for comparison operators changes semantics fix for bug 149803 was not good.; ; the right fix should do the following; if --> if --> if ; if ; if

y=Debug (score **-0.835**) top features

Contribution[?]	Feature
+0.017	Highlighted in text (sum)
-0.852	<BIAS>

exchange left and right operands for comparison operators changes semantics fix for bug 149803 was not good.; ; the right fix should do the following; if --> if --> if ; if ; if

y=Doc (score **-1.434**) top features

Contribution[?]	Feature
-0.050	Highlighted in text (sum)
-1.385	<BIAS>

exchange left and right operands for comparison operators changes semantics fix for bug 149803 was not good.; ; the right fix should do the following; if --> if --> if ; if ; if

y=Text (score **-1.221**) top features

Contribution[?]	Feature
-0.126	Highlighted in text (sum)
-1.095	<BIAS>

exchange left and right operands for comparison operators changes semantics fix for bug 149803 was not good.; ; the right fix should do the following; if --> if --> if ; if ; if

y=UI (score **-0.838**) top features

Contribution[?]	Feature
-0.363	<BIAS>
-0.476	Highlighted in text (sum)

exchange left and right operands for comparison operators changes semantics fix for bug 149803 was not good.; ; the right fix should do the following; if --> if --> if ; if ; if

This is a nice visualization for understanding which words contribute to the algorithm deciding the categories. Compared to the original LIME package, with ELI5 you need considerably less code, and you can use ELI5 for nonlinear SVM models. Depending on your classifier and use case, you might decide on LIME or ELI5. Due to the same method, the results should be comparable (if not identical).

Work in Progress

ELI5 is still under heavy development, and you might experience difficulties with new scikit-learn versions. We have used ELI5 version 0.10.1 in this chapter.

ELI5 is an easy-to-use software library for understanding and visualizing the decision logic of classifiers, but it also suffers from the shortcomings of the underlying LIME algorithm, such as explainability by example only. To make the black-box classification more transparent, it would be insightful to gain access to the "rules" that a model uses. That was the motivation for the group at Washington University to create a follow-up project called Anchor.

Blueprint: Using Anchor to Explain the Classification Results

Like LIME, Anchor (*https://oreil.ly/qSDMl*) is model agnostic and works for any black-box model. As a tool for explanations, it creates rules, the so-called *anchors*, which explain the behavior of the model. Reading these rules, you will not only be able to explain a prediction of the model but also predict in the same way as the model has learned to.

Compared to LIME, Anchor has considerable advantages for better explaining the models with the rules. However, the software itself is quite new and still a work in progress. Not all examples were working for us, so we chose a selection of methods that help in interpreting the classification model.

Using the Distribution with Masked Words

There are different ways Anchor can be used. We start with the so-called *unknown* distribution. Anchor will explain how a model makes a decision by replacing existing tokens that are supposed to be unimportant for the prediction with the word *unknown*.

Again, we will use the document with an ID of 21. In this case, the classifier has the difficult task of choosing between two categories that have roughly the same probability. This should make it an interesting example for studying.

To create (semantic) variance in the text, Anchor uses spaCy's word vectors and needs a spaCy model that includes these vectors, like en_core_web_lg.

As a prerequisite, you should therefore install anchor-exp and spacy (using either conda or pip) and load the model with the following:

```
python -m spacy download en_core_web_lg
```

In the first step, we can then instantiate our explainer. The explainer has some probabilistic elements, so it's better to restart the random-number generator at the same time:

```
np.random.seed(42)
explainer_unk = anchor_text.AnchorText(nlp, class_names, \
                use_unk_distribution=True)
```

Let's check the predicted results and alternatives and compare them to the ground truth. predicted_class_ids contains the indices of the predicted classes with decreasing probability, so the element 0 is the prediction, and element 1 is its closest competitor:

```
text = er.iloc[21]["text"]
actual = er.iloc[21]["actual"]
# we want the class with the highest probability and must invert the order
predicted_class_ids = np.argsort(pipeline.predict_proba([text])[0])[::-1]
pred = explainer_unk.class_names[predicted_class_ids[0]]
alternative = explainer_unk.class_names[predicted_class_ids[1]]
print(f'predicted {pred}, alternative {alternative}, actual {actual}')
```

Out:

```
predicted Core, alternative UI, actual UI
```

In the next step, we will let the algorithm find the rules for the predictions. The parameters are the same as for LIME earlier:

```
exp_unk = explainer_unk.explain_instance(text, pipeline.predict, threshold=0.95)
```

The calculation can take up to 60 minutes depending on the speed of your CPU.

Everything is now contained in the explainer, so we can query the explainer to find out about the inner workings of the model:

```
print(f'Rule: {" AND ".join(exp_unk.names())}')
print(f'Precision: {exp_unk.precision()}')
```

Out:

```
Rule: following AND comparison AND Bug AND semantics AND for
Precision: 0.9865771812080537
```

So, the rule tells us that an occurrence of the words *following* and *comparison* combined with *Bug* and *semantic* leads to a prediction of "Core" with more than 98% precision, which is unfortunately wrong. We can now also find typical examples that the model would classify as Core:

```
print(f'Made-up examples where anchor rule matches and model predicts {pred}\n')
print('\n'.join([x[0] for x in exp_unk.examples(only_same_prediction=True)]))
```

The UNK token shown next stands for "unknown" and means that the word at the corresponding position is not important:

```
Made-up examples where anchor rule matches and model predicts Core

UNK left UNK UNK UNK UNK comparison operators UNK semantics Fix for Bug UNK UNK
exchange left UNK UNK operands UNK comparison operators changes semantics Fix fo
exchange UNK and UNK operands UNK comparison UNK UNK semantics UNK for Bug UNK U
exchange UNK and right UNK for comparison UNK UNK semantics UNK for Bug 149803 U
UNK left UNK UNK operands UNK comparison UNK changes semantics UNK for Bug 14980
exchange left UNK right UNK UNK comparison UNK changes semantics Fix for Bug UNK
UNK UNK and right operands for comparison operators UNK semantics Fix for Bug 14
UNK left and right operands UNK comparison operators changes semantics UNK for B
exchange left UNK UNK operands UNK comparison operators UNK semantics UNK for Bu
UNK UNK UNK UNK operands for comparison operators changes semantics Fix for Bug
```

We can also ask for examples where the rule matches but the model predicts the wrong class:

```
print(f'Made-up examples where anchor rule matches and model predicts \
    {alternative}\n')
print('\n'.join([x[0] for x in exp_unk.examples(partial_index=0, \
    only_different_prediction=True)]))
```

Out:

```
Made-up examples where anchor rule matches and model predicts UI

exchange left and right UNK for UNK UNK UNK UNK Fix for UNK 149803 was not UNK .
exchange left UNK UNK UNK for UNK UNK UNK semantics Fix for Bug 149803 UNK not U
exchange left UNK UNK operands for comparison operators UNK UNK Fix UNK Bug 1498
exchange left UNK right operands UNK comparison UNK UNK UNK Fix for UNK UNK UNK U
exchange left and right operands UNK UNK operators UNK UNK Fix UNK UNK UNK UNK U
UNK UNK and UNK UNK UNK comparison UNK UNK UNK Fix for UNK UNK was not good UNK
exchange left and UNK UNK UNK UNK operators UNK UNK Fix UNK Bug 149803 was not U
exchange left and right UNK UNK UNK operators UNK UNK UNK for Bug 149803 UNK UNK
exchange left UNK right UNK for UNK operators changes UNK Fix UNK UNK UNK was no
UNK left UNK UNK operands UNK UNK operators changes UNK UNK for UNK 149803 was n
```

To be honest, this is not a good result for the model. We would have expected that the underlying rules learned by the models would be sensitive to words specific to the different components. However, there is no obvious reason why *following* and *Bug* would be specific to Core. More or less these are generic words that are not very characteristic of either of the categories.

The UNK tokens are a bit misleading. Even if they are not important in this sample, they might be replaced by other, realistic words that would influence the decision of the algorithm. Anchor can also help us illustrate that.

Working with Real Words

By substituting `use_unk_distribution=False` in the original constructor of the explainer, we can tell Anchor to use real words (similar to the one it is substituting by using the word vectors from spaCy) and observe the behavior of the model:

```
np.random.seed(42)
explainer_no_unk = anchor_text.AnchorText(nlp, class_names,
                    use_unk_distribution=False, use_bert=False)
exp_no_unk = explainer_no_unk.explain_instance(text, pipeline.predict,
            threshold=0.95)
print(f'Rule: {" AND ".join(exp_no_unk.names())}')
print(f'Precision: {exp_no_unk.precision()}')
```

Out:

```
Rule: following AND Bug AND comparison AND semantics AND left AND right
Precision: 0.9601990049751243
```

The rules are a bit different from the earlier unknown distribution. It seems that some of the words have become a bit more specific for the Core, like *left* and *right*, whereas other words like *for* have vanished.

Let's also ask Anchor to generate alternative texts that would also be (wrongly) classified as Core as the previous rule applies:

```
Examples where anchor applies and model predicts Core:

exchange left and right suffixes for comparison operators affects semantics NEED
exchange left and right operands for comparison operators depends semantics UPDA
exchange left and right operands for comparison operators indicates semantics so
exchange left and right operands for comparison operators changes semantics Firm
exchange left and right operands into comparison dispatchers changes semantics F
exchange left and right operands with comparison operators changes semantics Fix
exchange left and right operands beyond comparison operators changes semantics M
exchange left and right operands though comparison representatives changes seman
exchange left and right operands before comparison operators depends semantics M
exchange left and right operands as comparison operators changes semantics THING
```

Some words have changed and have not affected the result of the classification. In some cases, it is only prepositions, and normally this should not have an effect on the results. However, *operators* can also be replaced by *dispatchers* without affecting the results. Anchor shows you that it is stable against these modifications.

Compare the previous results to those where the model would (correctly) predict "UI." Again, the difference affects single words like *changes*, *metaphors*, and so on, which definitely carry more meaning than the smaller modifications in the previous example, but it is highly unlikely that you as a human would interpret these words as signals for a different category:

```
Examples where anchor applies and model predicts UI:

exchange left and good operands for comparison operators changes metaphors Fix i
exchange landed and right operands for comparison supervisors changes derivation
exchange left and happy operands for correlation operators changes equivalences
exchange left and right operands for scenario operators changes paradigms Fix be
exchange left and right operands for trade customers occurs semantics Fix as BoT
exchange did and right operands than consumer operators changes analogies Instal
exchange left and few operands for reason operators depends semantics Fix for Bu
exchange left and right operands for percentage operators changes semantics MESS
exchange left and right pathnames after comparison operators depends fallacies F
exchange left and right operands of selection operators changes descriptors Fix
```

Anchor also has an intuitive way of showing the results with the important words highlighted in the notebook and also includes the rules it has calculated:[2]

```
exp_unk.show_in_notebook()
```

Out:

Text with highlighted words

exchange left and right operands for comparison operators changes semantics Fix for Bug 149803 was not good.; ; The right fix should do the following; if --> if --> if ; if ; if
A.I. prediction
● Core
Explanation of A.I. prediction
If ALL of these words are in the text:

comparison	Bug	following	semantics	left	right

The A.I. will predict Core 95.8% of the time

As it's quite likely that you are also familiar with software development, it would be hard to determine the correct category from the rules alone. In other words, this means the model seems to be quite fragile when trained with the corpus. The "correct" category can probably be determined only by a project contributor who has a lot of context knowledge (which we will revisit later in Chapter 11). So, finding that a classifier works does not necessarily mean that it has really learned in a way that is transparent for us.

To summarize this section, Anchor is quite interesting. The authors of Anchor did not choose version number 0.0.1 by chance; the program is still in its infancy. During

---

2 We had a hard time getting this to work, as it was suited only for numerical categories. We plan to make some pull requests to get the upstream working for textual categories as well.

our experiments, we have seen quite a few quirks, and to make it work in production, a lot of things have to be improved. Conceptually, however, it is already really convincing for explaining single predictions and making models transparent. The calculated rules especially are almost unique and cannot be created by any other solution.

Closing Remarks

Using the techniques presented in this chapter will help make your model predictions more transparent.

From a technical perspective, this transparency can be a great help as it supports you in choosing among competing models or improving your feature models. The techniques presented in this chapter give you insights into the "inner workings" of a model and help to detect and improve untrustworthy models.

Considering the business perspective, explainability is a great selling proposition for projects. It is much easier to talk about models and present them if you don't exclusively pursue the black-box model but rather make your models transparent. Recent articles in Forbes (*https://oreil.ly/Xcfjx*) and VentureBeat (*https://oreil.ly/SIa-R*) have focused on this interesting development. Being able to "trust" a model will be more and more important when you want to build trustable machine learning solutions.

Explainable AI is a young field. We can expect to see tremendous progress, better algorithms, and improved tooling in the future.

For most of the book, machine learning methods have worked nicely as black-box models. This is fine, as long as the results are consistent and we don't have to justify the models. If either is challenged, as is becoming more common, then the time for explainable AI has arrived.

## CHAPTER 8

Unsupervised Methods: Topic Modeling and Clustering

When working with a large number of documents, one of the first questions you want to ask without reading all of them is "What are they talking about?" You are interested in the general topics of the documents, i.e., which (ideally semantic) words are often used together.

Topic modeling tries to solve that challenge by using statistical techniques for finding out topics from a corpus of documents. Depending on your vectorization (see Chapter 5), you might find different kinds of topics. Topics consist of a probability distribution of features (words, n-grams, etc.).

Topics normally overlap with each other; they are not clearly separated. The same is true for documents: it is not possible to assign a document uniquely to a single topic; a document always contains a mixture of different topics. The aim of topic modeling is not primarily to assign a topic to an arbitrary document but to find the global structure of the corpus.

Often, a set of documents has an explicit structure that is given by categories, keywords, and so on. If we want to take a look at the organic composition of the corpus, then topic modeling will help a lot to uncover the latent structure.

Topic modeling has been known for a long time and has gained immense popularity during the last 15 years, mainly due to the invention of LDA,[1] a stochastic method for discovering topics. LDA is flexible and allows many modifications. However, it is not the only method for topic modeling (although you might believe this by looking at

---

1 Blei, David M., et al. "Latent Dirichlet Allocation." *Journal of Machine Learning Research* 3 (4–5): 993–1022. doi:10.1162/jmlr.2003.3.4-5.993.

the literature, much of which is biased toward LDA). Conceptually simpler methods are non-negative matrix factorization, singular-value decomposition (sometimes called *LSI*), and a few others.

What You'll Learn and What We'll Build

In this chapter, we will take an in-depth look at the various methods of topic modeling, try to find differences and similarities between the methods, and run them on the same use case. Depending on your requirements, it might also be a good idea to not only try a single method but compare the results of a few.

After studying this chapter, you will know the different methods of topic modeling and their specific advantages and drawbacks. You will understand how topic modeling can be applied not only to find topics but also to create quick summaries of document corpora. You will learn about the importance of choosing the correct granularity of entities for calculating topic models. You have experimented with many parameters to find the optimal topic model. You are able to judge the quality of the resulting topic models by quantitative methods and numbers.

Our Dataset: UN General Debates

Our use case is to semantically analyze the corpus of the UN general debates. You might know this dataset from the earlier chapter about text statistics.

This time we are more interested in the meaning and in the semantic content of the speeches and how we can arrange them topically. We want to know what the speakers are talking about and answer questions like these: Is there a structure in the document corpus? What are the topics? Which of them is most prominent? Does this change over time?

Checking Statistics of the Corpus

Before starting with topic modeling, it is always a good idea to check the statistics of the underlying text corpus. Depending on the results of this analysis, you will often choose to analyze different entities, e.g., documents, sections, or paragraphs of text.

We are not so much interested in authors and additional information, so it's enough to work with one of the supplied *CSV* files:

```
import pandas as pd
debates = pd.read_csv("un-general-debates.csv")
debates.info()
```

Out:

```
<class 'pandas.core.frame.DataFrame'>
RangeIndex: 7507 entries, 0 to 7506
Data columns (total 4 columns):
session    7507 non-null int64
year       7507 non-null int64
country    7507 non-null object
text       7507 non-null object
dtypes: int64(2), object(2)
memory usage: 234.7+ KB
```

The result looks fine. There are no null values in the text column; we might use years and countries later, and they also have only non-null values.

The speeches are quite long and cover a lot of topics as each country is allowed only to deliver a single speech per year. Different parts of the speeches are almost always separated by paragraphs. Unfortunately, the dataset has some formatting issues. Compare the text of two selected speeches:

```
print(repr(df.iloc[2666]["text"][0:200]))
print(repr(df.iloc[4729]["text"][0:200]))
```

Out:

```
'\ufeffIt is indeed a pleasure for me and the members of my delegation to
extend to Ambassador Garba our sincere congratulations on his election to the
presidency of the forty-fourth session of the General '
'\ufeffOn behalf of the State of Kuwait, it\ngives me pleasure to congratulate
Mr. Han Seung-soo,\nand his friendly country, the Republic of Korea, on
his\nelection as President of the fifty-sixth session of t'
```

As you can see, in some speeches the newline character is used to separate paragraphs. In the transcription of other speeches, a newline is used to separate lines. To recover the paragraphs, we therefore cannot just split at newlines. It turns out that splitting at stops, exclamation points, or question marks occurring at line ends works well enough. We ignore spaces after the stops:

```
import re
df["paragraphs"] = df["text"].map(lambda text: re.split('[.?!]\s*\n', text))
df["number_of_paragraphs"] = df["paragraphs"].map(len)
```

From the analysis in Chapter 2, we already know that the number of speeches per year does not change much. Is this also true for the number of paragraphs?

```
%matplotlib inline
debates.groupby('year').agg({'number_of_paragraphs': 'mean'}).plot.bar()
```

Out:

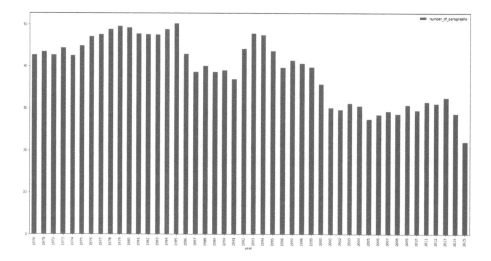

The average number of paragraphs has dropped considerably over time. We would have expected that, as the number of speakers per year increased and the total time for speeches is limited.

Apart from that, the statistical analysis shows no systematic problems with the dataset. The corpus is still quite up-to-date; there is no missing data for any year. We can now safely start with uncovering the latent structure and detect topics.

Preparations

Topic modeling is a machine learning method and needs vectorized data. All topic modeling methods start with the document-term matrix. Recalling the meaning of this matrix (which was introduced in Chapter 4), its elements are word frequencies (or often scaled as TF-IDF weights) of the words (columns) in the corresponding documents (rows). The matrix is sparse, as most documents contain only a small fraction of the vocabulary.

Let's calculate the TF-IDF matrix both for the speeches and for the paragraphs of the speeches. First, we have to import the necessary packages from scikit-learn. We start with a naive approach and use the standard spaCy stop words:

```
from sklearn.feature_extraction.text import TfidfVectorizer
from spacy.lang.en.stop_words import STOP_WORDS as stopwords
```

Calculating the document-term matrix for the speeches is easy; we also include bigrams:

```
tfidf_text = TfidfVectorizer(stop_words=stopwords, min_df=5, max_df=0.7)
vectors_text = tfidf_text.fit_transform(debates['text'])
vectors_text.shape
```

Out:

```
(7507, 24611)
```

For the paragraphs, it's a bit more complicated as we have to flatten the list first. In the same step, we omit empty paragraphs:

```
# flatten the paragraphs keeping the years
paragraph_df = pd.DataFrame([{ "text": paragraph, "year": year }
                    for paragraphs, year in \
                    zip(df["paragraphs"], df["year"])
                        for paragraph in paragraphs if paragraph])

tfidf_para_vectorizer = TfidfVectorizer(stop_words=stopwords, min_df=5,
                                    max_df=0.7)
tfidf_para_vectors = tfidf_para_vectorizer.fit_transform(paragraph_df["text"])
tfidf_para_vectors.shape
```

Out:

```
(282210, 25165)
```

Of course, the paragraph matrix has many more rows. The number of columns (words) is also different because min_df and max_df have an effect in selecting features, as the number of documents has changed.

Nonnegative Matrix Factorization (NMF)

The conceptually easiest way to find a latent structure in the document corpus is the factorization of the document-term matrix. Fortunately, the document-term matrix has only positive-value elements; therefore, we can use methods from linear algebra that allow us to represent the matrix as the product of two other nonnegative matrices (*https://oreil.ly/JVpFA*). Conventionally, the original matrix is called *V*, and the factors are *W* and *H*:

$$V \approx W \cdot H$$

Or we can represent it graphically (visualizing the dimensions necessary for matrix multiplication), as in Figure 8-1.

Depending on the dimensions, the factorization can be performed exactly. But as this is so much more computationally expensive, an approximate factorization is sufficient.

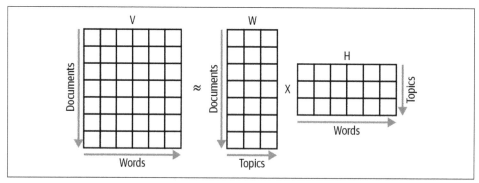

Figure 8-1. Schematic nonnegative matrix factorization; the original matrix V is decomposed into W and H.

In the context of text analytics, both W and H have an interpretation. The matrix W has the same number of rows as the document-term matrix and therefore maps documents to topics (document-topic matrix). H has the same number of columns as features, so it shows how the topics are constituted of features (topic-feature matrix). The number of topics (the columns of W and the rows of H) can be chosen arbitrarily. The smaller this number, the less exact the factorization.

Blueprint: Creating a Topic Model Using NMF for Documents

It's really easy to perform this decomposition for speeches in scikit-learn. As (almost) all topic models need the number of topics as a parameter, we arbitrarily choose 10 topics (which will later turn out to be a good choice):

```
from sklearn.decomposition import NMF

nmf_text_model = NMF(n_components=10, random_state=42)
W_text_matrix = nmf_text_model.fit_transform(tfidf_text_vectors)
H_text_matrix = nmf_text_model.components_
```

Similar to the TfidfVectorizer, NMF also has a fit_transform method that returns one of the positive factor matrices. The other factor can be accessed by the compo nents_ member variable of the NMF class.

Topics are word distributions. We are now going to analyze this distribution and see whether we can find an interpretation of the topics. Taking a look at Figure 8-1, we need to consider the H matrix and find the index of the largest values in each row (topic) that we then use as a lookup index in the vocabulary. As this is helpful for all topic models, we define a function for outputting a summary:

```
def display_topics(model, features, no_top_words=5):
    for topic, word_vector in enumerate(model.components_):
```

```
total = word_vector.sum()
largest = word_vector.argsort()[::-1] # invert sort order
print("\nTopic %02d" % topic)
for i in range(0, no_top_words):
    print("  %s (%2.2f)" % (features[largest[i]],
        word_vector[largest[i]]*100.0/total))
```

Calling this function, we get a nice summary of the topics that NMF detected in the speeches (the numbers are the percentage contributions of the words to the respective topic):

```
display_topics(nmf_text_model, tfidf_text_vectorizer.get_feature_names())
```

Out:

Topic 00	Topic 01	Topic 02	Topic 03	Topic 04
co (0.79)	terrorism (0.38)	africa (1.15)	arab (1.02)	american (0.33)
operation (0.65)	challenges (0.32)	african (0.82)	israel (0.89)	america (0.31)
disarmament (0.36)	sustainable (0.30)	south (0.63)	palestinian (0.60)	latin (0.31)
nuclear (0.34)	millennium (0.29)	namibia (0.36)	lebanon (0.54)	panama (0.21)
relations (0.25)	reform (0.28)	delegation (0.30)	israeli (0.54)	bolivia (0.21)

Topic 05	Topic 06	Topic 07	Topic 08	Topic 09
pacific (1.55)	soviet (0.81)	guinea (4.26)	european (0.61)	caribbean (0.98)
islands (1.23)	republic (0.78)	equatorial (1.75)	europe (0.44)	small (0.66)
solomon (0.86)	nuclear (0.68)	bissau (1.53)	cooperation (0.39)	bahamas (0.63)
island (0.82)	viet (0.64)	papua (1.47)	bosnia (0.34)	saint (0.63)
fiji (0.71)	socialist (0.63)	republic (0.57)	herzegovina (0.30)	barbados (0.61)

Topic 00 and Topic 01 look really promising as people are talking about nuclear disarmament and terrorism. These are definitely real topics in the UN general debates.

The subsequent topics, however, are more or less focused on different regions of the world. This is due to speakers mentioning primarily their own country and neighboring countries. This is especially evident in Topic 03, which reflects the conflict in the Middle East.

It's also interesting to take a look at the percentages with which the words contribute to the topics. Due to the large number of words, the individual contributions are quite small, except for *guinea* in Topic 07. As we will see later, the percentages of the words within a topic are a good indication for the quality of the topic model. If the percentage within a topic is rapidly decreasing, the topic is well-defined, whereas slowly decreasing word probabilities indicate a less-pronounced topic. It's much more difficult to intuitively find out how well the topics are separated; we will take a look at that later.

It would be interesting to find out how "big" the topics are, i.e., how many documents could be assigned mainly to each topic. This can be calculated using the document-topic matrix and summing the individual topic contributions over all documents.

Normalizing them with the total sum and multiplying by 100 gives a percentage value:

```
W_text_matrix.sum(axis=0)/W_text_matrix.sum()*100.0
```

`Out:`

```
array([11.13926287, 17.07197914, 13.64509781, 10.18184685, 11.43081404,
        5.94072639,  7.89602474,  4.17282682, 11.83871081,  6.68271054])
```

We can easily see that there are smaller and larger topics but basically no outliers. Having an even distribution is a quality indicator. If your topic models have, for example, one or two large topics compared to all the others, you should probably adjust the number of topics.

In the next section, we will use the paragraphs of the speeches as entities for topic modeling and try to find out if that improves the topics.

Blueprint: Creating a Topic Model for Paragraphs Using NMF

In UN general debates, as in many other texts, different topics are often mixed, and it is hard for the topic modeling algorithm to find a common topic of an individual speech. Especially in longer texts, it happens quite often that documents do not cover just one but several topics. How can we deal with that? One idea is to find smaller entities in the documents that are more coherent from a topic perspective.

In our corpus, paragraphs are a natural subdivision of speeches, and we can assume that the speakers try to stick to one topic within one paragraph. In many documents, paragraphs are a good candidate (if they can be identified as such), and we have already prepared the corresponding TF-IDF vectors. Let's try to calculate their topic models:

```
nmf_para_model = NMF(n_components=10, random_state=42)
W_para_matrix = nmf_para_model.fit_transform(tfidf_para_vectors)
H_para_matrix = nmf_para_model.components_
```

Our `display_topics` function developed earlier can be used to find the content of the topics:

```
display_topics(nmf_para_model, tfidf_para_vectorizer.get_feature_names())
```

```
Out:
```

Topic 00	Topic 01	Topic 02	Topic 03	Topic 04
nations (5.63)	general (2.87)	countries (4.44)	people (1.36)	nuclear (4.93)
united (5.52)	session (2.83)	developing (2.49)	peace (1.34)	weapons (3.27)
organization (1.27)	assembly (2.81)	economic (1.49)	east (1.28)	disarmament (2.01)
states (1.03)	mr (1.98)	developed (1.35)	middle (1.17)	treaty (1.70)
charter (0.93)	president (1.81)	trade (0.92)	palestinian (1.14)	proliferation (1.46)

Topic 05	Topic 06	Topic 07	Topic 08	Topic 09
rights (6.49)	africa (3.83)	security (6.13)	international (2.05)	development (4.47)
human (6.18)	south (3.32)	council (5.88)	world (1.50)	sustainable (1.18)
respect (1.15)	african (1.70)	permanent (1.50)	community (0.92)	economic (1.07)
fundamental (0.86)	namibia (1.38)	reform (1.48)	new (0.77)	social (1.00)
universal (0.82)	apartheid (1.19)	peace (1.30)	peace (0.67)	goals (0.93)

Compared to the previous results for topic modeling speeches, we have almost lost all countries or regions except for South Africa and the Middle East. These are due to the regional conflicts that sparked interest in other parts of the world. Topics in the paragraphs like "Human rights," "international relations," "developing countries," "nuclear weapons," "security council," "world peace," and "sustainable development" (the last one probably occurring only lately) look much more reasonable compared to the topics of the speeches. Taking a look at the percentage values of the words, we can observe that they are dropping much faster, and the topics are more pronounced.

Latent Semantic Analysis/Indexing

Another algorithm for performing topic modeling is based on the so-called singular value decomposition (SVD), another method from linear algebra.

Graphically, it is possible to conceive SVD as rearranging documents and words in a way to uncover a block structure in the document-term matrix. There is a nice visualization of that process at topicmodels.info (*https://oreil.ly/yJnWL*). Figure 8-2 shows the start of the document-term matrix and the resulting block diagonal form.

Making use of the principal axis theorem, orthogonal $n \times n$ matrices have an eigenvalue decomposition. Unfortunately, we do not have orthogonal square document-term matrices (except for rare cases). Therefore, we need a generalization called *singular value decomposition*. In its most general form, the theorem states that any $m \times n$ matrix $\mathbf{V}$ can be decomposed as follows:

$$V = U \cdot \Sigma \cdot V^\star$$

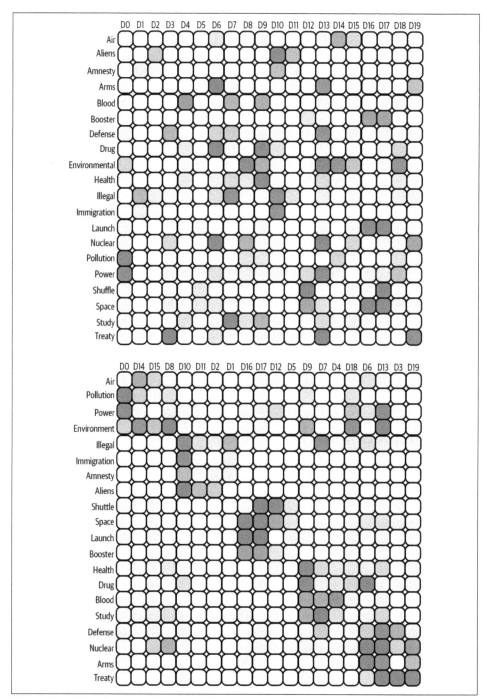

Figure 8-2. Visualization of topic modeling with SVD.

U is a unitary $m \times m$ matrix, V^* is an $n \times n$ matrix, and Σ is an $m \times n$ diagonal matrix containing the singular values. There are exact solutions for this equation, but as they take a lot of time and computational effort to find, we are looking for approximate solutions that can be found quickly. The approximation works by only considering the largest singular values. This leads to Σ becoming a $t \times t$ matrix; in turn, U has $m \times t$ and $V^* t \times n$ dimensions. Graphically, this is similar to the nonnegative matrix factorization, as shown in Figure 8-3.

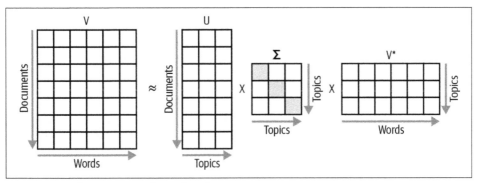

Figure 8-3. Schematic singular value decomposition.

The singular values are the diagonal elements of Σ. The document-topic relations are included in U, whereas the word-to-topic mapping is represented by V^*. Note that neither the elements of U nor the elements of V^* are guaranteed to be positive. The relative sizes of the contributions will still be interpretable, but the probability explanation is no longer valid.

Blueprint: Creating a Topic Model for Paragraphs with SVD

In scikit-learn the interface to SVD is identical to that of NMF. This time we start directly with the paragraphs:

```
from sklearn.decomposition import TruncatedSVD

svd_para_model = TruncatedSVD(n_components = 10, random_state=42)
W_svd_para_matrix = svd_para_model.fit_transform(tfidf_para_vectors)
H_svd_para_matrix = svd_para_model.components_
```

Our previously defined function for evaluating the topic model can also be used:

```
display_topics(svd_para_model, tfidf_para_vectorizer.get_feature_names())
```

Out:

Topic 00	Topic 01	Topic 02	Topic 03	Topic 04
nations (0.67)	general (14.04)	countries (19.15)	nations (4.41)	nuclear (21.13)
united (0.65)	assembly (13.09)	development (14.61)	united (4.06)	weapons (14.01)
international (0.58)	session (12.94)	economic (13.91)	development (0.95)	disarmament (9.02)
peace (0.46)	mr (10.02)	developing (13.00)	organization (0.84)	treaty (7.23)
world (0.46)	president (8.59)	session (10.29)	charter (0.80)	proliferation (6.31)
Topic 05	**Topic 06**	**Topic 07**	**Topic 08**	**Topic 09**
rights (29.50)	africa (8.73)	council (14.96)	world (48.49)	development (63.98)
human (28.81)	south (8.24)	security (13.38)	international (41.03)	sustainable (20.78)
nuclear (9.20)	united (3.91)	africa (8.50)	peace (32.98)	peace (20.74)
weapons (6.42)	african (3.71)	south (6.11)	community (23.27)	goals (15.92)
respect (4.98)	nations (3.41)	african (3.94)	africa (22.00)	africa (15.61)

Most of the resulting topics are surprisingly similar to those of the nonnegative matrix factorization. However, the Middle East conflict does not appear as a separate topic this time. As the topic-word mappings can also have negative values, the normalization varies from topic to topic. Only the relative sizes of the words constituting the topics are relevant.

Don't worry about the negative percentages. These arise as SVD does not guarantee positive values in W, so contributions of individual words might be negative. This means that words appearing in documents "reject" the corresponding topic.

If we want to determine the sizes of the topics, we now have to take a look at the singular values of the decomposition:

```
svd_para.singular_values_
```

Out:

```
array([68.21400653, 39.20120165, 36.36831431, 33.44682727, 31.76183677,
       30.59557993, 29.14061799, 27.40264054, 26.85684195, 25.90408013])
```

The sizes of the topics also correspond quite nicely with the ones from the NMF method for the paragraphs.

Both NMF and SVF have used the document-term matrix (with TF-IDF transformations applied) as a basis for the topic decomposition. Also, the dimensions of the *U* matrix are identical to those of *W*; the same is true for *V** and *H*. It is therefore not surprising that both of these methods produce similar and comparable results. As these methods are really fast to calculate, for real-life projects we recommend starting with the linear algebra methods.

We will now turn away from these linear-algebra-based methods and focus on probabilistic topic models, which have become immensely popular in the past 20 years.

Latent Dirichlet Allocation

LDA is arguably the most prominent method of topic modeling in use today. It has been popularized during the last 15 years and can be adapted in flexible ways to different usage scenarios.

How does it work?

LDA views each document as consisting of different topics. In other words, each document is a mix of different topics. In the same way, topics are mixed from words. To keep the number of topics per document low and to have only a few, important words constituting the topics, LDA initially uses a Dirichlet distribution (*https:// oreil.ly/Kkd9k*), a so-called *Dirichlet prior*. This is applied both for assigning topics to documents and for finding words for the topics. The Dirichlet distribution ensures that documents have only a small number of topics and topics are mainly defined by a small number of words. Assuming that LDA generated topic distributions like the previous ones, a topic could be made up of words like *nuclear*, *treaty*, and *disarmament*, while another topic would be sampled by *sustainable*, *development*, etc.

After the initial assignments, the generative process starts. It uses the Dirichlet distributions for topics and words and tries to re-create the words from the original documents with stochastic sampling. This process has to be iterated many times and is therefore computationally intensive.[2] On the other hand, the results can be used to generate documents for any identified topic.

Blueprint: Creating a Topic Model for Paragraphs with LDA

Scikit-learn hides all these differences and uses the same API as the other topic modeling methods:

```
from sklearn.feature_extraction.text import CountVectorizer

count_para_vectorizer = CountVectorizer(stop_words=stopwords, min_df=5,
                        max_df=0.7)
count_para_vectors = count_para_vectorizer.fit_transform(paragraph_df["text"])

from sklearn.decomposition import LatentDirichletAllocation

lda_para_model = LatentDirichletAllocation(n_components = 10, random_state=42)
W_lda_para_matrix = lda_para_model.fit_transform(count_para_vectors)
H_lda_para_matrix = lda_para_model.components_
```

---

2 For a more detailed description, see the Wikipedia page (*https://oreil.ly/yr5yA*).

Waiting Time

Due to the probabilistic sampling, the process takes a lot longer than NMF and SVD. Expect at least minutes, if not hours, of run-time.

Our utility function can again be used to visualize the latent topics of the paragraph corpus:

```
display_topics(lda_para_model, tfidf_para.get_feature_names())
```

Out:

Topic 00	Topic 01	Topic 02	Topic 03	Topic 04
africa (2.38)	republic (1.52)	general (4.22)	human (3.62)	world (2.22)
people (1.86)	government (1.39)	assembly (3.63)	rights (3.48)	people (1.14)
south (1.57)	united (1.21)	session (3.38)	international (1.83)	countries (0.94)
namibia (0.88)	peace (1.16)	president (2.33)	law (1.01)	years (0.88)
regime (0.75)	people (1.02)	mr (2.32)	terrorism (0.99)	today (0.66)

Topic 05	Topic 06	Topic 07	Topic 08	Topic 09
peace (1.76)	countries (3.19)	nuclear (3.14)	nations (5.50)	international (1.96)
security (1.63)	development (2.70)	weapons (2.32)	united (5.11)	world (1.91)
east (1.34)	economic (2.22)	disarmament (1.82)	international (1.46)	peace (1.60)
middle (1.34)	developing (1.61)	states (1.47)	security (1.45)	economic (1.00)
israel (1.24)	international (1.45)	arms (1.46)	organization (1.44)	relations (0.99)

It's interesting to observe that LDA has generated a completely different topic structure compared to the linear algebra methods described earlier. *People* is the most prominent word in three quite different topics. In Topic 04, South Africa is related to Israel and Palestine, while in Topic 00, Cyprus, Afghanistan, and Iraq are related. This is not easy to explain. This is also reflected in the slowly decreasing word weights of the topics.

Other topics are easier to comprehend, such as climate change, nuclear weapons, elections, developing countries, and organizational questions.

In this example, LDA does not yield much better results than either NMF or SVD. However, due to the sampling process, LDA is not limited to sample topics just consisting of words. There are several variations, such as author-topic models, that can also sample categorical features. Moreover, as there is so much research going on in LDA, other ideas are published quite frequently, which extend the focus of the method well beyond text analytics (see, for example, Minghui Qiu et al., "It Is Not Just What We Say, But How We Say Them: LDA-based Behavior-Topic Model" (*https://oreil.ly/dnqq5*) or Rahji Abdurehman, "Keyword-Assisted LDA: Exploring New Methods for Supervised Topic Modeling" (*https://oreil.ly/DDClf*)).

Blueprint: Visualizing LDA Results

As LDA is so popular, there is a nice package in Python to visualize the LDA results called pyLDAvis.[3] Fortunately, it can directly use the results from sciki-learn for its visualization.

Be careful, this takes some time:

```
import pyLDAvis.sklearn

lda_display = pyLDAvis.sklearn.prepare(lda_para_model, count_para_vectors,
                          count_para_vectorizer, sort_topics=False)
pyLDAvis.display(lda_display)
```

Out:

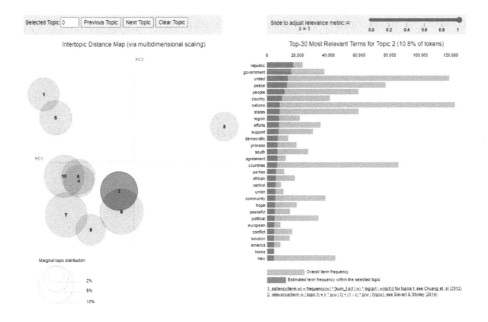

There is a multitude of information available in the visualization. Let's start with the topic "bubbles" and click the topic. Now take a look at the red bars, which symbolize the word distribution in the currently selected topic. As the length of the bars is not decreasing quickly, Topic 2 is not very pronounced. This is the same effect you can see in the table from "Blueprint: Creating a Topic Model for Paragraphs with LDA" on

---

3 pyLDAvis must be installed separately using **pip install pyldavis** or **conda install pyldavis**.

page 221 (look at Topic 1, where we have used the array indices, whereas pyLDAvis starts enumerating the topics with 1).

To visualize the results, the topics are mapped from their original dimension (the number of words) into two dimensions using principal component analysis (PCA), a standard method for dimension reduction. This results in a point; the circle is added to see the relative sizes of the topics. It is possible to use T-SNE instead of PCA by passing `mds="tsne"` as a parameter in the preparation stage. This changes the inter-topic distance map and shows fewer overlapping topic bubbles. This is, however, just an artifact of projecting the many word dimensions in just two for visualization. Therefore, it's always a good idea to look at the word distribution of the topics and not exclusively trust a low-dimensional visualization.

It's interesting to see the strong overlap of Topics 4, 6, and 10 ("international"), whereas Topic 3 ("general assembly") seems to be far away from all other topics. By hovering over the other topic bubbles or clicking them, you can take a look at their respective word distributions on the right side. Although not all the topics are per-fectly separated, there are some (like Topic 1 and Topic 7) that are far away from the others. Try to hover over them and you will find that their word content is also differ-ent from each other. For such topics, it might be useful to extract the most represen-tative documents and use them as a training set for supervised learning.

pyLDAvis is a nice tool to play with and is well-suited for screenshots in presenta-tions. Even though it looks explorative, the real exploration in the topic models takes place by modifying the features and the hyperparameters of the algorithms.

Using pyLDAvis gives us a good idea how the topics are arranged with respect to one another and which individual words are important. However, if we need a more qual-itative understanding of the topics, we can use additional visualizations.

Blueprint: Using Word Clouds to Display and Compare Topic Models

So far, we have used lists to display the topic models. This way, we could nicely identify how pronounced the different topics were. However, in many cases topic models are used to give you a first impression about the validity of the corpus and better visualizations. As we have seen in Chapter 1, word clouds are a qualitative and intuitive instrument to show this.

We can directly use word clouds to show our topic models. The code is easily derived from the previously defined `display_topics` function:

```
import matplotlib.pyplot as plt
from wordcloud import WordCloud

def wordcloud_topics(model, features, no_top_words=40):
    for topic, words in enumerate(model.components_):
        size = {}
        largest = words.argsort()[::-1] # invert sort order
        for i in range(0, no_top_words):
            size[features[largest[i]]] = abs(words[largest[i]])
        wc = WordCloud(background_color="white", max_words=100,
                    width=960, height=540)
        wc.generate_from_frequencies(size)
        plt.figure(figsize=(12,12))
        plt.imshow(wc, interpolation='bilinear')
        plt.axis("off")
        # if you don't want to save the topic model, comment the next line
        plt.savefig(f'topic{topic}.png')
```

By using this code, we can qualitatively compare the results of the NMF model (Figure 8-4) with those of the LDA model(Figure 8-5). Larger words are more important in their respective topics. If many words have roughly the same size, the topic is not well-pronounced:

```
wordcloud_topics(nmf_para_model, tfidf_para_vectorizer.get_feature_names())
wordcloud_topics(lda_para_model, count_para_vectorizer.get_feature_names())
```

Word Clouds Use Individual Scaling

The font sizes in the word clouds use scaling within each topic separately, and therefore it's important to verify with the actual numbers before drawing any final conclusions.

The presentation is now way more compelling. It is much easier to match topics between the two methods, like 0-NMF with 8-LDA. For most topics, this is quite obvious, but there are also differences. 1-LDA ("people republic") has no equivalent in NMF, whereas 9-NMF ("sustainable development") cannot be found in LDA.

As we have found a nice qualitative visualization of the topics, we are now interested in how that topic distribution has changed over time.

Figure 8-4. Word clouds representing the NMF topic model.

Figure 8-5. Word clouds representing the LDA topic model.

Blueprint: Calculating Topic Distribution of Documents and Time Evolution

As you can see in the analysis at the beginning of the chapter, the speech metadata changes over time. This leads to the interesting question of how the distribution of the topics changes over time. It turns out that this is easy to calculate and insightful.

Like the scikit-learn vectorizers, the topic models also have a `transform` method, which calculates the topic distribution of existing documents keeping the already fitted topic model. Let's use this to first separate speeches before 1990 from those after 1990. For this, we create NumPy arrays for the documents before and after 1990:

```
import numpy as np
before_1990 = np.array(paragraph_df["year"] < 1990)
after_1990  = ~ before_1990
```

Then we can calculate the respective *W* matrices:

```
W_para_matrix_early = nmf_para_model.transform(tfidf_para_vectors[before_1990])
W_para_matrix_late  = nmf_para_model.transform(tfidf_para_vectors[after_1990])
print(W_para_matrix_early.sum(axis=0)/W_para_matrix_early.sum()*100.0)
print(W_para_matrix_late.sum(axis=0)/W_para_matrix_late.sum()*100.0)
```

Out:

```
['9.34', '10.43', '12.18', '12.18', '7.82', '6.05', '12.10', '5.85', '17.36',
 '6.69']
['7.48', '8.34', '9.75', '9.75', '6.26', '4.84', '9.68', '4.68', '13.90',
 '5.36']
```

The result is interesting, as some percentages have changed considerably; specifically, the size of the second-to-last topic is much smaller in the later years. We will now try to take a deeper look at the topics and their changes over time.

Let's try to calculate the distribution for individual years and see whether we can find a visualization to uncover possible patterns:

```
year_data = []
years = np.unique(paragraph_years)
for year in tqdm(years):
    W_year = nmf_para_model.transform(tfidf_para_vectors[paragraph_years \
                                        == year])
    year_data.append([year] + list(W_year.sum(axis=0)/W_year.sum()*100.0))
```

To make the plots more intuitive, we first create a list of topics with their two most important words:

```
topic_names = []
voc = tfidf_para_vectorizer.get_feature_names()
for topic in nmf_para_model.components_:
    important = topic.argsort()
    top_word = voc[important[-1]] + " " + voc[important[-2]]
    topic_names.append("Topic " + top_word)
```

We then combine the results in a DataFrame with the previous topics as column
names, so we can easily visualize that as follows:

```
df_year = pd.DataFrame(year_data,
                columns=["year"] + topic_names).set_index("year")
df_year.plot.area()
```

Out:

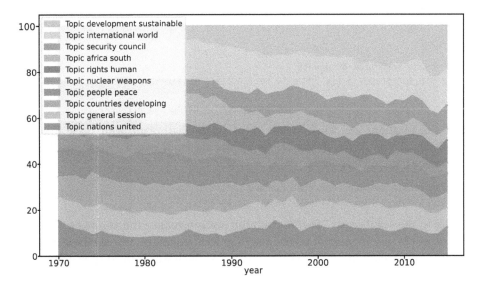

In the resulting graph you can see how the topic distribution changes over the
year. We can recognize that the "sustainable development" topic is continuously
increasing, while "south africa" has lost popularity after the apartheid regime ended.

Compared to showing the time development of single (guessed) words, topics seem
to be a more natural entity as they arise from the text corpus itself. Note that this
chart was generated with an unsupervised method exclusively, so there is no bias in it.
Everything was already in the debates data; we have just uncovered it.

So far, we have used scikit-learn exclusively for topic modeling. In the Python ecosystem, there is a specialized library for topic models called Gensim, which we will now
investigate.

Using Gensim for Topic Modeling

Apart from scikit-learn, *Gensim* (*https://oreil.ly/Ybn63*) is another popular tool for performing topic modeling in Python. Compared to scikit-learn, it offers more algorithms for calculating topic models and can also give estimates about the quality of the model.

Blueprint: Preparing Data for Gensim

Before we can start calculating the Gensim models, we have to prepare the data. Unfortunately, the API and the terminology are different from scikit-learn. In the first step, we have to prepare the vocabulary. Gensim has no integrated tokenizer and expects each line of a document corpus to be already tokenized:

```
# create tokenized documents
gensim_paragraphs = [[w for w in re.findall(r'\b\w\w+\b' , paragraph.lower())
                      if w not in stopwords]
                        for paragraph in paragraph_df["text"]]
```

After tokenization, we can initialize the Gensim dictionary with these tokenized documents. Think of the dictionary as a mapping from words to columns (like the features we used in Chapter 2):

```
from gensim.corpora import Dictionary
dict_gensim_para = Dictionary(gensim_paragraphs)
```

Similar to the scikit-learn `TfidfVectorizer`, we can reduce the vocabulary by filtering out words that appear not often enough or too frequently. To keep the dimensions low, we choose a minimum of five documents in which words must appear, but not in more than 70% of the documents. As we saw in Chapter 2, these parameters can be optimized and require some experimentation.

In Gensim, this is implemented via a filter with the parameters `no_below` and `no_above` (in scikit-learn, the analog would be `min_df` and `max_df`):

```
dict_gensim_para.filter_extremes(no_below=5, no_above=0.7)
```

With the dictionary read, we can now use Gensim to calculate the bag-of-words matrix (which is called a *corpus* in Gensim, but we will stick with our current terminology):

```
bow_gensim_para = [dict_gensim_para.doc2bow(paragraph) \
                     for paragraph in gensim_paragraphs]
```

Finally, we can perform the TF-IDF transformation. The first line fits the bag-of-words model, while the second line transforms the weights:

```
from gensim.models import TfidfModel
tfidf_gensim_para = TfidfModel(bow_gensim_para)
vectors_gensim_para = tfidf_gensim_para[bow_gensim_para]
```

The vectors_gensim_para matrix is the one that we will use for all upcoming topic modeling tasks with Gensim.

Blueprint: Performing Nonnegative Matrix Factorization with Gensim

Let's check first the results of NMF and see whether we can reproduce those of scikit-learn:

```
from gensim.models.nmf import Nmf
nmf_gensim_para = Nmf(vectors_gensim_para, num_topics=10,
                      id2word=dict_gensim_para, kappa=0.1, eval_every=5)
```

The evaluation can take a while. Although Gensim offers a show_topics method for directly displaying the topics, we have a different implementation to make it look like the scikit-learn results so it's easier to compare them:

```
display_topics_gensim(nmf_gensim_para)
```

Out:

Topic 00	Topic 01	Topic 02	Topic 03	Topic 04
nations (0.03)	africa (0.02)	economic (0.01)	countries (0.02)	israel (0.02)
united (0.02)	south (0.02)	development (0.01)	developing (0.02)	arab (0.02)
human (0.02)	people (0.02)	countries (0.01)	resources (0.01)	palestinian (0.02)
rights (0.02)	government (0.01)	social (0.01)	sea (0.01)	council (0.01)
role (0.01)	republic (0.01)	international (0.01)	developed (0.01)	security (0.01)
Topic 05	**Topic 06**	**Topic 07**	**Topic 08**	**Topic 09**
organization (0.02)	problem (0.01)	nuclear (0.02)	session (0.02)	world (0.02)
charter (0.02)	solution (0.01)	co (0.02)	general (0.02)	peace (0.02)
principles (0.02)	east (0.01)	operation (0.02)	assembly (0.02)	peoples (0.02)
member (0.01)	situation (0.01)	disarmament (0.02)	mr (0.02)	security (0.01)
respect (0.01)	problems (0.01)	weapons (0.02)	president (0.02)	states (0.01)

NMF is also a statistical method, so the results are not supposed to be identical to the ones that we calculated with scikit-learn, but they are similar enough. Gensim has code for calculating the coherence score for topic models, a quality indicator. Let's try this:

```
from gensim.models.coherencemodel import CoherenceModel

nmf_gensim_para_coherence = CoherenceModel(model=nmf_gensim_para,
```

```
                                    texts=gensim_paragraphs,
                                    dictionary=dict_gensim_para,
                                    coherence='c_v')
    nmf_gensim_para_coherence_score = nmf_gensim_para_coherence.get_coherence()
    print(nmf_gensim_para_coherence_score)
```

Out:

```
    0.6500661701098243
```

The score varies with the number of topics. If you want to find the optimal number of topics, a frequent approach is to run NMF for several different values, calculate the coherence score, and take the number of topics that maximizes the score.

Let's try the same with LDA and compare the quality indicators.

Blueprint: Using LDA with Gensim

Running LDA with Gensim is as easy as using NMF if we have the data prepared. The `LdaModel` class has a lot of parameters for tuning the model; we use the recommended values here:

```
from gensim.models import LdaModel
lda_gensim_para = LdaModel(corpus=bow_gensim_para, id2word=dict_gensim_para,
    chunksize=2000, alpha='auto', eta='auto', iterations=400, num_topics=10,
    passes=20, eval_every=None, random_state=42)
```

We are interested in the word distribution of the topics:

```
    display_topics_gensim(lda_gensim_para)
```

Out:

Topic 00	Topic 01	Topic 02	Topic 03	Topic 04
climate (0.12)	country (0.05)	nations (0.10)	international (0.03)	africa (0.06)
convention (0.03)	people (0.05)	united (0.10)	community (0.01)	african (0.06)
pacific (0.02)	government (0.03)	human (0.04)	efforts (0.01)	continent (0.02)
environmental (0.02)	national (0.02)	security (0.03)	new (0.01)	terrorist (0.02)
sea (0.02)	support (0.02)	rights (0.03)	global (0.01)	crimes (0.02)

Topic 05	Topic 06	Topic 07	Topic 08	Topic 09
world (0.05)	peace (0.03)	south (0.10)	general (0.10)	development (0.07)
years (0.02)	conflict (0.02)	sudan (0.05)	assembly (0.09)	countries (0.05)
today (0.02)	region (0.02)	china (0.04)	session (0.05)	economic (0.03)
peace (0.01)	people (0.02)	asia (0.04)	president (0.04)	sustainable (0.02)
time (0.01)	state (0.02)	somalia (0.04)	secretary (0.04)	2015 (0.02)

The topics are not as easy to interpret as the ones generated by NMF. Checking the coherence score as shown earlier, we find a lower score of 0.45270703180962374. Gensim also allows us to calculate the perplexity score of an LDA model. Perplexity measures how well a probability model predicts a sample. When we execute `lda_gensim_para.log_perplexity(vectors_gensim_para)`, we get a perplexity score of -9.70558947109483.

Blueprint: Calculating Coherence Scores

Gensim can also calculate topic coherence. The method itself is a four-stage process consisting of segmentation, probability estimation, a confirmation measure calculation, and aggregation. Fortunately, Gensim has a `CoherenceModel` class that encapsulates all these single tasks, and we can directly use it:

```
from gensim.models.coherencemodel import CoherenceModel

lda_gensim_para_coherence = CoherenceModel(model=lda_gensim_para,
    texts=gensim_paragraphs, dictionary=dict_gensim_para, coherence='c_v')
lda_gensim_para_coherence_score = lda_gensim_para_coherence.get_coherence()
print(lda_gensim_para_coherence_score)
```

Out:

```
0.5444930496493174
```

Substituting `nmf` for `lda`, we can calculate the same score for our NMF model:

```
nmf_gensim_para_coherence = CoherenceModel(model=nmf_gensim_para,
    texts=gensim_paragraphs, dictionary=dict_gensim_para, coherence='c_v')
nmf_gensim_para_coherence_score = nmf_gensim_para_coherence.get_coherence()
print(nmf_gensim_para_coherence_score)
```

Out:

```
0.6505110480127619
```

The score is quite a bit higher, which means that the NMF model is a better approximation to the real topics compared to LDA.

Calculating the coherence score of the individual topics for LDA is even easier, as it is directly supported by the LDA model. Let's take a look at the average first:

```
top_topics = lda_gensim_para.top_topics(vectors_gensim_para, topn=5)
avg_topic_coherence = sum([t[1] for t in top_topics]) / len(top_topics)
print('Average topic coherence: %.4f.' % avg_topic_coherence)
```

Out:

```
Average topic coherence: -2.4709.
```

We are also interested in the coherence scores of the individual topics, which is contained in `top_topics`. However, the output is verbose (check it!), so we try to condense it a bit by just printing the coherence scores together with the most important words of the topics:

```
[(t[1], " ".join([w[1] for w in t[0]])) for t in top_topics]
```

Out:

```
[(-1.5361194241843663, 'general assembly session president secretary'),
 (-1.7014902754187737, 'nations united human security rights'),
 (-1.8485895463251694, 'country people government national support'),
 (-1.9729985026779555, 'peace conflict region people state'),
 (-1.9743434414778658, 'world years today peace time'),
 (-2.0202823396586433, 'international community efforts new global'),
 (-2.7269347656599225, 'development countries economic sustainable 2015'),
 (-2.9089975883502706, 'climate convention pacific environmental sea'),
 (-3.8680684770508753, 'africa african continent terrorist crimes'),
 (-4.1515707817343195, 'south sudan china asia somalia')]
```

Coherence scores for topic models can easily be calculated using Gensim. The absolute values are difficult to interpret, but varying the methods (NMF versus LDA) or the number of topics can give you ideas about which way you want to proceed in your topic models. Coherence scores and coherence models are a big advantage of Gensim, as they are not (yet) included in scikit-learn.

As it's difficult to estimate the "correct" number of topics, we are now taking a look at an approach that creates hierarchical models and does not need a fixed number of topics as a parameter.

Blueprint: Finding the Optimal Number of Topics

In the previous sections, we have always worked with 10 topics. So far we have not compared the quality of this topic model to different ones with a lower or higher number of topics. We want to find the optimal number of topics in a structured way without having to go into the interpretation of each constellation.

It turns out there is a way to achieve this. The "quality" of a topic model can be measured by the previously introduced coherence score. To find the best coherence score, we will now calculate it for a different number of topics with an LDA model. We will try to find the highest score, which should give us the optimal number of topics:

```
from gensim.models.ldamulticore import LdaMulticore
lda_para_model_n = []
for n in tqdm(range(5, 21)):
    lda_model = LdaMulticore(corpus=bow_gensim_para, id2word=dict_gensim_para,
                             chunksize=2000, eta='auto', iterations=400,
                             num_topics=n, passes=20, eval_every=None,
                             random_state=42)
    lda_coherence = CoherenceModel(model=lda_model, texts=gensim_paragraphs,
                                   dictionary=dict_gensim_para, coherence='c_v')
    lda_para_model_n.append((n, lda_model, lda_coherence.get_coherence()))
```

Coherence Calculations Take Time

Calculating the LDA model (and the coherence) is computationally expensive, so in real life it would be better to optimize the algorithm to calculate only a minimal number of models and perplexities. Sometimes it might make sense if you calculate the coherence scores for only a few numbers of topics.

Now we can choose which number of topics produces a good coherence score. Note that typically the score grows with the number of topics. Taking too many topics makes interpretation difficult:

```
pd.DataFrame(lda_para_model_n, columns=["n", "model", \
    "coherence"]).set_index("n")[["coherence"]].plot(figsize=(16,9))
```

Out:

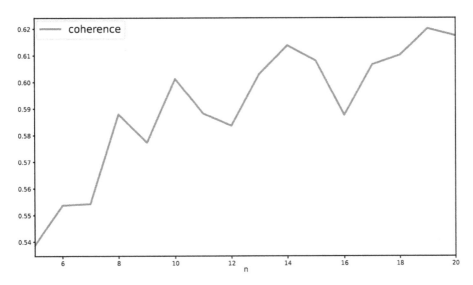

Overall, the graph grows with the number of topics, which is almost always the case. However, we can see "spikes" at 13 and 17 topics, so these numbers look like good choices. We will visualize the results for 17 topics:

```
display_topics_gensim(lda_para_model_n[12][1])
```

Out:

Topic 00	Topic 01	Topic 02	Topic 03	Topic 04	Topic 05
peace (0.02)	general (0.05)	united (0.04)	nations (0.07)	development (0.03)	international (0.03)
international (0.02)	assembly (0.04)	nations (0.04)	united (0.07)	general (0.02)	terrorism (0.03)
cooperation (0.01)	session (0.03)	states (0.03)	security (0.03)	conference (0.02)	states (0.01)
countries (0.01)	president (0.03)	european (0.02)	council (0.02)	assembly (0.02)	iraq (0.01)
region (0.01)	mr (0.03)	union (0.02)	international (0.02)	sustainable (0.01)	acts (0.01)

Topic 06	Topic 07	Topic 08	Topic 09	Topic 10	Topic 11
peace (0.03)	africa (0.08)	states (0.04)	world (0.03)	human (0.07)	climate (0.03)
east (0.02)	south (0.05)	small (0.04)	international (0.02)	rights (0.06)	change (0.03)
middle (0.02)	african (0.05)	island (0.03)	problems (0.01)	law (0.02)	global (0.02)
israel (0.02)	namibia (0.02)	sea (0.02)	war (0.01)	respect (0.02)	environment (0.01)
solution (0.01)	republic (0.01)	pacific (0.02)	peace (0.01)	international (0.01)	energy (0.01)

Topic 12	Topic 13	Topic 14	Topic 15	Topic 16	
world (0.03)	people (0.03)	people (0.02)	countries (0.05)	nuclear (0.06)	
people (0.02)	independence (0.02)	country (0.02)	development (0.03)	weapons (0.04)	
future (0.01)	peoples (0.02)	government (0.02)	economic (0.03)	disarmament (0.03)	
years (0.01)	struggle (0.01)	humanitarian (0.01)	developing (0.02)	arms (0.03)	
today (0.01)	countries (0.01)	refugees (0.01)	trade (0.01)	treaty (0.02)	

Most of the topics are easy to interpret, but quite a few are difficult (like 0, 3, 8) as they contain many words with small, but not too different, sizes. Is the topic model with 17 topics therefore easier to explain? Not really. The coherence measure is higher, but that does not necessarily mean a more obvious interpretation. In other words, relying solely on coherence scores can be dangerous if the number of topics gets too large. Although in theory higher coherence should contribute to better inter-pretability, it is often a trade-off, and choosing smaller numbers of topics can make life easier. Taking a look back at the coherence graph, 10 seems to be a good value as it is a *local maximum* of the coherence score.

As it's obviously difficult to find the "correct" number of topics, we will now take a look at an approach that creates hierarchical models and does not need a fixed number of topics as a parameter.

Blueprint: Creating a Hierarchical Dirichlet Process with Gensim

Take a step back and recall the visualization of the topics in "Blueprint: Using LDA with Gensim" on page 232. The sizes of the topics vary quite a bit, and some topics have a large overlap. It would be nice if the results gave us broader topics first and some subtopics below them. This is the exact idea of the hierarchical Dirichlet process (HDP). The hierarchical topic model should give us just a few broad topics that are well separated, then go into more detail by adding more words and getting more differentiated topic definitions.

HDP is still quite new and has not yet been extensively analyzed. Gensim is also often used in research and has an experimental implementation of HDP integrated. As we can directly use our already existing vectorization, it's not complicated to try it. Note that we are again using the bag-of-words vectorization as the Dirichlet processes themselves handle frequent words correctly:

```
from gensim.models import HdpModel
hdp_gensim_para = HdpModel(corpus=bow_gensim_para, id2word=dict_gensim_para)
```

HDP can estimate the number of topics and can show all that it identified:

```
hdp_gensim_para.print_topics(num_words=10)
```

Out:

	prob0	word0	prob1	word1	prob2	word2	prob3	word3	prob4	word4	prob5	word5	prob6	word6	prob7	word7
0	0.015	nations	0.014	united	0.012	international	0.010	world	0.009	countries	0.009	peace	0.007	states	0.006	security
1	0.010	united	0.009	international	0.009	nations	0.008	nuclear	0.008	world	0.008	states	0.008	people	0.007	countries
2	0.017	countries	0.013	development	0.012	international	0.011	economic	0.011	world	0.009	nations	0.008	united	0.007	developing
3	0.010	nations	0.010	united	0.009	international	0.009	countries	0.009	general	0.009	world	0.007	assembly	0.007	session
4	0.011	international	0.010	peace	0.009	united	0.009	nations	0.008	people	0.007	world	0.007	countries	0.006	security
5	0.010	international	0.010	united	0.010	nations	0.009	peace	0.008	countries	0.007	world	0.006	people	0.006	security
6	0.012	international	0.010	nations	0.010	united	0.008	countries	0.008	world	0.006	peace	0.006	people	0.006	states
7	0.011	international	0.010	nations	0.010	united	0.009	countries	0.009	world	0.007	peace	0.006	economic	0.006	states
8	0.011	international	0.010	nations	0.010	united	0.008	world	0.008	countries	0.007	peace	0.006	people	0.006	states
9	0.011	international	0.010	nations	0.010	united	0.008	world	0.008	countries	0.007	peace	0.006	states	0.006	people
10	0.010	international	0.010	nations	0.010	united	0.008	world	0.007	peace	0.007	countries	0.006	people	0.006	states
11	0.011	nations	0.011	united	0.010	international	0.008	world	0.007	peace	0.007	countries	0.006	states	0.006	people
12	0.011	nations	0.011	united	0.010	international	0.008	world	0.007	countries	0.007	peace	0.005	people	0.005	states
13	0.011	nations	0.011	united	0.010	international	0.008	world	0.007	countries	0.007	peace	0.005	people	0.005	development
14	0.010	nations	0.010	international	0.010	united	0.008	world	0.008	countries	0.007	peace	0.005	development	0.005	states
15	0.011	nations	0.011	united	0.010	international	0.008	world	0.007	peace	0.007	countries	0.006	states	0.005	security
16	0.011	nations	0.011	united	0.010	international	0.008	world	0.007	peace	0.007	countries	0.005	security	0.005	states
17	0.011	nations	0.010	united	0.010	international	0.008	world	0.007	countries	0.007	peace	0.005	development	0.005	states
18	0.011	nations	0.011	united	0.010	international	0.008	world	0.007	peace	0.007	countries	0.005	development	0.005	security
19	0.011	nations	0.010	united	0.010	international	0.008	world	0.007	peace	0.007	countries	0.005	security	0.005	development

The results are sometimes difficult to understand. It can be an option to first perform a "rough" topic modeling with only a few topics. If you find out that a topic is really big or suspect that it might have subtopics, you can create a subset of the original corpus where the only documents included are those that have a significant mixture of this topic. This needs some manual interaction but often yields much better results compared to HDP. At this stage of development, we would not recommend using HDP exclusively.

Topic models focus on uncovering the topic structure of a large corpus of documents. As all documents are modeled as a mixture of different topics, they are not well-suited for assigning documents to exactly one topic. This can be achieved using clustering.

Blueprint: Using Clustering to Uncover the Structure of Text Data

Apart from topic modeling, there is a multitude of other unsupervised methods. Not all are suitable for text data, but many clustering algorithms can be used. Compared to topic modeling, it is important for us to know that each document (or paragraph) gets assigned to exactly one cluster.

Clustering Works Well for Mono-Typical Texts

In our case, it is a reasonable assumption that each document belongs to exactly one cluster, as there are probably not too many different things contained in one paragraph. For larger text fragments, we would rather use topic modeling to take possible mixtures into account.

Most clustering methods need the number of clusters as a parameter, while there are a few (like mean-shift) that can guess the correct number of clusters. Most of the latter do not work well with sparse data and therefore are not suitable for text analytics. In our case, we decided to use k-means clustering, but birch or spectral clustering should work in a similar manner. There are a few nice explanations of how the k-means algorithm works.[4]

---

4 See, for example, Andrey A. Shabalin's k-means clustering page (*https://oreil.ly/OTGWX*) or Naftali Harris's "Visualizing K-Means Clustering" (*https://oreil.ly/Po3bL*).

Clustering Is Much Slower Than Topic Modeling

For most algorithms, clustering takes considerable time, much more than even LDA. So, be prepared to wait for roughly one hour when executing the clustering in the next code fragment.

The scikit-learn API for clustering is similar to what we have seen with topic models:

```
from sklearn.cluster import KMeans
k_means_text = KMeans(n_clusters=10, random_state=42)
k_means_text.fit(tfidf_para_vectors)

KMeans(n_clusters=10, random_state=42)
```

But now it's much easier to find out how many paragraphs belong to which cluster. Everything necessary is in the `labels_` field of the `k_means_para` object. For each document, it contains the label that was assigned by the clustering algorithm:

```
np.unique(k_means_para.labels_, return_counts=True)
```

Out:

```
(array([0, 1, 2, 3, 4, 5, 6, 7, 8, 9], dtype=int32),
 array([133370,  41705,  12396,   9142,  12674,  21080,  19727,  10563,
         10437,  11116]))
```

In many cases, you might already have found some conceptual problems here. If the data is too heterogeneous, most clusters tend to be small (containing a comparatively small vocabulary) and are accompanied by a large cluster that absorbs all the rest. Fortunately (and due to the short paragraphs), this is not the case here; cluster 0 is much bigger than the others, but it's not orders of magnitude. Let's visualize the distribution with the y-axis showing the size of the clusters (Figure 8-6):

```
sizes = []
for i in range(10):
    sizes.append({"cluster": i, "size": np.sum(k_means_para.labels_==i)})
pd.DataFrame(sizes).set_index("cluster").plot.bar(figsize=(16,9))
```

Visualizing the clusters works in a similar way to the topic models. However, we have to calculate the individual feature contributions manually. For this, we add up the TF-IDF vectors of all documents in the cluster and keep only the largest values.

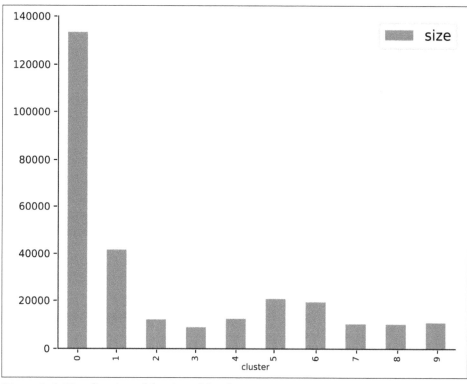

Figure 8-6. Visualization of the size of the clusters.

These are the weights for their corresponding words. In fact, that's the only change compared to the previous code:

```
def wordcloud_clusters(model, vectors, features, no_top_words=40):
    for cluster in np.unique(model.labels_):
        size = {}
        words = vectors[model.labels_ == cluster].sum(axis=0).A[0]
        largest = words.argsort()[::-1] # invert sort order
        for i in range(0, no_top_words):
            size[features[largest[i]]] = abs(words[largest[i]])
        wc = WordCloud(background_color="white", max_words=100,
                       width=960, height=540)
        wc.generate_from_frequencies(size)
        plt.figure(figsize=(12,12))
        plt.imshow(wc, interpolation='bilinear')
        plt.axis("off")
        # if you don't want to save the topic model, comment the next line
        plt.savefig(f'cluster{cluster}.png')

wordcloud_clusters(k_means_para, tfidf_para_vectors,
                   tfidf_para_vectorizer.get_feature_names())
```

Out:

As you can see, the results are (fortunately) not too different from the various topic modeling approaches; you might recognize the topics of nuclear weapons, South Africa, general assembly, etc. Note, however, that the clusters are more pronounced. In other words, they have more specific words. Unfortunately, this is not true for the biggest cluster, 1, which has no clear direction but many words with similar, smaller sizes. This is a typical phenomenon of clustering algorithms compared to topic modeling.

Clustering calculations can take quite long, especially compared to NMF topic models. On the positive side, we are now free to choose documents in a certain cluster (opposed to a topic model, this is well-defined) and perform additional, more sophisticated operations, such as hierarchical clustering, etc.

The quality of the clustering can be calculated by using coherence or the Calinski-Harabasz score. These metrics are not optimized for sparse data and take a long time to calculate, and therefore we skip this here.

Further Ideas

In this chapter, we have shown different methods for performing topic modeling. However, we have only scratched the surface of the possibilities:

- It's possible to add n-grams in the vectorization process. In scikit-learn this is straightforward by using the `ngram_range` parameter. Gensim has a special `Phrases` class for that. Due to the higher TF-IDF weights of n-grams, they can contribute considerably to the features of a topic and add a lot of context information.

- As we have used years to have time-dependent topic models, you could also use countries or continents and find the topics that are most relevant in the speeches of their ambassadors.

- Calculate the coherence score for an LDA topic model using the whole speeches instead of the paragraphs and compare the scores.

Summary and Recommendation

In your daily work, it might turn out that unsupervised methods such as topic modeling or clustering are often used as first methods to understand the content of unknown text corpora. It is further useful to check whether the right features have been chosen or this can still be optimized.

One of the most important decisions is the entity on which you will be calculating the topics. As shown in our blueprint example, documents don't always have to be the best choice, especially when they are quite long and consist of algorithmically determinable subentities.

Finding the correct number of topics is always a challenge. Normally, this must be solved iteratively by calculating the quality indicators. A frequently used, more pragmatic approach is to try with a reasonable number of topics and find out whether the results can be interpreted.

Using a (much) higher number of topics (like a few hundred), topic models are often used as techniques for the dimensionality reduction of text documents. With the resulting vectorizations, similarity scores can then be calculated in the latent space and frequently yield better results compared to the naive distance in TF-IDF space.

Conclusion

Topic models are a powerful technique and are not computationally expensive. Therefore, they can be used widely in text analytics. The first and foremost reason to use them is uncovering the latent structure of a document corpus.

Topic models are also useful for getting a summarization and an idea about the structure of large unknown texts. For this reason, they are often used routinely in the beginning of an analysis.

As there is a large number of different algorithms and implementations, it makes sense to experiment with the different methods and see which one yields the best results for a given text corpus. The linear-algebra-based methods are quite fast and make analyses possible by changing the number of topics combined with calculating the respective quality indicators.

Aggregating data in different ways before performing topic modeling can lead to interesting variations. As we have seen in the UN general debates dataset, paragraphs were more suited as the speakers talked about one topic after the other. If you have a corpus with texts from many authors, concatenating all texts per author will give you persona models for different types of authors.

## CHAPTER 9

Text Summarization

There is a massive amount of information on the internet on every topic. A Google search returns millions of search results containing text, images, videos, and so on. Even if we consider only the text content, it's not possible to read through it all. Text summarization methods are able to condense text information to a short summary of a few lines or a paragraph and make it digestible to most users. Applications of text summarization can be found not just on the internet but also in fields like paralegal case summaries, book synopses, etc.

What You'll Learn and What We'll Build

In this chapter, we will start with an introduction to text summarization and provide an overview of the methods used. We will analyze different types of text data and their specific characteristics that are useful in determining the choice of summarization method. We will provide blueprints that apply these methods to different use cases and analyze their performance. At the end of this chapter, you will have a good understanding of different text summarization methods and be able to choose the right approach for any application.

Text Summarization

It is likely that you have undertaken a summarization task knowingly or unknowingly at some point in life. Examples are telling a friend about a movie you watched last night and trying to explain your work to your family. We all like to provide a brief summary of our experiences to the rest of the world to share our feelings and motivate others. *Text summarization* is defined as the method used for generating a concise summary of longer text while still conveying useful information and without losing the overall context. This is a method that we are quite familiar with: when reading course textbooks, lecture notes, or even this book, many students will try to highlight important sentences or make short notes to capture the important concepts. Automatic text summarization methods allow us to use computers to do this task.

Summarization methods can be broadly classified into *extraction* and *abstraction* methods. In extractive summarization, important phrases or sentences are identified in a given body of text and combined to form the summary of the entire text. Such methods identify the important parts of text by assigning weights correctly, remove sentences that might convey redundant information, rank different parts of the text, and combine the most important ones as the summary. These methods select a part of the original text as the summary, so while each sentence would be grammatically accurate, it may not form a cohesive paragraph.

Abstractive summarization methods, on the other hand, try to paraphrase and generate a summary just like a human would. This typically involves the use of deep neural networks that are capable of generating phrases and sentences that provide a grammatically accurate summary of the text and not just picking out important words or sentences. However, the process of training deep neural networks requires a lot of training data and addresses multiple subdomains within NLP, like natural language generation, semantic segmentation, etc.

Abstractive summarization methods are an area of active research with several approaches (*https://oreil.ly/DxXd1*) looking to improve the state of the art. The Trans formers library (*https://oreil.ly/JS-x8*) from Hugging Face provides an implementation that uses a pre-trained model to perform the summarization task. We explore the concept of pre-trained models and the Transformers library in more detail in Chapter 11. Extractive summarization is preferred in many use cases because these methods are simple to implement and fast to run. In this chapter, we will focus on blueprints using extractive summarization.

Let's say you are working with a legal firm that wants to review historical cases to help prepare for a current case. Since case proceedings and judgments are very long, they want to generate summaries and review the entire case only if it's relevant. Such a summary helps them to quickly look at multiple cases and allocate their time efficiently. We can consider this an example of text summarization applied to long-form text. Another use case might be a media company that wants to send a newsletter to its subscribers every morning highlighting the important events of the previous day. Customers don't appreciate long emails, and therefore creating a short summary of each article is important to keep them engaged. In this use case, you need to summarize shorter pieces of text. While working on these projects, maybe you have to work in a team that uses a chat communication tool like Slack or Microsoft Teams. There are shared chat groups (or channels) where all team members can communicate with each other. If you are away for a few hours in a meeting, it can quickly get flooded with multiple messages and discussions. As a user, it's hard to go through 100+

unread messages, and you can't be sure if you missed something important. In such a situation, it can be beneficial to have a way to summarize these missed discussions with the help of an automated bot.

In each of the use cases, we see a different type of text that we are looking to summarize. Let's briefly present them again:

- Long-form text written in a structured manner, containing paragraphs, and spread across multiple pages. Examples include case proceedings, research papers, textbooks, etc.

- Short-form text such as news articles, and blogs where images, data, and other graphical elements might be present.

- Multiple, short pieces of text in the form of conversations that can contain special characters such as emojis and are not very structured. Examples include Twitter threads, online discussion forums, and group messaging applications.

Each of these types of text data presents information differently, and therefore the method used to summarize one may not work for the other. In our blueprints we present methods that work for these text types and provide guidance to determine the appropriate method.

Extractive Methods

All extractive methods follow these three basic steps:

1. Create an intermediate representation of the text.

2. Score the sentences/phrases based on the chosen representation.

3. Rank and choose sentences to create a summary of the text.

While most blueprints will follow these steps, the specific method that they use to create the intermediate representation or score will vary.

Data Preprocessing

Before proceeding to the actual blueprint, we will reuse the blueprint from Chapter 3 to read a given URL that we would like to summarize. In this blueprint we will focus on generating a summary using the text, but you can study Chapter 3 to get a detailed overview of extracting data from a URL. The output of the article has been shortened for brevity; to view the entire article, you can follow the URL:

```
import reprlib
r = reprlib.Repr()
r.maxstring = 800

url1 = "https://www.reuters.com/article/us-qualcomm-m-a-broadcom-5g/\
```

```
                what-is-5g-and-who-are-the-major-players-idUSKCN1GR1IN"
        article_name1 = download_article(url1)
        article1 = parse_article(article_name1)
        print ('Article Published on', r.repr(article1['time']))
        print (r.repr(article1['text']))
```

Out:

```
        Article Published on '2018-03-15T11:36:28+0000'
        'LONDON/SAN FRANCISCO (Reuters) - U.S. President Donald Trump has blocked
        microchip maker Broadcom Ltd's (AVGO.O) $117 billion takeover of rival Qualcomm
        (QCOM.O) amid concerns that it would give China the upper hand in the next
        generation of mobile communications, or 5G. A 5G sign is seen at the Mobile
        World Congress in Barcelona, Spain February 28, 2018. REUTERS/Yves HermanBelow
        are some facts... 4G wireless and looks set to top the list of patent holders
        heading into the 5G cycle. Huawei, Nokia, Ericsson and others are also vying to
        amass 5G patents, which has helped spur complex cross-licensing agreements like
        the deal struck late last year Nokia and Huawei around handsets. Editing by Kim
        Miyoung in Singapore and Jason Neely in LondonOur Standards:The Thomson Reuters
        Trust Principles.'
```

 We make use of the reprlib package, which allows us to customize the output of the print statement. In this case, printing the contents of the full article would not make sense. We limit the size of the output to 800 characters, and the reprlib package reformats the output to show a selected sequence of words from the beginning and end of the article.

Blueprint: Summarizing Text Using Topic Representation

Let's first try to summarize the example Reuters article ourselves. Having read through it, we could provide the following manually generated summary:

5G is the next generation of wireless technology that will rely on denser arrays of small antennas to offer data speeds up to 50 or 100 times faster than current 4G networks. These new networks are supposed to deliver faster data not just to phones and computers but to a whole array of sensors in cars, cargo, crop equipment, etc. Qualcomm is the dominant player in smartphone communications chips today, and the concern is that a takeover by Singapore-based Broadcom could see the firm cut research and development spending by Qualcomm or hive off strategically important parts of the company to other buyers, including in China. This risked weakening Qualcomm, which would boost China over the United States in the 5G race.

As humans, we understand what the article is conveying and then generate a summary of our understanding. However, an algorithm doesn't have this understanding and therefore has to rely on the identification of important topics to determine whether a sentence should be included in the summary. In the example article, topics could be broad themes like technology, telecommunications, and 5G, but to an algorithm this is nothing but a collection of important words. Our first method tries to distinguish between important and not-so-important words that allows us to then give a higher rank to sentences that contain important words.

Identifying Important Words with TF-IDF Values

The simplest approach would be to identify important sentences based on an aggregate of the TF-IDF values of the words in that sentence. A detailed explanation of TF-IDF is provided in Chapter 5, but for this blueprint, we apply the TF-IDF vectorization and then aggregate the values to a sentence level. We can generate a score for each sentence as a sum of the TF-IDF values for each word in that sentence. This would mean that a sentence with a high score contains many important words as compared to other sentences in the article:

```
from sklearn.feature_extraction.text import TfidfVectorizer
from nltk import tokenize

sentences = tokenize.sent_tokenize(article1['text'])
tfidfVectorizer = TfidfVectorizer()
words_tfidf = tfidfVectorizer.fit_transform(sentences)
```

In this case, there are approximately 20 sentences in the article, and we chose to create a condensed summary that is only 10% of the size of the original article (approximately two to three sentences). We sum up the TF-IDF values for each sentence and use np.argsort to sort them. This method sorts the indices of each sentence in ascending order, and we reverse the returned indices using [::-1]. To ensure the same flow of thoughts as presented in the article, we print the chosen summarized sentences in the same order in which they appear. We can see the results of our generated summary, as shown here:

```
# Parameter to specify number of summary sentences required
num_summary_sentence = 3

# Sort the sentences in descending order by the sum of TF-IDF values
sent_sum = words_tfidf.sum(axis=1)
important_sent = np.argsort(sent_sum, axis=0)[::-1]

# Print three most important sentences in the order they appear in the article
for i in range(0, len(sentences)):
    if i in important_sent[:num_summary_sentence]:
        print (sentences[i])
```

Out:

> LONDON/SAN FRANCISCO (Reuters) - U.S. President Donald Trump has blocked
> microchip maker Broadcom Ltd's (AVGO.O) $117 billion takeover of rival Qualcomm
> (QCOM.O) amid concerns that it would give China the upper hand in the next
> generation of mobile communications, or 5G.
> 5G networks, now in the final testing stage, will rely on denser arrays of
> small antennas and the cloud to offer data speeds up to 50 or 100 times faster
> than current 4G networks and serve as critical infrastructure for a range of
> industries.
> The concern is that a takeover by Singapore-based Broadcom could see the firm
> cut research and development spending by Qualcomm or hive off strategically
> important parts of the company to other buyers, including in China, U.S.
> officials and analysts have said.

In this method, we create an intermediate representation of the text using TF-IDF values, score the sentences based on this, and pick three sentences with the highest score. The sentences selected using this method agree with the manual summary we wrote earlier and capture the main points covered by the article. Some nuances like the importance of Qualcomm in the industry and the specific applications of 5G technology are missing. But this method serves as a good blueprint to quickly identify important sentences and automatically generate the summary for news articles. We wrap this blueprint into a function tfidf_summary that is defined in the accompanying notebook and reused later in the chapter.

LSA Algorithm

One of the modern methods used in extractive-based summarization is *latent semantic analysis* (LSA). LSA is a general-purpose method that is used for topic modeling, document similarity, and other tasks. LSA assumes that words that are close in meaning will occur in the same documents. In the LSA algorithm, we first represent the entire article in the form of a sentence-term matrix. The concept of a document-term matrix has been introduced in Chapter 8, and we can adapt the concept to fit a sentence-term matrix. Each row represents a sentence, and each column represents a word. The value of each cell in this matrix is the word frequency often scaled as TF-IDF weights. The objective of this method is to reduce all the words to a few topics by creating a modified representation of the sentence-term matrix. To create the modified representation, we apply the method of nonnegative matrix factorization that expresses this matrix as the product of two new decomposed matrices that have fewer rows/columns. You can refer to Chapter 8 for a more detailed understanding of this method. After the matrix decomposition step, we can generate the summary by choosing the top N important topics and then picking the most important sentences for each of these topics to form our summary.

Instead of applying LSA from scratch, we make use of the package sumy, which can be installed using the command **pip install sumy**. It provides multiple summarization methods within the same library. This library uses an integrated stop words list along with the tokenizer and stemmer functionality from NLTK but makes this configurable. In addition, it is also able to read input from plain text, HTML, and files. This gives us the ability to quickly test different summarization methods and change the default configurations to suit specific use cases. For now, we will go with the default options, including identifying the top three sentences:[1]

```
from sumy.parsers.plaintext import PlaintextParser
from sumy.nlp.tokenizers import Tokenizer
from sumy.nlp.stemmers import Stemmer
from sumy.utils import get_stop_words

from sumy.summarizers.lsa import LsaSummarizer

LANGUAGE = "english"
stemmer = Stemmer(LANGUAGE)

parser = PlaintextParser.from_string(article1['text'], Tokenizer(LANGUAGE))
summarizer = LsaSummarizer(stemmer)
summarizer.stop_words = get_stop_words(LANGUAGE)

for sentence in summarizer(parser.document, num_summary_sentence):
    print (str(sentence))
```

Out:

```
LONDON/SAN FRANCISCO (Reuters) - U.S. President Donald Trump has blocked
microchip maker Broadcom Ltd's (AVGO.O) $117 billion takeover of rival Qualcomm
(QCOM.O) amid concerns that it would give China the upper hand in the next
generation of mobile communications, or 5G.
Moving to new networks promises to enable new mobile services and even whole
new business models, but could pose challenges for countries and industries
unprepared to invest in the transition.
The concern is that a takeover by Singapore-based Broadcom could see the firm
cut research and development spending by Qualcomm or hive off strategically
important parts of the company to other buyers, including in China, U.S.
officials and analysts have said.
```

By analyzing the results, we see that there is a difference in only one sentence from the results of the TF-IDF, and that is sentence 2. While the LSA method chose to highlight a sentence that captures the topic about challenges, the TF-IDF method chose a sentence that provides more information about 5G. In this scenario, the summaries generated by the two methods are not very different, but let's analyze how this method works on a longer article.

---

1 You can find more information about the package, including the usage guidelines that we used while designing this blueprint on GitHub (*https://oreil.ly/IOFMA*).

We wrap this blueprint into a function `lsa_summary`, which is defined in the accompanying notebook and can be reused:

```
r.maxstring = 800
url2 = "https://www.reuters.com/article/us-usa-economy-watchlist-graphic/\
        predicting-the-next-u-s-recession-idUSKCN1V31JE"
article_name2 = download_article(url2)
article2 = parse_article(article_name2)
print ('Article Published', r.repr(article1['time']))
print (r.repr(article2['text']))
```

Out:

```
Article Published '2018-03-15T11:36:28+0000'
'NEW YORK A protracted trade war between China and the United States, the
world's largest economies, and a deteriorating global growth outlook has left
investors apprehensive about the end to the longest expansion in American
history. FILE PHOTO: Ships and shipping containers are pictured at the port of
Long Beach in Long Beach, California, U.S., January 30, 2019.   REUTERS/Mike
BlakeThe recent ...hton wrote in the June Cass Freight Index report.   12.
MISERY INDEX The so-called Misery Index adds together the unemployment rate and
the inflation rate. It typically rises during recessions and sometimes prior to
downturns. It has slipped lower in 2019 and does not look very miserable.
Reporting by Saqib Iqbal Ahmed; Editing by Chizu NomiyamaOur Standards:The
Thomson Reuters Trust Principles.'
```

Then:

```
summary_sentence = tfidf_summary(article2['text'], num_summary_sentence)
for sentence in summary_sentence:
    print (sentence)
```

Out:

```
REUTERS/Mike BlakeThe recent rise in U.S.-China trade war tensions has brought
forward the next U.S. recession, according to a majority of economists polled
by Reuters who now expect the Federal Reserve to cut rates again in September
and once more next year.
On Tuesday, U.S. stocks jumped sharply higher and safe-havens like the Japanese
yen and Gold retreated after the U.S. Trade Representative said additional
tariffs on some Chinese goods, including cell phones and laptops, will be
delayed to Dec. 15.
ISM said its index of national factory activity slipped to 51.2 last month, the
lowest reading since August 2016, as U.S. manufacturing activity slowed to a
near three-year low in July and hiring at factories shifted into lower gear,
suggesting a further loss of momentum in economic growth early in the third
quarter.
```

And finally:

```
summary_sentence = lsa_summary(article2['text'], num_summary_sentence)
for sentence in summary_sentence:
    print (sentence)
```

`Out:`

```
NEW YORK A protracted trade war between China and the United States, the
world's largest economies, and a deteriorating global growth outlook has left
investors apprehensive about the end to the longest expansion in American
history.
REUTERS/Mike BlakeThe recent rise in U.S.-China trade war tensions has brought
forward the next U.S. recession, according to a majority of economists polled
by Reuters who now expect the Federal Reserve to cut rates again in September
and once more next year.
Trade tensions have pulled corporate confidence and global growth to multi-year
lows and U.S. President Donald Trump's announcement of more tariffs have raised
downside risks significantly, Morgan Stanley analysts said in a recent note.
```

The difference in the chosen summarized sentences becomes more evident here. The main topic of the trade war tensions is captured by both methods, but the LSA summarizer also highlights important topics such as the apprehensiveness of investors and corporate confidence. While the TF-IDF tries to express the same idea in its chosen sentences, it does not pick the right sentences and therefore fails to convey the idea. There are other topic-based summarization methods, but we have chosen to highlight LSA as a simple and widely used method.

It's interesting to note that the sumy library also provides the implementation of one of the oldest methods for automatic text summarization (LuhnSummarizer), which was created by Hans Peter Luhn in 1958 (*https://oreil.ly/j6cQI*). This method is also based on topic representation by identifying important words using their counts and setting thresholds to get rid of extremely frequent and infrequent words. You can use this as a baseline method for your summarization experiments and compare improvements provided by other methods.

Blueprint: Summarizing Text Using an Indicator Representation

Indicator representation methods aim to create the intermediate representation of a sentence by using features of the sentence and its relationship to others in the document rather than using only the words in the sentence. TextRank (*https://oreil.ly/yY29h*) is one of the most popular examples of an indicator-based method. TextRank is inspired by PageRank, a "graph-based ranking algorithm that was originally used by Google to rank search results. As per the authors of the TextRank paper, graph-based algorithms rely on the collective knowledge of web architects rather than individual content analysis of web pages," which leads to improved performance. Applied to our context, we will rely on the features of a sentence and the linkages between them rather than on topics contained in each sentence.

We will first try to understand how the PageRank algorithm works and then adapt the methodology to the text summarization problem. Let's consider a list of web pages—(A, B, C, D, E, and F) and their links to one another. In Figure 9-1, page A contains a link to page D. Page B contains links to A and D and so on. We can also represent this in the form of a matrix with rows referring to each page and with columns referring to incoming links from other pages. The matrix shown in the figure represents our graph with rows representing each node, columns referring to incoming links from other nodes, and the value of the cell representing the weight of the edge between them. We start with a simple representation (1 indicates an incoming link, 0 indicates none). We can then normalize these values by dividing by the total number of outgoing links for each web page. For example, page C has two outgoing links (to pages E and F), and therefore the value of each outgoing link is 0.5.

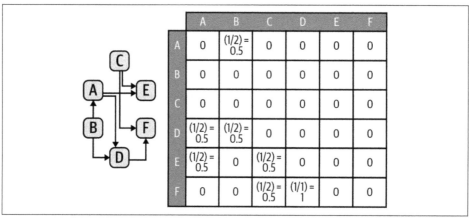

Figure 9-1. Web page links and corresponding PageRank matrix.

The PageRank for a given page is a weighted sum of the PageRank for all other pages that have a link to it. This also means that calculating the PageRank is an iterative function where we must start with some assumed values of PageRank for each page. If we assume all initial values to be 1 and multiply the matrices as shown in Figure 9-2, we arrive at the PageRank for each page after one iteration (not taking into consideration the damping factor for this illustration).

The research paper by Brin and Page (*https://oreil.ly/WjjFv*) showed that after repeating this calculation for many iterations the values stabilize, and hence we get the PageRank or importance for each page. TextRank adapts the previous approach by considering each sentence in the text to be analogous to a page and therefore a node in the graph. The weight of the edges between nodes is determined by the similarity between sentences, and the authors of TextRank suggest a simple approach by counting the number of shared lexical tokens, normalized by the size of both sentences. There are other similarity measures such as cosine distance and longest common substring that can also be used.

0	0.5	0	0	0	0
0	0	0	0	0	0
0	0	0	0	0	0
0.5	0.5	0	0	0	0
0.5	0	0.5	0	0	0
0	0	0.5	1	0	0

*

1
1
1
1
1
1

=

0.5
0
0
1.5
0.5
1.5

Figure 9-2. Application of one iteration of PageRank algorithm.

Since the sumy package also provides a TextRank implementation, we will use it to generate the summarized sentences for the article on the US recession that we saw previously:

```
from sumy.summarizers.text_rank import TextRankSummarizer

parser = PlaintextParser.from_string(article2['text'], Tokenizer(LANGUAGE))
summarizer = TextRankSummarizer(stemmer)
summarizer.stop_words = get_stop_words(LANGUAGE)

for sentence in summarizer(parser.document, num_summary_sentence):
    print (str(sentence))
```

```
REUTERS/Mike BlakeThe recent rise in U.S.-China trade war tensions has brought
forward the next U.S. recession, according to a majority of economists polled
by Reuters who now expect the Federal Reserve to cut rates again in September
and once more next year.
As recession signals go, this so-called inversion in the yield curve has a
solid track record as a predictor of recessions.
Markets turned down before the 2001 recession and tumbled at the start of the
2008 recession.
```

While one of the summarized sentences remains the same, this method has chosen to return two other sentences that are probably linked to the main conclusions drawn in this article. While these sentences themselves may not seem important, the use of a graph-based method resulted in selecting highly linked sentences that support the main theme of the article. We wrap this blueprint as a function textrank_summary, allowing us to reuse it.

We also want to see how this method works on the shorter article on 5G technology that we looked at previously:

```
parser = PlaintextParser.from_string(article1['text'], Tokenizer(LANGUAGE))
summarizer = TextRankSummarizer(stemmer)
summarizer.stop_words = get_stop_words(LANGUAGE)

for sentence in summarizer(parser.document, num_summary_sentence):
    print (str(sentence))
```

Out:

```
Acquiring Qualcomm would represent the jewel in the crown of Broadcom's
portfolio of communications chips, which supply wi-fi, power management, video
and other features in smartphones alongside Qualcomm's core baseband chips -
radio modems that wirelessly connect phones to networks.
Qualcomm (QCOM.O) is the dominant player in smartphone communications chips,
making half of all core baseband radio chips in smartphones.
Slideshow (2 Images)The standards are set by a global body to ensure all phones
work across different mobile networks, and whoever's essential patents end up
making it into the standard stands to reap huge royalty licensing revenue
streams.
```

We see that the results capture the central idea of the Qualcomm acquisition but do not contain any mention of 5G as a technology that was selected by the LSA method. TextRank generally works better in the case of longer text content as it is able to identify the most important sentences using the graph linkages. In the case of shorter text content, the graphs are not very large, and therefore the wisdom of the network plays a smaller role. Let's use an example of even longer content from Wikipedia to highlight this point further. We will reuse the blueprint from Chapter 2 to download the text content of a Wikipedia article. In this case, we choose an article that describes a historical event or series of events: the Mongol invasion of Europe. And since this is much longer text, we choose to summarize about 10 sentences to provide a better summary:

```
p_wiki = wiki_wiki.page('Mongol_invasion_of_Europe')
print (r.repr(p_wiki.text))
```

Out:

```
'The Mongol invasion of Europe in the 13th century occurred from the 1220s into
the 1240s. In Eastern Europe, the Mongols destroyed Volga Bulgaria, Cumania,
Alania, and the Kievan Rus\' federation. In Central Europe, the Mongol armies
launched a tw...tnotes\nReferences\nSverdrup, Carl (2010). "Numbers in Mongol
Warfare". Journal of Medieval Military History. Boydell Press. 8: 109-17 [p.
115]. ISBN 978-1-84383-596-7.\n\nFurther reading\nExternal links\nThe Islamic
World to 1600: The Golden Horde'
```

Then:

```
r.maxstring = 200

num_summary_sentence = 10
```

```
summary_sentence = textrank_summary(p_wiki.text, num_summary_sentence)

for sentence in summary_sentence:
    print (sentence)
```

We illustrate the results as highlighted sentences in the original Wikipedia page (Figure 9-3) to show that using the TextRank algorithm provides an almost accurate summarization of the article by picking the most important sentences from each section of the article. We can compare how this works with an LSA method, but we leave this as an exercise to the reader using the previous blueprint. Based on our experiences, when we want to summarize a large piece of text content, for example, scientific research papers, collection of writings, and speeches by world leaders or multiple web pages, then we would choose a graph-based method like TextRank.

Figure 9-3. Wikipedia page with selected summary sentences highlighted.

Measuring the Performance of Text Summarization Methods

In the blueprints so far, we have seen many methods that produce summaries of some given text. Each summary differs from the other in subtle ways, and we have to rely on our subjective evaluation. This is certainly a challenge in selecting a method that works best for a given use case. In this section, we will introduce commonly used accuracy metrics and show how they can be used to empirically select the best method for summarization.

We must understand that to automatically evaluate the summary of some given text, there must be a reference summary that it can be compared with. Typically, this is a summary written by a human and is referred to as the *gold standard*. Every automatically generated summary can be compared with the gold standard to get an accuracy measure. This also gives us the opportunity to easily compare multiple methods and choose the best one. However, we will often run into the issue that a human-generated summary may not exist for every use case. In such situations, we can choose a proxy measure to be considered as the gold standard. An example in the case of a news article would be the headline. While it is written by a human, it is a poor proxy as it can be quite short and is not an accurate summary but more of a leading statement to draw users. While this may not give us the best results, it is still useful to compare the performance of different summarization methods.

Recall-Oriented Understudy for Gisting Evaluation (ROUGE) is one of the most commonly used methods to measure the accuracy of a summary. There are several types of ROUGE metrics, but the basic idea is simple. It arrives at the measure of accuracy by comparing the number of shared terms between the automatically generated summary and the gold standard. ROUGE-N is a metric that measures the number of common n-grams (ROUGE-1 compares individual words, ROUGE-2 compares bigrams, and so on).

The original ROUGE paper (*https://oreil.ly/Tsncq*) compared how many of the words that appear in the gold standard also appear in the automatically generated summary. This is what we introduced in Chapter 6 as *recall*. So if most of the words present in the gold standard were also present in the generated summary, we would achieve a high score. However, this metric alone does not tell the whole story. Consider that we generate a verbose summary that is long but includes most of the words in the gold standard. This summary would have a high score, but it would not be a good summary since it doesn't provide a concise representation. This is why the ROUGE measure has been extended to compare the number of shared words to the total number of words in the generated summary as well. This indicates the precision: the number of words in the generated summary that are actually useful. We can combine these measures to generate the F-score.

Let's see an example of ROUGE for one of our generated summaries. Since we do not have a gold standard human-generated summary, we use the headline of the article as a proxy for the gold standard. While it is simple to calculate this independently, we make use of the Python package called rouge_scorer to make our life easier. This package implements all the ROUGE measures that we will use later, and it can be installed by executing the command **pip install rouge_scorer**. We make use of a print utility function print_rouge_score to present a concise view of the scores:

```
num_summary_sentence = 3
gold_standard = article2['headline']
summary = ""

summary = ''.join(textrank_summary(article2['text'], num_summary_sentence))
scorer = rouge_scorer.RougeScorer(['rouge1'], use_stemmer=True)
scores = scorer.score(gold_standard, summary)
print_rouge_score(scores)
```

Out:

```
rouge1 Precision: 0.06 Recall: 0.83 fmeasure: 0.11
```

The previous result shows us that the summary generated by TextRank has a high recall but low precision. This is an artifact of our gold standard being an extremely short headline, which is itself not the best choice but used here for illustration. The most important use of our metric is a comparison with another summarization method, and in this case, let's compare this with the LSA-generated summary:

```
summary = ''.join(lsa_summary(article2['text'], num_summary_sentence))
scores = scorer.score(gold_standard, summary)
print_rouge_score(scores)
```

Out:

```
rouge1 Precision: 0.04 Recall: 0.83 fmeasure: 0.08
```

The above result shows us that TextRank was the superior method in this case because it had a higher precision, while the recall of both methods was the same. We can easily extend ROUGE-1 to ROUGE-2, which would compare the number of common sequences of two words (bigrams). Another important metric is ROUGE-L, which measures the number of common sequences between the reference summary and the generated summary by identifying the longest common subsequences. A subsequence of a sentence is a new sentence that can be generated from the original sentence with some words deleted without changing the relative order of the remaining words. The advantage of this metric is that it does not focus on exact sequence matches but in-sequence matches that reflect sentence-level word order. Let's analyze the ROUGE-2 and ROUGE-L metrics for the Wikipedia page. Again, we do not have a gold standard, and therefore we will use the introductory paragraph as the proxy for our gold standard:

```
num_summary_sentence = 10
gold_standard = p_wiki.summary

summary = ''.join(textrank_summary(p_wiki.text, num_summary_sentence))

scorer = rouge_scorer.RougeScorer(['rouge2','rougeL'], use_stemmer=True)
scores = scorer.score(gold_standard, summary)
print_rouge_score(scores)
```

Out:

```
rouge2 Precision: 0.18 Recall: 0.46 fmeasure: 0.26
rougeL Precision: 0.16 Recall: 0.40 fmeasure: 0.23
```

Then:

```
summary = ''.join(lsa_summary(p_wiki.text, num_summary_sentence))

scorer = rouge_scorer.RougeScorer(['rouge2','rougeL'], use_stemmer=True)
```

```
scores = scorer.score(gold_standard, summary)
print_rouge_score(scores)
```

Out:

```
rouge2 Precision: 0.04 Recall: 0.08 fmeasure: 0.05
rougeL Precision: 0.12 Recall: 0.25 fmeasure: 0.16
```

Based on the results, we see that TextRank proves to be more accurate than LSA. We can use the same method as shown earlier to see which method works best for shorter Wikipedia entries, which we will leave as an exercise for the reader. When applying this to your use case, it is important that you choose the right summary for comparison. For instance, when working with news articles, instead of using the headline, you could look for a summary section contained within the article or generate one yourself for a small number of articles. This would allow you to have a fair comparison between different methods.

Blueprint: Summarizing Text Using Machine Learning

Many of you might have participated in online discussion forums for topics such as travel planning, programming, etc. Users on these platforms communicate in the form of threads. Anybody can start a thread, and other members provide their responses on this thread. Threads can become long, and the key message might be lost. In this blueprint, we will use data extracted from a travel forum used in the research paper,[2] which contains the text for all posts in a thread along with the summary for that thread, as shown in Figure 9-4.

In this blueprint, we are going to use machine learning to help us automatically identify the most important posts across the entire thread that accurately summarize it. We will first use the summary by the annotator to create target labels for our dataset. We will then generate features that can be useful to determine whether a particular post should be in the summary and finally train a model and evaluate the accuracy. The task at hand is similar to text classification but performed at a post level.

While the forum threads are used to illustrate this blueprint, it can easily be used for other use-cases. For example, consider the CNN and Daily Mail news summarization task (*https://oreil.ly/T_RNc*), DUC (*https://oreil.ly/0Hlov*), or SUMMAC (*https://oreil.ly/Wg322*) datasets. In each of these datasets, you will find the text of each article

---

2 Sansiri Tarnpradab, et al. "Toward Extractive Summarization of Online ForumDiscussions via Hierarchical Attention Networks." *https://arxiv.org/abs/1805.10390*. See the data set (*.zip*) (*https://oreil.ly/cqU_O*) as well.

and the highlighted summary sentences. These are analogous to the text of each thread and the summary as presented in this blueprint.

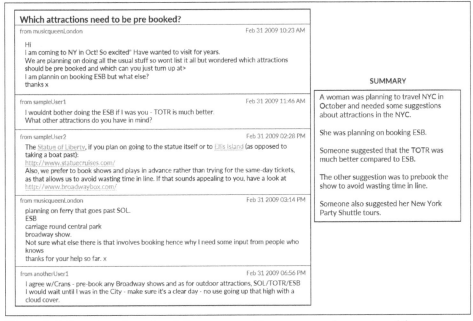

Figure 9-4. Posts in a thread and the corresponding summary from a travel forum.

Step 1: Creating Target Labels

The first step is to load the dataset, understand its structure, and create target labels using the provided summary. We have performed the initial data preparation steps to create a well-formatted DataFrame, shown next. Please refer to the Data_Preparation notebook in the GitHub repo of the book for a detailed look at the steps:

```
import pandas as pd
import numpy as np


df = pd.read_csv('travel_threads.csv', sep='|', dtype={'ThreadID': 'object'})
df[df['ThreadID']=='60763_5_3122150'].head(1).T
```

	170
Date	29 September 2009, 1:41
Filename	thread41_system20
ThreadID	60763_5_3122150
Title	which attractions need to be pre booked?
postNum	1

	170
text	Hi I am coming to NY in Oct! So excited" Have wanted to visit for years. We are planning on doing all the usual stuff so wont list it all but wondered which attractions should be pre booked and which can you just turn up at> I am plannin on booking ESB but what else? thanks x
userID	musicqueenLon...
summary	A woman was planning to travel NYC in October and needed some suggestions about attractions in the NYC. She was planning on booking ESB.Someone suggested that the TOTR was much better compared to ESB. The other suggestion was to prebook the show to avoid wasting time in line.Someone also suggested her New York Party Shuttle tours.

Each row in this dataset refers to a post in a thread. Each thread is identified by a unique `ThreadID`, and it's possible that multiple rows in the `DataFrame` have the same `ThreadID`. The column `Title` refers to the name with which the user started the thread. The content of each post is in the `text` column, along with additional details like the name of the user who created the post (`userID`), the time when the post was created (`Date`), and its position in the thread (`postNum`). For this dataset, human-generated summaries for each thread are provided in the `summary` column.

We will reuse the regular expression cleaning and spaCy pipeline blueprints from Chapter 4 to remove special formatting, URLs, and other punctuation from the posts. We will also generate the lemmatized representation of the text, which we will use for prediction. You can find the function definitions in the accompanying notebook for this chapter. Since we are making use of the spaCy lemmatization function, it might take a couple of minutes to complete execution:

```
# Applying regex based cleaning function
df['text'] = df['text'].apply(regex_clean)
# Extracting lemmas using spacy pipeline
df['lemmas'] = df['text'].apply(clean)
```

Each observation in our dataset contains a post that is part of a thread. If we were to apply a train-test split at this level, it is possible that two posts belonging to the same thread would end up in the train and test datasets, which would lead to inaccurate training. As a result, we use `GroupShuffleSplit` to group all posts into their respective threads and then randomly select 80% of the threads to create the training dataset, with the rest of the threads forming part of the test dataset. This function ensures that posts belonging to the same thread are part of the same dataset. The `GroupShuffleSplit` function does not actually split the data but provides a set of indices that split the data identified by `train_split` and `test_split`. We use these indices to create the two datasets:

```
from sklearn.model_selection import GroupShuffleSplit

gss = GroupShuffleSplit(n_splits=1, test_size=0.2)
train_split, test_split = next(gss.split(df, groups=df['ThreadID']))
```

```
train_df = df.iloc[train_split]
test_df = df.iloc[test_split]

print ('Number of threads for Training ', train_df['ThreadID'].nunique())
print ('Number of threads for Testing ', test_df['ThreadID'].nunique())
```

Out:

```
Number of threads for Training  559
Number of threads for Testing  140
```

Our next step is to determine the target label for each of our posts. The target label defines whether a particular post should be included in the summary. We determine this by comparing each post to the annotator summary and picking posts that are most similar to be included in the summary. There are several metrics that can be used to determine the similarity of two sentences, but in our use case we are working with short texts and therefore choose the Jaro-Winkler distance (*https://oreil.ly/ b5q0B*). We use the `textdistance` package that also provides implementations of other distance metrics. This can be easily installed using the command **pip install textdistance**. You can also easily modify the blueprint and choose a metric based on your use case.

In the following step, we determine the similarity and rank all the posts within a thread based on the chosen metric. We then create our target label named summary Post that contains a True or False value indicating whether this post is part of the summary. This is based on the rank of the post and the compression factor. We choose a compression factor of 30%, which means that we pick the top 30% of all posts ordered by their similarity to be included in the summary:

```
import textdistance

compression_factor = 0.3

train_df['similarity'] = train_df.apply(
    lambda x: textdistance.jaro_winkler(x.text, x.summary), axis=1)
train_df["rank"] = train_df.groupby("ThreadID")["similarity"].rank(
    "max", ascending=False)

topN = lambda x: x <= np.ceil(compression_factor * x.max())
train_df['summaryPost'] = train_df.groupby('ThreadID')['rank'].apply(topN)

train_df[['text','summaryPost']][train_df['ThreadID']=='60763_5_3122150'].head(3)
```

Out:

text	summaryPost
170 Hi I am coming to NY in Oct! So excited" Have wanted to visit for years. We are planning on doing all the usual stuff so wont list it all but wondered which attractions should be pre booked and which can you just turn up at> I am plannin on booking ESB but what else? thanks x	True

	text	summaryPost
171	I wouldnt bother doing the ESB if I was you TOTR is much better. What other attractions do you have in mind?	False
172	The Statue of Liberty, if you plan on going to the statue itself or to Ellis Island (as opposed to taking a boat past): http://www.statuecruises.com/ Also, we prefer to book shows and plays in advance rather than trying for the same-day tickets, as that allows us to avoid wasting time in line. If that sounds appealing to you, have a look at http://www.broadwaybox.com/	True

As you can see in the previous results for a given thread, the first and third posts are tagged as summaryPost, but the second post is not considered important and would not be included in the summary. Because of the way we defined our target label, it is possible in rare situations that very short posts are also included in the summary. This might happen when a short post contains the same words as the thread title. This is not useful to the summary, and we correct this by setting all posts containing 20 words or less to not be included in the summary:

```
train_df.loc[train_df['text'].str.len() <= 20, 'summaryPost'] = False
```

Step 2: Adding Features to Assist Model Prediction

Since we are dealing with forum threads in this blueprint, there are some additional features that we can generate to help our model in the prediction. The title of the thread conveys the topic succinctly and can be helpful in identifying which post should actually be selected in the summary. We cannot directly include the title as a feature since it would be the same for each post in the thread, but instead we calculate the similarity between the post and the title as one of the features:

```
train_df['titleSimilarity'] = train_df.apply(
    lambda x: textdistance.jaro_winkler(x.text, x.Title), axis=1)
```

Another useful feature could be the length of the post. Short posts could be asking clarifying questions and would not capture the most useful knowledge of the thread. Longer posts could indicate that a lot of useful information is being shared. The position of where the post appears in the thread could also be a useful indicator of whether it should be in the summary. This might vary depending on the way in which the forum threads are organized. In the case of the travel forum, the posts are chronologically ordered, and the occurrence of the post is given by the column post Num, which we can readily use as a feature:

```
# Adding post length as a feature
train_df['textLength'] = train_df['text'].str.len()
```

As a final step, let's create the vectorized representation of the lemmas that we extracted earlier using the *TfidfVectorizer*. We then create a new DataFrame, train_df_tf, which contains the vectorized lemmas and the additional features that we created earlier:

```
feature_cols = ['titleSimilarity','textLength','postNum']

train_df['combined'] = [
    ' '.join(map(str, l)) for l in train_df['lemmas'] if l is not '']
tfidf = TfidfVectorizer(min_df=10, ngram_range=(1, 2), stop_words="english")
tfidf_result = tfidf.fit_transform(train_df['combined']).toarray()

tfidf_df = pd.DataFrame(tfidf_result, columns=tfidf.get_feature_names())
tfidf_df.columns = ["word_" + str(x) for x in tfidf_df.columns]
tfidf_df.index = train_df.index
train_df_tf = pd.concat([train_df[feature_cols], tfidf_df], axis=1)
```

This step of adding features can be extended or customized depending on the use case. For example, if we are looking to summarize longer text, then the paragraph that a sentence belongs to will be important. Normally, each paragraph or section tries to capture an idea, and sentence similarity metrics at that level would be relevant. If we are looking at generating summaries of scientific papers, then the number of citations and the sentences used for those citations have proven to be useful. We must also repeat the same feature engineering steps on the test dataset, which we show in the accompanying notebook but exclude here.

Step 3: Build a Machine Learning Model

Now that we've generated features, we will reuse the text classification blueprint from Chapter 6 but use a `RandomForestClassifier` model instead of the SVM model. While building a machine learning model for summarization, we might have additional features other than the vectorized text representation. Particularly in situations where a combination of numeric and categorical features are present, a tree-based classifier might perform better:

```
from sklearn.ensemble import RandomForestClassifier

model1 = RandomForestClassifier()
model1.fit(train_df_tf, train_df['summaryPost'])
```

Out:

```
RandomForestClassifier(bootstrap=True, ccp_alpha=0.0, class_weight=None,
                       criterion='gini', max_depth=None, max_features='auto',
                       max_leaf_nodes=None, max_samples=None,
                       min_impurity_decrease=0.0, min_impurity_split=None,
                       min_samples_leaf=1, min_samples_split=2,
                       min_weight_fraction_leaf=0.0, n_estimators=100,
                       n_jobs=None, oob_score=False, random_state=20, verbose=0,
                       warm_start=False)
```

Let's apply this model on the test threads and predict the summary posts. To determine the accuracy, we concatenate all identified summary posts and generate the ROUGE-1 score by comparing it with the annotator summary:

```
# Function to calculate rouge_score for each thread
def calculate_rouge_score(x, column_name):
    # Get the original summary - only first value since they are repeated
    ref_summary = x['summary'].values[0]

    # Join all posts that have been predicted as summary
    predicted_summary = ''.join(x['text'][x[column_name]])

    # Return the rouge score for each ThreadID
    scorer = rouge_scorer.RougeScorer(['rouge1'], use_stemmer=True)
    scores = scorer.score(ref_summary, predicted_summary)
    return scores['rouge1'].fmeasure
test_df['predictedSummaryPost'] = model1.predict(test_df_tf)
print('Mean ROUGE-1 Score for test threads',
      test_df.groupby('ThreadID')[['summary','text','predictedSummaryPost']] \
      .apply(calculate_rouge_score, column_name='predictedSummaryPost').mean())
```

Out:

```
Mean ROUGE-1 Score for test threads 0.3439714323225145
```

We see that the mean ROUGE-1 score for all threads in the test set is 0.34, which is comparable with extractive summarization scores on other public summarization tasks (*https://oreil.ly/SaCk2*). You will also notice on the leaderboard that the use of pretrained models such as BERT improves the score, and we explore this technique in detail in Chapter 11.

```
random.seed(2)
random.sample(test_df['ThreadID'].unique().tolist(), 1)
```

Out:

```
['60974_588_2180141']
```

Let's also take a look at one of the summarized results produced by this model to understand how useful it might be:

```
example_df = test_df[test_df['ThreadID'] == '60974_588_2180141']
print('Total number of posts', example_df['postNum'].max())
print('Number of summary posts',
      example_df[example_df['predictedSummaryPost']].count().values[0])
print('Title: ', example_df['Title'].values[0])
example_df[['postNum', 'text']][example_df['predictedSummaryPost']]
```

Out:

```
Total number of posts 9
Number of summary posts 2
Title:  What's fun for kids?
```

postNum	text
551 4	Well, you're really in luck, because there's a lot going on, including the Elmwood Avenue Festival of the Arts (http://www.elmwoodartfest.org), with special activities for youngsters, performances (including one by Nikki Hicks, one of my favorite local vocalists), and food of all kinds. Elmwood Avenue is one of the area's most colorful and thriving neighborhoods, and very walkable. The Buffalo Irish Festival is also going on that weekend in Hamburg, as it happens, at the fairgrounds: www.buf...
552 5	Depending on your time frame, a quick trip to Niagara Falls would be great. It is a 45 minute drive from Hamburg and well worth the investment of time. Otherwise you have some beaches in Angola to enjoy. If the girls like to shop you have the Galleria, which is a great expansive Mall. If you enjoy a more eclectic afternoon, lunch on Elmwood Avenue, a stroll through the Albright Know Art gallery, and hitting some of the hip shops would be a cool afternoon. Darien Lake Theme Park is 40 minutes...

In the previous example, the original thread consisted of nine posts, two of which have been picked to summarize the thread, as shown earlier. Reading through the summary posts shows that the thread is about activities for youngsters, and there are already some specific suggestions, such as Elmwood Avenue, Darien Lake Theme Park, etc. Imagine that while scrolling through the forum search results, this information is provided on a mouse hover. It gives the user an accurate enough summary to decide whether it's interesting and click through for more details or continue looking at other search results. You could also easily reuse this blueprint with other datasets as mentioned at the start and customize the distance function, introduce additional features, and then train the model.

Closing Remarks

In this chapter, we introduced the concept of text summarization and provided blueprints that can be used to generate summaries for different use cases. If you are looking to generate summaries from short text such as web pages, blogs, and news articles, then the first blueprint based on topic representation using the LSA summarizer would be a good choice. If you are working with much larger text such as speeches, book chapters, or scientific articles, then the blueprint using TextRank would be a better choice. These blueprints are great as the first step in your journey toward automatic text summarization as they are simple and fast. However, the third blueprint using machine learning provides a more custom solution for your specific use case. Provided you have the necessary annotated data, this method can be tailored by adding features and optimizing the machine learning model to improve performance. For example, your company or product might have multiple policy documents that govern user data, terms and conditions, and other such processes that you want to summarize for a new user or employee. You could start with the third blueprint and customize the second step by adding features such as the number of clauses, usage of block letters, presence of bold or underlined text, etc., that will help the model summarize the important points in the policy documents.

Further Reading

Allahyari, Mehdi, et al. "Text Summarization Techniques: A Brief Survey." *https://arxiv.org/pdf/1707.02268.pdf*.

Bhatia, Sumit, et al. "Summarizing Online Forum Discussions—Can Dialog Acts of Individual Messages Help?" *http://sumitbhatia.net/papers/emnlp14.pdf*.

Collins, Ed, et al. "A Supervised Approach to Extractive Summarisation of Scientific Papers." *https://arxiv.org/pdf/1706.03946.pdf*.

Tarnpradab, Sansiri, et al. "Toward Extractive Summarization of Online ForumDiscussions via Hierarchical Attention Networks." *https://aaai.org/ocs/index.php/FLAIRS/FLAIRS17/paper/viewFile/15500/14945*.

## CHAPTER 10

Exploring Semantic Relationships with Word Embeddings

The concept of similarity is fundamental to all machine learning tasks. In Chapter 5, we explained how to compute text similarity based on the bag-of-words model. Given two TF-IDF vectors for documents, their cosine similarity can be easily computed, and we can use this information to search, cluster, or classify similar documents.

However, the concept of similarity in the bag-of-words model is completely based on the number of common words in two documents. If documents do not share any tokens, the dot product of the document vectors and hence the cosine similarity will be zero. Consider the following two comments about a new movie, which could be found on a social platform:

"What a wonderful movie."

"The film is great."

Obviously, the comments have a similar meaning even though they use completely different words. In this chapter, we will introduce word embeddings as a means to capture the semantics of words and use them to explore semantic similarities within a corpus.

What You'll Learn and What We'll Build

For our use case we assume that we are market researchers and want to use texts about cars to better understand some relationships in the car market. Specifically, we want to explore similarities among car brands and models. For example, which models of brand A are most similar to a given model of brand B?

Our corpus consists of the 20 subreddits in the autos category of the Reddit Self-Posts dataset, which was already used in Chapter 4. Each of these subreddits contains 1,000 posts on cars and motorcycles with brands such as Mercedes, Toyota, Ford, and Harley-Davidson. Since those posts are questions, answers, and comments written by users, we will actually get an idea of what these users implicitly *consider* as being similar.

We will use the Gensim library (*https://oreil.ly/HaYkR*) again, which was introduced in Chapter 8. It provides a nice API to train different types of embeddings and to use those models for semantic reasoning.

After studying this chapter, you will be able to use word embeddings for semantic analysis. You will know how to use pretrained embeddings, how to train your own embeddings, how to compare different models, and how to visualize them. You can find the source code for this chapter along with some of the images in our GitHub repository (*https://oreil.ly/W1ztU*).

The Case for Semantic Embeddings

In the previous chapters, we used the TF-IDF vectorization for our models. It is easy to compute, but it has some severe disadvantages:

- The document vectors have a very high dimensionality that is defined by the size of the vocabulary. Thus, the vectors are extremely sparse; i.e., most entries are zero.
- It does not work well for short texts like Twitter messages, service comments, and similar content because the probability for common words is low for short texts.
- Advanced applications such as sentiment analysis, question answering, or machine translation require capturing the real meaning of the words to work correctly.

Still, the bag-of-words model works surprisingly well for tasks such as classification or topic modeling, but only if the texts are sufficiently long and enough training data is available. Remember that similarity in the bag-of-words model is solely based on the existence of significant common words.

An *embedding*, in contrast, is a dense numerical vector representation of an object that captures some kind of *semantic* similarity. When we talk of embeddings in the context of text analysis, we have to distinguish word and document embeddings. A *word embedding* is a vector representation for a single word, while a *document embedding* is a vector representing a document. By *document* we mean any sequence of words, be it a short phrase, a sentence, a paragraph, or even a long article. In this chapter, we will focus on dense vector representations for words.

Word Embeddings

The target of an embedding algorithm can be defined as follows: given a dimensionality d, find vector representations for words such that words with similar meanings have similar vectors. The dimensionality d is a hyperparameter of any word embedding algorithm. It is typically set to a value between 50 and 300.

The dimensions themselves have no predefined or human-understandable meaning. Instead, the model learns latent relations among the words from the text. Figure 10-1 (left) illustrates the concept. We have five-dimensional vectors for each word. Each of these dimensions represents some relation among the words so that words similar in that aspect have similar values in this dimension. Dimension names shown are possible interpretations of those values.

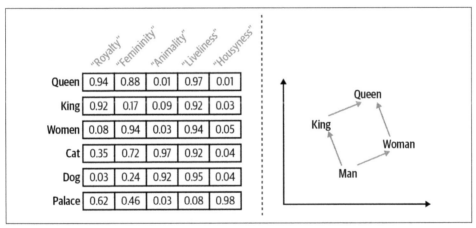

Figure 10-1. Dense vector representations captioning semantic similarity of words (left) can be used to answer analogy questions (right). We gave the vector dimensions hypothetical names like "Royalty" to show possible interpretations.[1]

The basic idea for training is that words occurring in similar contexts have similar meanings. This is called the *distributional hypothesis*. Take, for example, the following sentences describing *tesgüino*:[2]

- A bottle of ___ is on the table.
- Everybody likes ___ .
- Don't have ___ before you drive.
- We make ___ out of corn.

---

1 Inspired by Adrian Colyer's "The Amazing Power of Word Vectors" blog post (*https://oreil.ly/8iMPF*).

2 This frequently cited example originally came from the linguist Eugene Nida in 1975.

Even without knowing the word *tesgüino*, you get a pretty good understanding of its meaning by analyzing typical contexts. You could also identify semantically similar words because you know it's an alcoholic beverage.

Analogy Reasoning with Word Embeddings

What's really amazing is that word vectors built this way allow us to detect analogies like "queen is to king like woman is to man" with vector algebra (Figure 10-1, right). Let $v(w)$ be the word embedding for a word w. Then the analogy can be expressed mathematically like this:

$$v(queen) - v(king) \approx v(woman) - v(man)$$

If this approximate equation holds, we can reformulate the analogy as a question: What is to *king* like "woman" is to "man"? Or mathematically:[3]

$$v(woman) + [v(king) - v(man)] \approx ?$$

This allows some kind of fuzzy reasoning to answer analogy questions like this one: "Given that Paris is the capital of France, what is the capital of Germany?" Or in a market research scenario as the one we will explore: "Given that F-150 is a pickup truck from Ford, what is the similar model from Toyota?"

Types of Embeddings

Several algorithms have been developed to train word embeddings. Gensim allows you to train Word2Vec and FastText embeddings. GloVe embeddings can be used for similarity queries but not trained with Gensim. We introduce the basic ideas of these algorithms and briefly explain the more advanced but also more complex contextualized embedding methods. You will find the references to the original papers and further explanations at the end of this chapter.

Word2Vec

Even though there have been approaches for word embeddings before, the work of Tomáš Mikolov at Google (Mikolov et al., 2013) marks a milestone because it dramatically outperformed previous approaches, especially on analogy tasks such as the ones just explained. There exist two variants of Word2Vec, the *continuous bag-of-words model* (CBOW) and the *skip-gram model* (see Figure 10-2).

---

3 Jay Alammar's blog post entitled "The Illustrated Word2Vec" (*https://oreil.ly/TZNTT*) gives a wonderful visual explanation of this equation.

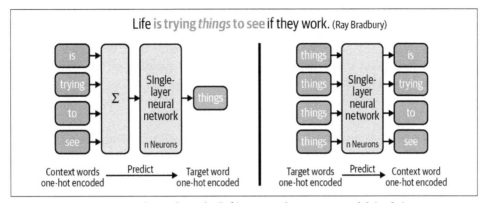

Figure 10-2. Continuous bag-of words (left) versus skip-gram model (right).

Both algorithms use a sliding window over the text, defined by a target word w_t and the size of the context window c. In the example, $c = 2$, i.e., the training samples consist of the five words $w_{t-2}, \cdots, w_{t+2}$. One such training sample is printed in bold: ... **is trying *things* to see** .... In the CBOW architecture (left), the model is trained to predict the target words from their context words. Here, a training sample consists of the sum or average of the one-hot encoded vectors of the context words and the target word as the label. In contrast, the skip-gram model (right) is trained to predict the context words given the target word. In this case, each target word generates a separate training sample for each context word; there is no vector averaging. Thus, skip-gram trains slower (much slower for large window sizes!) but often gives better results for infrequent words.

Both embedding algorithms use a simple single-layer neural network and some tricks for fast and scalable training. The learned embeddings are actually defined by the weight matrix of the hidden layer. Thus, if you want to learn 100-dimensional vector representations, the hidden layer has to consist of 100 neurons. The input and output words are represented by one-hot vectors. The dimensionality of the embeddings and size of the context window c are hyperparameters in all of the embedding methods presented here. We will explore their impact on the embeddings later in this chapter.

GloVe

The GloVe (global vectors) approach (*https://oreil.ly/7hIGW*), developed in 2014 by Stanford's NLP group, uses a global co-occurrence matrix to compute word vectors instead of a prediction task (Pennington et al., 2014). A co-occurrence matrix for a vocabulary of size V has the dimensionality $V \times V$. Each cell (i, j) in the matrix contains the number of co-occurrences of the words w_i and w_j based again on a fixed context window size. The embeddings are derived using a matrix factorization technique similar to those used for topic modeling or dimensionality reduction.

The model is called *global* because the co-occurrence matrix captures global corpus statistics in contrast to Word2Vec, which uses only the local context window for its prediction task. GloVe does not generally perform better than Word2Vec but produces similarly good results with some differences depending on the training data and the task (see Levy et al., 2014, for a discussion).

FastText

The third model we introduce was developed again by a team with Tomáš Mikolov, this time at Facebook (Joulin et al., 2017). The main motivation was to handle out-of-vocabulary words. Both Word2Vec and GloVe produce word embeddings only for words contained in the training corpus. FastText (*https://fasttext.cc*), in contrast, uses subword information in the form of character n-grams to derive vector representations. The character trigrams for *fasttext* are, for example, *fas*, *ast*, *stt*, *tte*, *tex*, and *ext*. The lengths of n-grams used (minimum and maximum) are hyperparameters of the model.

Any word vector is built from the embeddings of its character n-grams. And that does work even for words previously unseen by the model because most of the character n-grams have embeddings. For example, the vector for *fasttext* will be similar to *fast* and *text* because of the common n-grams. Thus, FastText is pretty good at finding embeddings for misspelled words that are usually out-of-vocabulary.

Deep contextualized embeddings

The semantic meaning of a word often depends on its context. Think of different meanings of the word *right* in "I am right" and "Please turn right."[4] All three models (Word2Vec, GloVe, and FastText) have just one vector representation per word; they cannot distinguish between context-dependent semantics.

Contextualized embeddings like *Embedding from Language Models* (ELMo) take the context, i.e., the preceding and following words, into account (Peters et al., 2018). There is not one word vector stored for each word that can simply be looked up. Instead, ELMo passes the whole sentence through a multilayer bidirectional long short-term memory neural network (LSTM) and assembles the vectors for each word from weights of the internal layers. Recent models such as BERT and its successors improve the approach by using attention transformers instead of bidirectional LSTMs. The main benefit of all these models is transfer learning: the ability to use a pretrained language model and fine-tune it for specific downstream tasks such as classification or question answering. We will cover this concept in more detail in Chapter 11.

---

4 Words having the same pronunciation but different meanings are called *homonyms*. If they are spelled identically, they are called *homographs*.

Blueprint: Using Similarity Queries on Pretrained Models

After all this theory, let's start some practice. For our first examples, we use pretrained embeddings. These have the advantage that somebody else spent the training effort, usually on a large corpus like Wikipedia or news articles. In our blueprint, we will check out available models, load one of them, and do some reasoning with word vectors.

Loading a Pretrained Model

Several models are publicly available for download.[5] We will describe later how to load custom models, but here we will use Gensim's convenient downloader API instead.

Per the default, Gensim stores models under ~/gensim-data. If you want to change this to a custom path, you can set the environment variable GENSIM_DATA_DIR before importing the downloader API. We will store all models in the local directory models:

```
import os
os.environ['GENSIM_DATA_DIR'] = './models'
```

Now let's take a look at the available models. The following lines transform the dictionary returned by api.info()['models'] into a DataFrame to get a nicely formatted list and show the first five of a total of 13 entries:

```
import gensim.downloader as api

info_df = pd.DataFrame.from_dict(api.info()['models'], orient='index')
info_df[['file_size', 'base_dataset', 'parameters']].head(5)
```

	file_size	base_dataset	parameters
fasttext-wiki-news-subwords-300	1005007116	Wikipedia 2017, UMBC webbase corpus and statmt.org news dataset (16B tokens)	{'dimension': 300}
conceptnet-numberbatch-17-06-300	1225497562	ConceptNet, word2vec, GloVe, and OpenSubtitles 2016	{'dimension': 300}
word2vec-ruscorpora-300	208427381	Russian National Corpus (about 250M words)	{'dimension': 300, 'window_size': 10}

---

5 For example, from RaRe Technologies (*https://oreil.ly/twoOR*) and 3Top (*https://oreil.ly/4DwDy*).

	file_size	base_dataset	parameters
word2vec-google-news-300	1743563840	Google News (about 100 billion words)	{'dimension': 300}
glove-wiki-gigaword-50	69182535	Wikipedia 2014 + Gigaword 5 (6B tokens, uncased)	{'dimension': 50}

We will use the *glove-wiki-gigaword-50* model. This model with 50-dimensional word vectors is small in size but still quite comprehensive and fully sufficient for our purposes. It was trained on roughly 6 billion lowercased tokens. api.load downloads the model if required and then loads it into memory:

```
model = api.load("glove-wiki-gigaword-50")
```

The file we downloaded actually does not contain a full GloVe model but just the plain word vectors. As the internal states of the model are not included, such reduced models cannot be trained further.

Similarity Queries

Given a model, the vector for a single word like *king* can be accessed simply via the property model.wv['king'] or even more simply by the shortcut model['king']. Let's take a look at the first 10 components of the 50-dimensional vectors for *king* and *queen*.

```
v_king = model['king']
v_queen = model['queen']

print("Vector size:", model.vector_size)
print("v_king  =", v_king[:10])
print("v_queen =", v_queen[:10])
print("similarity:", model.similarity('king', 'queen'))
```

Out:

```
Vector size: 50
v_king  = [ 0.5   0.69 -0.6  -0.02  0.6  -0.13 -0.09  0.47 -0.62 -0.31]
v_queen = [ 0.38  1.82 -1.26 -0.1   0.36  0.6  -0.18  0.84 -0.06 -0.76]
similarity: 0.7839043
```

As expected, the values are similar in many dimensions, resulting in a high similarity score of over 0.78. So *queen* is quite similar to *king*, but is it the most similar word? Well, let's check the three words most similar to *king* with a call to the respective function:

```
model.most_similar('king', topn=3)
```

Out:

```
[('prince', 0.824), ('queen', 0.784), ('ii', 0.775)]
```

In fact, the male *prince* is more similar than *queen*, but *queen* is second in the list, followed by the roman numeral II, because many kings have been named "the second."

Similarity scores on word vectors are generally computed by cosine similarity, which was introduced in Chapter 5. Gensim provides several variants of similarity functions. For example, the `cosine_similarities` method computes the similarity between a word vector and an array of other word vectors. Let's compare *king* to some more words:

```
v_lion = model['lion']
v_nano = model['nanotechnology']

model.cosine_similarities(v_king, [v_queen, v_lion, v_nano])
```

Out:

```
array([ 0.784,  0.478, -0.255], dtype=float32)
```

Based on the training data for the model (Wikipedia and Gigaword), the model assumes the word *king* to be similar to *queen*, still a little similar to *lion*, but not at all similar to *nanotechnology*. Note, that in contrast to nonnegative TF-IDF vectors, word embeddings can also be negative in some dimensions. Thus, the similarity values range from $+1$ to -1.

The function `most_similar()` used earlier allows also two parameters, `positive` and `negative`, each a list of vectors. If $positive = [pos_1, \cdots, pos_n]$ and $negative = [neg_1, \cdots, neg_m]$, then this function finds the word vectors most similar to $\sum_{i=1}^{n} pos_i - \sum_{j=1}^{m} neg_j$.

Thus, we can formulate our analogy query about the royals in Gensim this way:

```
model.most_similar(positive=['woman', 'king'], negative=['man'], topn=3)
```

Out:

```
[('queen', 0.852), ('throne', 0.766), ('prince', 0.759)]
```

And the question for the German capital:

```
model.most_similar(positive=['paris', 'germany'], negative=['france'], topn=3)
```

Out:

```
[('berlin', 0.920), ('frankfurt', 0.820), ('vienna', 0.818)]
```

We can also leave out the negative list to find the word closest to the sum of *france* and *capital*:

```
model.most_similar(positive=['france', 'capital'], topn=1)
```

Out:

```
[('paris', 0.784)]
```

It is indeed `paris`! That's really amazing and shows the great power of word vectors. However, as always in machine learning, the models are not perfect. They can learn only what's in the data. Thus, by far not all similarity queries yield such staggering results, as the following example demonstrates:

```
model.most_similar(positive=['greece', 'capital'], topn=3)
```

Out:

```
[('central', 0.797), ('western', 0.757), ('region', 0.750)]
```

Obviously, there has not been enough training data for the model to derive the relation between Athens and Greece.

 Gensim also offers a variant of cosine similarity, `most_similar_cos mul`. This is supposed to work better for analogy queries than the one shown earlier because it smooths the effects of one large similarity term dominating the equation (Levy et al., 2015). For the previous examples, however, the returned words would be the same, but the similarity scores would be higher.

If you train embeddings with redacted texts from Wikipedia and news articles, your model will be able to capture factual relations like capital-country quite well. But what about the market research question comparing products of different brands? Usually you won't find this information on Wikipedia but rather on up-to-date social platforms where people discuss products. If you train embeddings on user comments from a social platform, your model will learn word associations from user discussions. This way, it becomes a representation of what people *think* about a relationship, independent of whether this is objectively true. This is an interesting side effect you should be aware of. Often you want to capture exactly this application specific bias, and this is what we are going to do next. But be aware that every training corpus contains some bias, which may also lead to unwanted side effects (see "Man Is to Computer Programmer as Woman Is to Homemaker").

Man Is to Computer Programmer as Woman Is to Homemaker

Most state-of-the-art approaches for NLP tasks ranging from classification to machine translation use semantic embeddings for better results. Thus, the quality of the embeddings has a direct impact on the quality of the final model. Unfortunately, machine learning algorithms have the tendency to amplify biases present in the training data. This is also true for word embeddings.

Bolukbasi et al., showed that "even word embeddings trained on Google News articles exhibit female/male gender stereotypes to a disturbing extent." This is problematic, as a common approach is to use pretrained word embeddings for downstream tasks such as classification. Thus, debiasing training data is a hot topic in research nowadays.

Blueprints for Training and Evaluating Your Own Embeddings

In this section, we will train and evaluate domain-specific embeddings on 20,000 user posts on autos from the Reddit Selfposts dataset. Before we start training, we have to consider the options for data preparation as they always have a significant impact on the usefulness of a model for a specific task.

Data Preparation

Gensim requires sequences of tokens as input for the training. Besides tokenization there are some other aspects to consider for data preparation. Based on the distributional hypothesis, words frequently appearing together or in similar context will get similar vectors. Thus, we should make sure that co-occurrences are actually identified as such. If you do not have very many training sentences, as in our example here, you should include these steps in your preprocessing:

1. Clean text from unwanted tokens (symbols, tags, etc.).
2. Put all words into lowercase.
3. Use lemmas.

All this keeps the vocabulary small and training times short. Of course, inflected and uppercase words will be out-of-vocabulary if we prune our training data according to these rules. This is not a problem for semantic reasoning on nouns as we want to do, but it could be, if we wanted to analyze, for example, emotions. In addition, you should consider these token categories:

Stop words
    Stop words can carry valuable information about the context of non-stop words. Thus, we prefer to keep the stop words.

Numbers
    Depending on the application, numbers can be valuable or just noise. In our example, we are looking at auto data and definitely want to keep tokens like 328

because it's a BMW model name. You should keep numbers if they carry relevant information.

Another question is whether we should split on sentences or just keep the posts as they are. Consider the imaginary post "I like the BMW 328. But the Mercedes C300 is also great." Should these sentences be treated like two different posts for our similarity task? Probably not. Thus, we will treat the list of all lemmas in one user post as a single "sentence" for training.

We already prepared the lemmas for the 20,000 Reddit posts on autos in Chapter 4. Therefore, we can skip that part of data preparation here and just load the lemmas into a Pandas `DataFrame`:

```
db_name = "reddit-selfposts.db"
con = sqlite3.connect(db_name)
df = pd.read_sql("select subreddit, lemmas, text from posts_nlp", con)
con.close()

df['lemmas'] = df['lemmas'].str.lower().str.split() # lower case tokens
sents = df['lemmas'] # our training "sentences"
```

Phrases

Especially in English, the meaning of a word may change if the word is part of a compound phrase. Take, for example, *timing belt*, *seat belt*, or *rust belt*. All of these compounds have different meanings, even though all of them can be found in our corpus. So, it may better to treat such compounds as single tokens.

We can use any algorithm to detect such phrases, for example, spaCy's detection of noun chunks (see "Linguistic Processing with spaCy" on page 104). A number of statistical algorithms also exist to identify such collocations, such as extraordinary frequent n-grams. The original Word2Vec paper (Mikolov et al., 2013) uses a simple but effective algorithm based on *pointwise mutual information* (PMI), which basically measures the statistical dependence between the occurrences of two words.

For the model that we are now training, we use an advanced version called *normalized pointwise mutual information* (NPMI) because it gives more robust results. And given its limited value range from −1 to +1, it is also easier to tune. The NPMI threshold in our initial run is set to a rather low value of 0.3. We choose a hyphen as a delimiter to connect the words in a phrase. This generates compound tokens like *harley-davidson*, which will be found in the text anyway. The default underscore delimiter would result in a different token:

```
from gensim.models.phrases import Phrases, npmi_scorer

phrases = Phrases(sents, min_count=10, threshold=0.3,
                  delimiter=b'-', scoring=npmi_scorer)
```

With this phrase model we can identify some interesting compound words:

```
sent = "I had to replace the timing belt in my mercedes c300".split()
phrased = phrases[sent]
print('|'.join(phrased))
```

Out:

```
I|had|to|replace|the|timing-belt|in|my|mercedes-c300
```

timing-belt is good, but we do not want to build compounds for combinations of brands and model names, like *mercedes c300*. Thus, we will analyze the phrase model to find a good threshold. Obviously, the chosen value was too low. The following code exports all phrases found in our corpus together with their scores and converts the result to a `DataFrame` for easy inspection:

```
phrase_df = pd.DataFrame(phrases.export_phrases(sents),
                         columns =['phrase', 'score'])
phrase_df = phrase_df[['phrase', 'score']].drop_duplicates() \
            .sort_values(by='score', ascending=False).reset_index(drop=True)
phrase_df['phrase'] = phrase_df['phrase'].map(lambda p: p.decode('utf-8'))
```

Now we can check what would be a good threshold for *mercedes*:

```
phrase_df[phrase_df['phrase'].str.contains('mercedes')]
```

	phrase	score
83	mercedes benz	0.80
1417	mercedes c300	0.47

As we can see, it should be larger than 0.5 and less than 0.8. Checking with a few other brands like *bmw*, *ford*, or *harley davidson* lets us identify 0.7 as a good threshold to identify compound vendor names but keep brands and models separate. In fact, with the rather stringent threshold of 0.7, the phrase model still keeps many relevant word combinations, for example, *street glide* (Harley-Davidson), *land cruiser* (Toyota), *forester xt* (Subaru), *water pump*, *spark plug*, or *timing belt*.

We rebuild our phraser and create a new column in our `DataFrame` with single tokens for compound words:

```
phrases = Phrases(sents, min_count=10, threshold=0.7,
                  delimiter=b'-', scoring=npmi_scorer)

df['phrased_lemmas'] = df['lemmas'].map(lambda s: phrases[s])
sents = df['phrased_lemmas']
```

The result of our data preparation steps are sentences consisting of lemmas and phrases. We will now train different embedding models and check which insights we can gain from them.

Blueprint: Training Models with Gensim

Word2Vec and FastText embeddings can be conveniently trained by Gensim. The following call to `Word2Vec` trains 100-dimensional Word2Vec embeddings on the corpus with a window size of 2, i.e., target word ±2 context words. Some other relevant hyperparameters are passed as well for illustration. We use the skip-gram algorithm and train the network in four threads for five epochs:

```
from gensim.models import Word2Vec

model = Word2Vec(sents,        # tokenized input sentences
                 size=100,     # size of word vectors (default 100)
                 window=2,     # context window size (default 5)
                 sg=1,         # use skip-gram (default 0 = CBOW)
                 negative=5,   # number of negative samples (default 5)
                 min_count=5,  # ignore infrequent words (default 5)
                 workers=4,    # number of threads (default 3)
                 iter=5)       # number of epochs (default 5)
```

This takes about 30 seconds on an i7 laptop for the 20,000 sentences, so it is quite fast. More samples and more epochs, as well as longer vectors and larger context windows, will increase the training time. For example, training 100-dimensional vectors with a context window size of 30 requires about 5 minutes in this setting for skip-gram. The CBOW training time, in contrast, is rather independent of the context window size.

The following call saves the full model to disk. *Full model* means the complete neural network, including all internal states. This way, the model can be loaded again and trained further:

```
model.save('./models/autos_w2v_100_2_full.bin')
```

The choice of the algorithm as well as those hyperparameters have quite an impact on the resulting models. Therefore, we provide a blueprint to train and inspect different models. A parameter grid defines which algorithm variant (CBOW or skip-gram) and window sizes will be trained for Word2Vec or FastText. We could also vary vector size here, but that parameter does not have such a big impact. In our experience, 50- or 100-dimensional vectors work well on smaller corpora. So, we fix the vector size to 100 in our experiments:

```
from gensim.models import Word2Vec, FastText

model_path = './models'
model_prefix = 'autos'

param_grid = {'w2v': {'variant': ['cbow', 'sg'], 'window': [2, 5, 30]},
```

```
                'ft': {'variant': ['sg'], 'window': [5]}}
size = 100

for algo, params in param_grid.items():
    for variant in params['variant']:
        sg = 1 if variant == 'sg' else 0
        for window in params['window']:
            if algo == 'w2v':
                model = Word2Vec(sents, size=size, window=window, sg=sg)
            else:
                model = FastText(sents, size=size, window=window, sg=sg)

            file_name = f"{model_path}/{model_prefix}_{algo}_{variant}_{window}"
            model.wv.save_word2vec_format(file_name + '.bin', binary=True)
```

As we just want to analyze the similarities within our corpus, we do not save the complete models here but just the plain word vectors. These are represented by the class KeyedVectors and can be accessed by the model property model.wv. This generates much smaller files and is fully sufficient for our purpose.

Beware of information loss! When you reload models consisting only of the word vectors, they cannot be trained further. Moreover, FastText models lose the ability to derive embeddings for out-of-vocabulary words.

Blueprint: Evaluating Different Models

Actually, it is quite hard to algorithmically identify the best hyperparameters for a domain-specific task and corpus. Thus, it is not a bad idea to inspect the models manually and check how they perform to identify some already-known relationships.

The saved files containing only the word vectors are small (about 5 MB each), so we can load many of them into memory and run some comparisons. We use a subset of five models to illustrate our findings. The models are stored in a dictionary indexed by the model name. You could add any models you'd like to compare, even the pre-trained GloVe model from earlier:

```
from gensim.models import KeyedVectors

names = ['autos_w2v_cbow_2', 'autos_w2v_sg_2',
         'autos_w2v_sg_5', 'autos_w2v_sg_30', 'autos_ft_sg_5']
models = {}

for name in names:
```

```
        file_name = f"{model_path}/{name}.bin"
        models[name] = KeyedVectors.load_word2vec_format(file_name, binary=True)
```

We provide a small blueprint function for the comparison. It takes a list of models and a word and produces a `DataFrame` with the most similar words according to each model:

```
def compare_models(models, **kwargs):

    df = pd.DataFrame()
    for name, model in models:
        df[name] = [f"{word} {score:.3f}"
                    for word, score in model.most_similar(**kwargs)]
    df.index = df.index + 1 # let row index start at 1
    return df
```

Now let's see what effect the parameters have on our computed models. As we are going to analyze the car market, we check out the words most similar to *bmw*:

```
compare_models([(n, models[n]) for n in names], positive='bmw', topn=10)
```

	autos_w2v_cbow_2	autos_w2v_sg_2	autos_w2v_sg_5	autos_w2v_sg_30	autos_ft_sg_5
1	mercedes 0.873	mercedes 0.772	mercedes 0.808	xdrive 0.803	bmws 0.819
2	lexus 0.851	benz 0.710	335i 0.740	328i 0.797	bmwfs 0.789
3	vw 0.807	porsche 0.705	328i 0.736	f10 0.762	m135i 0.774
4	benz 0.806	lexus 0.704	benz 0.723	335i 0.760	335i 0.773
5	volvo 0.792	merc 0.695	x-drive 0.708	535i 0.755	mercedes_benz 0.765
6	harley 0.783	mercede 0.693	135i 0.703	bmws 0.745	mercedes 0.760
7	porsche 0.781	mercedes-benz 0.680	mercede 0.690	x-drive 0.740	35i 0.747
8	subaru 0.777	audi 0.675	e92 0.685	5-series 0.736	merc 0.747
9	mb 0.769	335i 0.670	mercedes-benz 0.680	550i 0.728	135i 0.746
10	volkswagen 0.768	135i 0.662	merc 0.679	435i 0.726	435i 0.744

Interestingly, the first models with the small window size of 2 produce mainly other car brands, while the model with window size 30 produces basically lists of different BMW models. In fact, shorter windows emphasize paradigmatic relations, i.e., words that can be substituted for each other in a sentence. In our case, this would be brands as we are searching for words similar to *bmw*. Larger windows capture more syntagmatic relations, where words are similar if they frequently show up in the same context. Window size 5, which is the default, produced a mix of both. For our data, paradigmatic relations are best represented by the CBOW model, while syntagmatic relations require a large window size and are therefore better captured by the skipgram model. The outputs of the FastText model demonstrate its property that similarly spelled words get similar scores.

Looking for similar concepts

The CBOW vectors with window size 2 are pretty precise on paradigmatic relations. Starting from some known terms, we can use such a model to identify the central terms and concepts of a domain. Table 10-1 shows the output of some similarity queries on model `autos_w2v_cbow_2`. The column `concept` was added by us to highlight what kind of words we would expect as output.

Table 10-1. Most similar neighbors for selected words using the CBOW model with window size 2

Word	Concept	Most Similar
toyota	car brand	ford mercedes nissan certify dodge mb bmw lexus chevy honda
camry	car model	corolla f150 f-150 c63 is300 ranger 335i 535i 328i rx
spark-plug	car part	water-pump gasket thermostat timing-belt tensioner throttle-body serpentine-belt radiator intake-manifold fluid
washington	location	oregon southwest ga ottawa san_diego valley portland mall chamber county

Of course, the answers are not always correct with regard to our expectations; they are just similar words. For example, the list for *toyota* contains not only car brands but also several models. In real-life projects, however, domain experts from the business department can easily identify the wrong terms and still find interesting new associations. But manual curation is definitely necessary when you work with word embeddings this way.

Analogy reasoning on our own models

Now let's find out how our different models are capable of detecting analogous concepts. We want to find out if Toyota has a product comparable to Ford's F-150 pickup truck. So our question is: What is to "toyota" as "f150" is to "ford"? We use our function `compare_models` from earlier and transpose the result to compare the results of `wv.most_similar()` for different models:

```
compare_models([(n, models[n]) for n in names],
               positive=['f150', 'toyota'], negative=['ford'], topn=5).T
```

Out:

	1	2	3	4	5
autos_w2v_cbow_2	f-150 0.850	328i 0.824	s80 0.820	93 0.819	4matic 0.817
autos_w2v_sg_2	f-150 0.744	f-250 0.727	dodge-ram 0.716	tacoma 0.713	ranger 0.708
autos_w2v_sg_5	tacoma 0.724	tundra 0.707	f-150 0.664	highlander 0.644	4wd 0.631
autos_w2v_sg_30	4runner 0.742	tacoma 0.739	4runners 0.707	4wd 0.678	tacomas 0.658
autos_ft_sg_5	toyotas 0.777	toyo 0.762	tacoma 0.748	tacomas 0.745	f150s 0.744

In reality, the Toyota Tacoma is a direct competitor to the F-150 as well as the Toyota Tundra. With that in mind, the skip-gram model with the window size 5 gives the best results.[6] In fact, if you exchange *toyota* for *gmc*, you get the *sierra*, and if you ask for *chevy*, you get *silverado* as the most similar to this model. All of these are competing full-size pickup trucks. This also works quite well for other brands and models, but of course it works best for those models that are heavily discussed in the Reddit forum.

Blueprints for Visualizing Embeddings

If we explore our corpus on the basis of word embeddings, as we do in this chapter, we are not interested in the actual similarity scores because the whole concept is inherently fuzzy. What we want to understand are semantic relations based on the concepts of closeness and similarity. Therefore, visual representations can be extremely helpful for the exploration of word embeddings and their relations. In this section, we will first visualize embeddings by using different dimensionality reduction techniques. After that, we will show how to visually explore the semantic neighborhood of given keywords. As we will see, this type of data exploration can reveal quite interesting relationships between domain-specific terms.

Blueprint: Applying Dimensionality Reduction

High-dimensional vectors can be visualized by projecting the data into two or three dimensions. If the projection works well, it is possible to visually detect clusters of related terms and get a much deeper understanding of semantic concepts in the corpus. We will look for clusters of related words and explore the semantic neighborhood of certain keywords in the model with window size 30, which favors syntagmatic relations. Thus, we expect to see a "BMW" cluster with BMW terms, a "Toyota" cluster with Toyota terms, and so on.

Dimensionality reduction also has many use cases in the area of machine learning. Some learning algorithms have problems with high-dimensional and often sparse data. Dimensionality reduction techniques such as PCA, t-SNE, or UMAP (see "Dimensionality Reduction Techniques" on page 287) try to preserve or even highlight important aspects of the data distribution by the projection. The general idea is to project the data in a way that objects close to each other in high-dimensional

---

6 If you run the code yourself, the results may be slightly different than the ones printed in the book because of random initialization.

space are close in the projection and, similarly, distant objects remain distant. In our examples, we will use the UMAP algorithm because it provides the best results for visualization. But as the umap library implements the scikit-learn estimator interface, you can easily replace the UMAP reducer with scikit-learn's PCA or TSNE classes.

Dimensionality Reduction Techniques

There are many different algorithms for dimensionality reduction. Frequently used for visualization are PCA, t-SNE, and UMAP.

Principal Component Analysis (PCA) performs a linear projection of the data such that most of the variance in the data points is preserved. Mathematically, it is based on the eigenvectors of the largest eigenvalues of the covariance matrix (the principal components). PCA only takes the global data distribution into account. Independent of local structures, all data points are transformed in the same way. Except for the number of dimensions in the target space (n_components), PCA has no hyperparameters to tune.

Nonlinear algorithms such as t-SNE and UMAP try to balance local and global aspects in the mapping. Thus, different areas of the original space get projected differently dependent on the local data distribution. Both algorithms provide hyperparameters that need to be carefully selected to produce good results. For t-SNE this is the perplexity (roughly the effective number of nearest neighbors of each point). For UMAP you need to specify the size of the local neighborhood (n_neighbors) and in addition the minimum distance of points in the projection (min_dist). t-SNE, published in 2008, is very popular but has some severe limitations. It preserves the local structure much better than the global structure, it does not scale well, and it works practically only for two or three dimensions. UMAP, published in 2018, is faster and retains the global data structure much better.

The following code block contains the basic operations to project the embeddings into two-dimensional space with UMAP, as shown in Figure 10-3. After the selection of the embedding models and the words to plot (in this case we take the whole vocabulary), we instantiate the UMAP dimensionality reducer with target dimensionality n_components=2. Instead of the standard Euclidean distance metric, we use the cosine as usual. The embeddings are then projected to 2D by calling reducer.fit_transform(wv).

```
from umap import UMAP

model = models['autos_w2v_sg_30']
words = model.vocab
wv = [model[word] for word in words]
```

```
reducer = UMAP(n_components=2, metric='cosine', n_neighbors = 15, min_dist=0.1)
reduced_wv = reducer.fit_transform(wv)
```

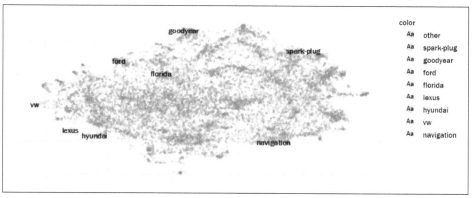

Figure 10-3. Two-dimensional UMAP projections of all word embeddings of our model. A few words and their most similar neighbors are highlighted to explain some of the clusters in this scatter plot.

We use Plotly Express here for visualization instead of Matplotlib because it has two nice features. First, it produces interactive plots. When you hover with the mouse over a point, the respective word will be displayed. Moreover, you can zoom in and out and select regions. The second nice feature of Plotly Express is its simplicity. All you need to prepare is a `DataFrame` with the coordinates and the metadata to be displayed. Then you just instantiate the chart, in this case the scatter plot (`px.scatter`):

```
import plotly.express as px

plot_df = pd.DataFrame.from_records(reduced_wv, columns=['x', 'y'])
plot_df['word'] = words
params = {'hover_data': {c: False for c in plot_df.columns},
          'hover_name': 'word'}

fig = px.scatter(plot_df, x="x", y="y", opacity=0.3, size_max=3, **params)
fig.show()
```

You can find a more general blueprint function `plot_embeddings` in the `embeddings` package in our GitHub repository (*https://oreil.ly/gX6Ti*). It allows you to choose the dimensionality reduction algorithm and highlight selected search words with their most similar neighbors in the low-dimensional projection. For the plot in Figure 10-3 we inspected some clusters manually beforehand and then explicitly named a few typical search words to colorize the clusters.[7] In the interactive view, you could see the words when you hover over the points.

---

7 You'll find the colorized figures in the electronic versions and on GitHub (*https://oreil.ly/MWJLd*).

Here is the code to produce this diagram:

```
from blueprints.embeddings import plot_embeddings

search = ['ford', 'lexus', 'vw', 'hyundai',
          'goodyear', 'spark-plug', 'florida', 'navigation']

plot_embeddings(model, search, topn=50, show_all=True, labels=False,
                algo='umap', n_neighbors=15, min_dist=0.1)
```

For data exploration, it might be more interesting to visualize only the set of search words and their most similar neighbors, without all other points. Figure 10-4 shows an example generated by the following lines. Displayed are the search words and their top 10 most similar neighbors:

```
search = ['ford', 'bmw', 'toyota', 'tesla', 'audi', 'mercedes', 'hyundai']

plot_embeddings(model, search, topn=10, show_all=False, labels=True,
                algo='umap', n_neighbors=15, min_dist=10, spread=25)
```

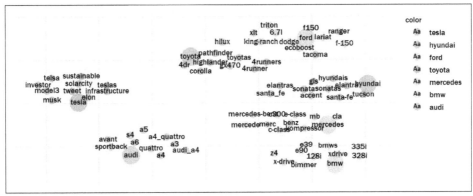

Figure 10-4. Two-dimensional UMAP projection of selected keywords words and their most similar neighbors.

Figure 10-5 shows the same keywords but with many more similar neighbors as a three-dimensional plot. It is nice that Plotly allows you to rotate and zoom into the point cloud. This way it is easy to investigate interesting areas. Here is the call to generate that diagram:

```
plot_embeddings(model, search, topn=30, n_dims=3,
                algo='umap', n_neighbors=15, min_dist=.1, spread=40)
```

To visualize analogies such as *tacoma is to toyota like f150 is to ford*, you should use the linear PCA transformation. Both UMAP and t-SNE distort the original space in a nonlinear manner. Therefore, the direction of difference vectors in the projected space can be totally unrelated to the original direction. Even PCA distorts because of shearing, but the effect is not as strong as in UMAP or t-SNE.

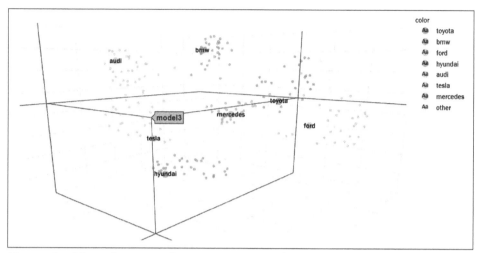

Figure 10-5. *Three-dimensional UMAP projection of selected keywords and their most similar neighbors.*

Blueprint: Using the TensorFlow Embedding Projector

A nice alternative to a self-implemented visualization function is the TensorFlow Embedding Projector. It also supports PCA, t-SNE, and UMAP and offers some convenient options for data filtering and highlighting. You don't even have to install TensorFlow to use it because there is an online version available (*https://oreil.ly/VKLxe*). A few datasets are already loaded as a demo.

To display our own word embeddings with the TensorFlow Embedding Projector, we need to create two files with tabulator-separated values: one file with the word vectors and an optional file with metadata for the embeddings, which in our case are simply the words. This can be achieved with a few lines of code:

```python
import csv

name = 'autos_w2v_sg_30'
model = models[name]

with open(f'{model_path}/{name}_words.tsv', 'w', encoding='utf-8') as tsvfile:
    tsvfile.write('\n'.join(model.vocab))

with open(f'{model_path}/{name}_vecs.tsv', 'w', encoding='utf-8') as tsvfile:
    writer = csv.writer(tsvfile, delimiter='\t',
                        dialect=csv.unix_dialect, quoting=csv.QUOTE_MINIMAL)
```

```
for w in model.vocab:
    _ = writer.writerow(model[w].tolist())
```

Now we can load our embeddings into the projector and navigate through the 3D visualization. For the detection of clusters, you should use UMAP or t-SNE. Figure 10-6 shows a cutout of the UMAP projection for our embeddings. In the projector, you can click any data point or search for a word and get the first 100 neighbors highlighted. We chose *harley* as a starting point to explore the terms related to Harley-Davidson. As you can see, this kind of visualization can be extremely helpful when exploring important terms of a domain and their semantic relationship.

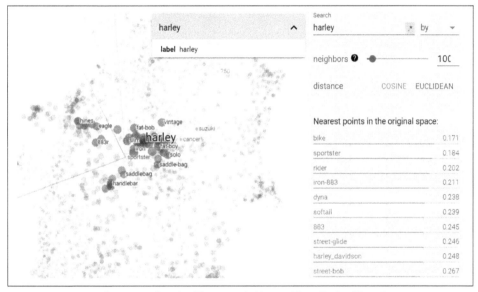

Figure 10-6. Visualization of embeddings with TensorFlow Embedding Projector.

 Blueprint: Constructing a Similarity Tree

The words with their similarity relations can be interpreted as a network graph in the following way: the words represent the nodes of the graph, and an edge is created whenever two nodes are "very" similar. The criterion for this could be either that the nodes are among their top-n most-similar neighbors or a threshold for the similarity score. However, most of the words in the vicinity of a word are similar not only to that word but also to each other. Thus, the complete network graph even for a small subset of words would have too many edges for comprehensible visualization. Therefore, we start with a slightly different approach and create a subgraph of this network, a similarity tree. Figure 10-7 shows such a similarity tree for the root word *noise*.

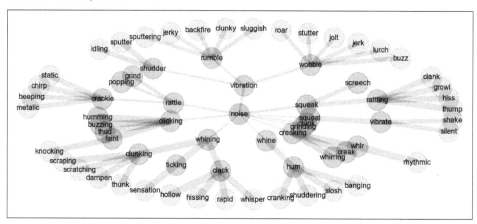

Figure 10-7. Similarity tree of words most similar to noise.

We provide two blueprint functions to create such visualizations. The first one, sim_tree, generates the similarity tree starting from a root word. The second one, plot_tree, creates the plot. We use Python's graph library networkx in both functions.

Let's first look at sim_tree. Starting from a root word, we look for the top-n most-similar neighbors. They are added to the graph with the according edges. Then we do the same for each of these newly discovered neighbors, and their neighbors, and so on, until a maximum distance to the root node is reached. Internally, we use a queue (collections.deque) to implement a breadth-first search. The edges are weighted by similarity, which is used later to style the line width:

```
import networkx as nx
from collections import deque

def sim_tree(model, word, top_n, max_dist):

    graph = nx.Graph()
    graph.add_node(word, dist=0)

    to_visit = deque([word])
    while len(to_visit) > 0:
        source = to_visit.popleft() # visit next node
        dist = graph.nodes[source]['dist']+1

        if dist <= max_dist: # discover new nodes
            for target, sim in model.most_similar(source, topn=top_n):
                if target not in graph:
                    to_visit.append(target)
```

```
              graph.add_node(target, dist=dist)
              graph.add_edge(source, target, sim=sim, dist=dist)
      return graph
```

The function `plot_tree` consists of just a few calls to create the layout and to draw the nodes and edges with some styling. We used Graphviz's `twopi` layout to create the snowflake-like positioning of nodes. A few details have been left out here for the sake of simplicity, but you can find the full code on GitHub (*https://oreil.ly/W-zbu*):

```
from networkx.drawing.nx_pydot import graphviz_layout

def plot_tree(graph, node_size=1000, font_size=12):

    pos = graphviz_layout(graph, prog='twopi', root=list(graph.nodes)[0])

    colors = [graph.nodes[n]['dist'] for n in graph] # colorize by distance
    nx.draw_networkx_nodes(graph, pos, node_size=node_size, node_color=colors,
                           cmap='Set1', alpha=0.4)
    nx.draw_networkx_labels(graph, pos, font_size=font_size)

    for (n1, n2, sim) in graph.edges(data='sim'):
        nx.draw_networkx_edges(graph, pos, [(n1, n2)], width=sim, alpha=0.2)

    plt.show()
```

Figure 10-7 was generated with these functions using this parametrization:

```
model = models['autos_w2v_sg_2']
graph = sim_tree(model, 'noise', top_n=10, max_dist=3)
plot_tree(graph, node_size=500, font_size=8)
```

It shows the most similar words to *noise* and their most similar words up to an imagined distance of 3 to *noise*. The visualization suggests that we created a kind of a taxonomy, but actually we didn't. We just chose to include only a subset of the possible edges in our graph to highlight the relationships between a "parent" word and its most similar "child" words. The approach ignores possible edges among siblings or to grandparents. The visual presentation nevertheless helps to explore the specific vocabulary of an application domain around the root word. However, Gensim also implements Poincaré embeddings (*https://oreil.ly/mff7p*) for learning hierarchical relationships among words.

The model with the small context window of 2 used for this figure brings out the different kinds and synonyms of noises. If we choose a large context window instead, we get more concepts related to the root word. Figure 10-8 was created with these parameters:

```
model = models['autos_w2v_sg_30']
graph = sim_tree(model, 'spark-plug', top_n=8, max_dist=2)
plot_tree(graph, node_size=500, font_size=8)
```

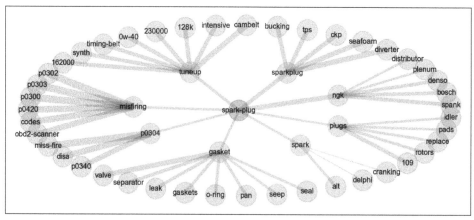

Figure 10-8. Similarity tree of words most similar to spark-plug's most similar words.

Here, we chose *spark-plug* as root word and selected the model with window size 30. The generated diagram gives a nice overview about domain-specific terms related to *spark-plugs*. For example, the codes like *p0302*, etc., are the standardized OBD2 error codes for misfires in the different cylinders.

Of course, these charts also bring up some the weaknesses of our data preparation. We see four nodes for *spark-plug*, *sparkplug*, *spark*, and *plugs*, all of which are representing the same concept. If we wanted to have a single embedding for all of these, we would have to merge the different forms of writing into a single token.

Closing Remarks

Exploring the similar neighbors of certain key terms in domain-specific models can be a valuable technique to discover latent semantic relationships among words in a domain-specific corpus. Even though the whole concept of word similarity is inherently fuzzy, we produced really interesting and interpretable results by training a simple neural network on just 20,000 user posts about cars.

As in most machine learning tasks, the quality of the results is strongly influenced by data preparation. Depending on the task you are going to achieve, you should decide consciously which kind of normalization and pruning you apply to the original texts. In many cases, using lemmas and lowercase words produces good embeddings for similarity reasoning. Phrase detection can be helpful, not only to improve the result but also to identify possibly important compound terms in your application domain.

We used Gensim to train, store, and analyze our embeddings. Gensim is very popular, but you may also want to check possibly faster alternatives like (Py)Magnitude (*https://oreil.ly/UlRzX*) or finalfusion (*https://oreil.ly/TwM4h*). Of course, you can also use TensorFlow and PyTorch to train different kinds of embeddings.

Today, semantic embeddings are fundamental for all complex machine learning tasks. However, for tasks such as sentiment analysis or paraphrase detection, you don't need embeddings for words but for sentences or complete documents. Many different approaches have been published to create document embeddings (Wolf, 2018; Palachy, 2019). A common approach is to compute the average of the word vectors in a sentence. Some of spaCy's models include word vectors (*https://oreil.ly/zI1wm*) in their vocabulary and allow the computation of document similarities based on average word vectors out of the box. However, averaging word vectors only works reasonably well for single sentences or very short documents. In addition, the whole approach is limited to the bag-of-words idea where the word order is not considered.

State-of-the-art models utilize both the power of semantic embeddings and the word order. We will use such a model in the next chapter for sentiment classification.

Further Reading

Bolukbasi, Tolga, Kai-Wei Chang, James Zou, Venkatesh Saligrama, and Adam Kalai. *Man Is to Computer Programmer as Woman Is to Homemaker? Debiasing Word Embeddings.* 2016. *https://arxiv.org/abs/1607.06520.*

Joulin, Armand, Edouard Grave, Piotr Bojanowski, and Tomáš Mikolov. *Bag of Tricks for Efficient Text Classification.* 2017. *https://www.aclweb.org/anthology/E17-2068.*

Levy, Omer, Yoav Goldberg, and Ido Dagan. *Improving Distributional Similarity with Lessons Learned from Word Embeddings.* *https://www.aclweb.org/anthology/Q15-1016.*

McCormick, Chris. *Word2Vec Tutorial.* *http://mccormickml.com/2016/04/19/word2vec-tutorial-the-skip-gram-model* and *http://mccormickml.com/2017/01/11/word2vec-tutorial-part-2-negative-sampling.*

Mikolov, Tomáš, Kai Chen, Greg Corrado, and Jeffrey Dean. *Efficient Estimation of Word Representations in Vector Space.* 2013. *https://arxiv.org/abs/1301.3781.*

Mikolov, Tomáš, Ilya Sutskever, Kai Chen, Greg Corrado, and Jeffrey Dean. *Distributed Representations of Words and Phrases and Their Compositionality.* 2013. *https://arxiv.org/abs/1310.4546.*

Palachy, Shay. *Beyond Word Embedding: Key Ideas in Document Embedding.* *https://www.kdnuggets.com/2019/10/beyond-word-embedding-document-embedding.html.*

Pennington, Jeffrey, Richard Socher, and Christopher Manning. *Glove: Global Vectors for Word Representation.* 2014. *https://nlp.stanford.edu/pubs/glove.pdf.*

Peters, Matthew E., Mark Neumann, Mohit Iyyer, et al. *Deep contextualized word representations.* 2018. *https://arxiv.org/abs/1802.05365.*

Wolf, Thomas. *The Current Best of Universal Word Embeddings and Sentence Embeddings.* 2018. *https://medium.com/huggingface/universal-word-sentence-embeddings-ce48ddc8fc3a.*

## CHAPTER 11

Performing Sentiment Analysis on Text Data

In every interaction that we have in the real world, our brain subconsciously registers feedback not just in the words said but also using facial expressions, body language, and other physical cues. However, as more of our communication becomes digital, it increasingly appears in the form of text, where we do not have the possibility of evaluating physical cues. Therefore, it's important to understand the mood or sentiment felt by a person through the text they write in order to form a complete understanding of their message.

For example, a lot of customer support is now automated through the use of a software ticketing system or even an automated chatbot. As a result, the only way to understand how a customer is feeling is by understanding the sentiment from their responses. Therefore, if we are dealing with a particularly irate customer, it's important to be extra careful with our responses to not annoy them further. Similarly, if we want to understand what customers think about a particular product or brand, we can analyze the sentiment from their posts, comments, or reviews about that brand in social media channels and understand how they feel about the brand.

Understanding sentiment from text is challenging because there are several aspects that need to be inferred that are not directly evident. A simple example is the following customer review for a laptop purchased on Amazon:

> This laptop is full of series problem. Its speed is exactly as per specifications which is very slow! Boot time is more."

If a human were to read it, they could detect the irony expressed about the speed of the laptop and the fact that it takes a long time to boot up, which leads us to conclude that this is a negative review. However, if we analyze only the text, it's clear that the speed is exactly as specified. The fact that the boot time is high might also be perceived as a good thing unless we know that this is a parameter that needs to be small. The task of sentiment analysis is also specific to the type of text data being used. For example, a newspaper article is written in a structured manner, whereas tweets and other social media text follow a loose structure with the presence of slang and incorrect punctuation. As a result, there isn't one blueprint that might work for every scenario. Instead, we will present a set of blueprints that can be used to produce a successful sentiment analysis.

What You'll Learn and What We'll Build

In this chapter, we will explore multiple techniques to estimate the sentiment from a snippet of text data. We will start with simple rule-based techniques and work our way through more complex methods, finally using state-of-the-art language models such as BERT from Google. The purpose of walking through these techniques is to improve our understanding of customer sentiment and provide you with a set of blueprints that can be used for various use cases. For example, combined with the Twitter API blueprint from Chapter 2, you could determine the public sentiment about a certain personality or political issue. You could also use these blueprints within your organization to analyze the sentiment in customer complaints or support emails and determine how happy your clients are.

Sentiment Analysis

A lot of information is available in the form of text, and based on the context of the communication, the information can be categorized into objective texts and subjective texts. *Objective texts* contain a simple statement of facts, like we might find in a textbook or Wikipedia article. Such texts generally present the facts and do not express an opinion or sentiment. *Subjective texts*, on the other hand, convey someone's reaction or contain information about emotion, mood, or feelings. This might be typically found in social media channels in tweets or where customers express their opinions, such as in product reviews. We undertake a study of sentiment in order to understand the state of mind of an individual expressed through the medium of text. Therefore, sentiment analysis works best on subjective texts that contain this kind of information rather than objective texts. Before starting our analysis, we must ensure that we have the right kind of dataset that captures the sentiment information we are looking for.

The sentiment of a piece of text can be determined at the phrase, sentence, or document level. For example, if we take the case of a customer writing an email to a company, there will be several paragraphs, with each paragraph containing multiple sentences. Sentiment can be calculated for each sentence and also for each paragraph. While paragraph 1 may be positive, paragraphs 3 and 4 could be negative. So, if we want to determine the overall sentiment expressed by this customer, we would have to determine the best way to aggregate the sentiment for each paragraph up to the document level. In the blueprints that we present, we calculate sentiment at a sentence level.

The techniques for performing sentiment analysis can be broken down into simple rule-based techniques and supervised machine learning approaches. Rule-based techniques are easier to apply since they do not require annotated training data. Supervised learning approaches provide better results but include the additional effort of labeling the data. There might be simple ways to work around this requirement as we will show in our use case. In this chapter, we will provide the following set of blueprints:

- Sentiment analysis using lexicon-based approaches
- Sentiment analysis by building additional features from text data and applying a supervised machine learning algorithm
- Sentiment analysis using transfer learning technique and pretrained language models like BERT

Introducing the Amazon Customer Reviews Dataset

Let's assume you are an analyst working in the marketing department of a leading consumer electronics company and would like to know how your smartphone products compare with competitors. You can easily compare the technical specifications, but it is more interesting to understand the consumer perception of the product. You could determine this by analyzing the sentiment expressed by customers in product reviews on Amazon. Using the blueprints and aggregating the sentiment for each review for a brand, you would be able to identify how customers perceive each brand. Similarly, what if your company is looking to expand their business by introducing products in an adjacent category? You could analyze customer reviews for all products in a segment, such as media tablets, smartwatches, or action cameras, and based on the aggregated sentiment determine a segment with poor customer satisfaction and therefore higher potential success of your product.

For our blueprints, we will use a dataset containing a collection of Amazon customer reviews for different products across multiple product categories. This dataset of Amazon customer reviews has already been scraped and compiled by researchers at Stanford University.[1] The last updated version (*https://oreil.ly/QcMIz*) consists of product reviews from the Amazon website between 1996 and 2018 across several categories. It includes product reviews, product ratings, and other information such as

---

[1] J. McAuley and J. Leskovec. "Hidden Factors and Hidden Topics: Understanding Rating Dimensions with Review Text." RecSys, 2013. *https://snap.stanford.edu/data/web-Amazon.html*.

helpfulness votes and product metadata. For our blueprints, we are going to focus on product reviews and use only those that are one sentence long. This is to keep the blueprint simple and remove the step of aggregation. A review containing multiple sentences can include both positive and negative sentiment. Therefore, if we tag all sentences in a review with the same sentiment, this would be incorrect. We only use data for some of the categories so that it can fit in memory and reduce processing time. This dataset has already been prepared, but you can refer to the `Data_Prepara tion` notebook present in the repository to understand the steps and possibly extend it. The blueprints work on any kind of dataset, and therefore if you have access to powerful hardware or cloud infrastructure, then you can choose more categories.

Let's now take a look at the dataset:

```
df = pd.read_json('reviews.json', lines=True)
df.sample(5)
```

Out:

	overall	verified	reviewerID	asin	text	summary
163807	5	False	A2A8GHFXUG1B28	B0045Z4JAI	Good Decaf... it has a good flavour for a decaf :)	Nice!
195640	5	True	A1VU337W6PKAR3	B00K0TIC56	I could not ask for a better system for my small greenhouse, easy to set up and nozzles do very well	I could not ask for a better system for my small greenhouse
167820	4	True	A1Z5TT1BBSDLRM	B0012ORBT6	good product at a good price and saves a trip to the store	Four Stars
104268	1	False	A4PRXX2G8900X	B005SPI45U	I like the principle of a raw chip - something I can eat with my homemade salsa and guac - but these taste absolutely revolting.	No better alternatives but still tastes bad.
51961	1	True	AYETYLNYDIS2S	B00D1HLUP8	Fake China knockoff, you get what you pay for.	Definitely not OEM

Looking at a summary of the dataset, we can see that it contains the following columns:

Overall

This is the final rating provided by the reviewer to the product. Ranges from 1 (lowest) to 5 (highest).

Verified

This indicates whether the product purchase has been verified by Amazon.

ReviewerID

This is the unique identifier allocated by Amazon to each reviewer.

ASIN

This is a unique product code that Amazon uses to identify the product.

Text

The actual text in the review provided by the user.

Summary

This is the headline or summary of the review that the user provided.

The column `text` contains the main content of the customer review and expresses the user's opinion. While the rest of the information can be useful, we will focus on using this column in the blueprints.

Blueprint: Performing Sentiment Analysis Using Lexicon-Based Approaches

As an analyst working on the Amazon customer reviews data, the first challenge that might come up is the absence of target labels. We do not automatically know whether a particular review is positive or negative. Does the text express happiness because the product worked perfectly or anger because the product has broken at the first use? We cannot determine this until we actually read the review. This is challenging because we would have to read close to 300,000 reviews and manually assign a target sentiment to each of the reviews. We overcome this problem by using a lexicon-based approach.

What is a lexicon? A *lexicon* is like a dictionary that contains a collection of words and has been compiled using expert knowledge. The key differentiating factor for a lexicon is that it incorporates specific knowledge and has been collected for a specific purpose. We will use sentiment lexicons that contain commonly used words and capture the sentiment associated with them. A simple example of this is the word *happy*, with a sentiment score of 1, and another is the word *frustrated*, which would have a score of -1. Several standardized lexicons are available for the English language, and the popular ones are AFINN Lexicon, SentiWordNet, Bing Liu's lexicon, and VADER lexicon, among others. They differ from each other in the size of their vocabulary and their representation. For example, the AFINN Lexicon (*https://oreil.ly/YZ9WB*) comes in the form of a single dictionary with 3,300 words, with each word assigned a signed sentiment score ranging from -3 to +3. Negative/positive indicate the polarity, and the magnitude indicates the strength. On the other hand, if we look at Bing Liu lexicon (*https://oreil.ly/jTj_u*), it comes in the form of two lists: one for positive words and another for negative, with a combined vocabulary of 6,800 words. Most sentiment lexicons are available for English, but there are also lexicons available for German[2] and for 81 other languages as generated by this research paper.[3]

The sentiment of a sentence or phrase is determined by first identifying the sentiment score for each word from the chosen lexicon and then adding them up to arrive at the overall sentiment. By using this technique, we avoid the need to manually look at each review and assign the sentiment label. Instead, we rely on the lexicon that provides expert sentiment scores for each word. For our first blueprint, we will use the Bing Liu lexicon, but you are free to extend the blueprint to use other lexicons as well. The lexicons normally contain several variants of the word and exclude stop words, and therefore the standard preprocessing steps are not essential in this approach. Only those words that are present in the lexicon will actually be scored. This also leads to one of the disadvantages of this method, which we will discuss at the end of the blueprint.

Bing Liu Lexicon

The Bing Liu lexicon has been compiled by dividing the words into those that express positive opinion and those that express negative opinion. This lexicon also contains misspelled words and is more suitable to be used on text that has been extracted from online discussion forums, social media, and other such sources and should therefore produce better results on the Amazon customer reviews data.

The Bing Liu lexicon is available from the authors' website as a zip file (*https://oreil.ly/A_O4Q*) that contains a set of positive and negative words. It is also available within the NLTK library as a corpus that we can use after downloading. Once we have extracted the lexicon, we will create a dictionary that can hold the lexicon words and their corresponding sentiment score. Our next step is to generate the score for each review in our dataset. We convert the contents of text to lowercase first; then using the word_tokenize function from the NLTK package, we split the sentence into words and check whether this word is part of our lexicon, and if so, we add the corresponding sentiment score of the word to the total sentiment score for the review. As the final step, we normalize this score based on the number of words in the sentence. This functionality is encapsulated in the function bing_liu_score and is applied to every review in our dataset:

```
from nltk.corpus import opinion_lexicon
from nltk.tokenize import word_tokenize
nltk.download('opinion_lexicon')
```

---

2 "Interest Group on German Sentiment Analysis, Multi-Domain Sentiment Lexicon for German," *https://oreil.ly/WpMhF*.

3 Yanqing Chen and Steven Skiena. *Building Sentiment Lexicons for All Major Languages* (*https://oreil.ly/Inbs8*). Lexicons available on Kaggle (*https://oreil.ly/xTeH4*).

```
print('Total number of words in opinion lexicon', len(opinion_lexicon.words()))
print('Examples of positive words in opinion lexicon',
      opinion_lexicon.positive()[:5])
print('Examples of negative words in opinion lexicon',
      opinion_lexicon.negative()[:5])
```

Out:

```
Total number of words in opinion lexicon 6789
Examples of positive words in opinion lexicon ['a+', 'abound', 'abounds',
'abundance', 'abundant']
Examples of negative words in opinion lexicon ['2-faced', '2-faces',
'abnormal', 'abolish', 'abominable']
```

Then:

```
# Let's create a dictionary which we can use for scoring our review text
df.rename(columns={"reviewText": "text"}, inplace=True)
pos_score = 1
neg_score = -1
word_dict = {}

# Adding the positive words to the dictionary
for word in opinion_lexicon.positive():
        word_dict[word] = pos_score

# Adding the negative words to the dictionary
for word in opinion_lexicon.negative():
        word_dict[word] = neg_score

def bing_liu_score(text):
    sentiment_score = 0
    bag_of_words = word_tokenize(text.lower())
    for word in bag_of_words:
        if word in word_dict:
            sentiment_score += word_dict[word]
    return sentiment_score / len(bag_of_words)

df['Bing_Liu_Score'] = df['text'].apply(bing_liu_score)
df[['asin','text','Bing_Liu_Score']].sample(2)
```

Out:

	asin	text	Bing_Liu_Score
188097	B00099QWOU	As expected	0.00
184654	B000RW1X08	Works as designed...	0.25

Now that we have calculated the sentiment score, we would like to check whether the calculated score matches the expectation based on the rating provided by the customer. Instead of checking this for each review, we could compare the sentiment score across reviews that have different ratings. We would expect that a review that has a five-star rating would have a higher sentiment score than a review with a one-star rating. In the next step, we scale the score for each review between 1 and -1 and compute the average sentiment scores across all reviews for each type of star rating:

```
df['Bing_Liu_Score'] = preprocessing.scale(df['Bing_Liu_Score'])
df.groupby('overall').agg({'Bing_Liu_Score':'mean'})
```

Out:

overall	Bing_Liu_Score
1	-0.587061
2	-0.426529
4	0.344645
5	0.529065

The previous blueprint allows us to use any kind of sentiment lexicon to quickly determine a sentiment score and can also serve as a baseline to compare other sophisticated techniques, which should improve the accuracy of sentiment prediction.

Disadvantages of a Lexicon-Based Approach

While the lexicon-based approach is simple, it has some obvious disadvantages that we observed:

- First, we are bound by the size of the lexicon; if a word does not exist in the chosen lexicon, then we are unable to use this information while determining the sentiment score for this review. In the ideal scenario, we would like to use a lexicon that captures all the words in the language, but this is not feasible.

- Second, we assume that the chosen lexicon is a gold standard and trust the sentiment score/polarity provided by the author(s). This is a problem because a particular lexicon may not be the right fit for a given use case. In the previous example, the Bing Liu lexicon is relevant because it captures the online usage of language and includes common typos and slang in its lexicon. But if we were working on a dataset of tweets, then the VADER lexicon would be better suited since it includes support for popular acronyms (e.g., LOL) and emojis.

- Finally, one of the biggest disadvantages of lexicons is that they overlook negation. Since the lexicon only matches words and not phrases, this would result in a negative score for a sentence that contains *not bad* when it actually is more neutral.

To improve our sentiment detection, we must explore the use of supervised machine learning approaches.

Supervised Learning Approaches

The use of a supervised learning approach is beneficial because it allows us to model the patterns in the data and create a prediction function that is close to reality. It also gives us the flexibility to choose from different techniques and identify the one that provides maximum accuracy. A more detailed overview of supervised machine learning is provided in Chapter 6.

To use such an approach, we would need labeled data that may not be easily available. Often, it involves two or more human annotators looking at each review and determining the sentiment. If the annotators do not agree, then a third annotator might be needed to break the deadlock. It is common to have five annotators, with three of them agreeing on the opinion to confirm the label. This can be tedious and expensive but is the preferred approach when working with real business problems.

However, in many cases we will be able to test a supervised learning approach without going through the expensive labeling process. A simpler option is to check for any proxy indicators within the data that might help us annotate it automatically. Let's illustrate this in the case of the Amazon reviews. If somebody has given a five-star product rating, then we can assume that they liked the product they used, and this should be reflected in their review. Similarly, if somebody has provided a one-star rating for a product, then they are dissatisfied with it and would have some negative things to say. Therefore, we could use the product rating as a proxy measure of whether a particular review would be positive or negative. The higher the rating, the more positive a particular review should be.

Preparing Data for a Supervised Learning Approach

Therefore, as the first step in converting our dataset into a supervised machine learning problem, we will automatically annotate our reviews using the rating. We have chosen to annotate all reviews with a rating of 4 and 5 as positive and with ratings 1 and 2 as negative based on the reasoning provided earlier. In the data preparation process, we also filtered out reviews with a rating of 3 to provide a clearer separation between positive and negative reviews. This step can be tailored based on your use case.

```
df = pd.read_json('reviews.json', lines=True)

# Assigning a new [1,0] target class label based on the product rating
df['sentiment'] = 0
df.loc[df['overall'] > 3, 'sentiment'] = 1
df.loc[df['overall'] < 3, 'sentiment'] = 0

# Removing unnecessary columns to keep a simple DataFrame
df.drop(columns=[
    'reviewTime', 'unixReviewTime', 'overall', 'reviewerID', 'summary'],
```

```
        inplace=True)
    df.sample(3)
```

Out:

	verified	asin	text	sentiment
176400	True	B000C5BN72	everything was as listed and is in use all appear to be in good working order	1
65073	True	B00PK03IVI	this is not the product i received.	0
254348	True	B004AIKVPC	Just like the dealership part.	1

As you can see from the selection of reviews presented, we have created a new column named sentiment that contains a value of 1 or 0 depending on the rating provided by the user. We can now treat this as a supervised machine learning problem where we will use the content present in text to predict the sentiment: positive (1) or negative (0).

Blueprint: Vectorizing Text Data and Applying a Supervised Machine Learning Algorithm

In this blueprint, we will build a supervised machine learning algorithm by first cleaning the text data, then performing vectorization, and finally applying a support vector machine model for the classification.

Step 1: Data Preparation

To preprocess the data, we will apply the regex blueprint from Chapter 4 to remove any special characters, HTML tags, and URLs:

```
df['text_orig'] = df['text'].copy()
df['text'] = df['text'].apply(clean)
```

Then, we will apply the data preparation blueprint from the same chapter that uses the spaCy pipeline. This ensures that the text is standardized to lowercase, does not include numerals and punctuations, and is in a format that can be used by subsequent steps. Please note that it might take a couple of minutes to complete execution. In a few cases, it's possible that all tokens in a review are removed during the cleaning step, and it doesn't make sense to include such reviews anymore:

```
df["text"] = df["text"].apply(clean_text)

# Remove observations that are empty after the cleaning step
df = df[df['text'].str.len() != 0]
```

Step 2: Train-Test Split

We split the data so that the next step of vectorization is performed using only the training dataset. We create an 80-20 split of the data and confirm that the positive and negative classes show a similar distribution across the two splits by specifying the target variable, sentiment, as the `stratify` argument:

```
from sklearn.model_selection import train_test_split
X_train, X_test, Y_train, Y_test = train_test_split(df['text'],
                                                    df['sentiment'],
                                                    test_size=0.2,
                                                    random_state=42,
                                                    stratify=df['sentiment'])

print ('Size of Training Data ', X_train.shape[0])
print ('Size of Test Data ', X_test.shape[0])

print ('Distribution of classes in Training Data :')
print ('Positive Sentiment ', str(sum(Y_train == 1)/ len(Y_train) * 100.0))
print ('Negative Sentiment ', str(sum(Y_train == 0)/ len(Y_train) * 100.0))

print ('Distribution of classes in Testing Data :')
print ('Positive Sentiment ', str(sum(Y_test == 1)/ len(Y_test) * 100.0))
print ('Negative Sentiment ', str(sum(Y_test == 0)/ len(Y_test) * 100.0))
```

Out:

```
Size of Training Data  234108
Size of Test Data  58527
Distribution of classes in Training Data :
Positive Sentiment  50.90770071932612
Negative Sentiment  49.09229928067388
Distribution of classes in Testing Data :
Positive Sentiment  50.9081278726058
Negative Sentiment  49.09187212739419
```

Step 3: Text Vectorization

The next step is where we convert the cleaned text to usable features. Machine learning models do not understand text data and are capable of working only with numeric data. We reuse the TF-IDF vectorization blueprint from Chapter 5 to create the vectorized representation. We select the parameters of `min_df` as 10 and do not include bigrams. In addition, our previous step has already removed stop words, and therefore we do not need to take care of this during vectorization. We will use the same vectorizer to transform the test split, which will be used during evaluation:

```
from sklearn.feature_extraction.text import TfidfVectorizer

tfidf = TfidfVectorizer(min_df = 10, ngram_range=(1,1))
X_train_tf = tfidf.fit_transform(X_train)
X_test_tf = tfidf.transform(X_test)
```

Step 4: Training the Machine Learning Model

As described in Chapter 6, support vector machines are the preferred machine learning algorithms when working with text data. SVMs are known to work well with datasets with a large number of numeric features, and in particular the LinearSVC module we use is quite fast. We can also select tree-based methods like random forest or XGBoost, but in our experience the accuracy is comparable, and thanks to quick training times, experimentation can be faster:

```
from sklearn.svm import LinearSVC

model1 = LinearSVC(random_state=42, tol=1e-5)
model1.fit(X_train_tf, Y_train)
```

Out:

```
LinearSVC(C=1.0, class_weight=None, dual=True, fit_intercept=True,
          intercept_scaling=1, loss='squared_hinge', max_iter=1000,
          multi_class='ovr', penalty='l2', random_state=42, tol=1e-05,
          verbose=0)
```

Then:

```
from sklearn.metrics import accuracy_score
from sklearn.metrics import roc_auc_score

Y_pred = model1.predict(X_test_tf)
print ('Accuracy Score - ', accuracy_score(Y_test, Y_pred))
print ('ROC-AUC Score - ', roc_auc_score(Y_test, Y_pred))
```

Out:

```
Accuracy Score -  0.8658396979172006
ROC-AUC Score -  0.8660667427476778
```

As we can see, this model achieves an accuracy of around 86%. Let's look at some of the model predictions and the review text to perform a sense check of the model:

```
sample_reviews = df.sample(5)
sample_reviews_tf = tfidf.transform(sample_reviews['text'])
sentiment_predictions = model1.predict(sample_reviews_tf)
sentiment_predictions = pd.DataFrame(data = sentiment_predictions,
                                     index=sample_reviews.index,
                                     columns=['sentiment_prediction'])
sample_reviews = pd.concat([sample_reviews, sentiment_predictions], axis=1)
print ('Some sample reviews with their sentiment - ')
sample_reviews[['text_orig','sentiment_prediction']]
```

Out:

```
Some sample reviews with their sentiment -
```

---

	text_orig	sentiment_prediction
29500	Its a nice night light, but not much else apparently!	1
98387	Way to small, do not know what to do with them or how to use them	0
113648	Didn't make the room "blue" enough - returned with no questions asked	0
281527	Excellent	1
233713	fit like oem and looks good	1

We can see that this model is able to predict the reviews reasonably well. For example, review 98387 where the user found the product to be too small and unusable is marked as negative. Consider review 233713 where the user says that the product was fitting well and looks good is marked as positive. How does the model compare with a baseline that uses the Bing Liu lexicon?

```
def baseline_scorer(text):
    score = bing_liu_score(text)
    if score > 0:
        return 1
    else:
        return 0

Y_pred_baseline = X_test.apply(baseline_scorer)
acc_score = accuracy_score(Y_pred_baseline, Y_test)
print (acc_score)
```

Out:

```
0.7521998393903668
```

It does provide an uplift on the lexicon baseline of 75%, and while the accuracy can be improved further, this is a simple blueprint that provides quick results. For example, if you're looking to determine the customer perception of your brand versus competitors, then using this blueprint and aggregating sentiments for each brand will give you a fair understanding. Or let's say you want to create an app that helps people decide whether to watch a movie. Using this blueprint on data collected from Twitter or YouTube comments, you could determine whether people feel more positively or negatively and use that to provide a suggestion. In the next blueprint, we will describe a more sophisticated technique that can be used to improve the accuracy.

Pretrained Language Models Using Deep Learning

Languages have evolved over centuries and are still continuously changing. While there are rules of grammar and guidelines to forming sentences, these are often not strictly followed and depend heavily on context. The words that a person chooses while tweeting would be quite different when writing an email to express the same thought. And in many languages (including English) the exceptions to the rules are far too many! As a result, it is difficult for a computer program to understand text-based communication. This can be overcome by giving algorithms a deeper language understanding by making use of language models.

Language models are a mathematical representation of natural language that allows us to understand the structure of a sentence and the words in it. There are several types of language models, but we will focus on the use of pretrained language models in this blueprint. The most important characteristic of these language models is that they make use of deep neural network architectures and are trained on a large corpus of data. The use of language models greatly improves the performance of NLP tasks such as language translation, automatic spelling correction, and text summarization.

Deep Learning and Transfer Learning

Deep learning is commonly used to describe a set of machine learning methods that leverage artificial neural networks (ANNs). ANNs were inspired by the human brain and try to mimic the connections and information processing activity between neurons in biological systems. Simply explained, it tries to model a function using an interconnected network of nodes spanning several layers with the weights of the network edges learned with the help of data. For a more detailed explanation, please refer to Section II of *Hands-On Machine Learning* (O'Reilly, 2019) by Aurélien Géron.

Transfer learning is a technique within deep learning that allows us to benefit from pretrained, widely available language models by *transferring* a model to our specific use case. It gives us the ability to use the knowledge and information obtained in one task and apply it to another problem. As humans, we are good at doing this. For example, we initially learn to play the guitar but can then relatively easily apply that knowledge to pick up the cello or harp more quickly (than a complete beginner). When the same concepts are applied with regard to a machine learning algorithm, then it's referred to as *transfer learning*.

This idea was first popularized in the computer vision industry, where a large-scale image recognition challenge (*https://oreil.ly/ISv5j*) led to several research groups competing to build complex neural networks that are several layers deep to reduce the error on the challenge. Other researchers discovered that these complex models work well not just for that challenge but also on other image recognition tasks with small tweaks. These large models had already learned basic features about images (think of edges, shapes, etc.) and could be fine-tuned for the specific application without the need to train from scratch. In the last two years, the same techniques have been successfully applied to text analytics. First, a deep neural network is trained on a large text corpus (often derived from publicly available data sources like Wikipedia). The chosen model architecture is a variant of LSTM or Transformer.[4] When training these models, one word is removed (masked) in the sentence, and the prediction task is to determine the masked word given all the other words in the sentence. To go back to our human analogy, there might be far more YouTube videos that teach you how to play the guitar than the harp or cello. Therefore, it would be beneficial to first learn to play the guitar because of the large number of resources available and then apply this knowledge to a different task, like playing the harp or cello.

Such large models take a lot of time to train and can be time-consuming. Fortunately, many research groups have made such pretrained models publicly available, including ULMFiT (*https://oreil.ly/ukMdf*) from fastai, BERT (*https://oreil.ly/GtSpY*) from Google, GPT-2 (*https://oreil.ly/LVwyy*) from OpenAI, and Turing (*https://mstur ing.org*) from Microsoft. Figure 11-1 shows the final step of applying transfer learning, where the initial layers of the pretrained models are kept fixed, and the final layers of the model are retrained to better suit the task at hand. In this way, we can apply a pretrained model to specific tasks such as text classification and sentiment analysis.

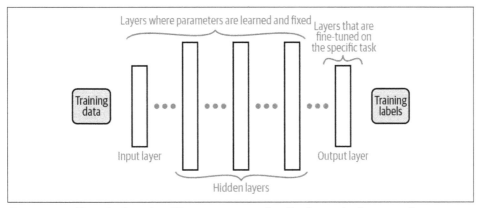

Figure 11-1. Transfer learning. The parameters of earlier layers in the network are learned by training the model on the large corpus, and the parameters of the final layers are unfrozen and allowed to be fine-tuned during the training on the specific dataset.

For our blueprint we will use the BERT pretrained model released by Google. BERT is an acronym for *Bidirectional Encoder Representations from Transformers*. It uses the Transformers architecture and trains a model using a large corpus of text data. The model that we use in this blueprint (`bert-base-uncased`) is trained on the combined English Wikipedia and Books corpus using a Masked Language Model (MLM). There are other versions of the BERT model that can be trained on different corpora. For

---

4 Ashish Vaswani et al. "Attention Is All You Need." 2017. *https://arxiv.org/abs/1706.03762*.

example, there is a BERT model trained on German Wikipedia articles. The masked language model randomly masks (hides) some of the tokens from the input, and the objective is to predict the original vocabulary ID of the masked word based only on its context (surrounding words). Since it's bidirectional, the model looks at each sentence in both directions and is able to understand context better. In addition, BERT also uses subwords as tokens, which provides more granularity when identifying the meaning of a word. Another advantage is that BERT generates context-aware embeddings. For example, depending on the surrounding words in a sentence where the word *cell* is used, it can have a biological reference or actually refer to a prison cell. For a much more detailed understanding of how BERT works, please see "Further Reading" on page 322.

Blueprint: Using the Transfer Learning Technique and a Pretrained Language Model

This blueprint will show you how we can leverage pretrained language models to perform sentiment classification. Consider the use case where you would like to take action based on the sentiment expressed. For example, if a customer is particularly unhappy, you would like to route them to your best customer service representative. It's important that you are able to detect the sentiment accurately or else you risk losing them. Or let's say you are a small business that relies heavily on reviews and ratings on public websites like Yelp (*https://yelp.com*). To improve your ratings, you would like to follow up with unhappy customers by offering them coupons or special services. It's important to be accurate so that you target the right customers. In such use cases, we may not have a lot of data to train the model, but having a high accuracy is important. We know that sentiment is influenced by the context in which a word is used, and the use of a pretrained language model can improve our sentiment predictions. This gives us the ability to go beyond the limited dataset that we have to incorporate knowledge from general usage.

In our blueprint we will use the Transformers library because of its easy-to-use functionality and wide support for multiple pretrained models. "Choosing the Transformers Library" provides more details about this topic. The Transformers library is continuously updated, with multiple researchers contributing.

Choosing the Transformers Library

While there are several excellent deep learning models produced by multiple research groups, at this point in time they are fragmented and not compatible across different frameworks. For example, the BERT model was developed by the Google research team primarily on TensorFlow and does not work automatically on PyTorch. So if someone is more comfortable using PyTorch, they will need to port/rewrite all of this code. The deep learning models also do not use a standard input format and other naming conventions, which makes a standardized approach much more difficult. This is where the Transformers library by Hugging Face (*https://oreil.ly/F0Vy7*) comes in. There are two primary advantages in making use of this library:

- The Transformers library allows us to easily choose between different pretrained models by just changing a parameter value. Most of the benchmark models developed in the last two years, like BERT and GPT-2, are already implemented and available.
- It works in PyTorch and TensorFlow. These are the two most popular deep learning frameworks as of 2020, and the Transformers library gives us the ability to choose either of them as the underlying processing framework.

The Transformers library has provided a standardized approach to reuse all the models with minimum effort and code changes. Our blueprint will make use of this library to choose a BERT pretrained model, fine-tune the training on the Amazon reviews dataset, and then evaluate the result. We have put together this blueprint by using the SST-2 task example provided in the Transformers repository (*https://oreil.ly/bDMQV*) and the primary trainer class implementation (*https://oreil.ly/cBeBK*).

Step 1: Loading Models and Tokenization

The first step when using the Transformers library is to import the three classes needed for the chosen model. This includes the *config* class, used to store important model parameters; the *tokenizer*, to tokenize and prepare the text for model training; and the *model* class, which defines the model architecture and weights. These classes are specific to the model architecture, and if we want to use a different architecture, then the appropriate classes need to be imported instead. We instantiate these classes from a pretrained model and choose the smallest BERT model, `bert-base-uncased`, which is 12 layers deep and contains 110 million parameters!

The advantage of using the Transformers library is that it already provides multiple pretrained models for many model architectures, which you can check here (*https://oreil.ly/QdC7E*). When we instantiate a model class from a pretrained model, the model architecture and weights are downloaded from an AWS S3 bucket hosted by Hugging Face. This might take a while the first time, but it is then cached on your machine, which removes the need for subsequent downloads. Note that since we are using the pretrained model to predict the sentiment (positive versus negative), we specify `finetuning_task='binary'`. We have provided additional instructions in the accompanying notebook to ensure that additional Python packages are installed before running this blueprint.

```
from transformers import BertConfig, BertTokenizer, BertForSequenceClassification

config = BertConfig.from_pretrained('bert-base-uncased',finetuning_task='binary')
tokenizer = BertTokenizer.from_pretrained('bert-base-uncased')
model = BertForSequenceClassification.from_pretrained('bert-base-uncased')
```

We have to transform the input text data into a standard format required by the model architecture. We define a simple get_tokens method to convert the raw text of our reviews to numeric values. The pretrained model accepts each observation as a fixed length sequence. So, if an observation is shorter than the maximum sequence length, then it is padded with empty (zero) tokens, and if it's longer, then it is truncated. Each model architecture has a maximum sequence length that it supports. The tokenizer class provides a tokenize function that splits the sentence to tokens, pads the sentence to create the fixed-length sequence, and finally represents it as a numerical value that can be used during model training. This function also adds an attention mask to differentiate those positions where we have actual words from those that contain padding characters. Here is an example of how this process works:

```
def get_tokens(text, tokenizer, max_seq_length, add_special_tokens=True):
    input_ids = tokenizer.encode(text,
                                 add_special_tokens=add_special_tokens,
                                 max_length=max_seq_length,
                                 pad_to_max_length=True)
    attention_mask = [int(id > 0) for id in input_ids]
    assert len(input_ids) == max_seq_length
    assert len(attention_mask) == max_seq_length
    return (input_ids, attention_mask)

text = "Here is the sentence I want embeddings for."
input_ids, attention_mask = get_tokens(text,
                                       tokenizer,
                                       max_seq_length=30,
                                       add_special_tokens = True)
input_tokens = tokenizer.convert_ids_to_tokens(input_ids)
print (text)
print (input_tokens)
print (input_ids)
print (attention_mask)
```

Out:

```
Here is the sentence I want embeddings for.
['[CLS]', 'here', 'is', 'the', 'sentence', 'i', 'want', 'em', '##bed',
'##ding', '##s', 'for', '.', '[SEP]', '[PAD]', '[PAD]', '[PAD]', '[PAD]',
'[PAD]', '[PAD]', '[PAD]', '[PAD]', '[PAD]', '[PAD]', '[PAD]', '[PAD]',
'[PAD]', '[PAD]', '[PAD]', '[PAD]']
[101, 2182, 2003, 1996, 6251, 1045, 2215, 7861, 8270, 4667, 2015, 2005, 1012,
102, 0, 0, 0, 0, 0, 0, 0, 0, 0, 0, 0, 0, 0, 0, 0, 0]
[1, 1, 1, 1, 1, 1, 1, 1, 1, 1, 1, 1, 1, 0, 0, 0, 0, 0, 0, 0, 0, 0, 0, 0, 0,
0, 0, 0, 0]
```

The first token that we observe is the [CLS] token, which stands for classification, which is one of the pretraining tasks of the BERT model. This token is used to identify the start of a sentence and stores the aggregated representation of the entire sentence within the model. We also see the [SEP] token at the end of the sentence, which stands for *separator*. When BERT is used for nonclassification tasks like language translation, each observation would include a pair of texts (for example, text in English and text in French), and the [SEP] token is used to separate the first text from the second. However, since we are building a classification model, the separator token is followed by [PAD] tokens. We specified the sequence length to be 30, and since our test observation was not that long, multiple padding tokens have been added at the end. Another interesting observation is that a word like *embedding* is not one token but actually split into em, ##bed, ##ding, and ##s. The ## is used to identify tokens that are subwords, which is a special characteristic of the BERT model. This allows the model to have a better distinction between root words, prefixes, and suffixes and also try to infer the meaning of words that it may not have seen before.

An important point to note is that since deep learning models use a context-based approach, it is advisable to use the text in the original form without any preprocessing, thus allowing the tokenizer to produce all possible tokens from its vocabulary. As a result, we must split the data again using the original text_orig column rather than the cleaned text column. After that, let's apply the same function to our train and test data and this time use a max_seq_length of 50:

```
X_train, X_test, Y_train, Y_test = train_test_split(df['text_orig'],
                                                    df['sentiment'],
                                                    test_size=0.2,
                                                    random_state=42,
                                                    stratify=df['sentiment'])
X_train_tokens = X_train.apply(get_tokens, args=(tokenizer, 50))
X_test_tokens = X_test.apply(get_tokens, args=(tokenizer, 50))
```

Deep learning models are trained on GPUs using frameworks like TensorFlow (*https://tensorflow.org*) and PyTorch (*https://pytorch.org*). A tensor is the basic data structure used by these frameworks to represent and work with data and can store data in N dimensions. A simple way to visualize a tensor is by drawing an analogy with a chessboard. Let's suppose that we mark an unoccupied position with 0, a position occupied by a white piece with 1, and a position occupied by a black piece with 2. We get an 8 × 8 matrix denoting the status of the chessboard at a given point in time. If we now want to track and store this over several moves, then we get multiple 8 × 8 matrices, which can be stored in what we call a *tensor*. Tensors are n-dimensional representations of data, containing an array of components that are functions of the coordinates of a space. The tensor that tracks the historical chess moves would be a rank 3 tensor, whereas the initial 8 × 8 matrix could also be considered a tensor, but with rank 2.

This is a simplistic explanation, but to get a more in-depth understanding, we would recommend reading "An Introduction to Tensors for Students of Physics and Engineering" (*https://oreil.ly/VC_80*) by Joseph C. Kolecki. In our case, we create three tensors that contain the tokens (tensors containing multiple arrays of size 50), input masks (tensors containing arrays of size 50), and target labels (tensors containing scalars of size 1):

```
import torch
from torch.utils.data import TensorDataset

input_ids_train = torch.tensor(
    [features[0] for features in X_train_tokens.values], dtype=torch.long)
input_mask_train = torch.tensor(
    [features[1] for features in X_train_tokens.values], dtype=torch.long)
label_ids_train = torch.tensor(Y_train.values, dtype=torch.long)

print (input_ids_train.shape)
print (input_mask_train.shape)
print (label_ids_train.shape)
```

Out:

```
torch.Size([234104, 50])
torch.Size([234104, 50])
torch.Size([234104])
```

We can take a peek at what is in this tensor and see that it contains a mapping to the BERT vocabulary for each of the tokens in a sentence. The number 101 indicates the start, and 102 indicates the end of the review sentence. We combine these tensors together into a TensorDataset, which is the basic data structure used to load all observations during model training:

```
input_ids_train[1]
```

Out:

```
tensor([ 101, 2009, 2134, 1005, 1056, 2147, 6314, 2055, 2009, 1037, 5808, 1997,
        2026, 2769,  102,    0,    0,    0,    0,    0,    0,    0,    0,    0,
           0,    0,    0,    0,    0,    0,    0,    0,    0,    0,    0,    0,
           0,    0,    0,    0,    0,    0,    0,    0,    0,    0,    0,    0,
           0,    0])
```

Then:

```
train_dataset = TensorDataset(input_ids_train,input_mask_train,label_ids_train)
```

Step 2: Model Training

Now that we have preprocessed and tokenized the data, we are ready to train the model. Because of the large memory usage and computation demands of deep learning models, we follow a different approach compared to the SVM model used in the

---

previous blueprint. All training observations are split into batches (defined by `train_batch_size` and randomly sampled from all observations using `RandomSam pler`) and passed forward through the layers of the model. When the model has seen all the training observations by going through the batches, it is said to have been trained for one epoch. An epoch is therefore one pass through all the observations in the training data. The combination of `batch_size` and number of epochs determines how long the model takes to train. Choosing a larger `batch_size` reduces the number of forward passes in an epoch but might result in higher memory consumption. Choosing a larger number of epochs gives the model more time to learn the right value of the parameters but will also result in a longer training time. For this blueprint we have defined `batch_size` to be 64 and `num_train_epochs` to be 2:

```python
from torch.utils.data import DataLoader, RandomSampler

train_batch_size = 64
num_train_epochs = 2

train_sampler = RandomSampler(train_dataset)
train_dataloader = DataLoader(train_dataset,
                             sampler=train_sampler,
                             batch_size=train_batch_size)
t_total = len(train_dataloader) // num_train_epochs

print ("Num examples = ", len(train_dataset))
print ("Num Epochs = ", num_train_epochs)
print ("Total train batch size  = ", train_batch_size)
print ("Total optimization steps = ", t_total)
```

Out:

```
Num examples =  234104
Num Epochs =  2
Total train batch size  =  64
Total optimization steps =  1829
```

When all the observations in one batch have passed forward through the layers of the model, the backpropagation algorithm is applied in the backward direction. This technique allows us to automatically compute the gradients for each parameter in the neural network, giving us a way to tweak the parameters to reduce the error. This is similar to how stochastic gradient descent works, but we do not attempt a detailed explanation. Chapter 4 of *Hands-On Machine Learning* (O'Reilly, 2019) provides a good introduction and mathematical explanation. The key thing to note is that when training a deep learning algorithm, parameters that influence backpropagation like the learning rate and choice of optimizer determine how quickly the model is able to learn the parameters and reach higher accuracies. However, there isn't a scientific reason for why a certain method or value is better, but a lot of researchers[5] attempt to determine what the best options could be. We make informed choices for the blueprint based on the parameters in the BERT paper and recommendations in the Transformers library, as shown here:

```
from transformers import AdamW, get_linear_schedule_with_warmup

learning_rate = 1e-4
adam_epsilon = 1e-8
warmup_steps = 0

optimizer = AdamW(model.parameters(), lr=learning_rate, eps=adam_epsilon)
scheduler = get_linear_schedule_with_warmup(optimizer,
                                            num_warmup_steps=warmup_steps,
                                            num_training_steps=t_total)
```

Before setting up the training loop, we check whether a GPU is available (see "Using GPUs for Free with Google Colab"). If so, the model and input data are transferred to the GPU, and then we set up the forward pass by running the inputs through the model to produce outputs. Since we have specified the labels, we already know the deviation from actual (loss), and we adjust the parameters using backpropagation that calculates gradients. The optimizer and scheduler steps are used to determine the amount of parameter adjustment. Note the special condition to clip the gradients to a max value to prevent the problem of exploding gradients (*https://oreil.ly/Ry0Vi*).

Using GPUs for Free with Google Colab

One of the primary drivers for the popularity of neural network architectures and the success of models like BERT has been the use of graphics processing units (GPUs). The use of a GPU allows parallel operations, specifically matrix multiplication that a deep neural network relies on. This gives us the capability to train complex neural network architectures with multiple layers that a CPU can never provide. If your laptop or desktop does not come with one of the latest (NVIDIA) GPUs, this makes it harder to experiment with these pretrained models, and one has to choose cloud providers like AWS and rent a machine with GPU on a usage basis.

But with Google Colab (Colaboratory), we have a free alternative. Google Colab is a Jupyter notebook type of environment that runs on Google Cloud. One can access it via a browser, just like Jupyter notebooks, and run commands in a cell interface. The biggest advantage is that you can change the runtime environment to a GPU, and all the code will execute using a GPU for free. There are limitations to how long you can run your notebook with the free option, but it also comes with a paid monthly subscription that enhances these limits.

---

5 Robin M. Schmidt, Frank Schneider, and Phillipp Hennig. "Descending through a Crowded Valley: Benchmarking Deep Learning Optimizers." 2020. *https://arxiv.org/pdf/2007.01547.pdf*.

To use this, you must have a Google account and then log in at *https://colab.research.google.com*, create a new notebook, and then choose Edit > Runtime Settings. From the drop-down for Hardware Accelerator, choose GPU. Once you are finished running your code, you can also save this notebook to your Google Drive or download it as a Jupyter notebook.

We will now wrap all these steps in nested for loops—one for each epoch and another for each batch in the epoch—and use the TQDM library introduced earlier to keep track of the training progress while printing the loss value:

```
from tqdm import trange, notebook

device = torch.device("cuda" if torch.cuda.is_available() else "cpu")
train_iterator = trange(num_train_epochs, desc="Epoch")

# Put model in 'train' mode
model.train()

for epoch in train_iterator:
    epoch_iterator = notebook.tqdm(train_dataloader, desc="Iteration")
    for step, batch in enumerate(epoch_iterator):

        # Reset all gradients at start of every iteration
        model.zero_grad()

        # Put the model and the input observations to GPU
        model.to(device)
        batch = tuple(t.to(device) for t in batch)

        # Identify the inputs to the model
        inputs = {'input_ids':      batch[0],
                  'attention_mask': batch[1],
                  'labels':         batch[2]}

        # Forward Pass through the model. Input -> Model -> Output
        outputs = model(**inputs)

        # Determine the deviation (loss)
        loss = outputs[0]
        print("\r%f" % loss, end='')

        # Back-propogate the loss (automatically calculates gradients)
        loss.backward()

        # Prevent exploding gradients by limiting gradients to 1.0
        torch.nn.utils.clip_grad_norm_(model.parameters(), 1.0)

        # Update the parameters and learning rate
        optimizer.step()
        scheduler.step()
```

The steps we have performed up to now have fine-tuned the parameters of the BERT model that we downloaded to fit the sentiment analysis of the Amazon customer reviews. If the model is learning the parameter values correctly, you should observe that the loss value reduces over multiple iterations. At the end of the training step, we can save the model and tokenizer into a chosen output folder:

```
model.save_pretrained('outputs')
```

Step 3: Model Evaluation

Evaluating our model on the test data is similar to the training steps, with only minor differences. First, we have to evaluate the entire test dataset and therefore don't need to make random samples; instead, we use the SequentialSampler class to load observations. However, we are still constrained by the number of observations we can load at a time and therefore must use test_batch_size to determine this. Second, we do not need a backward pass or adjustment of parameters and only perform the forward pass. The model provides us with output tensors that contain the value of loss and output probabilities. We use the np.argmax function to determine the output label with maximum probability and calculate the accuracy by comparing with actual labels:

```
import numpy as np
from torch.utils.data import SequentialSampler

test_batch_size = 64
test_sampler = SequentialSampler(test_dataset)
test_dataloader = DataLoader(test_dataset,
                             sampler=test_sampler,
                             batch_size=test_batch_size)

# Load the pretrained model that was saved earlier
# model = model.from_pretrained('/outputs')

# Initialize the prediction and actual labels
preds = None
out_label_ids = None

# Put model in "eval" mode
model.eval()

for batch in notebook.tqdm(test_dataloader, desc="Evaluating"):

    # Put the model and the input observations to GPU
    model.to(device)
    batch = tuple(t.to(device) for t in batch)

    # Do not track any gradients since in 'eval' mode
    with torch.no_grad():
        inputs = {'input_ids':      batch[0],
```

```
                    'attention_mask': batch[1],
                    'labels':         batch[2]}

        # Forward pass through the model
        outputs = model(**inputs)

        # We get loss since we provided the labels
        tmp_eval_loss, logits = outputs[:2]

        # There maybe more than one batch of items in the test dataset
        if preds is None:
            preds = logits.detach().cpu().numpy()
            out_label_ids = inputs['labels'].detach().cpu().numpy()
        else:
            preds = np.append(preds, logits.detach().cpu().numpy(), axis=0)
            out_label_ids = np.append(out_label_ids,
                                    inputs['labels'].detach().cpu().numpy(),
                                    axis=0)

    # Get final loss, predictions and accuracy
    preds = np.argmax(preds, axis=1)
    acc_score = accuracy_score(preds, out_label_ids)
    print ('Accuracy Score on Test data ', acc_score)
```

Out:

```
Accuracy Score on Test data  0.9535086370393152
```

The results for our test data show an increase in model accuracy to 95%—a 10 percentage point jump compared to our previous baseline with TF-IDF and SVM. These are the benefits of using a state-of-the-art language model and is most likely a result of BERT being trained using a large corpus of data. The reviews are quite short, and the earlier model has only that data to learn a relationship. BERT, on the other hand, is context aware and can *transfer* the prior information it has about the words in the review. The accuracy can be improved by fine-tuning the hyperparameters like learning_rate or by training for more epochs. Because the number of parameters for pretrained language models far exceeds the number of observations we use for fine-tuning, we must be careful to avoid overfitting during this process!

Using Saved Models

If you are running the evaluation separately, you can load the fine-tuned model directly without the need to train again. Note that this is the same function that we initially used to load the pretrained model from transformers, but this time we are using the fine-tuned model that we trained ourselves.

As you can see, using a pretrained language model improves the accuracy of our model but also involves many additional steps and can incur costs like the use of a GPU (training a useful model on CPU can take 50–100 times longer). The pretrained models are quite large and not memory efficient. Using these models in production is often more complicated because of the time taken to load millions of parameters in memory, and they are inefficient for real-time scenarios because of longer inference times. Some pretrained models like DistilBERT (*https://oreil.ly/o4xEU*) and ALBERT (*https://oreil.ly/m715P*) have been specifically developed for a more favorable trade-off between accuracy and model simplicity. You can easily try this by reusing the blueprint and changing the appropriate model classes to choose the `distil-bert-uncased` or `albert-base-v1` model, which is available in the Transformers library, to check the accuracy.

Closing Remarks

In this chapter, we introduced several blueprints that can be used for sentiment analysis. They range from simple lexicon-based approaches to complex state-of-the-art language models. If your use case is a one-time analysis to determine the sentiment of a particular topic using Twitter data, then the first blueprint would be most suitable. If you are looking to create a ranking of products/brands using sentiment expressed in customer reviews or route customer complaints based on their sentiment, then a supervised machine learning approach as described in the second and third blueprints would be more suitable. If accuracy is of utmost importance, the best results are obtained by using a pretrained language model, but this is also a more complicated and expensive technique. Each blueprint is appropriate for a given use case, and the crucial thing is to determine which approach is suitable for your needs. In general, you must find a method that works well for your use case, and the suggestion would always be to keep it simple at the start and then increase the complexity to get better results.

Further Reading

Kolecki, Joseph C. "An Introduction to Tensors for Students of Physics and Engineering." *https://www.grc.nasa.gov/WWW/k-12/Numbers/Math/documents/Tensors_TM2002211716.pdf*.

McCormick, Chris, and Nick Ryan. "BERT Word Embedding Tutorial." *http://mccormickml.com/2019/05/14/BERT-word-embeddings-tutorial*.

Olah, Christopher. "Understanding LSTMs." *https://colah.github.io/posts/2015-08-Understanding-LSTMs.*

Uszkoreit, Jakob. "Transformer: A Novel Neural Network Architecture for Language Understanding." *https://ai.googleblog.com/2017/08/transformer-novel-neural-network.html.*

## CHAPTER 12

Building a Knowledge Graph

In this book, we have been working through many blueprints for text analysis. Our goal was always to identify patterns in the data with the help of statistics and machine learning. In Chapter 10 we explained how embeddings can be used to answer questions like "What is to Germany like Paris is to France?" Embeddings represent some kind of implicit knowledge that was learned from the training documents based on a notion of similarity.

A knowledge base, in contrast, consists of structured statements of the form "Berlin capital-of Germany." In this case, "capital-of" is a precisely defined relation between the two specific entities *Berlin* and *Germany*. The network formed by many entities and their relations is a graph in the mathematical sense, a *knowledge graph*. Figure 12-1 shows a simple knowledge graph illustrating the example. In this chapter, we will introduce blueprints to extract structured information from unstructured text and build a basic knowledge graph.

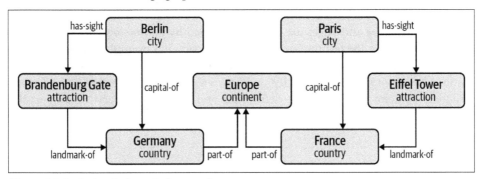

Figure 12-1. A simple knowledge graph.

What You'll Learn and What We'll Build

Information extraction is one of the hardest tasks in natural language processing because of the complexity and inherent ambiguity of language. Thus, we need to apply a sequence of different steps to discover the entities and relationships. Our example use case in this section is the creation of a knowledge graph based on business news articles about companies.

In the course of the chapter, we will take a deep dive into the advanced language processing features of spaCy. We will use the pretrained neural models in combination with custom rules for named-entity recognition, coreference resolution, and relation extraction. We will also explain the necessary steps to perform entity linking, but we won't go into the implementation details.

After reading this chapter, you will have the basic linguistic and technical knowledge to start building your own knowledge base. You will find the source code for this chapter and additional information in our GitHub repository (*https://oreil.ly/5dF4g*).

Knowledge Graphs

A knowledge graph is a large semantic network. It consists of nodes that are entities such as persons, places, events, or companies, and edges that represent formalized relations between those nodes, as shown in Figure 12-1.

All the big players such as Google, Microsoft, Facebook, etc., use knowledge graphs to power their search engines and query services.[1] And nowadays more and more companies are building their own knowledge graphs to gain market insights or power chatbots. But the largest knowledge graph is distributed all over the world: *Linked Open Data* refers to all the available data on the web that can be identified by a uniform resource identifier (URI). It is the result of 20 years of academic development in the area of the Semantic Web (see "Semantic Web and RDF" on page 327).

The types of nodes and edges are precisely defined by an *ontology*, which is itself a knowledge base for the terminology used in a domain. For example, the public ontology Wikidata provides definitions for all types used in Figure 12-1.[2] Each of these definitions has a unique URI (e.g., "city" is *http://www.wikidata.org/wiki/Q515.*). In fact, Wikidata contains both, the type definitions and the actual objects in a queryable format.

---

1 See Natasha Noy, Yuqing Gao, Anshu Jain, Anant Narayanan, Alan Patterson, and Jamie Taylor. *Industry-scale Knowledge Graphs: Lessons and Challenges.* 2019. *https://queue.acm.org/detail.cfm?id=3332266.*

2 See *https://oreil.ly/nzhUR* for details.

Semantic Web and RDF

The vision of Tim Berners-Lee, who coined the term *Semantic Web* in 2001, was to make the data on the web understandable to computers.[3] Today, a lot of knowledge is available in public knowledge graphs. For example, Wikidata (*https://wikidata.org*) and DBpedia (*https://wiki.dbpedia.org*) are two huge knowledge bases related to Wikipedia.

RDF, the resource description framework, is a W3C standard that defines notations for entities and their attributes and relationships. Its intention is to simplify the interlinking of knowledge between knowledge bases. The basic concepts in RDF are *resources* and *statements*. The resources are "things" like entities, types, or literal values. A *statement* is a subject-predicate-object *triple* of resources, like *Berlin(Q64) capital-of(P1376) Germany(Q183)*. The numbers in the example are the unique Wikidata identifiers for the mentioned entities and the relation "capital-of." Unique identifiers and standardized definitions are the basis to interlink public and private knowledge bases.

Public knowledge bases like Wikidata provide the possibility to query their data with SPARQL. SPARQL is an RDF-based query language. You could, for example, visit the Wikidata SPARQL (*https://query.wikidata.org*) endpoint and request a list of relevant entities for your domain. In the notebook on GitHub for this chapter (*https://oreil.ly/FKJ2D*), you will find an additional blueprint that queries the Wikidata SPARQL endpoint. It request the list of all US departments with their alias names and returns the result as a Pandas dataframe.

Information Extraction

There are several typical steps needed to extract structured information from text, as shown in Figure 12-2. As a first step, *named-entity recognition*, finds *mentions* of named entities in the text and labels them with the correct type, e.g., person, organization, or location. The same entity is usually referenced multiple times in a document by different variants of the name or by pronouns. The second step, *coreference resolution*, identifies and resolves those *coreferences* to prevent duplicates and information loss.

Closely related to coreference resolution, and usually the next step, is the task of *entity linking*. Here, the goal is to link a mention in the text to a unique real-world entity in an ontology, for example, *Berlin* to the URI *http://www.wikidata.org/entity/Q64*. Thus, any ambiguities are removed: Q64 is the Berlin in Germany and not the

---

3 Tim Berners-Lee et al., "The Semantic Web: a New Form of Web Content that is Meaningful to Computers Will Unleash a Revolution of New Possibilities." *Scientific American* 284 No. 5: May 2001.

one in New Hampshire (which is, by the way, Q821244 in Wikidata). This is essential to connect information from different sources and really build a knowledge base.

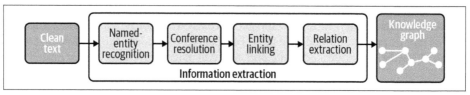

Figure 12-2. The process of information extraction.

The last step, *relation extraction*, identifies the relations between those entities. In an application scenario, you will usually consider only a few relations of interest because it is hard to extract this kind of information correctly from arbitrary text.

Finally, you could store the graph in a graph database as the backend of a knowledge-based application. Such graph databases store the data either as RDF triples (*triple stores*) or in the form of a property graph, where nodes and edges can have arbitrary attributes. Commonly used graph databases are, for example, GraphDB (triple store), Neo4j, and Grakn (property graphs).

For each of the steps, you have the choice between a rule-based approach and machine learning. We will use available models of spaCy and rules in addition. We will not train our own models, though. The usage of rules for the extraction of domain-specific knowledge has the advantage that you can get started quickly without training data. As we will see, the results allow some really interesting analyses. But if you plan to build a corporate knowledge base on a large scale, you may have to train your own models for named-entity and relationship detection as well as for entity linking.

Introducing the Dataset

Assume you are working in the financial business and want to track news on mergers and acquisitions. It would be great if you could automatically identify company names and the kind of deals they are involved in and make the results available in a knowledge base. In this chapter, we will explain the building blocks to extract some information about companies. For example, we will extract the relation "Company1 acquires Company2."

To simulate such a scenario, we use a publicly available dataset, the well-known Reuters-21578 (*https://oreil.ly/lltWo*) news corpus. It contains more than 20,000 news articles of 90 categories published by Reuters in 1987. This dataset was chosen because it is free and easy to get. In fact, it is available as one of the NLTK standard corpora, and you can simply download it with NLTK:

```
import nltk
nltk.download('reuters')
```

We will work only with articles from the acquisitions category (acq). To prepare it for our purposes, we loaded all articles into a single DataFrame and did some data cleaning following the blueprints in "Cleaning Text Data" on page 94. Clean data is crucial to recognize named-entities and relationships as the neural models benefit from well-structured sentences. For this dataset, we substituted HTML escapes, removed stock ticker symbols, replaced abbreviations like *mln* for *million*, and corrected some spelling mistakes. We also dropped the headlines because they are written in capital letters only. The complete article bodies are retained, though. All cleaning steps can be found in the notebook on GitHub (*https://oreil.ly/21p8d*). Let's take a look at a sample of the cleaned articles in our DataFrame:

```
USAir Group Inc said a U.S. District Court in Pittsburgh issued a temporary
restraining order to prevent Trans World Airlines Inc from buying additional
USAir shares. USAir said the order was issued in response to its suit, charging
TWA chairman Carl Icahn and TWA violated federal laws and made misleading
statements. TWA last week said it owned 15 % of USAir's shares. It also offered
to buy the company for 52 dollars a share cash or 1.4 billion dollars.
```

So, this is the data we have in mind when we develop the blueprints for information extraction. However, most of the sentences in the following sections are simplified examples to better explain the concepts.

Named-Entity Recognition

After data cleaning, we can start with the first step of our information extraction process: named-entity recognition. Named-entity recognition was briefly introduced in Chapter 4 as part of spaCy's standard pipeline. spaCy is our library of choice for all the blueprints in this chapter because it is fast and has an extensible API that we will utilize. But you could also use Stanza or Flair (see "Alternatives for NER: Stanza and Flair" on page 331).

spaCy provides trained NER models for many languages. The English models have been trained on the large OntoNotes5 corpus (*https://oreil.ly/gyOiH*) containing 18 different entity types. Table 12-1 lists a subset of these. The remaining types are for numeric entities.

Table 12-1. Subset of NER types of the OntoNotes 5 corpus

NER Type	Description	NER Type	Description
PERSON	People, including fictional	PRODUCT	Vehicles, weapons, foods, etc. (Not services)
NORP	Nationalities or religious or political groups	EVENT	Named hurricanes, battles, wars, sports events, etc.

NER Type	Description	NER Type	Description
FAC	Facilities: buildings, airports, highways, bridges, etc.	WORK_OF_ART	Titles of books, songs, etc.
ORG	Organizations: companies, agencies, institutions, etc.	LAW	Named documents made into laws
GPE	Countries, cities, states	LANGUAGE	Any named language
LOCATION	Non-GPE locations, mountain ranges, bodies of water		

The NER tagger is enabled by default when you load a language model. Let's start by initializing an nlp object with the standard (small) English model en_core_web_sm and print the components of the NLP pipeline:[4]

```
nlp = spacy.load('en_core_web_sm')
print(*nlp.pipeline, sep='\n')
```

Out:

```
('tagger', <spacy.pipeline.pipes.Tagger object at 0x7f98ac6443a0>)
('parser', <spacy.pipeline.pipes.DependencyParser object at 0x7f98ac7a07c0>)
('ner', <spacy.pipeline.pipes.EntityRecognizer object at 0x7f98ac7a0760>)
```

Once the text is processed, we can access the named entities directly with doc.ents. Each entity has a text and a label describing the entity type. These attributes are used in the last line in the following code to print the list of entities recognized in this text:

```
text = """Hughes Tool Co Chairman W.A. Kistler said its merger with
Baker International Corp was still under consideration.
We hope to come soon to a mutual agreement, Kistler said.
The directors of Baker filed a law suit in Texas to force Hughes
to complete the merger."""
doc = nlp(text)

print(*[(e.text, e.label_) for e in doc.ents], sep=' ')
```

Out:

```
(Hughes Tool Co, ORG) (W.A. Kistler, PERSON) (Baker International Corp, ORG)
(Kistler, ORG) (Baker, PERSON) (Texas, GPE) (Hughes, ORG)
```

With spaCy's neat visualization module displacy, we can generate a visual representation of the sentence and its named entities. This is helpful to inspect the result:

```
from spacy import displacy
displacy.render(doc, style='ent')
```

---

4 The asterisk operator (*) unpacks the list into separate arguments for print.

```
Out:
```

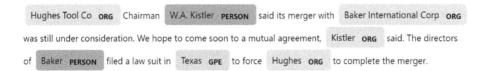

In general, spaCy's named-entity recognizer does a good job. In our example, it was able to detect all named entities. The labels of *Kistler* and *Baker* in the second and third sentence, however, are not correct. In fact, distinguishing between persons and organizations is quite a challenge for NER models because those entity types are used very similarly. We will resolve such problems later in the blueprint for name-based coreference resolution.

Alternatives for NER: Stanza and Flair

Previously known as StanfordNLP, Stanza 1.0.0 (*https://oreil.ly/MupNu*) was released in March 2020. Similar to spaCy, it was designed to support many languages in a coherent way. It also includes a Python API for additional linguistic functions in the well-known CoreNLP Java package.

Stanza's API is very similar to spaCy's. Even better, the `spacy_stanza` library (*https://oreil.ly/2Q2E1*), which is officially maintained by spaCy's development team from Explosion, provides a wrapper for the Stanza NLP pipeline. So, you can use the spaCy-based blueprints of this chapter and still leverage the models of Stanza if you want. As of the time of writing this book, Stanza's English models are more accurate than the models of spaCy 2.3.2 in our example. But they are huge in size and therefore much slower. The models in spaCy 3.0 are reported to be as accurate as Stanza's and significantly faster.

Another popular NLP library with excellent NER models is Flair (*https://oreil.ly/hKFSk*). Flair was developed by people from Humboldt University in Berlin and Zalando Research and is now part of the PyTorch ecosystem. It is definitely worth checking out.

Blueprint: Using Rule-Based Named-Entity Recognition

If you want to identify domain-specific entities on which the model has not been trained, you can of course train your own model with spaCy (*https://oreil.ly/6EMig*). But training a model requires a lot of training data. Often it is sufficient to specify simple rules for custom entity types. In this section, we will show how to use rules to detect government organizations like the "Department of Justice" (or alternatively the "Justice Department") in the Reuters dataset.

spaCy provides an `EntityRuler` (*https://oreil.ly/A6MZ8*) for this purpose, a pipeline component that can be used in combination with or instead of the statistical named-entity recognizer. Compared to regular expression search, spaCy's matching engine is more powerful because patterns are defined on sequences of spaCy's tokens instead of just strings. Thus, you can use any token property like the lemma or the part-of-speech tag to build your patterns.

So, let's define some pattern rules to match departments of the US government and the "Securities and Exchange Commission," which is frequently mentioned in our corpus:

```
from spacy.pipeline import EntityRuler

departments = ['Justice', 'Transportation']
patterns = [{"label": "GOV",
             "pattern": [{"TEXT": "U.S.", "OP": "?"},
                         {"TEXT": "Department"}, {"TEXT": "of"},
                         {"TEXT": {"IN": departments}, "ENT_TYPE": "ORG"}]},
            {"label": "GOV",
             "pattern": [{"TEXT": "U.S.", "OP": "?"},
                         {"TEXT": {"IN": departments}, "ENT_TYPE": "ORG"},
                         {"TEXT": "Department"}]},
            {"label": "GOV",
             "pattern": [{"TEXT": "Securities"}, {"TEXT": "and"},
                         {"TEXT": "Exchange"}, {"TEXT": "Commission"}]}]
```

Each rule consists of a dictionary with a label, in our case the custom entity type `GOV`, and a pattern that the token sequence must match. You can specify multiple rules for the same label, as we did here.[5] The first rule, for example, matches sequences of tokens with the texts `"U.S."` (optional, denoted by `"OP": "?"`), `"Department"`, `"of"`, and either `"Justice"` or `"Transportation"`. Note that this and the second rule refine already recognized entities of type `ORG`. Thus, these patterns must be applied on top and not instead of spaCy's named-entity model.

Based on these patterns, we create an `EntityRuler` and add it to our pipeline:

```
entity_ruler = EntityRuler(nlp, patterns=patterns, overwrite_ents=True)
nlp.add_pipe(entity_ruler)
```

Now, when we call `nlp`, those organizations will automatically be labeled with the new type `GOV`:

---

[5] See spaCy's rule-based matching usage docs (*https://oreil.ly/Hvtgs*) for an explanation of the syntax, and check out the interactive pattern explorer on *https://explosion.ai/demos/matcher*.

```
text = """Justice Department is an alias for the U.S. Department of Justice.
Department of Transportation and the Securities and Exchange Commission
are government organisations, but the Sales Department is not."""

doc = nlp(text)
displacy.render(doc, style='ent')
```

`Out:`

Justice Department **GOV** is an alias for U.S. Department of Justice **GOV** .

Department of Transportation **GOV** and the Securities and Exchange Commission **GOV**

are government organisations, but the Sales Department **ORG** is not.

Blueprint: Normalizing Named Entities

One approach to simplify the resolution of different entity mentions to a single name is the normalization or standardization of mentions. Here, we will do a first normalization, which is generally helpful: the removal of unspecific suffixes and prefixes. Take a look at this example:

```
text = "Baker International's shares climbed on the New York Stock Exchange."

doc = nlp(text)
print(*[([t.text for t in e], e.label_) for e in doc.ents], sep='\n')
```

`Out:`

```
(['Baker', 'International', "'s"], 'ORG')
(['the', 'New', 'York', 'Stock', 'Exchange'], 'ORG')
```

In the first sentence, the token sequence `Baker International's` was detected as an entity even though the genitive-s is not part of the company name. A similar case is the article in `the New York Stock Exchange`. Regardless of whether the article is actually part of the name or not, entities will likely be referenced sometimes with and sometimes without the article. Thus, the general removal of the article and an apostrophe-s simplifies the linking of mentions.

As with any rules, there is a potential of errors: think of `The Wall Street Journal` or `McDonald's`. If you need to preserve the article or the apostrophe-s in such cases, you must define exceptions for the rules.

Our blueprint function shows how to implement normalizations such as removing a leading article and a trailing apostrophe-s in spaCy. As we are not allowed to update entities in place, we create a copy of the entities and apply our modifications to this copy:

```
from spacy.tokens import Span

def norm_entities(doc):
    ents = []
    for ent in doc.ents:
        if ent[0].pos_ == "DET": # leading article
            ent = Span(doc, ent.start+1, ent.end, label=ent.label)
        if ent[-1].pos_ == "PART": # trailing particle like 's
            ent = Span(doc, ent.start, ent.end-1, label=ent.label)
        ents.append(ent)
    doc.ents = tuple(ents)
    return doc
```

An entity in spaCy is a Span object with a defined start and end plus an additional label denoting the type of the entity. We loop through the entities and adjust the position of the first and last token of the entity if necessary. Finally, we replace doc.ents with our modified copy.

The function takes a spaCy Doc object (named doc) as a parameter and returns a Doc. Therefore, we can use it as a another pipeline component and simply add it to the existing pipeline:

```
nlp.add_pipe(norm_entities)
```

Now we can repeat the process on the example sentences and check the result:

```
doc = nlp(text)
print(*[([t.text for t in e], e.label_) for e in doc.ents], sep='\n')
```

Out:

```
(['Baker', 'International'], 'ORG')
(['New', 'York', 'Stock', 'Exchange'], 'ORG')
```

Merging Entity Tokens

In many cases, it makes sense to treat compound names like the ones from the previous example as single tokens because it simplifies the sentence structure. spaCy provides a built-in pipeline function merge_entities for that purpose. We add it to our NLP pipeline and get exactly one token per named-entity:

```
from spacy.pipeline import merge_entities
nlp.add_pipe(merge_entities)
```

```
doc = nlp(text)
print(*[(t.text, t.ent_type_) for t in doc if t.ent_type_ != ''])
```

Out:

```
('Baker International', 'ORG') ('New York Stock Exchange', 'ORG')
```

Even though merging entities simplifies our blueprints later in this chapter, it may not always be a good idea. Think, for example, about compound entity names like London Stock Exchange. After merging into a single token, the implicit relation of this entity to the city of London will be lost.

Coreference Resolution

One of the greatest obstacles in information extraction is the fact that entity mentions appear in many different spellings (also called *surface forms*). Look at the following sentences:

> Hughes Tool Co Chairman W.A. Kistler said its merger with Baker International Corp. was still under consideration. We hope to come to a mutual agreement, Kistler said. Baker will force Hughes to complete the merger. A review by the U.S. Department of Justice was completed today. The Justice Department will block the merger after consultation with the SEC.

As we can see, entities are frequently introduced by their full name, while later mentions use abbreviated versions. This is one type of coreference that must resolved to understand what's going on. Figure 12-3 shows a co-occurrence graph without (left) and with (right) unified names. Such a co-occurrence graph, as we will build in the next section, is a visualization of entity pairs appearing in the same article.

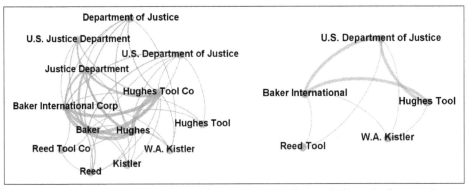

Figure 12-3. A co-occurrence graph of the same articles before (left) and after coreference resolution (right).

Coreference resolution is the task of determining the different mentions of an entity within a single text, for example, abbreviated names, aliases, or pronouns. The result of this step is a group of coreferencing mentions called a *mention cluster*, for example,

{Hughes Tool Co, Hughes, its}. Our target in this section is to identify related mentions and link them within a document.

For this purpose, we develop a couple of blueprints for coreference resolution and name unification (see Figure 12-4). We will restrict ourselves to organizations and persons, as these are the entity types we are interested in. First, we will resolve aliases like *SEC* by a dictionary lookup. Then we will match names within a document to the first mention. For example, we will create a link from "Kistler" to "W.A. Kistler." After that, indirect references (*anaphora*) like the pronoun *its* in the first sentence will be resolved. Finally, we will normalize again the names of the resolved entities. All of these steps will be implemented as additional pipeline functions.

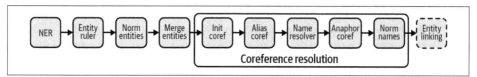

Figure 12-4. Pipeline for named-entity recognition and coreference resolution.

Entity linking goes one step further. Here the mentions of an entity are disambiguated on a semantic level and linked to a unique entry in an existing knowledge base. Because entity linking is itself a challenging task, we will not provide a blueprint for that but just discuss it at the end of this section.

Blueprint: Using spaCy's Token Extensions

We need a way to technically create the link from the different mentions of an entity to the main reference, the *referent*. After coreference resolution, the token for "Kistler" of the example article should point to "(W.A. Kistler, PERSON)." spaCy's extension mechanism allows us to define custom attributes, and this is the perfect way to store this kind of information with tokens. Thus, we create two token extensions ref_n (referent's name) and ref_t (referent's type). The attributes will be initialized for each token with the specified default values by spaCy for each token:

```
from spacy.tokens import Token
Token.set_extension('ref_n', default='')
Token.set_extension('ref_t', default='')
```

The function init_coref shown next ensures that each entity mention of type ORG, GOV, and PERSON gets an initial reference to itself. This initialization is required for the succeeding functions:

```
def init_coref(doc):
    for e in doc.ents:
```

```
    if e.label_ in ['ORG', 'GOV', 'PERSON']:
        e[0]._.ref_n, e[0]._.ref_t = e.text, e.label_
return doc
```

The custom attributes are accessed via the underscore property of the token. Note that after merge_entities, each entity mention e consists of a single token e[0] where we set the attributes. We could also define the attributes on the entity spans instead of tokens, but we want to use the same mechanism for pronoun resolution later.

Blueprint: Performing Alias Resolution

Our first targets are well-known domain aliases like *Transportation Department* for "U.S. Department of Transportation" and acronyms like SEC or TWA. A simple solution to resolve such aliases is to use a lookup dictionary. We prepared such a dictionary for all the acronyms and some common aliases of the Reuters corpus and provided it as part of the blueprints module for this chapter.[6] Here are some example lookups:

```
from blueprints.knowledge import alias_lookup

for token in ['Transportation Department', 'DOT', 'SEC', 'TWA']:
    print(token, ':', alias_lookup[token])
```

Out:

```
Transportation Department : ('U.S. Department of Transportation', 'GOV')
DOT : ('U.S. Department of Transportation', 'GOV')
SEC : ('Securities and Exchange Commission', 'GOV')
TWA : ('Trans World Airlines Inc', 'ORG')
```

Each token alias is mapped to a tuple consisting of an entity name and a type. The function alias_resolver shown next checks whether an entity's text is found in the dictionary. If so, its ref attributes are updated to the looked-up value:

```
def alias_resolver(doc):
    """Lookup aliases and store result in ref_t, ref_n"""
    for ent in doc.ents:
        token = ent[0].text
        if token in alias_lookup:
            a_name, a_type = alias_lookup[token]
            ent[0]._.ref_n, ent[0]._.ref_t = a_name, a_type
    return propagate_ent_type(doc)
```

---

6 You will find an additional blueprint for acronym detection in the notebook for this chapter on GitHub (*https://oreil.ly/LlPHm*).

Once we have resolved the aliases, we can also correct the type of the named-entity in case it was misidentified. This is done by the function `propagate_ent_type`. It updates all resolved aliases and will also be used in the next blueprint for name-based coreference resolution:

```
def propagate_ent_type(doc):
    """propagate entity type stored in ref_t"""
    ents = []
    for e in doc.ents:
        if e[0]._.ref_n != '': # if e is a coreference
            e = Span(doc, e.start, e.end, label=e[0]._.ref_t)
        ents.append(e)
    doc.ents = tuple(ents)
    return doc
```

Again, we add the `alias_resolver` to our pipeline:

```
nlp.add_pipe(alias_resolver)
```

Now we can inspect the results. For this purpose, our provided blueprints package includes a utility function `display_ner` that creates a `DataFrame` for the tokens in a doc object with the relevant attributes for this chapter:

```
from blueprints.knowledge import display_ner
text = """The deal of Trans World Airlines is under investigation by the
U.S. Department of Transportation.
The Transportation Department will block the deal of TWA."""
doc = nlp(text)
display_ner(doc).query("ref_n != ''")[['text', 'ent_type', 'ref_n', 'ref_t']]
```

Out:

	text	ent_type	ref_n	ref_t
3	Trans World Airlines	ORG	Trans World Airlines Inc	ORG
9	U.S. Department of Transportation	GOV	U.S. Department of Transportation	GOV
12	Transportation Department	GOV	U.S. Department of Transportation	GOV
18	TWA	ORG	Trans World Airlines Inc	ORG

Blueprint: Resolving Name Variations

Alias resolution works only if the aliases are known up front. But because articles contain variations of almost any names, it is not feasible to build a dictionary for all of them. Take a look again at the recognized named entities in the first sentences of our introductory example:

Hughes Tool Co `ORG` Chairman W.A. Kistler `PERSON` said its merger with Baker International Corp. `ORG` was still under consideration. We hope to come to a mutual agreement, Kistler `ORG` said. Baker `PERSON` will force Hughes `ORG` to complete the merger.

Here you find the coreference "Kistler" for W.A. Kistler (PERSON), "Baker" for Baker International Corp (ORG), and "Hughes" for Hughes Tool Co (ORG). And as you can see, abbreviated company names are often mistaken for people, especially when they are used in impersonated form, as in the examples. In this blueprint, we will resolve those coreferences and assign the correct entity types to each mention.

For that, we will exploit a common pattern in news articles. An entity is usually introduced first by its full name, while later mentions use abbreviated versions. Thus, we will resolve the secondary references by matching the names to the first mention of an entity. Of course, this is a heuristic rule that could produce false matches. For example, *Hughes* could also refer in the same article to the company and to the legendary entrepreneur Howard Hughes (who indeed founded Hughes Tool Co.). But such cases are rare in our dataset, and we decide to accept that uncertainty in favor of the many cases where our heuristics works correctly.

We define a simple rule for name matching: a secondary mention matches a primary mention if all of its words appear in the primary mention in the same order. To check this, the function `name_match` shown next transforms a secondary mention m2 into a regular expression and searches for a match in the primary mention m1:

```
def name_match(m1, m2):
    m2 = re.sub(r'[()\.]', '', m2) # ignore parentheses and dots
    m2 = r'\b' + m2 + r'\b' # \b marks word boundary
    m2 = re.sub(r'\s+', r'\\b.*\\b', m2)
    return re.search(m2, m1, flags=re.I) is not None
```

The secondary mention of Hughes Co., for example, would be converted into `'\bHughes\b.*\bCo\b'`, which matches Hughes Tool Co. The \b ensures that only whole words match and not subwords like *Hugh*.

Based on this matching logic, the function `name_resolver` shown next implements the name-based coreference resolution for organizations and persons:

```
def name_resolver(doc):
    """create name-based reference to e1 as primary mention of e2"""
    ents = [e for e in doc.ents if e.label_ in ['ORG', 'PERSON']]
    for i, e1 in enumerate(ents):
        for e2 in ents[i+1:]:
            if name_match(e1[0]._.ref_n, e2[0].text):
                e2[0]._.ref_n = e1[0]._.ref_n
                e2[0]._.ref_t = e1[0]._.ref_t
    return propagate_ent_type(doc)
```

First, we create a list of all organization and person entities. Then all pairs of entities e1 and e2 are compared against each other. The logic ensures that entity e1 always comes before e2 in the document. If e2 matches e1, its referent is set to the same as in e1. Thus, the first matching entity is automatically propagated to its subsequent coreferences.

We add this function to the nlp pipeline and check the result:

```
nlp.add_pipe(name_resolver)

doc = nlp(text)
displacy.render(doc, style='ent')
```

Out:

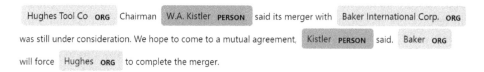

Now each named-entity in our example has the correct type. We can also check that the entities are mapped to their first mention:

```
display_ner(doc).query("ref_n != ''")[['text', 'ent_type', 'ref_n', 'ref_t']]
```

Out:

	text	ent_type	ref_n	ref_t
0	Hughes Tool Co	ORG	Hughes Tool Co	ORG
2	W.A. Kistler	PERSON	W.A. Kistler	PERSON
7	Baker International Corp.	ORG	Baker International Corp.	ORG
22	Kistler	PERSON	W.A. Kistler	PERSON
25	Baker	ORG	Baker International Corp.	ORG
28	Hughes	ORG	Hughes Tool Co	ORG

Blueprint: Performing Anaphora Resolution with NeuralCoref

In linguistics, *anaphora* are words whose interpretation depends on the preceding text. Consider this variation of our example sentences:

```
text = """Hughes Tool Co said its merger with Baker
was still under consideration. Hughes had a board meeting today.
```

```
W.A. Kistler mentioned that the company hopes for a mutual agreement.
He is reasonably confident."""
```

Here *its*, *the company*, and *he* are anaphora. NeuralCoref (*https://oreil.ly/kQRhE*) from Hugging Face is a library to resolve these kind of coreferences. The algorithm uses feature vectors based on word embeddings (see Chapter 10) in combination with two neural networks to identify coreference clusters and their main mentions.[7]

NeuralCoref is implemented as a pipeline extension for spaCy, so it fits perfectly into our process. We create the neural coreference resolver with a greedyness value of 0.45 and add it to our pipeline. The greedyness controls the sensitivity of the model, and after some experiments, we decided to choose a little more restrictive (better accuracy, lower recall) value than the default 0.5:

```
from neuralcoref import NeuralCoref
neural_coref = NeuralCoref(nlp.vocab, greedyness=0.45)
nlp.add_pipe(neural_coref, name='neural_coref')
```

NeuralCoref uses also spaCy's extension mechanism to add custom attributes to Doc, Span, and Token objects. When a text is processed, we can access the detected coreference clusters with the doc._.coref_clusters attribute. In our example, three such clusters have been identified:

```
doc = nlp(text)
print(*doc._.coref_clusters, sep='\n')
```

Out:

```
Hughes Tool Co: [Hughes Tool Co, its]
Hughes: [Hughes, the company]
W.A. Kistler: [W.A. Kistler, He]
```

NeuralCoref works on Span objects (sequences of token) because coreferences in general are not limited to named entities. Thus, the blueprint function anaphor_coref retrieves for each token the first coreference cluster and searches for the first named-entity with a value in its ref_n attribute. In our case, this will be organizations and people only. Once found, it sets the values in ref_n and ref_t of the anaphor token to the same values as in the primary reference:

```
def anaphor_coref(doc):
    """anaphora resolution"""
    for token in doc:
        # if token is coref and not already dereferenced
        if token._.in_coref and token._.ref_n == '':
            ref_span = token._.coref_clusters[0].main # get referred span
            if len(ref_span) <= 3: # consider only short spans
```

---

7 See Wolf (2017), "State-Of-The-Art Neural Coreference Resolution For Chatbots" (*https://oreil.ly/VV4Uy*) for more.

```
                    for ref in ref_span: # find first dereferenced entity
                        if ref._.ref_n != '':
                            token._.ref_n = ref._.ref_n
                            token._.ref_t = ref._.ref_t
                            break
        return doc
```

Again, we add this resolver to our pipeline and check the result:

```
nlp.add_pipe(anaphor_coref)
doc = nlp(text)
display_ner(doc).query("ref_n != ''") \
  [['text', 'ent_type', 'main_coref', 'ref_n', 'ref_t']]
```

Out:

	text	ent_type	main_coref	ref_n	ref_t
0	Hughes Tool Co	ORG	Hughes Tool Co	Hughes Tool Co	ORG
2	its		Hughes Tool Co	Hughes Tool Co	ORG
5	Baker	PERSON	None	Baker	PERSON
11	Hughes	ORG	Hughes	Hughes Tool Co	ORG
18	W.A. Kistler	PERSON	W.A. Kistler	W.A. Kistler	PERSON
21	the		Hughes	Hughes Tool Co	ORG
22	company		Hughes	Hughes Tool Co	ORG
29	He		W.A. Kistler	W.A. Kistler	PERSON

Now our pipeline consists of all the steps shown in Figure 12-4.

Beware of long runtimes! NeuralCoref increases the total processing time by a factor of 5–10. So, you should use anaphora resolution only if necessary.

Name Normalization

Even though our name resolution unifies company mentions within an article, the company names are still inconsistent across articles. We find *Hughes Tool Co.* in one article and *Hughes Tool* in another one. An entity linker can be used to link different entity mentions to a unique canonical representation, but in absence of an entity linker we will use the (resolved) name entity as its unique identifier. Because of the previous steps for coreference resolution, the resolved names are always the first, and thus usually most complete, mentions in an article. So, the potential for errors is not that large.

Still, we have to harmonize company mentions by removing the legal suffixes like *Co.* or *Inc.* from company names. The following function uses a regular expression to achieve this:

```
def strip_legal_suffix(text):
    return re.sub(r'(\s+and)?(\s+|\b(Co|Corp|Inc|Plc|Ltd)\b\.?)*$', '', text)

print(strip_legal_suffix('Hughes Tool Co'))
```

Out:

```
Hughes Tool
```

The last pipeline function `norm_names` applies this final normalization to each of the coreference-resolved organization names stored in the `ref_n` attributes. Note that Hughes (PERSON) and Hughes (ORG) will still remain separate entities with this approach.

```
def norm_names(doc):
    for t in doc:
        if t._.ref_n != '' and t._.ref_t in ['ORG']:
            t._.ref_n = strip_legal_suffix(t._.ref_n)
            if t._.ref_n == '':
                t._.ref_t = ''
    return doc

nlp.add_pipe(norm_names)
```

Sometimes the named-entity recognizer misclassifies a legal suffix like *Co.* or *Inc.* by itself as named-entity. If such an entity name gets stripped to the empty string, we just ignore it for later processing.

Entity Linking

In the previous sections we developed a pipeline of operations with the purpose of unifying the different mentions of named entities. But all this is string based, and except for the syntactical representation, we have no connection between the string *U.S. Department of Justice* and the represented real-world entity. The task of an entity linker, in contrast, is to resolve named entities globally and link them to a uniquely identified real-world entity. Entity linking makes the step from "strings to things."[8]

Technically, this means that each mention is mapped to a URI. URIs, in turn, address entities in an existing knowledge base. This can be a public ontology, like Wikidata or DBpedia, or a private knowledge base in your company. URIs can be URLs (e.g., web pages) but do not have to be. The U.S. Department of Justice, for example, has the Wikidata URI *http://www.wikidata.org/entity/Q1553390*, which is also a web page

---

8 This slogan was coined by Google when it introduced its knowledge graph in 2012.

where you find information about this entity. If you build your own knowledge base, it is not necessary to have a web page for each URI; they just must be unique. DBpedia and Wikidata, by the way, use different URIs, but you will find the Wikidata URI on DBpedia as a cross-reference. Both, of course, contain links to the Wikipedia web page.

Entity linking is simple if an entity is mentioned by a fully qualified name, like the *U.S. Department of Justice*. But the term *Department of Justice* without *U.S.* is already quite ambiguous because many states have a "Department of Justice." The actual meaning depends on the context, and the task of an entity linker is to map such an ambiguous mention context-sensitively to the correct URI. This is quite a challenge and still an area of ongoing research. A common solution for entity linking in business projects is the usage of a public service (see "Services for Entity Linking").

Services for Entity Linking

There are several web services for named-entity resolution and linking. DBpedia Spotlight (*https://dbpedia-spotlight.org*), for example, is an open service that links to DBpedia resources. You can either use the public web service or deploy a copy in your own environment. A commercial alternative for such a service is TextRazor (*https://textrazor.com/demo*), which even provides a nice Python library for easy integration into your own project.

Alternatively, you could create your own entity linker. A simple solution would be a name-based lookup dictionary. But that does not take the context into account and would not resolve ambiguous names for different entities. For that, you need a more sophisticated approach. State-of-the-art solutions use embeddings and neural models for entity linking. spaCy also provides such an entity linking functionality (*https://oreil.ly/bqs8E*). To use spaCy's entity linker, you first have to create embeddings (see Chapter 10) for the real-world entities, which capture their semantics based on descriptions you specify. Then you can train a model to learn the context-sensitive mapping of mentions to the correct URI. The setup and training of an entity linker are, however, beyond the scope of this chapter.

Blueprint: Creating a Co-Occurrence Graph

In the previous sections, we spent much effort to normalize named entities and to resolve at least the in-document coreferences. Now we are finally ready to analyze a first relationship among pairs of entities: their joint mention in an article. For this, we will create a co-occurrence graph, the simplest form of a knowledge graph. The nodes in the co-occurrence graph are the entities, e.g., organizations. Two entities share an (undirected) edge if they are mentioned in the same context, for example, within an article, a paragraph, or a sentence.

Figure 12-5 shows part of the co-occurrence graph for companies mentioned together in articles of the Reuters corpus. The width of the edges visualizes the co-occurrence frequency. The *modularity* (*https://oreil.ly/pGZ-s*), a structural measure to identify closely related groups or communities in a network, was used to colorize the nodes and edges.[9]

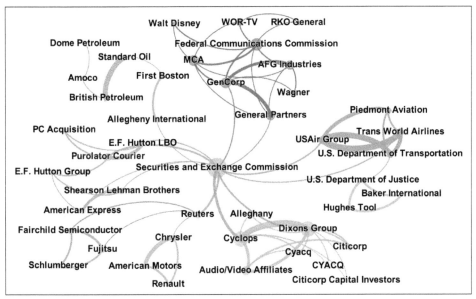

Figure 12-5. Largest connected component of the co-occurrence graph generated from the Reuters corpus.

Of course, we don't know anything about the type of relationship here. In fact, the joint mentioning of two entities merely indicates that there *might be some* relationship. We won't know for sure unless we really analyze the sentences, and we will do that in the next section. But even the simple exploration of co-occurrences can already be revealing. For example, the central node in Figure 12-5 is the "Securities and Exchange Commission" because it is mentioned in many articles together with a great variety of other entities. Obviously, this entity plays a major role in mergers and acquisitions. The different clusters give us an impression about groups of companies (or communities) involved in certain deals.

---

9 You'll find the colorized figures in the electronic versions of this book and in our GitHub repository (*https:// oreil.ly/2ju0k*).

To plot a co-occurrence graph, we have to extract entity pairs from a document. For longer articles covering multiple topic areas, it may be better to search for co-occurrences within paragraphs or even sentences. But the Reuters articles on mergers and acquisitions are very focused, so we stick to the document level here. Let's briefly walk through the process to extract and visualize co-occurrences.

Extracting Co-Occurrences from a Document

The function `extract_coocs` returns the list of entities pairs of the specified types from a given `Doc` object:

```
from itertools import combinations

def extract_coocs(doc, include_types):
    ents = set([(e[0]._.ref_n, e[0]._.ref_t)
                    for e in doc.ents if e[0]._.ref_t in include_types])
    yield from combinations(sorted(ents), 2)
```

We first create a set of the coreference-resolved entity names and types. Having this, we use the function `combinations` from the Python standard library `itertools` to create all the entity pairs. Each pair is sorted lexicographically (`sorted(ents)`) to prevent duplicate entries like "(Baker, Hughes)" and "(Hughes, Baker)."

To process the whole dataset efficiently, we use again spaCy's streaming by calling `nlp.pipe` (introduced in Chapter 4). As we do not need anaphora resolution to find in-document co-occurrences, we disable the respective components here:

```
batch_size = 100

coocs = []
for i in range(0, len(df), batch_size):
    docs = nlp.pipe(df['text'][i:i+batch_size],
                    disable=['neural_coref', 'anaphor_coref'])
    for j, doc in enumerate(docs):
        coocs.extend([(df.index[i+j], *c)
                        for c in extract_coocs(doc, ['ORG', 'GOV'])])
```

Let's take a look at the identified co-occurrences of the first article:

```
print(*coocs[:3], sep='\n')
```

Out:

```
(10, ('Computer Terminal Systems', 'ORG'), ('Sedio N.V.', 'ORG'))
(10, ('Computer Terminal Systems', 'ORG'), ('Woodco', 'ORG'))
(10, ('Sedio N.V.', 'ORG'), ('Woodco', 'ORG'))
```

In information extraction, it is always recommended to have some kind of traceability that allows you to identify the source of the information in the case of problems. Therefore, we retain the index of the article, which in our case is the file ID of the Reuters corpus, with each co-occurrence tuple (here the ID 10). Based on this list, we generate a `DataFrame` with exactly one entry per entity combination, its frequency, and the article IDs (limited to five) where this co-occurrence was found.

```
coocs = [([id], *e1, *e2) for (id, e1, e2) in coocs]
cooc_df = pd.DataFrame.from_records(coocs,
            columns=('article_id', 'ent1', 'type1', 'ent2', 'type2'))
cooc_df = cooc_df.groupby(['ent1', 'type1', 'ent2', 'type2'])['article_id'] \
            .agg(['count', 'sum']) \
            .rename(columns={'count': 'freq', 'sum': 'articles'}) \
            .reset_index().sort_values('freq', ascending=False)
cooc_df['articles'] = cooc_df['articles'].map(
            lambda lst: ','.join([str(a) for a in lst[:5]]))
```

Here are the three most frequent entity pairs we found in the corpus:

```
cooc_df.head(3)
```

`Out:`

	ent1	type1	ent2	type2	freq	articles
12667	Trans World Airlines	ORG	USAir Group	ORG	22	1735,1771,1836,1862,1996
5321	Cyclops	ORG	Dixons Group	ORG	21	4303,4933,6093,6402,7110
12731	U.S. Department of Transportation	GOV	USAir Group	ORG	20	1735,1996,2128,2546,2799

Visualizing the Graph with Gephi

Actually, this `DataFrame` already represents the list of edges for our graph. For the visualization we prefer Gephi (*https://gephi.org*), an open source tool for graph analysis. Because it is interactive, it is much better to use than Python's graph library NetworkX.[10] To work with Gephi, we need to save the list of nodes and edges of the graph in Graph Exchange XML format. Fortunately, NetworkX provides a function to export graphs in this format. So, we can simply convert our `DataFrame` into a NetworkX graph and save it as a `.gexf` file. We discard rare entity pairs to keep the graph compact and rename the frequency column because Gephi automatically uses a `weight` attribute to adjust the width of edges:

```
import networkx as nx

graph = nx.from_pandas_edgelist(
            cooc_df[['ent1', 'ent2', 'articles', 'freq']] \
            .query('freq > 3').rename(columns={'freq': 'weight'}),
            source='ent1', target='ent2', edge_attr=True)
```

---

10 You can find a NetworkX version of the graph in the notebook for this chapter on GitHub (*https://oreil.ly/OWTcO*).

```
nx.readwrite.write_gexf(graph, 'cooc.gexf', encoding='utf-8',
                        prettyprint=True, version='1.2draft')
```

After importing the file into Gephi, we selected only the largest component (connected subgraph) and removed some nodes with only a few connections manually for the sake of clarity.[11] The result is presented in Figure 12-5.

 Sometimes the most interesting relations are the ones that are not frequent. Take, for example, the first announcement on an upcoming merger or surprising relations that were mentioned a few times in the past but then forgotten. A sudden co-occurrence of entities that were previously unrelated can be a signal to start a deeper analysis of the relation.

Relation Extraction

Even though the co-occurrence graph already gave us some interesting insights about company networks, it does not tell us anything about the types of the relations. Take, for example, the subgraph formed by the companies Schlumberger, Fairchild Semiconductor, and Fujitsu in the lower-left corner of Figure 12-5. So far, we know nothing about the relations between those companies; the information is still hidden in sentences like these:

Fujitsu wants to expand. It plans to acquire 80% of Fairchild Corp, an industrial unit of Schlumberger.

In this section, we will introduce two blueprints for pattern-based relation extraction. The first and simpler blueprint searches for token phrases of the form "subject-predicate-object." The second one uses the syntactical structure of a sentence, the dependency tree, to get more precise results at the price of more complex rules. In the end, we will generate a knowledge graph based on the four relations: *acquires*, *sells*, *subsidiary-of*, and *chairperson-of*. To be honest, we will use relaxed definitions of *acquires* and *sells*, which are easier to identify. They will also match sentences like "Fujitsu *plans to acquire 80%* of Fairchild Corp" or even "Fujitsu *withdraws the option to acquire* Fairchild Corp."

Relation extraction is a complicated problem because of the ambiguity of natural language and the many different kinds and variations of relations. Model-based approaches to relation extraction are a current topic in research.[12] There are also

---

11 We provide more details on that in our GitHub repository (*https://oreil.ly/nri01*) for this chapter.

12 See an overview of the state of the art (*https://oreil.ly/l6DIH*).

some training datasets like FewRel (*http://zhuhao.me/fewrel*) publicly available. However, training a model to identify relations is still pretty much in the research stage and out of the scope of this book.

Blueprint: Extracting Relations Using Phrase Matching

The first blueprint works like rule-based entity recognition: it tries to identify relations based on patterns for token sequences. Let's start with a simplified version of the introductory example to explain the approach.

```
text = """Fujitsu plans to acquire 80% of Fairchild Corp, an industrial unit
of Schlumberger."""
```

We could find the relations in this sentence by searching for patterns like these:

```
ORG {optional words, not ORG} acquire {optional words, not ORG} ORG
ORG {optional words, not ORG} unit of {optional words, not ORG} ORG
```

spaCy's rule-based matcher (*https://oreil.ly/Mxd3m*) allows us to find patterns that not only can involve the textual tokens but also their properties, like the lemma or part of speech. To use it, we must first define a matcher object. Then we can add rules with token patternsto the matcher:

```
from spacy.matcher import Matcher

matcher = Matcher(nlp.vocab)

acq_synonyms = ['acquire', 'buy', 'purchase']
pattern = [{'_': {'ref_t': 'ORG'}}, # subject
           {'_': {'ref_t': {'NOT_IN': ['ORG']}}, 'OP': '*'},
           {'POS': 'VERB', 'LEMMA': {'IN': acq_synonyms}},
           {'_': {'ref_t': {'NOT_IN': ['ORG']}}, 'OP': '*'},
           {'_': {'ref_t': 'ORG'}}] # object
matcher.add('acquires', None, pattern)

subs_synonyms = ['subsidiary', 'unit']
pattern = [{'_': {'ref_t': 'ORG'}}, # subject
           {'_': {'ref_t': {'NOT_IN': ['ORG']}},
            'POS': {'NOT_IN': ['VERB']}, 'OP': '*'},
           {'LOWER': {'IN': subs_synonyms}}, {'TEXT': 'of'},
           {'_': {'ref_t': {'NOT_IN': ['ORG']}},
            'POS': {'NOT_IN': ['VERB']}, 'OP': '*'},
           {'_': {'ref_t': 'ORG'}}] # object
matcher.add('subsidiary-of', None, pattern)
```

The first pattern is for the `acquires` relation. It returns all spans consisting of an organization, followed by arbitrary tokens that are not organizations, a verb matching several synonyms of *acquire*, again arbitrary tokens, and finally the second organization. The second pattern for `subsidiary-of` works similarly.

Granted, the expressions are hard to read. One reason is that we used the custom attribute `ref_t` instead of the standard `ENT_TYPE`. This is necessary to match coreferences that are not marked as entities, e.g., pronouns. Another one is that we have included some `NOT_IN` clauses. This is because rules with the asterisk operator (*) are always dangerous as they search patterns of unbounded length. Additional conditions on the tokens can reduce the risk for false matches. For example, we want to match "Fairchild, an industrial unit of Schlumberger" for the `subsidiary-of` relation, but not "Fujitsu mentioned a unit of Schlumberger." When developing rules, you always have to pay for precision with complexity. We will discuss the problems of the `acquires` relation on that aspect in a minute.

The blueprint function `extract_rel_match` now takes a processed `Doc` object and a matcher and transforms all matches to subject-predicate-object triples:

```
def extract_rel_match(doc, matcher):
    for sent in doc.sents:
        for match_id, start, end in matcher(sent):
            span = sent[start:end]  # matched span
            pred = nlp.vocab.strings[match_id] # rule name
            subj, obj = span[0], span[-1]
            if pred.startswith('rev-'): # reversed relation
                subj, obj = obj, subj
                pred = pred[4:]
            yield ((subj._.ref_n, subj._.ref_t), pred,
                   (obj._.ref_n, obj._.ref_t))
```

The predicate is determined by the name of the rule; the involved entities are simply the first and last tokens of the matched span. We restrict the search to the sentence level because in a whole document we would have a high risk of finding false positives spanning multiple sentences.

Usually, the rules match in the order "subject-predicate-object," but often the entities appear in the text in reversed order, like in "the Schlumberger unit Fairchild Corp." Here, the order of entities with regard to the `subsidiary-of` relation is "object-predicate-subject." `extract_rel_match` is prepared to handle this and switches the subject and object if a rule has the prefix `rev-` like this one:

```
pattern = [{'_': {'ref_t': 'ORG'}}, # subject
           {'LOWER': {'IN': subs_synonyms}}, # predicate
           {'_': {'ref_t': 'ORG'}}] # object
matcher.add('rev-subsidiary-of', None, pattern)
```

Now we are able to detect `acquires` and both variants of `subsidiary-of` in sentences like these:

```
text = """Fujitsu plans to acquire 80% of Fairchild Corp, an industrial unit
of Schlumberger. The Schlumberger unit Fairchild Corp received an offer."""
doc = nlp(text)
print(*extract_rel_match(doc, matcher), sep='\n')
```

Out:

```
(('Fujitsu', 'ORG'), 'acquires', ('Fairchild', 'ORG'))
(('Fairchild', 'ORG'), 'subsidiary-of', ('Schlumberger', 'ORG'))
(('Fairchild', 'ORG'), 'subsidiary-of', ('Schlumberger', 'ORG'))
```

Although the rules work nicely for our examples, the rule for *acquires* is not very reliable. The verb *acquire* can appear in many different constellations of entities. Thus, there is a high probability for false matches like this one:

```
text = "Fairchild Corp was acquired by Fujitsu."
print(*extract_rel_match(nlp(text), matcher), sep='\n')
```

Out:

```
(('Fairchild', 'ORG'), 'acquires', ('Fujitsu', 'ORG'))
```

Or this one:

```
text = "Fujitsu, a competitor of NEC, acquired Fairchild Corp."
print(*extract_rel_match(nlp(text), matcher), sep='\n')
```

Out:

```
(('NEC', 'ORG'), 'acquires', ('Fairchild', 'ORG'))
```

Obviously, our rule wasn't made for passive clauses ("was acquired by") where the subject and object switch positions. We also cannot handle insertions containing named entities or negations because they produce false matches. To treat those cases correctly, we need knowledge about the syntactical structure of the sentence. And we get that from the dependency tree.

But let's first remove the unreliable rule for *acquires* from the matcher:

```
if matcher.has_key("acquires"):
    matcher.remove("acquires")
```

Blueprint: Extracting Relations Using Dependency Trees

The grammatical rules of a language impose a syntactical structure on each sentence. Each word serves a certain role in relation to the other words. A noun, for example, can be the subject or the object in a sentence; it depends on its relation to the verb. In linguistic theory, the words of a sentence are hierarchically interdependent, and the task of the parser in an NLP pipeline is to reconstruct these dependencies.[13] The result is a *dependency tree*, which can also be visualized by `displacy`:

```
text = "Fujitsu, a competitor of NEC, acquired Fairchild Corp."
doc = nlp(text)
displacy.render(doc, style='dep',
                options={'compact': False, 'distance': 100})
```

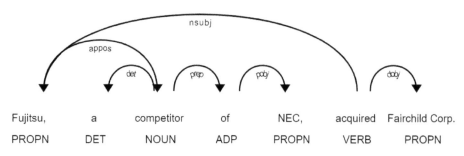

Each node in the dependency tree represents a word. The edges are labeled with the dependency information. The root is usually the predicate of the sentence, in this case *acquired*, having a subject (`nsubj`) and an object (`obj`) as direct children. This first level, root plus children, already represents the essence of the sentence "Fujitsu acquired Fairchild Corp."

Let's also take a look at the example with the passive clause. In this case, the auxiliary verb (`auxpass`) signals that *acquired* was used in passive form and *Fairchild* is the passive subject (`nsubjpass`):

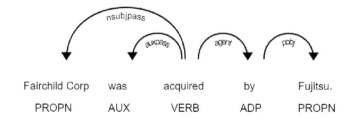

 The values of the dependency labels depend on the corpus the parser model was trained on. They are also language dependent because different languages have different grammar rules. So, you definitely need to check which tag set is used by the dependency parser.

---

13 Constituency parsers, in contrast to dependency parsers, create a hierarchical sentence structure based on nested phrases.

The function `extract_rel_dep` implements a rule to identify verb-based relations like *acquires* based on the dependencies:

```
def extract_rel_dep(doc, pred_name, pred_synonyms, excl_prepos=[]):
    for token in doc:
        if token.pos_ == 'VERB' and token.lemma_ in pred_synonyms:
            pred = token
            passive = is_passive(pred)
            subj = find_subj(pred, 'ORG', passive)
            if subj is not None:
                obj = find_obj(pred, 'ORG', excl_prepos)
                if obj is not None:
                    if passive: # switch roles
                        obj, subj = subj, obj
                    yield ((subj._.ref_n, subj._.ref_t), pred_name,
                           (obj._.ref_n, obj._.ref_t))
```

The main loop iterates through all tokens in a doc and searches for a verb signaling our relationship. This condition is the same as in the flat pattern rule we used before. But when we detect a possible predicate, we now traverse the dependency tree to find the correct subject and the object. `find_subj` searches the left subtree, and `find_obj` searches the right subtree of the predicate. Those functions are not printed in the book, but you can find them in the GitHub notebook for this chapter. They use breadth-first search to find the closest subject and object, as nested sentences may have multiple subjects and objects. Finally, if the predicate indicates a passive clause, the subject and object will be swapped.

Note, that this function also works for the *sells* relation:

```
text = """Fujitsu said that Schlumberger Ltd has arranged
to sell its stake in Fairchild Inc."""
doc = nlp(text)
print(*extract_rel_dep(doc, 'sells', ['sell']), sep='\n')
```

Out:

```
(('Schlumberger', 'ORG'), 'sells', ('Fairchild', 'ORG'))
```

In this case, *Fairchild Inc.* is the closest object in the dependency tree to *sell* and identified correctly as the object of the investigated relation. But to be the "closest" is not always sufficient. Consider this example:

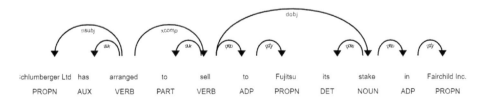

Actually, we have a three-way relation here: Schlumberger sells Fairchild to Fujitsu. Our *sells* relation is intended to have the meaning "one company sells [whole or parts of] another company." The other part is covered by the *acquires* relation. But how can we detect the right object here? Both Fujitsu and Fairchild are prepositional objects in this sentence (dependency `pobj`), and Fujitsu is the closest. The preposition is the key: Schlumberger sells something "to" Fujitsu, so that's not the relation we are looking for. The purpose of the parameter `excl_prepos` in the extraction function is to skip objects with the specified prepositions. Here is the output without (A) and with (B) preposition filter:

```
print("A:", *extract_rel_dep(doc, 'sells', ['sell']))
print("B:", *extract_rel_dep(doc, 'sells', ['sell'], ['to', 'from']))
```

Out:

```
A: (('Schlumberger', 'ORG'), 'sells', ('Fujitsu', 'ORG'))
B:
```

Let's check how our new relation extraction function works on a few variations of the examples:

```
texts = [
    "Fairchild Corp was bought by Fujitsu.", # 1
    "Fujitsu, a competitor of NEC Co, acquired Fairchild Inc.", # 2
    "Fujitsu is expanding." +
    "The company made an offer to acquire 80% of Fairchild Inc.", # 3
    "Fujitsu plans to acquire 80% of Fairchild Corp.", # 4
    "Fujitsu plans not to acquire Fairchild Corp.", # 5
    "The competition forced Fujitsu to acquire Fairchild Corp." # 6
]

acq_synonyms = ['acquire', 'buy', 'purchase']
for i, text in enumerate(texts):
    doc = nlp(text)
    rels = extract_rel_dep(doc, 'acquires', acq_synonyms, ['to', 'from'])
    print(f'{i+1}:', *rels)
```

Out:

```
1: (('Fujitsu', 'ORG'), 'acquires', ('Fairchild', 'ORG'))
2: (('Fujitsu', 'ORG'), 'acquires', ('Fairchild', 'ORG'))
3: (('Fujitsu', 'ORG'), 'acquires', ('Fairchild', 'ORG'))
4: (('Fujitsu', 'ORG'), 'acquires', ('Fairchild', 'ORG'))
5: (('Fujitsu', 'ORG'), 'acquires', ('Fairchild', 'ORG'))
6:
```

As we can see, the relations in the first four sentences have been correctly extracted. Sentence 5, however, contains a negation and still returns `acquires`. This is a typical case of a false positive. We could extend our rules to handle this case correctly, but negations are rare in our corpus, and we accept the uncertainty in favor of the simpler algorithm. Sentence 6, in contrast, is an example for a possible false negative. Even though the relation was mentioned, it was not detected because the subject in this sentence is *competition* and not one of the companies.

Actually, dependency-based rules are inherently complex, and every approach to make them more precise results in even more complexity. It is a challenge to find a good balance between precision (fewer false positives) and recall (fewer false negatives) without making the code too complex.

Despite those deficiencies, the dependency-based rule still yields good results. This last step in the process, however, depends on the correctness of named-entity recognition, coreference resolution, and dependency parsing, all of which are not working with 100% accuracy. So, there will always be some false positives and false negatives. But the approach is good enough to produce highly interesting knowledge graphs, as we will do in the next section.

Creating the Knowledge Graph

Now that we know how to extract certain relationships, we can put everything together and create a knowledge graph from the entire Reuters corpus. We will extract organizations, persons and the four relations "acquires," "sells," "subsidiary-of," and "executive-of." Figure 12-6 shows the resulting graph with some selected subgraphs.

To get the best results in dependency parsing and named-entity recognition, we use spaCy's large model with our complete pipeline. If possible, we will use the GPU to speed up NLP processing:

```
if spacy.prefer_gpu():
    print("Working on GPU.")
else:
    print("No GPU found, working on CPU.")
nlp = spacy.load('en_core_web_lg')

pipes = [entity_ruler, norm_entities, merge_entities,
         init_coref, alias_resolver, name_resolver,
         neural_coref, anaphor_coref, norm_names]
for pipe in pipes:
    nlp.add_pipe(pipe)
```

Before we start the information extraction process, we create two additional rules for the "executive-of" relation similar to the "subsidiary-of" relation and add them to our rule-based matcher:

```
ceo_synonyms = ['chairman', 'president', 'director', 'ceo', 'executive']
pattern = [{'ENT_TYPE': 'PERSON'},
           {'ENT_TYPE': {'NOT_IN': ['ORG', 'PERSON']}, 'OP': '*'},
           {'LOWER': {'IN': ceo_synonyms}}, {'TEXT': 'of'},
```

```
                {'ENT_TYPE': {'NOT_IN': ['ORG', 'PERSON']}, 'OP': '*'},
                {'ENT_TYPE': 'ORG'}]
matcher.add('executive-of', None, pattern)

pattern = [{'ENT_TYPE': 'ORG'},
           {'LOWER': {'IN': ceo_synonyms}},
           {'ENT_TYPE': 'PERSON'}]
matcher.add('rev-executive-of', None, pattern)
```

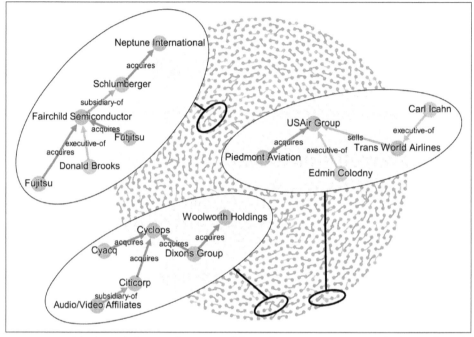

Figure 12-6. The knowledge graph extracted from the Reuters corpus with three selected subgraphs (visualized with the help of Gephi).

We then define one function to extract all relationships. Two of our four relations are covered by the matcher, and the other two by the dependency-based matching algorithm:

```
def extract_rels(doc):
    yield from extract_rel_match(doc, matcher)
    yield from extract_rel_dep(doc, 'acquires', acq_synonyms, ['to', 'from'])
    yield from extract_rel_dep(doc, 'sells', ['sell'], ['to', 'from'])
```

The remaining steps to extract the relations, convert them into a NetworkX graph, and store the graph in a gexf file for Gephi are basically following "Blueprint: Creating a Co-Occurrence Graph" on page 344. We skip them here, but you will find the full code again in the GitHub repository.

Here are a few records of the final data frame containing the nodes and edges of the graph as they are written to the gexf file:

	subj	subj_type	pred	obj	obj_type	freq	articles
883	Trans World Airlines	ORG	acquires	USAir Group	ORG	7	2950,2948,3013,3095,1862,1836,7650
152	Carl Icahn	PERSON	executive-of	Trans World Airlines	ORG	3	1836,2799,3095
884	Trans World Airlines	ORG	sells	USAir Group	ORG	1	9487

The visualization of the Reuters graph in Figure 12-6 was again created with the help of Gephi. The graph consists of many rather small components (disconnected subgraphs); because most companies got mentioned in only one or two news articles and we extracted only the four relations, simple co-occurrences are not included here. We manually magnified three of those subgraphs in the figure. They represent company networks that already appeared in the co-occurrence graph (Figure 12-5), but now we know the relation types and get a much clearer picture.

Don't Blindly Trust the Results

Each processing step we went through has a potential of errors. Thus, the information stored in the graph is not completely reliable. In fact, this starts with data quality in the articles themselves. If you look carefully at the upper-left example in Figure 12-6, you will notice that the two entities "Fujitsu" and "Futjitsu" appear in the graph. This is indeed a spelling error in the original text.

In the magnified subnetwork to the right in Figure 12-6 you can spot the seemingly contradictory information that "Piedmont acquires USAir" and "USAir acquires Piedmont." In fact, both are true because both enterprises acquired parts of the shares of the other one. But it could also be a mistake by one of the involved rules or models. To track this kind of problem, it is indispensable to store some information about the source of the extracted relations. That's why we included the list of articles in every record.

Finally, be aware that our analysis did not consider one aspect at all: the timeliness of information. The world is constantly changing and so are the relationships. Each edge in our graph should therefore get time stamped. So, there is still much to be done to create a knowledge base with trustable information, but our blueprint provides a solid foundation for getting started.

Closing Remarks

In this chapter, we explored how to build a knowledge graph by extracting structured information from unstructured text. We went through the whole process of information extraction, from named-entity recognition via coreference resolution to relation extraction.

As you have seen, each step is a challenge in itself, and we always have the choice between a rule-based and a model-based approach. Rule-based approaches have the advantage that you don't need training data. So, you can start right away; you just need to define the rules. But if the entity type or relationship you try to capture is complex to describe, you end up either with rules that are too simple and return a lot of false matches or with rules that are extremely complex and hard to maintain. When using rules, it is always difficult to find a good balance between recall (find most of the matches) and precision (find only correct matches). And you need quite a bit of technical, linguistic, and domain expertise to write good rules. In practice, you will also have to test and experiment a lot until your rules are robust enough for your application.

Model-based approaches, in contrast, have the great advantage that they learn those rules from the training data. Of course, the downside is that you need lots of high-quality training data. And if those training data are specific to your application domain, you have to create them yourself. The manual labeling of training data is especially cumbersome and time-consuming in the area of text because somebody has to read and understand the text before the labels can be set. In fact, getting good training data is the biggest bottleneck today in machine learning.

A possible solution to the problem of missing training data is weak supervision. The idea is to create a large dataset by rules like the ones we defined in this chapter or even to generate them programmatically. Of course, this dataset will be noisy, as the rules are not perfect. But, surprisingly, it is possible to train a high-quality model on low-quality data. Weak supervision learning for named-entity recognition and relationship extraction is, like many other topics covered in this section, a current topic of research. If you want to learn more about the state of the art in information extraction and knowledge graph creation, you can check out the following references. They provide good starting points for further reading.

Further Reading

Barrière, Caroline. *Natural Language Understanding in a Semantic Web Context.* Switzerland: Springer Publishing. 2016. *https://www.springer.com/de/book/9783319413358.*

Gao, Yuqing, Jisheng Liang, Benjamin Han, Mohamed Yakout, and Ahmed Mohamed. *Building a Large-scale, Accurate and Fresh Knowledge Graph.* Tutorial at KDD. 2018. *https://kdd2018tutorialt39.azurewebsites.net.*

Han, Xu, Hao Zhu, Pengfei Yu, Ziyun Wang, Yuan Yao, Zhiyuan Liu, and Maosong Sun. *FewRel: A Large-Scale Supervised Few-Shot Relation Classification Dataset with State-of-the-Art Evaluation.* Proceedings of EMNLP, 2018. *https://arxiv.org/abs/1810.10147.*

Jurafsky, Dan, and James H. Martin. *Speech and Language Processing.* 3rd Edition (draft), Chapters 18 and 22. 2019. *https://web.stanford.edu/~jurafsky/slp3.*

Lison, Pierre, Aliaksandr Hubin, Jeremy Barnes, and Samia Touileb. *Named-Entity Recognition without Labelled Data: A Weak Supervision Approach.* Proceedings of ACL, 2020 *https://arxiv.org/abs/2004.14723.*

## CHAPTER 13

Using Text Analytics in Production

We have introduced several blueprints so far and understood their application to multiple use cases. Any analysis or machine learning model is most valuable when it can be used easily by others. In this chapter, we will provide blueprints that will allow you to share the text classifier from one of our earlier chapters and also deploy to a cloud environment allowing anybody to make use of what we've built.

Consider that you used one of the blueprints in Chapter 10 in this book to analyze various car models using data from Reddit. If one of your colleagues was interested in doing the same analysis for the motorcycle industry, it should be simple to change the data source and reuse the code. In practice, this can prove much more difficult because your colleague will first have to set up an environment similar to the one you used by installing the same version of Python and all the required packages. It's possible that they might be working on a different operating system where the installation steps are different. Or consider that the clients to whom you presented the analysis are extremely happy and come back three months later asking you to cover many more industries. Now you have to repeat the same analysis but ensure that the code and environment remain the same. The volume of data for this analysis could be much larger, and your system resources may not be sufficient enough, prompting a move to use cloud computing resources. You would have to go through the installation steps on a cloud provider, and this can quickly become time-consuming.

What You'll Learn and What We'll Build

Often what happens is that you are able to produce excellent results, but they remain unusable because other colleagues who want to use them are unable to rerun the code and reproduce the results. In this chapter, we will show you some techniques that can ensure that your analysis or algorithm can be easily repeated by anyone else, including yourself at a later stage. What if we are able to make it even easier for others to use the output of our analysis? This removes an additional barrier and increases the accessibility of our results. We will show you how you can deploy your machine learning model as a simple REST API that allows anyone to use the predictions from your model in their own work or applications. Finally, we will show you how to make use of cloud infrastructure for faster runtimes or to serve multiple applications and users. Since most production servers and services run Linux, this chapter includes a lot of executable commands and instructions that run best in a Linux shell or terminal. However, they should work just as well in Windows PowerShell.

Blueprint: Using Conda to Create Reproducible Python Environments

The blueprints introduced in this book use Python and the ecosystem of packages to accomplish several text analytics tasks. As with any programming language, Python (*https://python.org/downloads*) has frequent updates and many supported versions. In addition, commonly used packages like Pandas, NumPy, and SciPy also have regular release cycles when they upgrade to a new version. While the maintainers try to ensure that newer versions are backward compatible, there is a risk that an analysis you completed last year will no longer be able to run with the latest version of Python. Your blueprint might have used a method that is deprecated in the latest version of a library, and this would make your analysis nonreproducible without knowing the version of the library used.

Let's suppose that you share a blueprint with your colleague in the form of a Jupyter notebook or a Python module; one of the common errors they might face when trying to run is as shown here:

```
import spacy
```

Out:

```
--------------------------------------------------------------------
ModuleNotFoundError                       Traceback (most recent call last)
<ipython-input-1-76a01d9c502b> in <module>
----> 1 import spacy
ModuleNotFoundError: No module named 'spacy'
```

In most cases, ModuleNotFoundError can be easily resolved by manually installing the required package using the command **pip install <module_name>**. But imagine having to do this for every nonstandard package! This command also installs the latest version, which might not be the one you originally used. As a result, the best way to ensure reproducibility is to have a standardized way of sharing the Python environment that was used to run the analysis. We make use of the conda package manager along with the Miniconda distribution of Python to solve this problem.

There are several ways to solve the problem of creating and sharing Python environments, and conda is just one of them. pip (*https:// oreil.ly/Dut6o*) is the standard Python package installer that is included with Python and is widely used to install Python packages. venv (*https://oreil.ly/k5m6A*) can be used to create virtual environments where each environment can have its own version of Python and set of installed packages. Conda combines the functionality of a package installer and environment manager and therefore is our preferred option. It's important to distinguish conda from the Anaconda/Miniconda distributions. These distributions include Python and conda along with essential packages required for working with data. While conda can be installed directly with pip, the easiest way is to install Miniconda, which is a small bootstrap version that contains conda, Python, and some essential packages they depend on.

First, we must install the Miniconda distribution with the following steps (*https:// oreil.ly/GZ4b-*). This will create a base installation containing just Python, conda, and some essential packages like pip, zlib, etc. We can now create separate environments for each project that contains only the packages we need and are isolated from other such environments. This is useful since any changes you make such as installing additional packages or upgrading to a different Python version does not impact any other project or application as they use their own environment. We can do so by using the following command:

```
conda create -n env_name [list_of_packages]
```

Executing the previous command will create a new Python environment with the default version that was available when Miniconda was installed the first time. Let's create our environment called blueprints where we explicitly specify the version of Python and the list of additional packages that we would like to install as follows:

```
$ conda create -n blueprints numpy pandas scikit-learn notebook python=3.8
Collecting package metadata (current_repodata.json): - done
Solving environment: \ done
 Package Plan
  environment location: /home/user/miniconda3/envs/blueprints
  added / updated specs:
    - notebook
    - numpy
    - pandas
    - python=3.8
    - scikit-learn

The following packages will be downloaded:

    package                    |            build
    ---------------------------|-----------------
```

```
blas-1.0                    |          mkl        6 KB
intel-openmp-2020.1         |          217      780 KB
joblib-0.16.0               |         py_0      210 KB
libgfortran-ng-7.3.0        |    hdf63c60_0     1006 KB
mkl-2020.1                  |          217    129.0 MB
mkl-service-2.3.0           |  py37he904b0f_0    218 KB
mkl_fft-1.1.0               |  py37h23d657b_0    143 KB
mkl_random-1.1.1            |  py37h0573a6f_0    322 KB
numpy-1.18.5                |  py37ha1c710e_0      5 KB
numpy-base-1.18.5           |  py37hde5b4d6_0    4.1 MB
pandas-1.0.5                |  py37h0573a6f_0    7.8 MB
pytz-2020.1                 |         py_0      184 KB
scikit-learn-0.23.1         |  py37h423224d_0    5.0 MB
scipy-1.5.0                 |  py37h0b6359f_0   14.4 MB
threadpoolctl-2.1.0         |   pyh5ca1d4c_0     17 KB
------------------------------------------------------------
                                    Total:     163.1 MB

The following NEW packages will be INSTALLED:

_libgcc_mutex     pkgs/main/linux-64::_libgcc_mutex-0.1-main
attrs             pkgs/main/noarch::attrs-19.3.0-py_0
backcall          pkgs/main/noarch::backcall-0.2.0-py_0
blas              pkgs/main/linux-64::blas-1.0-mkl
bleach            pkgs/main/noarch::bleach-3.1.5-py_0
ca-certificates   pkgs/main/linux-64::ca-certificates-2020.6.24-0

(Output truncated)
```

Once the command has been executed, you can activate it by executing **conda acti
vate <env_name>**, and you will notice that the command prompt is prefixed with the
name of the environment. You can further verify that the version of Python is the
same as you specified:

```
$ conda activate blueprints
(blueprints) $ python --version
Python 3.8
```

You can see the list of all environments on your system by using the command **conda
env list**, as shown next. The output will include the base environment, which is the
default environment created with the installation of Miniconda. An asterisk against a
particular environment indicates the currently active one, in our case the environment we just created. Please make sure that you continue to use this environment
when you work on your blueprint:

```
(blueprints) $ conda env list
# conda environments:
#
base                       /home/user/miniconda3
blueprints             *   /home/user/miniconda3/envs/blueprints
```

conda ensures that each environment can have its own versions of the same package, but this could come at the cost of increased storage since the same version of each package will be used in more than one environment. This is mitigated to a certain extent with the use of hard links, but it may not work in cases where a package uses hard-coded paths (*https://oreil.ly/bN8Dl*). However, we recommend creating another environment when you switch projects. But it is a good practice to remove unused environments using the command **conda remove --name <env_name> --all**.

The advantage of this approach is that when you want to share the code with someone else, you can specify the environment in which it should run. You can export the environment as a YAML file using the command **conda env export > environment.yml**. Ensure that you are in the desired environment (by running **conda activate <environment_name>**) before running this command:

```
(blueprints) $ conda env export > environment.yml
(blueprints) $ cat environment.yml
name: blueprints
channels:
  - defaults
dependencies:
  - _libgcc_mutex=0.1=main
  - attrs=19.3.0=py_0
  - backcall=0.2.0=py_0
  - blas=1.0=mkl
  - bleach=3.1.5=py_0
  - ca-certificates=2020.6.24=0
  - certifi=2020.6.20=py37_0
  - decorator=4.4.2=py_0
  - defusedxml=0.6.0=py_0
  - entrypoints=0.3=py37_0
  - importlib-metadata=1.7.0=py37_0
  - importlib_metadata=1.7.0=0
  - intel-openmp=2020.1=217
  - ipykernel=5.3.0=py37h5ca1d4c_0
(output truncated)
```

As shown in the output, the environment.yml file creates a listing of all the packages and their dependencies used in the environment. This file can be used by anyone to re-create the same environment by running the command **conda env create -f environment.yml**. However, this method can have cross-platform limitations since the dependencies listed in the YAML file are specific to the platform. So if you were working on a Windows system and exported the YAML file, it may not necessarily work on a macOS system.

This is because some of the dependencies required by a Python package are platform-dependent. For instance, the Intel MKL optimizations (*https://oreil.ly/ND7_H*) are specific to a certain architecture and can be replaced with the OpenBLAS (*http://open blas.net*) library. To provide a generic environment file, we can use the command `conda env export --from-history > environment.yml`, which generates a listing of only the packages that were explicitly requested by you. You can see the following output of running this command, which lists only the packages we installed when creating the environment. Contrast this with the previous environment file that also listed packages like `attrs` and `backcall`, which are part of the conda environment but not requested by us. When such a YAML file is used to create an environment on a new platform, the default packages and their platform-specific dependencies will be identified and installed automatically by conda. In addition, the packages that we explicitly specified and their dependencies will be installed:

```
(blueprints) $ conda env export --from-history > environment.yml
(blueprints) $ cat environment.yml
name: blueprints
channels:
  - defaults
dependencies:
  - scikit-learn
  - pandas
  - notebook
  - python=3.8
  - numpy
prefix: /home/user/miniconda3/envs/blueprints
```

The disadvantage of using the `--from-history` option is that the created environment is not a replica of the original environment since the base packages and dependencies are platform specific and hence different. If the platform where this environment is to be used is the same, then we do not recommend using this option.

Blueprint: Using Containers to Create Reproducible Environments

While a package manager like conda helps in installing multiple packages and managing dependencies, there are several platform-dependent binaries that can still hinder reproducibility. To make things simpler, we make use of a layer of abstraction called *containers*. The name is derived from the shipping industry, where standard-sized shipping containers are used to transport all kinds of goods by ships, trucks, and rail. Regardless of the type of items or the mode of transport, the shipping container ensures that anyone adhering to that standard can transport those items. In a similar fashion, we use a Docker container to standardize the environment we work in and guarantee that an identical environment is re-created every time regardless of where it runs or who runs it. Docker (*https://docker.com*) is one of the most popular tools that enables this functionality, and we will make use of it in this blueprint. Figure 13-1 shows a high-level overview of how Docker works.

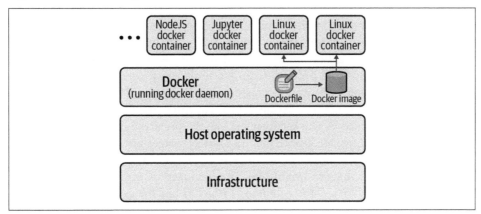

Figure 13-1. Workflow of Docker.

We need to start by installing Docker from the download link (*https://oreil.ly/ CJWKF*). Once it has been set up, please run `sudo docker run hello-world` from the command line to test that everything has been set up correctly, and you should see the output as shown. Please note that the Docker daemon binds to a Unix socket that is owned by the root user, hence the need to run all commands with `sudo`. If you are unable to provide root access, there is an experimental version (*https://oreil.ly/ X7lzt*) of Docker that you can also try:

```
$ sudo docker run hello-world

Hello from Docker!
This message shows that your installation appears to be working correctly.

To generate this message, Docker took the following steps:
 1. The Docker client contacted the Docker daemon.
 2. The Docker daemon pulled the "hello-world" image from the Docker Hub.
    (amd64)
 3. The Docker daemon created a new container from that image which runs the
    executable that produces the output you are currently reading.
 4. The Docker daemon streamed that output to the Docker client, which sent it
    to your terminal.

To try something more ambitious, you can run an Ubuntu container with:
 $ docker run -it ubuntu bash

Share images, automate workflows, and more with a free Docker ID:
 https://hub.docker.com/

For more examples and ideas, visit:
 https://docs.docker.com/get-started/
```

We can draw an analogy between building a Docker container and purchasing a car. We start by choosing from one of the preconfigured options. These configurations already have some components selected, such as the type of engine (displacement, fuel-type), safety features, level of equipment, etc. We can customize many of these components, for example, upgrade to a more fuel-efficient engine or add additional components like a navigation system or heated seats. At the end, we decide on our preferred configuration and order the car. In a similar way, we specify the configuration of the environment we want to create in the *Dockerfile*. These are described in the form of a set of instructions, executed in a sequential manner resulting in the creation of a *Docker image*. A Docker image is like the preferred car configuration that can be created based on our Dockerfile. All Docker images are extensible, so instead of defining all steps, we could extend an existing Docker image and customize it by adding specific steps that we would like. The final step of running a Docker image results in the creation of a *Docker container*, which is like the car with your preferred configuration delivered to you. In this case, it is a full-fledged environment including an operating system and additional utilities and packages as specified in the Dockerfile. It runs on the hardware and uses the interfaces provided by the host system but is completely isolated from it. In effect, it is a minimal version of a server running the way you designed it. Each Docker container instantiated from the same image will be the same regardless of which host system it is running on. This is powerful as it allows you to encapsulate your analysis and environment and run it on your laptop, in the cloud, or on your organization's server and expect the same behavior.

We are going to create a Docker image with the same Python environment as used in our analysis so that anyone else can reproduce our analysis by pulling the image and instantiating it as a container. While we can start by specifying our Docker image from scratch, it would be preferable to start with an existing image and customize certain parts of it to create our version. Such an image is referred to as a *parent image*. A good place to search for parent images is the Docker Hub registry (*https:// hub.docker.com*), which is a public repository containing prebuilt Docker images. You will find officially supported images like the Jupyter Data Science (*https://oreil.ly/ kKLXU*) notebook as well as user-created images (*https://oreil.ly/K5SMy*) like the one we have created for Chapter 9 that can be accessed here. Every image in the Docker repository can also be used as is to run containers. You can search for images using the **sudo docker search** command and add arguments to format results, as shown here where we search for available Miniconda images:

```
$ sudo docker search miniconda
NAME                              STARS
continuumio/miniconda3            218
continuumio/miniconda             77
conda/miniconda3                  35
conda/miniconda3-centos7          7
yamitzky/miniconda-neologd        3
```

```
conda/miniconda2                        2
atavares/miniconda-rocker-geospatial    2
```

We see that there is an image for Miniconda3 that would be a good starting point for our own Dockerfile. Note that all Dockerfiles have to start with the FROM keyword specifying which image they are deriving from. If you are specifying a Dockerfile from the start, then you would use the FROM scratch keyword. The details of the Miniconda image and the Dockerfile (*https://oreil.ly/ddYff*) show how this image derives from a Debian parent image and only adds additional steps to install and set up the conda package manager. When using a parent Docker image, it's important to check that it's from a trusted source. Docker Hub provides additional criteria like "Official Images" that can be helpful in identifying an official source.

Let's walk through the steps defined in our Dockerfile. We start with the Miniconda3 image and then add a step to create our custom environment. We use the ARG instruction to specify the argument for the name of our conda environment (blueprints). We then use ADD to copy the environment.yml file from the build context to the image. Finally, we create the conda environment by providing the **conda create** command as an argument to RUN:

```
FROM continuumio/miniconda3

# Add environment.yml to the build context and create the environment
ARG conda_env=blueprints
ADD environment.yml /tmp/environment.yml
RUN conda env create -f /tmp/environment.yml
```

In the next set of steps, we want to ensure that the environment is activated in the container. Therefore, we add it to the end of the .bashrc script, which will always run when the container starts. We also update the PATH environment variable using the ENV instruction to ensure that the conda environment is the version of Python used everywhere within the container:

```
# Activating the environment and starting the jupyter notebook
RUN echo "source activate ${conda_env}" > ~/.bashrc
ENV PATH /opt/conda/envs/${conda_env}/bin:$PATH
```

In the final step, we want to automatically start a Jupyter notebook that will allow the users of this Docker container to run the analysis in an interactive fashion. We use the ENTRYPOINT instruction, which is used to configure a container that will run as an executable. There can be only one such instruction in a Dockerfile (if there are multiple, only the last one will be valid), and it will be the last command to run when a container comes up and is typically used to start a server like the Jupyter notebook that we want to run. We specify additional arguments to run the server on the IP address of the container itself (0.0.0.0), on a particular port (8888), as the root user (--allow-root), and not open a browser by default (--no-browser). When the container starts, we don't want it to open the Jupyter server in its browser. Instead, we will attach the host machine to this container using the specified port and access it via the browser there:

```
# Start jupyter server on container
EXPOSE 8888
ENTRYPOINT ["jupyter","notebook","--ip=0.0.0.0", \
      "--port=8888","--allow-root","--no-browser"]
```

We use the `docker build` command to create the image from our Dockerfile. We specify the name of our image with the `-t` parameter and add a username followed by the name of the image. This is useful in identifying our image when we want to refer to it later. It is not mandatory to specify a username, but we will see later why this is useful. The Dockerfile to be used while building the image is specified with the `-f` parameter. If nothing is specified, then Docker will pick the file named *Dockerfile* in the directory specified by the argument PATH. The PATH argument also specifies where to find the files for the "context" of the build on the Docker daemon. All the files in this directory are packaged with `tar` and sent to the daemon during the build process. This must include all the files and artifacts that have to be added to the image, e.g., the `environment.yml` file, which will be copied to the image to create the conda environment.

```
docker build -t username/docker_project -f Dockerfile [PATH]
```

On executing this command, the Docker daemon starts creating an image by running the steps specified in the Dockerfile. Typically, you would execute the command in the same directory that already contains all the files and the Dockerfile as well. We specify the PATH argument using `.` referring to the current directory:

```
$ sudo docker build -t textblueprints/ch13:v1 .
Sending build context to Docker daemon  5.363MB
Step 1/8 : FROM continuumio/miniconda3
 ---> b4adc22212f1
Step 2/8 : ARG conda_env=blueprints
 ---> 959ed0c16483
Step 3/8 : ADD environment.yml /tmp/environment.yml
 ---> 60e039e09fa7
Step 4/8 : RUN conda env create -f /tmp/environment.yml
 ---> Running in 85d2f149820b
Collecting package metadata (repodata.json): ...working... done
Solving environment: ...working... done

Downloading and Extracting Packages

(output truncated)

Removing intermediate container 85d2f149820b
Step 5/8 : RUN echo "source activate ${conda_env}" > ~/.bashrc
 ---> e0ed2b448211
Step 6/8 : ENV PATH /opt/conda/envs/${conda_env}/bin:$PATH
 ---> 7068395ce2cf
```

```
Step 7/8 : EXPOSE 8888
 ---> Running in f78ac4aa0569
Removing intermediate container f78ac4aa0569
 ---> 06cfff710f8e
Step 8/8 : ENTRYPOINT ["jupyter","notebook","--ip=0.0.0.0",
                       "--port=8888","--allow-root","--no-browser"]
 ---> Running in 87852de682f4
Removing intermediate container 87852de682f4
 ---> 2b45bb18c071
Successfully built 2b45bb18c071
Successfully tagged textblueprints/ch13:v1
```

After the build completes, you can check whether the image was created successfully by running the command **sudo docker images**. You will notice that continuumio/miniconda3 image has been downloaded, and in addition, the image specified with your username and docker_project has also been created. Building a Docker will take longer the first time since the parent images have to be downloaded, but subsequent changes and rebuilds will be much faster:

```
$ sudo docker images
REPOSITORY                      TAG        IMAGE ID
textblueprints/ch13             v1         83a05579afe6
jupyter/minimal-notebook        latest     d94723ae86d1
continuumio/miniconda3          latest     b4adc22212f1
hello-world                     latest     bf756fb1ae65
```

We can create a running instance of this environment, also called *container*, by running:

```
docker run -p host_port:container_port username/docker_project:tag_name
```

The -p argument allows port forwarding, essentially sending any requests received on the host_port to the container_port. By default, the Jupyter server can only access the files and directories within the container. However, we would like to access the Jupyter notebooks and code files present in a local directory from the Jupyter server running inside the container. We can attach a local directory to the container as a volume by using -v host_volume:container_volume, which will create a new directory within the container pointing to a local directory. This ensures that any changes made to the Jupyter notebooks are not lost when the container shuts down. This is the recommended approach to work with files locally but using a Docker container for the reproducible environment. Let's start our Docker container by running the following command:

```
sudo docker run -p 5000:8888 -v \
/home/user/text-blueprints/ch13/:/work textblueprints/ch13:v1
```

Out:

```
[NotebookApp] Writing notebook server cookie secret to
/root/.local/share/jupyter/runtime/notebook_cookie_secret
[NotebookApp] Serving notebooks from local directory: /
```

```
[NotebookApp] The Jupyter Notebook is running at:
[NotebookApp] http://aaef990b90a3:8888/?token=xxxxxx
[NotebookApp]  or http://127.0.0.1:8888/?token=xxxxxx
[NotebookApp] Use Control-C to stop this server and shut down all kernels
(twice to skip confirmation).
[NotebookApp]

    To access the notebook, open this file in a browser:
        file:///root/.local/share/jupyter/runtime/nbserver-1-open.html
    Or copy and paste one of these URLs:
        http://aaef990b90a3:8888/?token=xxxxxx
     or http://127.0.0.1:8888/?token=xxxxxx
```

The logs you see now are actually the logs of the Jupyter server starting in port 8888 within the container. Since we have mapped the host port 5000, you can copy the URL and only replace the port number to 5000 to access the Jupyter server. You will also find here a directory called work, which should contain all the files from the local directory that was mapped. You can also check the status of all running containers by running the command **sudo docker container ps**. We can also specify the name for each running container by using the --name argument, and if this is not used, the Docker daemon will assign a randomly created one, as you see here:

```
$ sudo docker container ls
CONTAINER ID     IMAGE                    STATUS             NAMES
862e5b0570fe     textblueprints/ch13:v1   Up About a minute  musing_chaum
```

If you quit the terminal window where you ran this command, then the container will also be shut down. To run it in a detached mode, just add the -d option to the run command. When the container starts, it will print the container ID of the started container, and you can monitor the logs using sudo docker logs <container-id>. We have reproduced the complete environment used to run our analysis in this Docker container, and in the next blueprint, let's see the best techniques to share it.

The easiest way to share this image with anyone is by pushing this to the Docker Hub registry. You can sign up (*https://oreil.ly/vyi-2*) for a free account. Docker Hub is a public repository for Docker images, and each image is uniquely identified by the username, the name of the image, and a tag. For example, the miniconda3 package that we used as our parent image is identified as continuumio/miniconda3:latest, and any images that you share will be identified with your username. Therefore, when we built our image earlier, the username we specified must have been the same as the one used to log in to Docker Hub. Once you have created your credentials, you can click Create a Repository and choose a name and provide a description for your repository. In our case we created a repository called "ch13" that will contain a Docker image for this chapter. Once done, you can log in using the command **sudo docker login** and enter your username and password. For added security, please follow the instructions (*https://oreil.ly/m95HO*) to securely store your password.

By default, during the build process of a Docker image, all of the directories and files present in the PATH argument are part of the build context. In a previous command, we indicated the path to be the current directory using the . symbol. This is not necessary since we need to include only the selected list of files that are needed for the build and later the container. For instance, we need environment.yml but not the Jupyter notebook (.ipynb) file. It's important to specify the list of excluded files in the .dockerignore file to ensure that unwanted files do not automatically get added to the container. Our .dockerignore file is as shown here:

```
.git
.cache
figures
**/*.html
**/*.ipynb
**/*.css
```

Another thing to ensure is that the host_port (specified as 5000 in the blueprint) is open and not used by any other application on your system. Ideally, you must use a port number between 1024–49151 as these are user ports (*https://oreil.ly/F-Qps*), but you can also check this easily by running the command **sudo ss -tulw**, which will provide the list of used ports.

The next step is to tag the image that you would like to share with a tag_name to identify what it contains. In our case, we tag the image with v1 to signify that it is the first version for this chapter. We run the command sudo docker tag 2b45bb18c071 textblueprints/ch13:v1, where 2b45bb18c071 is the image ID. We can push our file now with the command sudo docker push textblueprints/ch13. Now anyone who wants to run your project can simply run the command docker pull your_username/docker_project:tag_name to create the same environment as you, irrespective of the system they might be personally working on. As an example, you can start working on blueprints in Chapter 9 by simply running the command docker pull textblueprints/ch09:v1. You can then attach the volume of the directory containing the cloned repository. Docker Hub is a popular public registry and configured as default with Docker, but each cloud provider also has their own version, and many organizations set up private registries for use within their internal applications and teams.

When working with conda environments with multiple scientific computing packages, Docker images can get large and therefore create a strain on bandwidth while pushing to Docker Hub. A much more efficient way is to include the Dockerfile in the base path of your repository. For example, the GitHub repo containing the code for this chapter contains a Dockerfile, which can be used to create the exact environment required to run the code. This blueprint easily allows you to move an analysis from your local system to a cloud machine with additional resources by re-creating the same working environment. This is especially useful when the size of the data increases or an analysis takes too long to finish.

Blueprint: Creating a REST API for Your Text Analytics Model

Let's say you used the blueprint provided in Chapter 11 to analyze the sentiment of customer support tickets in your organization. Your company is running a campaign to improve customer satisfaction where they would like to provide vouchers to unhappy customers. A colleague from the tech team reaches out to you for help with automating this campaign. While they can pull the Docker container and reproduce your analysis, they would prefer a simpler method where they provide the text of the support ticket and get a response of whether this is an unhappy customer. By encapsulating our analysis in a REST API, we can create a simple method that is accessible to anyone without them having to rerun the blueprint. They don't even necessarily need to know Python since a REST API can be called from any language. In Chapter 2, we made use of REST APIs provided by popular websites to extract data, whereas in this blueprint we are going to create our own.

We will make use of the following three components to host our REST API:

- FastAPI: A fast web framework for building APIs
- Gunicorn: A Web Service Gateway Interface server that handles all the incoming requests
- Docker: Extending the Docker container that we used in the previous blueprint

Let's create a new folder called *app* where we will place all the code that we require in order to serve sentiment predictions. It will follow the directory structure and contain files as shown next. *main.py* is where we will create the FastAPI app and the sentiment prediction method, and *preprocessing.py* is where our helper functions are included. The *models* directory contains the trained models we need to use to calculate our predictions, in our case the `sentiment_vectorizer` and `sentiment_classification`. Finally, we have the Dockerfile, *environment.yml*, and *start_script.sh*, which will be used to deploy our REST API:

```
├── app
│   ├── main.py
│   ├── Dockerfile
│   ├── environment.yml
```

```
|   ├── models
|   |   ├── sentiment_classification.pickle
|   |   └── sentiment_vectorizer.pickle
|   ├── preprocessing.py
|   └── start_script.sh
```

FastAPI (*https://oreil.ly/fastapi*) is a fast Python framework used to build APIs. It is capable of redirecting requests from a web server to specific functions defined in Python. It also takes care of validating the incoming requests against specified schema and is useful for creating a simple REST API. We will encapsulate the predict function of the model we trained in Chapter 11 in this API. Let's walk through the code in the file *main.py* step-by-step and explain how it works. You can install FastAPI by running `pip install fastapi` and Gunicorn by running `pip install gunicorn`.

Once FastAPI is installed, we can create an app using the following code:

```
from fastapi import FastAPI
app = FastAPI()
```

The FastAPI library runs this app using the included web server and can route requests received at an endpoint to a method in the Python file. This is specified by adding the `@app.post` attribute at the start of the function definition. We specify the endpoint to be *api/v1/sentiment*, the first version of our Sentiment API, which accepts HTTP POST requests. An API can evolve over time with changes to functionality, and it's useful to separate them into different versions to ensure that users of the older version are not affected:

```
class Sentiment(Enum):
    POSITIVE = 1
    NEGATIVE = 0

@app.post("/api/v1/sentiment", response_model=Review)
def predict(review: Review, model = Depends(load_model())):
    text_clean = preprocessing.clean(review.text)
    text_tfidf = vectorizer.transform([text_clean])
    sentiment = prediction_model.predict(text_tfidf)
    review.sentiment = Sentiment(sentiment.item()).name
    return review
```

The `predict` method retrieves the text field from the input and performs the preprocessing and vectorization steps. It uses the model we trained earlier to predict the sentiment of the product review. The returned sentiment is specified as an `Enum` class to restrict the possible return values for the API. The input parameter `review` is defined as an instance of the class `Review`. The class is as specified next and contains the text of the review, a mandatory field along with `reviewerID`, `productID`, and `sentiment`. FastAPI uses "type hints" (*https://oreil.ly/eErFf*) to guess the type of the field (`str`) and perform the necessary validation. As we will see, FastAPI automatically generates a web documentation for our API following the OpenAPI (*https://openapis.org*)

specification from which the API can be tested directly. We add the schema_extra as an example to act as a guide to developers who want to use the API:

```
class Review(BaseModel):
    text: str
    reviewerID: Optional[str] = None
    asin: Optional[str] = None
    sentiment: Optional[str] = None

    class Config:
        schema_extra = {
            "example": {
                "text": "This was a great purchase, saved me much time!",
                "reviewerID": "A1VU337W6PKAR3",
                "productID": "B00K0TIC56"
            }
        }
```

You would have noticed the use of the Depends keyword in the function definition. This allows us to load dependencies or other resources that are required before the function is called. This is treated as another Python function and is defined here:

```
def load_model():
    try:
        print('Calling Depends Function')
        global prediction_model, vectorizer
        prediction_model = pickle.load(
            open('models/sentiment_classification.pickle', 'rb'))
        vectorizer = pickle.load(open('models/tfidf_vectorizer.pickle', 'rb'))
        print('Models have been loaded')
    except Exception as e:
        raise ValueError('No model here')
```

Pickle is a Python serialization framework that is one of the common ways in which models can be saved/exported. Other standardized formats include joblib (*https://oreil.ly/iyl7W*) and ONNX (*https://onnx.ai*). Some deep learning frameworks use their own export formats. For example, TensorFlow uses SavedModel, while PyTorch uses pickle but implements its own save() function. It's important that you adapt the load and predict functions based on the type of model save/export you have used.

During development, FastAPI can be run with any web server (like uvicorn (*https://uvicorn.org*)), but it is recommended to use a full-fledged Web Service Gateway Interface (WSGI) server, which is production ready and supports multiple worker threads. We choose to use Gunicorn (*https://gunicorn.org*) as our WSGI server as it provides us with an HTTP server that can receive requests and redirect to the FastAPI app.

Once installed, it can be run by entering:

```
gunicorn -w 3 -b :5000 -t 5 -k uvicorn.workers.UvicornWorker main:app
```

The -w argument is used to specify the number of worker processes to run, three workers in this case. The -b parameter specifies the port that WSGI server listens on, and the -t indicates a timeout value of five seconds after which the server will kill and restart the app in case it's not responsive. The -k argument specifies the instance of worker class (uvicorn) that must be called to run the app, which is specified by referring to the Python module (main) and the name (app).

Before deploying our API, we have to revisit the *environment.yml* file. In the first blueprint, we described ways to generate and share the *environment.yml* file to ensure that your analysis is reproducible. However, it is not recommended to follow this method when deploying code to production. While the exported *environment.yml* file is a starting point, we must inspect it manually and ensure that it does not contain unused packages. It's also important to specify the exact version number of a package to ensure that package updates do not interfere with your production deployment. We use a Python code analysis tool called Vulture (*https://oreil.ly/fC71i*) that identifies unused packages as well as other dead code fragments. Let's run this analysis for the *app* folder:

```
vulture app/
```

Out:

```
app/main.py:11: unused variable 'POSITIVE' (60% confidence)
app/main.py:12: unused variable 'NEGATIVE' (60% confidence)
app/main.py:16: unused variable 'reviewerID' (60% confidence)
app/main.py:17: unused variable 'asin' (60% confidence)
app/main.py:20: unused class 'Config' (60% confidence)
app/main.py:21: unused variable 'schema_extra' (60% confidence)
app/main.py:40: unused variable 'model' (100% confidence)
app/main.py:44: unused attribute 'sentiment' (60% confidence)
app/preprocessing.py:30: unused import 'spacy' (90% confidence)
app/preprocessing.py:34: unused function 'display_nlp' (60% confidence)
```

Along with the list of potential issues, Vulture also provides a confidence score. Please use the identified issues as pointers to check the use of these imports. In the previous example, we know that the class variables we have defined are used to validate the input to the API and are definitely used. We can see that even though spacy and dis play_nlp are part of the preprocessing module, they are not used in our app. We can choose to remove them and the corresponding dependencies from the YAML file.

You can also determine the version of each package used in the conda environment by running the **conda list** command and then use this information to create the final cleaned-up environment YAML file, as shown here:

```
name: sentiment-app
channels:
  - conda-forge
dependencies:
  - python==3.8
  - fastapi==0.59.0
  - pandas==1.0.5
  - scikit-learn==0.23.2
  - gunicorn==20.0.4
  - uvicorn==0.11.3
```

As the final step, we can Dockerize the API so that it's easier to run the entire app in its own container, which is especially beneficial when we want to host it on a cloud provider, as we will see in the next blueprint. We make two changes in the Dockerfile from the previous blueprint as follows:

```
# Copy files required for deploying service to app folder in container
COPY . /app
WORKDIR /app
```

The previous instruction is used to COPY all of the contents of the current *app* folder to the Docker image, which contains all of the files needed to deploy and run the REST API. The current directory in the container is then changed to the *app* folder by using the WORKDIR instruction:

```
# Start WSGI server on container
EXPOSE 5000
RUN ["chmod", "+x", "start_script.sh"]
ENTRYPOINT [ "/bin/bash", "-c" ]
CMD ["./start_script.sh"]
```

We then provide the steps to run the WSGI server by first exposing port 5000 on the container. Next, we enable permissions on the start_script so that the Docker daemon can execute it at container startup. We use a combination of ENTRYPOINT (used to start the bash shell in which the script is to be run) and CMD (used to specify the actual script as an argument to the bash shell), which activates the conda environment and starts the Gunicorn server. Since we are running the server within a Docker container, we make a small change to specify the *access-logfile* to be written to STDOUT (-) to ensure we can still view them:

```
#!/bin/bash
source activate my_env_name
GUNICORN_CMD_ARGS="--access-logfile -" gunicorn -w 3 -b :5000 -t 5 \
        -k uvicorn.workers.UvicornWorker main:app -
```

We build the Docker image and run it following the same steps as in the previous blueprint. This will result in a running Docker container where the Gunicorn WSGI server is running the FastAPI app. We have to make sure that we forward a port from the host system where the container is running:

```
$ sudo docker run -p 5000:5000 textblueprints/sentiment-app:v1
    [INFO] Starting gunicorn 20.0.4
    [INFO] Listening at: http://0.0.0.0:5000 (11)
    [INFO] Using worker: sync
    [INFO] Booting worker with pid: 14
```

We can make a call to the container running the API from a different program. In a separate terminal window or IDE, create a test method that calls the API and passes in a sample review to check the response. We make a call to port 5000 with the local IP, which is forwarded to port 5000 of the container from which we receive the response, as shown here:

```
import requests
import json

url = 'http://0.0.0.0:5000/api/v1/sentiment'
data = {
    'text':
    'I could not ask for a better system for my small greenhouse, \
     easy to set up and nozzles do very well',
    'reviewerID': 'A1VU337W6PKAR3',
    'productID': 'B00K0TIC56'
}
input_data = json.dumps(data)
headers = {'content-type': 'application/json', 'Accept-Charset': 'UTF-8'}
r = requests.post(url, data=input_data, headers=headers)
print(r.text)
```

Out:

```
{
   "prediction": "POSITIVE"
}
```

We can see that our API has generated the expected response. Let's also check the documentation of this API, which we can find at *http://localhost:5000/docs*. It should generate a page as shown in Figure 13-2, and clicking the link for our /api/v1/senti ment method will provide additional details on how the method is to be called and also has the option to try it out. This allows others to provide different text inputs and view the results generated by the API without writing any code.

Docker containers are always started in unprivileged mode, meaning that even if there is a terminal error, it would only be restricted to the container without any impact to the host system. As a result, we can run the server as a root user safely within the container without worrying about an impact on the host system.

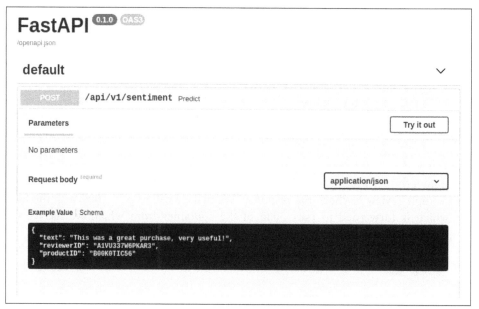

Figure 13-2. API specification and testing provided by FastAPI.

You can run a combination of the sudo docker tag and sudo docker push commands discussed earlier to share the REST API. Your colleague could easily pull this Docker image to run the API and use it to identify unhappy customers by providing their support tickets. In the next blueprint, we will run the Docker image on a cloud provider and make it available on the internet.

Blueprint: Deploying and Scaling Your API Using a Cloud Provider

Deploying machine learning models and monitoring their performance is a complex task and includes multiple tooling options. This is an area of constant innovation that is continuously looking to make it easier for data scientists and developers. There are several cloud providers and multiple ways to deploy and host your API using one of them. This blueprint introduces a simple way to deploy the Docker container we created in the previous blueprint using Kubernetes (*https://oreil.ly/ C2KX2*). Kubernetes is an open source technology that provides functionality to deploy and manage Docker containers to any underlying physical or virtual infrastructure. In this blueprint, we will be using Google Cloud Platform (GCP), but most major providers have support for Kubernetes. We can deploy the Docker container directly to a cloud service and make the REST API available to anyone. However, we choose to deploy this within a Kubernetes cluster since it gives us the flexibility to scale up and down the deployment easily.

You can sign up for a free account with GCP (*https://oreil.ly/H1jQS*). By signing up with a cloud provider, you are renting computing resources from a third-party provider and will be asked to provide your billing details. During this blueprint, we will stay within the free-tier limit, but it's important to keep a close track of your usage to ensure that you are not charged for some cloud resources that you forgot to shut down! Once you've completed the sign-up process, you can check this by visiting the Billing section from the GCP console (*https://oreil.ly/wX4wd*). Before using this blueprint, please ensure that you have a Docker image containing the REST API pushed and available in Docker Hub or any other container registry.

Let's start by understanding how we are going to deploy the REST API, which is illustrated in Figure 13-3. We will create a scalable compute cluster using GCP. This is nothing but a collection of individual servers that are called *nodes*. The compute cluster shown has three such nodes but can be scaled when needed. We will use Kubernetes to deploy the REST API to each node of the cluster. Assuming we start with three nodes, this will create three replicas of the Docker container, each running on one node. These containers are still not exposed to the internet, and we make use of Kubernetes to run a load balancer service, which provides a gateway to the internet and also redirects requests to each container depending on its utilization. In addition to simplifying our deployment process, the use of Kubernetes ensures that node failures and traffic spikes can be handled by automatically creating additional instances.

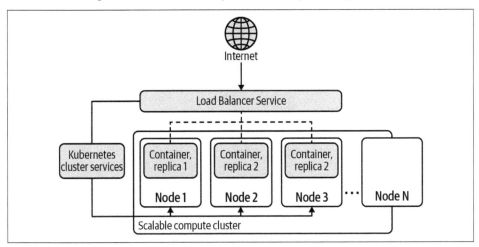

Figure 13-3. Kubernetes architecture diagram.

Let's create a project in GCP that we will use for our deployment. Visit Google Cloud (*https://oreil.ly/5mCaQ*), choose the Create Project option on the top right, and create a project with your chosen name (we choose sentiment-rest-api). Once the project has been created, click the navigation menu on the top left and navigate to the service called Kubernetes Engine, as shown in Figure 13-4. You have to click the Enable Billing link and select the payment account that you set up when you signed up. You can also click the Billing tab directly and set it up for your project as well. Assuming you are using the free trial to run this blueprint, you will not be charged. It will take a few minutes before it gets enabled for our project. Once this is complete, we are ready to proceed with our deployment.

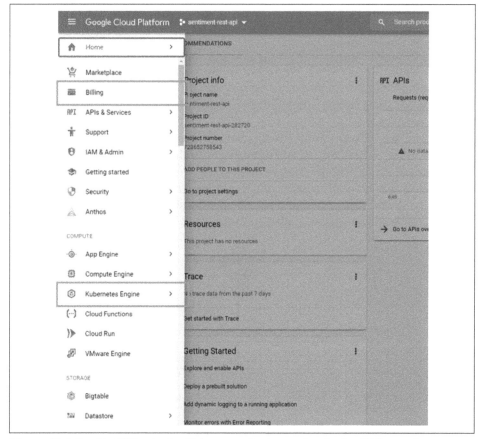

Figure 13-4. Enable Billing in the Kubernetes Engine option in the GCP console.

We can continue to work with Google Cloud Platform using the web console (*https://oreil.ly/-eZ-W*) or the command-line tool. While the functionality offered remains the same, we choose to describe the steps in the blueprint with the help of the command-line interface in the interest of brevity and to enable you to copy the commands.

Please install the Google Cloud SDK by following the instructions (*https://oreil.ly/ G3_js*) and then use the Kubernetes command-line tool by running:

```
gcloud components install kubectl
```

In a new terminal window, we first authenticate our user account by running **gcloud auth login**. This will open the browser and redirect you to the Google authentication page. Once you have completed this, you won't be asked for this again in this terminal window. We configure the project and compute zone where we would like to deploy our cluster. Use the project that we just created, and pick a location close to you from all the available options (*https://oreil.ly/SnRc8*); we chose us-central1-a:

```
gcloud config set project sentiment-rest-api
```

```
gcloud config set compute/zone us-central1-a
```

Our next step is to create a Google Kubernetes Engine compute cluster. This is the compute cluster that we will use to deploy our Docker containers. Let's create a cluster with three nodes and request a machine of type n1-standard-1. This type of machine comes with 3.75GB of RAM and 1 CPU. We can request a more powerful machine, but for our API this should suffice:

```
gcloud container clusters create \  sentiment-app-cluster --num-nodes 3 \
--machine-type n1-standard-1
```

Every container cluster in GCP comes with `HorizontalPodAutoscaling`, which takes care of monitoring the CPU utilization and adding machines if required. The requested machines will be provisioned and assigned to the cluster, and once it's executed, you can verify by checking the running compute instances with `gcloud compute instances list`:

```
$ gcloud compute instances list
NAME                                    ZONE          MACHINE_TYPE   STATUS
gke-sentiment-app-cluste-default-pool   us-central1-a n1-standard-1  RUNNING
gke-sentiment-app-cluste-default-pool   us-central1-a n1-standard-1  RUNNING
gke-sentiment-app-cluste-default-pool   us-central1-a n1-standard-1  RUNNING
```

Now that our cluster is up and running, we will deploy the Docker image we created in the previous blueprint to this cluster with the help of Kubernetes. Our Docker image is available on Docker Hub and is uniquely identified by `username/ project_name:tag`. We give the name of our deployment as `sentiment-app` by running the following command:

```
kubectl create deployment sentiment-app --image=textblueprints/sentiment-app:v0.1
```

Once it has been started, we can confirm that it's running with the command `kubectl get pods`, which will show us that we have one pod running. A pod is analogous here to the container; in other words, one pod is equivalent to a running container of the provided image. However, we have a three-node cluster, and we can easily deploy more instances of our Docker image. Let's scale this to three replicas with the following command:

```
kubectl scale deployment sentiment-app --replicas=3
```

You can verify that the other pods have also started running now. Sometimes there might be a delay as the container is deployed to the nodes in the cluster, and you can find detailed information by using the command kubectl describe pods. By having more than one replica, we enable our REST API to be continuously available even in the case of failures. For instance, let's say one of the pods goes down because of an error; there would be two instances still serving the API. Kubernetes will also automatically create another pod in case of a failure to maintain the desired state. This is also the case since the REST API is stateless and would need additional failure handling in other scenarios.

While we have deployed and scaled the REST API, we have not made it available to the internet. In this final step, we will add a LoadBalancer service called sentiment-app-loadbalancer, which acts as the HTTP server exposing the REST API to the internet and directing requests to the three pods based on the traffic. It's important to distinguish between the parameter port, which is the port exposed by the LoadBa lancer and the target-port, which is the port exposed by each container:

```
kubectl expose deployment sentiment-app --name=sentiment-app-loadbalancer
    --type=LoadBalancer --port 5000 --target-port 5000
```

If you run the kubectl get service command, it provides a listing of all Kubernetes services that are running, including the sentiment-app-loadbalancer. The parameter to take note of is EXTERNAL-IP, which can be used to access our API. The sentiment-app can be accessed using the link *http://[EXTERNAL-IP]:5000/apidocs*, which will provide the Swagger documentation, and a request can be made to *http://[EXTERNAL-IP]:5000/api/v1/sentiment*:

```
$ kubectl expose deployment sentiment-app --name=sentiment-app-loadbalancer \
--type=LoadBalancer --port 5000 --target-port 5000
service "sentiment-app-loadbalancer" exposed
$ kubectl get service
NAME                         TYPE          CLUSTER-IP    EXTERNAL-IP
kubernetes                   ClusterIP     10.3.240.1    <none>
sentiment-app-loadbalancer   LoadBalancer  10.3.248.29   34.72.142.113
```

Let's say you retrained the model and want to make the latest version available via the API. We have to build a new Docker image with a new tag (v0.2) and then set the image to that tag with the command kubectl set image, and Kubernetes will automatically update pods in the cluster in a rolling fashion. This ensures that our REST API will always be available but also deploy the new version using a rolling strategy.

When we want to shut down our deployment and cluster, we can run the following commands to first delete the LoadBalancer service and then tear down the cluster. This will also release all the compute instances you were using:

```
kubectl delete service sentiment-app-loadbalancer

gcloud container clusters delete sentiment-app-cluster
```

This blueprint provides a simple way to deploy and scale your machine learning model using cloud resources and does not cover several other aspects that can be crucial to production deployment. It's important to keep track of the performance of your model by continuously monitoring parameters such as accuracy and adding triggers for retraining. To ensure the quality of predictions, one must have enough test cases and other quality checks before returning a result from the API. In addition, good software design must provide for authentication, identity management, and security, which should be part of any publicly available API.

Blueprint: Automatically Versioning and Deploying Builds

In the previous blueprint, we created the first deployment of our REST API. Consider that you now have access to additional data and retrained your model to achieve a higher level of accuracy. We would like to update our REST API with this new version so that the results of our prediction improve. In this blueprint, we will provide an automated way to deploy updates to your API with the help of GitHub actions. Since the code for this book and also the sentiment-app (*https://oreil.ly/SesD8*) is hosted on GitHub, it made sense to use GitHub actions, but depending on the environment, you could use other tools, such as GitLab (*https://oreil.ly/vBS8i*).

We assume that you have saved the model files after retraining. Let's check in our new model files and make any additional changes to main.py. You can see these additions on the Git repository (*https://oreil.ly/ktwYX*). Once all the changes are checked in, we decide that we are satisfied and ready to deploy this new version. We have to tag the current state as the one that we want to deploy by using the git tag v0.2 command. This binds the tag name (v0.2) to the current point in the commit history. Tags should normally follow Semantic Versioning (*https://semver.org*), where version numbers are assigned in the form MAJOR.MINOR.PATCH and are often used to identify updates to a given software module. Once a tag has been assigned, additional changes can be made but will not be considered to be part of the already-tagged state. It will always point to the original commit. We can push the created tag to the repository by running git push origin tag-name.

Using GitHub actions, we have created a deployment pipeline that uses the event of tagging a repository to trigger the start of the deployment pipeline. This pipeline is defined in the *main.yml* file located in the folder *.github/workflow/* and defines the steps to be run each time a new tag is assigned. So whenever we want to release a new version of our API, we can create a new tag and push this to the repository.

Let's walk through the deployment steps:

```
name: sentiment-app-deploy

on:
  push:
    tags:
      - '*'

jobs:
  build:
    name: build
    runs-on: ubuntu-latest
    timeout-minutes: 10
    steps:
```

The file starts with a name to identify the GitHub workflow, and the on keyword specifies the events that trigger the deployment. In this case, we specify that only Git push commands that contain a tag will start this deployment. This ensures that we don't deploy with each commit and control a deployment to the API by using a tag. We can also choose to build only on specific tags, for example, major version revisions. The jobs specifies the series of steps that must be run and sets up the environment that GitHub uses to perform the actions. The build parameter defines the kind of build machine to be used (ubuntu) and a time-out value for the entire series of steps (set to 10 minutes).

Next, we specify the first set of actions as follows:

```
- name: Checkout
  uses: actions/checkout@v2

- name: build and push image
  uses: docker/build-push-action@v1
  with:
    username: ${{ secrets.DOCKER_USERNAME }}
    password: ${{ secrets.DOCKER_PASSWORD }}
    repository: sidhusmart/sentiment-app
    tag_with_ref: true
    add_git_labels: true
    push: ${{ startsWith(github.ref, 'refs/tags/') }}

- name: Get the Tag Name
  id: source_details
```

```
run: |-
  echo ::set-output name=TAG_NAME::${GITHUB_REF#refs/tags/}
```

The first step is typically always checkout, which checks out the latest code on the build machine. The next step is to build the Docker container using the latest commit from the tag and push this to the Docker Hub registry. The docker/build-push-action@v1 is a GitHub action that is already available in GitHub Marketplace (*https://oreil.ly/dHiai*), which we reuse. Notice the use of secrets to pass in the user credentials. You can encrypt and store the user credentials that your deployment needs by visiting the Settings > Secrets tab of your GitHub repository, as shown in Figure 13-5. This allows us to maintain security and enable automatic builds without any password prompts. We tag the Docker image with the same tag as the one we used in the Git commit. We add another step to get the tag and set this as an environment variable, TAG_NAME, which will be used while updating the cluster.

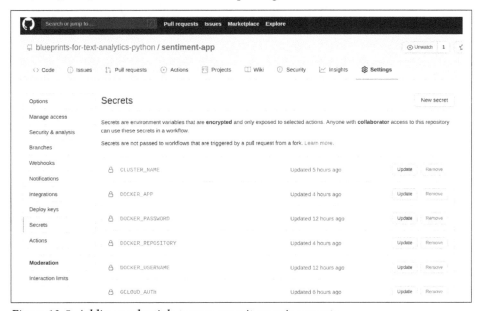

Figure 13-5. Adding credentials to your repository using secrets.

For the deployment steps, we have to connect to our running GCP cluster and update the image that we use for the deployment. First, we have to add PROJECT_ID, LOCA TION_NAME, CLUSTER_NAME, and GCLOUD_AUTH to the secrets to enable this action. We encode these as secrets to ensure that project details of our cloud deployments are not stored publicly. You can get the GCLOUD_AUTH by using the provided instructions (*https://oreil.ly/EDELL*) and adding the values in the downloaded key as the secret for this field.

The next steps for deployment include setting up the `gcloud` utility on the build machine and using this to get the Kubernetes configuration file:

```
# Setup gcloud CLI
- uses: GoogleCloudPlatform/github-actions/setup-gcloud@master
  with:
    version: '290.0.1'
    service_account_key: ${{ secrets.GCLOUD_AUTH }}
    project_id: ${{ secrets.PROJECT_ID }}

# Get the GKE credentials so we can deploy to the cluster
- run: |-
    gcloud container clusters get-credentials ${{ secrets.CLUSTER_NAME }} \
                        --zone ${{ secrets.LOCATION_ZONE }}
```

Finally, we update the Kubernetes deployment with the latest Docker image. This is where we use the `TAG_NAME` to identify the latest release that we pushed in the second step. Finally, we add an action to monitor the status of the rollout in our cluster:

```
# Deploy the Docker image to the GKE cluster
- name: Deploy
  run: |-
    kubectl set image --record deployment.apps/sentiment-app \
            sentiment-app=textblueprints/sentiment-app:\
            ${{ steps.source_details.outputs.TAG_NAME }}

# Verify that deployment completed
- name: Verify Deployment
  run: |-
    kubectl rollout status deployment.apps/sentiment-app
    kubectl get services -o wide
```

You can follow the various stages of the build pipeline using the Actions tab of your repository, as shown in Figure 13-6. At the end of the deployment pipeline, an updated version of the API should be available at the same URL and can also be tested by visiting the API documentation.

This technique works well when code and model files are small enough to be packaged into the Docker image. If we use deep learning models, this is often not the case, and creating large Docker containers is not recommended. In such cases, we still use Docker containers to package and deploy our API, but the model files reside on the host system and can be attached to the Kubernetes cluster. For cloud deployments, this makes use of a persistent storage like Google Persistent Disk (*https://oreil.ly/ OZ4Ru*). In such cases, we can perform model updates by performing a cluster update and changing the attached volume.

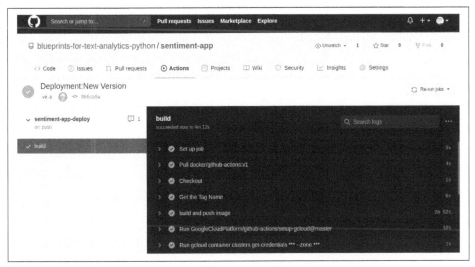

Figure 13-6. GitHub deployment workflow initiated by pushing a Git tag.

Closing Remarks

We introduced a number of blueprints with the aim of allowing you to share the analysis and projects you created using previous chapters in this book. We started by showing you how to create reproducible conda environments that will allow your teammate or a fellow learner to easily reproduce your results. With the help of Docker environments, we make it even easier to share your analysis by creating a complete environment that works regardless of the platform or infrastructure that your collaborators are using. If someone would like to integrate the results of your analysis in their product or service, we can encapsulate the machine learning model into a REST API that can be called from any language or platform. Finally, we provided a blueprint to easily create a cloud deployment of your API that can be scaled up or down based on usage. This cloud deployment can be updated easily with a new version of your model or additional functionality. While adding each layer of abstraction, we make the analysis accessible to a different (and broader) audience and reduce the amount of detail that is exposed.

Further Reading

Scully, D, et al. *Hidden Technical Debt in Machine Learning Systems. https:// papers.nips.cc/paper/2015/file/86df7dcfd896fcaf2674f757a2463eba-Paper.pdf.*

Index

A

ABC news headlines, 136-137, 143, 145-151
absolute versus relative term frequencies, 31
abstractive methods for text summarization, 246
accuracy metrics, 166
acronyms, resolution of, 337-338
ALBERT pretrained model, 322
aliases, resolution of, 336, 337-338
Amazon customer reviews dataset, 299-301
analogy reasoning, 272, 285
anaphora, resolution of, 336, 340-342, 346
Anchor model, 203-208
APIs (application programming interfaces), 33-34, 56, 62
    (see also GitHub API; REST (Representational State Transfer) API; text data extraction with APIs)
apply function, 13, 96
artificial neural networks (ANNs), 310
Atom feeds for URLs, 66
authenticated API requests, 44, 54
automatic deploying of REST API updates, 385-388

B

backpropagation algorithm, 317
backups, 81, 93, 346, 375
bag-of-words models, 15, 118, 120, 124, 131-134, 230, 269
bandwidth, saving, 67
batches and epochs in model training, 317
Beautiful Soup library (Python), 71-73, 83, 87
benchmarking, 151

Berners-Lee, Tim, 327
BERT (Bidirectional Encoder Representations from Transformers) model, xvi, 266, 274, 311-320, 321
bias in training data, 278
bigrams, 26-28, 113, 143-145
binary classification, 159
Bing Liu lexicon , 302-304, 309
block calculation approach, 149
box plots, 7, 8

C

case-folding, 13
CBOW (continuous bag-of-words) model, 272, 282
CDNs (content distribution networks), 67
character n-grams, 274
character normalization, 90, 98
class imbalance, 157, 170-172, 182
classification (see text classification algorithms)
classification_report function, 170
cleaning text data, 94-101, 120, 262, 306, 329
cloud providers, 380-385
clustering of text data, 238-242
co-occurrence analysis, 151
co-occurrence graphs, 335, 344-347
coefficients in predictive models, 191-193
coherence scores for topic models, 231, 233-236, 242
CoherenceModel (Gensim), 233
collocated words, 26, 28
Common Crawl dataset, 59
compound phrases/names, 25, 280-281, 334
compression for downloads, 67

compute clusters, 380-385
conda commands, 363-366
conda for reproducing Python environments, 362-366
confusion matrix, 167
containers for creating reproducible environments, 366-374
content distribution networks (CDNs), 67
contextualized embeddings, 274
copies for traceability, 81, 93, 346, 375
coreference resolution, 327, 335-343
corpus, 2
    (see also datasets)
cosine similarity, 139, 146, 150, 277-278
cosine_similarity function, 133, 146, 277
Counter (Python library), 15-17
CountVectorizer, 23, 101, 131-133, 143
count_keywords_by function, 29
count_words function, 17, 22, 96
crawling websites for URLs, 61, 66
cross-validation for accuracy metrics, 175-177
cross_val_score , 176
CSS selectors, 72-76, 86
Cursor object (Tweepy), 48

D

data cleaning, 90, 94-101, 120, 262, 306, 329
data masking, 99-100
data preprocessing
    for deep learning models, 315
    pipelines for, 10-14, 89-90, 104-107, 306
    for text classification, 160
    for text summarization, 247, 261-264
    for topic modeling, 230
    for word embeddings, 279-281, 294
DataFrame (Pandas), 5, 9, 14, 16, 58, 78, 91, 93, 132, 136, 280
datasets, examples of
    ABC news headlines, 136-137, 143, 145-151
    Amazon customer reviews dataset, 299-301
    JDT (Java Development Tools) bugs dataset, 154-158
    from Kaggle, 3, 91, 136
    market research on cars, 269, 279
    overview of, xiv, 58
    Reddit Self-Posts, 91-93, 119, 270, 279
    Reuters News Archive, 57, 59, 63-66, 70, 78, 82, 247-256, 328, 345, 355-357
    for sentiment analysis, 58

    travel forum, 260-267
    Twitter tweets, 48-55
    UN General Debates, 3, 5-9, 20, 28-31, 210-212
    Wikipedia articles, 55, 256, 259
datetime values, 9
DBpedia, 327, 343
DBpedia Spotlight, 344
debiasing training data, 278
deep contextualized embeddings, 274
deep learning, 310-312, 317, 376, 388
density-based text extraction, 82-83
dependency parser, 106, 119
dependency trees for extracting relations, 351-355
dimensionality reduction, 243, 286-289
displacy (spaCy), 114, 330, 352
display_ner function, 338
distance metrics, 263
DistilBERT pretrained model, 322
distributional hypothesis, 271
Docker commands, 371-373
Docker containers, 366-374, 378-385, 387-389
Docker Hub registry, 368, 372, 381, 383
Docker images, 368-371, 373, 379-380, 383-384
Docker, installation of, 367
Dockerfile, 368-371, 373
.dockerignore file, 373
document embedding, 270, 295
document extraction, standardized parts for, 77
document-term matrix, 128, 132, 150, 212-214, 217, 220
documents
    calculating similarities of, 128-130, 133-134
    topic modeling for, 214-216
    vectorizing, 124, 126-136, 141
dot product calculation, 128, 133, 269
downloading data, legal issues with, 61, 68, 86
downloading HTML pages, 57, 66-69, 84-86
downloading with spidering, 78-81, 84, 85
downsampling techniques, 171
dt (datetime) functions, 10

E

ELI5 ("Explain it to me like I'm 5") library, 200-203
ELMo (Embedding from Language Models), 274
embedding, 271

entity linking, 327, 336, 343-348
EntityRuler (spaCy), 332
enumeration of vocabulary, 125-127
environment.yml file, 365, 369, 377
epochs in model training, 317
error handling, 81
exception handling, 81
excl_prepos function, 354
execution time, 105, 117-119, 149, 151, 195, 223, 235, 239, 342
explainability (see text classification results, explaining)
explainer in LIME and Anchor, 195-200, 204
exploratory data analysis, 2
extensions (spaCy), 336, 341
extract.words function (textacy), 112
extraction of data (see text data extraction from web; text data extraction with APIs)
extractive methods for text summarization, 246, 247, 250
extract_coocs function, 346
extract_rel_dep function, 353
extract_rel_match function, 350

F

F1 score, 168
FastAPI, 374-376, 379
FastText, 119, 272, 274, 282, 284
feature engineering and vectorization
    about, 123-124, 138, 152, 159
    with bag-of-words models, 124, 131-134
    by building vectorizer, 125-130
    datasets for, 125, 136-137, 145-151
    syntactic similarities in, 145-152
    with TF-IDF models, 134-145
    use cases for, 134, 136, 140, 141, 144
    by vectorizing documents, 126-136, 141
feature extraction with spaCy, 115-119
feature importance, predicting, 191-193
feature names as vocabulary, 131
feature vectors, 159, 172, 195
FileStreamListener (Tweepy), 54
fit_transform method, 137, 214
Flair, xvii, 329, 331
frequency diagrams, 18
frequency heatmaps, 30-31
frequency timelines, 28-30
function words, 111

G

gcloud instructions, 383, 387
GCP (Google Cloud Platform), 380-383, 387
Gensim
    about, xvi
    for semantic embeddings, 270, 272, 277-278, 279, 282, 293, 294
    for topic modeling, 230-238, 242
Gephi, 347, 355
gexf file format, 347, 356
GitHub API
    archives in, 70
    data extraction from, 35-44
    LIME on, 195
    Rate Limiting policy of, 41
GloVe (global vectors) embedding, 272, 273-276
Google Colab, xviii, 118, 318
GPUs (graphics processing units), 117, 119, 315, 318, 355
graph databases, 328
GraphQL (Graph Query Language), 35
Graphviz, 293
grid search for hyperparameter tuning, 177-179, 182
GridSearchCV method, 178
GroupShuffleSplit function, 262
Gunicorn WSGI server, 374, 376-379

H

hashtags in tweets, 50
HDP (hierarchical Dirichlet process), 237-238
headers object, 37, 41
headlines, extracting, 72
headlines, finding similar, 145-149
heatmaps, 30, 169
hierarchical relationships, 293
HorizontalPodAutoscaling, 383
HTML pages, downloading, 57, 66-69, 84-86
HTML parser for extracting data, 71-77
HTML websites, scraping of (see scraping websites)
HTTPAdapter library, 42
HTTPS/TLS protocol, 67
Hugging Face, xvi, 246, 313, 341
hyperparameters, 177-179, 273, 282, 287

relation extraction, 328, 348-355

replace functions in textacy, 98-100

requests library (Python), 35, 67, 69

resample() function, 10

resampling time, 9

response object, 37-40, 41

REST (Representational State Transfer) API
    about, 35
    creating, 374-380
    deploying and scaling, 380-385

Reuters News Archive, 57, 59, 63-66, 70, 78, 82, 247-256, 328, 345, 355-357

robot exclusion standard (robots.txt), 61, 62

ROUGE (Recall-Oriented Understudy for Gisting Evaluation) score, 258-260, 266

rouge_scorer package (Python), 258, 265

row vectors, 126-128

RSS feeds, 62, 65-66

rule-based heuristics for knowledge graphs, 328, 331-333, 339, 349-356, 358

rule-based matcher (spaCy), 113, 120, 349-351, 355

rule-based named-entity recognition, 331-333

S

sample function (Pandas), 4

sampling with results, 25

scalar product calculation, 128, 133

scatter plots, 288

Scattertext library, 32

scikit-learn
    about, xvi
    classification_report function of, 170
    clustering with, 239
    cosine_similarity function of, 133, 146, 277
    CountVectorizer of, 23, 101, 131-133, 143
    dataset in, 59
    max_df and min_df parameters of, 13, 139, 141, 213, 230
    MultiLabelBinarizer of, 130
    TfidfVectorizer of, 23, 136, 143-144, 148, 212, 264
    topic modeling with, 212, 214, 219, 229, 234
    vectorization with, 128, 130-134, 137, 144, 200, 242
    with visualization of results, 223, 287

scoring of corpus, 2

scraping websites
    about, 57-59, 87

blocks and bans as result of, 67, 69, 87

downloading HTML pages for, 58, 66-69, 84-86

downloading robots.txt for, 61, 62

extracting data and (see text data extraction from web)

legal issues with, 61, 68, 86

problems with, 34, 86

with Reuters News Archive, 59, 78

RSS feeds for, 65-66

Scrapy all-in-one approach for, 84-86

URL generation for, 58, 61-62

use cases for, 58, 78

Scrapy package, 84-86

Seaborn library, 8, 30

Search API of Twitter, 34, 48-50

search engines for data sources, 60

secrets for GitHub repository, 387

select in Beautiful Soup, 73

selectors, CSS, 72-76, 86

semantic relationships (see word embeddings for semantic analysis)

Semantic Web, 326

sentence-term matrix, 250

sentiment analysis of text data
    about, 297-299
    Bing Liu lexicon for, 302-304, 309
    datasets for, 58, 299-301, 305
    deep learning and transfer learning for, 310-312
    further reading on, 310, 316, 322
    lexicon-based approaches for , 301-304
    pretrained language models for, 309-322
    supervised learning approaches to, 305-309
    transfer learning technique for, 312-322
    Transformers library for, 311-313, 318, 322
    use cases for, 298, 304, 309, 312, 322

serialization format of Python, 93

set operators (Python), 12

SGDClassifier, 165

similar concepts, 285

similarities
    calculations for document, 128-130, 133-134, 146-149
    syntactic, 145-152

similarity matrix , 129-130, 146

similarity queries for semantic analysis, 275-279

similarity trees, constructing, 291-294

extractive methods for, 246, 247, 250

further reading on, 267

indicator representation (TextRank) for, 253-257, 267

LSA algorithm for, 250-253, 267

machine learning for, 260-267

    step 1: target labels, 261-264

    step 2: features for model prediction, 264

    step 3: building model, 265-267

measuring, 257-260

TF-IDF method for, 249, 251, 253

topic representation for, 248-253

use cases for, 246, 257, 260, 260, 265, 267

textacy functions, 98

textacy library, 24, 32, 98-100, 112-115, 120

textdistance package, 263

TextRank method, 253, 254-257, 259, 267

textrank_summary function, 255

TF-IDF (Term-Frequency Inverse Document Frequency) weighting

    for data preparation in Gensim, 230

    limitations of, 270

    with similarity matrix calculations, 147

    of stop words, 13

    text data analysis with, 21-23, 27

    for text summarization, 249, 251, 253

    vectorization with, 134-145, 164, 178, 212, 230, 239, 270, 307

TfidfTransformer, 135

TfidfVectorizer, 23, 136, 143-144, 148, 212, 264

tfidf_summary function, 250

three-dimensional plot, 289

time evolution and topic distribution of documents, 228-229

time, execution, 105, 117-119, 149, 151, 195, 223, 235, 239, 342

time-series resampling, 9

timestamp of news article, extracting, 76

titles, extraction of, 72, 77

titleSimilarity function, 264

Token objects, 104, 106

tokenization/tokens

    for coreference resolution, 336

    in data preparation, 101-103, 230, 279

    defined, 11, 101

    with initial text analyses, 11, 14, 17, 27

    in named-entity recognition, 332, 334

    with NLTK, 101, 102

    normalization in, 120

with pretrained models, 313-316

recommendations for, 24, 103, 109

with regular expressions, 11, 101-103

in spaCy linguistic processing, 101, 104-115, 332, 336

topic modeling

    about, 209, 242

    changes over time in, 228-229

    clustering as alternative to, 238-242

    coherence scores, calculating and using, 231, 233-236, 242

    data preparation with Gensim for, 230

    for documents using NMF, 214-216

    Gensim for, 230-238, 242

    hierarchical Dirichlet process for, 237-238

    LDA for, 221-224, 225-225, 232-235, 242

    LDA with Gensim for, 232

    NMF for, 213-217, 220, 225-225, 231, 233

    NMF with Gensim for, 231

    with optimal number of topics, 232, 234-236

    SVD for, 217-220

    with UN general debates, 210-212

    use case for, 210

    visualizations for, 217, 223-224, 228

    word clouds for display and comparing of, 224-225, 239-242

topic representation for text summarization, 248-253

tqdm library, 14, 119, 319

train-test split, 161-163, 175, 262, 307

training

    data for, 123, 158-159, 270, 277-279, 307, 349, 358

    of machine learning models, 158, 163-165, 282, 308-309, 328, 358

    of deep learning models, 316-320

    of pretrained models, 276-279

    in supervised learning, 158-159, 305-309

transfer learning, 274, 310-312, 321

transform method, 228

Transformers library, xvi, 246, 311-313, 318, 322

transparency of models, 185, 208

travel forum threads, 260-267

tree-based classifiers, 265

trigrams, 26

triple stores for graph databases, 327, 328

Tweepy for data extraction, 45, 47-55

tweet_mode=extended parameter, 49

Twisted environment (Scrapy), 85, 86
Twitter
    about, 45-46
    data extraction from, 47-55
    Search API of , 34, 48-50
    Streaming API of, 53-55
    user's timelines on, 51-53
two-dimensional projections, 287-289

U

UMAP algorithm, 287-291
UN General Debates dataset, 3, 5-9, 20, 28-31, 210-212
underfitting of trained model, 175
universal part-of-speech tagset, 110
UNK token, 205
unknown distribution with Anchor, 203-206, 205
unprivileged mode of Docker containers, 379
unsupervised methods, 229, 238, 242
upsampling techniques, 171
URIs (uniform resource identifiers), 326, 343
URL generation, 58, 61-62
URLs for downloading HTML pages, 68-69
URLs, extraction of, 74, 77
use cases
    for feature dimensions, 134, 136, 140, 141, 144
    for knowledge graphs, 326
    overview of, xiv
    for replication of models, 361, 374
    for scraping websites, 58, 78
    for semantic analysis, 269
    for sentiment analysis of text data, 298, 304, 309, 312, 322
    for text classification, 153
    for text data extraction, 33-35, 39, 44-45, 51-55
    for text summarization, 246, 257, 260, 260, 265, 267
    for topic modeling, 210
user-generated content (UGC), 91

V

VADER lexicon, 304
value distributions, plotting, 7-9
vector algebra, 272
vector dimensions of word embeddings, 271
vectorizers/vectorization

bag-of-words models for, 131-134, 269-270
blueprint for building, 125-130
of documents, 124, 126-136, 141
with finding syntactic similarity, 145-151
with text classification, 159, 163-165, 177-179, 186, 195, 204
of text data for sentiment analysis, 306-309
with TF-IDF weighting, 134-145, 147, 164, 178, 212, 230, 270, 307
with topic modeling, 209, 212-216, 231, 237, 239, 242
vectors, 123
vectors_gensim_para matrix, 231
VERBOSE option, 102
violin plots, 8
visualization of data
    of developments over time, 9
    with frequency diagrams, 18
    with heatmaps, 30-31, 169
    with highlighted text, 199, 207
    with knowledge graphs, 330, 345, 347, 351-355, 355
    with spaCy display module, 114, 330, 352
    with topic modeling, 217, 223-224, 228
    with word clouds , 18-20, 22, 27, 32, 52, 224-225, 239-242
    with word embeddings, 286-294
vocabulary
    enumeration of, 125-127
    feature dimensions of, 138-145
    feature names as, 131
    filtering of, 142-145, 230
Vulture code analysis tool, 377

W

wait_on_rate_limit parameter, 49
Wayback Machine, 70
weak supervision learning, 358
Web Inspector in browsers, 72, 75
web services for entity linking, 344
wget tool for downloading, 69
Wikidata, 326, 343
Wikipedia articles, 55, 256, 259, 277-278, 327
wikipediaapi (Python), 55
Windows PowerShell, 362
word clouds , 18-20, 22, 27, 32, 52, 224-225, 239-242
word embeddings for semantic analysis
    about, 269, 294

About the Authors

Jens Albrecht is a full-time professor in the Computer Science Department at the Nuremberg Institute of Technology. His work focuses on data management and analytics, especially on text. He holds a PhD in computer science. Before he rejoined academia in 2012, he worked for more than a decade in the industry as a consultant and data architect. He is the author of several articles on big data management and analysis.

Sidharth Ramachandran currently leads a team of data scientists building data products for the consumer goods industry. He has more than 10 years of experience in software engineering and data science across the telecom, banking, and marketing industries. Sidharth also co-founded WACAO, a smart personal assistant on Whatsapp that was featured on Techcrunch. He holds an undergraduate engineering degree from IIT Roorkee and an MBA from IIM Kozhikode. Sidharth is passionate about solving real problems through technology and loves to hack through personal projects in his free time.

Christian Winkler is a data scientist and machine learning architect. He holds a PhD in theoretical physics and has been working in the field of large data volumes and artificial intelligence for 20 years, with a particular focus on scalable systems and intelligent algorithms for mass text processing. He is the founder of datanizing GmbH, a speaker at conferences, and the author of machine learning/text analytics articles.

Colophon

The animal on the cover of *Blueprints for Text Analytics Using Python* is a Palestine saw-scaled viper (*Echis coloratus*).

Also known as the painted saw-scaled viper, the painted carpet viper, and the Arabian saw-scaled viper (among other monikers), this venomous snake can be found in the Middle East and parts of northeastern Africa. It is the most common venomous snake in rocky desert habitats in the Negev and the Judean Deserts, and can be found in habitats ranging from sea level to altitudes upwards of 2,500 meters. It has a triangle-shaped head, a rust-colored body, and a distinctive saw-tooth pattern on its back. It typically grows to a maximum length of 75 cm and hunts using thermal cues to identify its prey. Many of the animals on O'Reilly covers are endangered; all of them are important to the world.

The cover illustration is by Jose Marzan, based on a black and white engraving from Lydekker's *Royal Natural History*. The cover fonts are Gilroy Semibold and Guardian Sans. The text font is Adobe Minion Pro; the heading font is Adobe Myriad Condensed; and the code font is Dalton Maag's Ubuntu Mono.

O'REILLY®

There's much more where this came from.

Experience books, videos, live online training courses, and more from O'Reilly and our 200+ partners—all in one place.

Learn more at oreilly.com/online-learning